A Survey of Historic Costume

A Survey of Historic Costume

PHYLLIS TORTORA

Professor and Chair, Home Economics Department
Queens College of The City
University of New York

KEITH EUBANK

Professor, History Department
Queens College of The City
University of New York

FAIRCHILD PUBLICATIONS

New York

Book Design: Lynn Fischer

Cover Art: Embroidered suit, French, c. 1770. *Photograph courtesy of The Philadelphia Museum of Art, gift of Charles F. Saake.*

Standard Book Number: 87005–632–8

Library of Congress Catalog Number: 88–81830

Printed in the United States of America

Contents

Preface

This book is intended for use as a basic text for college students making a survey of the history of costume. It is the purpose of the authors to present an overview of this vast subject rather than an infinitely detailed picture. At the same time it is the authors' intention to make that picture as complete as possible within the limitations of space.

Costume of each period must be viewed within the context of the period. To assist students who may have a limited background in history, a brief summary of the major historical developments related to the chapter will be provided. In every society clothing is a part of the basic equipment for everyday life and so in each chapter brief note will be made of some of the important aspects of the life of people of the time. The technology and economy of the production and distribution of fabrics often influences clothing, so changes in technology for the making of cloth and clothes and in the economic system by which they are produced and distributed are cited where these are appropriate.

The specific styles of each period are presented separately from the historical material as an overview of the clothing worn by men, by women, and by children. The authors have chosen to present this material in summary form, without references to or descriptions of specific costumes in the body of the text as they believe this kind of organization will be most clear to students. At the same time, given the tremendously confusing differences to be found in historic costume reference books and materials, particularly in some of the early periods where actual records are confusing, contradictory,

and scarce, the authors have attempted to present as accurate a summary as possible and one we hope is free from the tendency to present some of the largely apocryphal stories of the origins of styles as fact. When such material is introduced it is clearly labeled as questionable or as legend.

The authors also believe that it is important for students to have illustrations of original source materials available not only to provide illustrations of some of the unfamiliar terms, but also to supplement the general, survey approach of the text. The captions of the illustrations will not only identify various parts of the costume and provide the contemporary names for elements of the styles, but also will identify the aspects of the pictures that provide supporting evidence to the costume historian of the nature of costume at this period.

In this text the terms *garment*, *clothes*, and *clothing* are synonymous and used to mean wearing apparel. *Style* is the predominant form of dress of any given period or culture. Styles may persist for very long or shorter periods of time. *Fashion* is synonymous with style after the latter part of the Medieval Period but implies styles of relatively short duration. *Costume* is the style of dress peculiar to a nation, a class, or a period.

Two types of bibliographies are included: those following each chapter and a lengthy bibliography at the end of the book. The bibliographies at the end of each chapter are intended to serve three purposes. They list books that contain a good cross-section of illustrations of original source materials for costumes of the period covered in that chapter.

They identify books that provide a more complete picture of life in the period covered so that those who desire can learn more about the period. Finally, periodical articles dealing with costume or related topics are cited. The purpose of including such articles is to introduce students to some of the journals that are sources of further information about costume and also to provide some of the detailed analyses of costume topics that are not possible in a text which surveys so broad a topic.

The bibliography at the end of the book is a listing of books written about historic costume, and is organized by topic. This bibliography does not duplicate materials listed at the end of each chapter, nor does it include books dealing with techniques of theatrical costuming or socio-cultural aspects of dress.

Acknowledgments

No person, even after a lifetime of study, can be expert in all aspects of historic costume solely on the basis of his or her own research. Fortunately there are many individuals who have specialized in certain countries or periods and whose work is invaluable in the preparation of a broad survey of this type. It is important that these sources be given special acknowledgment beyond a citation in footnotes or a listing in the bibliography.

For materials dealing with costume of the ancient world, the books of Mary Houston and Lillian Wilson were of inestimable help. The work of Larissa Bonfante served as a basis for the material on Etruscan costume and related Greek styles.

For the Medieval period, Joan Evans' work on costume of the Middle Ages and the fine handbook by Phillis and Cecil Willet Cunnington were invaluable. Goddard's work on French costume of the 11th and 12th centuries also provided useful information.

Elizabeth Birbiri's fine study of Italian Renaissance costume provided not only detailed information but a wealth of excellent illustrative materials. For the 16th through the 19th centuries, the several volumes of handbooks on costume done by the Cunningtons, and that by Mrs. Cunnington and Alan Mansfield for the 20th century were among the most useful of the materials cited. Not only were they a superlative source for detailed information, but they were a helpful tool for cross-checking conflicting information.

For men's wear of the 20th century the *Esquire Encyclopedia of Men's Clothing* was by far the most useful secondary source an author or researcher could find with its wealth of detailed information quoted directly from the fashion press and its many illustrations from the periods covered in this book.

Underclothing has been thoroughly illustrated and explored in the books by C. W. Cunnington, Nora Waugh, and Elizabeth Ewing. Waugh's work is especially helpful in its inclusion of quotations from the literature of various periods concerning different types of undergarments.

The works of Boucher and Davenport should be noted for their wealth of illustrative material drawn from sources of the period, although the authors recommend that students approach these books armed with a magnifying glass.

For some specialized material in the area of bathing costume, Claudia Kidwell's monograph was useful, as was the work she and Christman did on American ready-to-wear.

Having begun by citing some of the books to which the authors are indebted, it is perhaps appropriate to acknowledge next the various libraries that were especially helpful. Gordon Stone, formerly librarian of the Costume Institute Library of the Metropolitan Museum, was most kind and helpful, as was Mrs. Evelyn Semler of the Morgan Library in New York City. The staff of the Queens College Library, both the Art Library and the main library, and the personnel of the Port Washington Public Library should be acknowledged. Mitzi Caputo of the Huntington Historical Society was most helpful in locating photographs, as was Frances Saha of the Cleveland Museum and the personnel of the Metropolitan Museum Photographic Services Department. And to the New York City Public Library, gratitude for maintaining the fine picture collection that is available to researchers.

Grateful thanks, also, to a number of anonymous reviewers who offered suggestions over the many years during which the manuscript was developed. And to one known reviewer, Elizabeth Ann Coleman, curator of the Costumes and Textiles Department of the Brooklyn Museum, thanks for a careful reading and excellent suggestions on the 19th and 20th century parts.

Finally, to family and colleagues and friends, thanks for the many kinds of assistance that could not ever be adequately acknowledged: photographs taken and printed, bibliographies alphabetized, typing done, phone calls made, messages taken, and a cheerful willingness to pick up other tasks so that we could complete the work.

Phyllis Tortora
Keith Eubank
New York

CHAPTER 1

Introduction

The Origins of Dress

The earliest pictorial records of clothing are found in the prehistoric cave paintings from the Old Stone Age, or Early Paleolithic Period, some 30,000 years ago. These paintings show little detail, so one can say only that people did wear clothing, and that the clothing appears to have taken the form of draped skirts, cut and sewn trousers, and a cape-like garment, probably all of which were made from skins. Supporting evidence for this conclusion comes from archeologists who have found needles for sewing, bone scrapers for preparing skins, and bone devices that were probably used for fastening clothing in sites dating from the same general period.

Archeologists have found evidence from later periods of textile weaving in the form of implements used in weaving and samples of fabric that have been preserved. What appears to be one of the earliest examples of skill in textile weaving has been found in excavations at Catal Huyuk in Anatolia (modern Turkey) where actual woven fabrics dating from 8500 years ago have been found.[1] The construction of these fabrics required rather complex weaving techniques and so archeologists have concluded that the weaving of fabrics must have begun well before this date in order to have evolved to the relatively high level of skill needed to make these particular fabrics. If cloth was woven, it was probably made into clothing, but no records exist of the form this clothing took.

Psychologists and sociologists have attempted to identify the motivations that cause people to dress themselves. There are places in the world where clothing is not essential for survival, and yet most cultures do use some form of clothing. The most basic reasons that have been suggested for the wearing of clothing are these: (1) clothing was worn for protection, (2) clothing was worn for decoration, (3) clothing was worn out of modesty, (4) clothing was worn to denote status. Of these four reasons, that of decoration is generally acknowledged to be primary.

It is true that most cultures use clothing to denote status, but it is argued that this function probably became attached to clothing at some time *after* it first came into use. Modesty differs markedly from society to society, and what is modest in one part of the world is immodest in another. Modesty, too, may have become associated with clothing after its use became widespread. Protection from the elements is needed, it would seem, for survival, but mankind seems to have had its origins in warm, not cold climates. Then, too, there are places in

1. J. Mellaart. "Catal Huyuk in Anatolia." *Illustrated London Daily News.* Feb. 9, 1963. p. 196 ff

which even though climatic conditions are inhospitable, clothing is not worn. The Indians of Tierra del Fuego protect themselves against the cold not with clothing, but with large shields held up against the winds. Instead of wearing clothing, they decorate themselves with body paint.[2]

Another type of protection may be related to the origins and functions of clothing. This is psychic protection, or protection against the spiritual dangers that are thought to surround each individual. Good luck amulets and charms are worn in most cultures. Aprons to protect the genitals not only from physical harm but also from witchcraft may have evolved into skirts or loincloths in some areas.

The reasons given for believing decoration to be a primary if not the most primary motive in human dress are compelling. Although dress as protection against the elements and evil spirits is not universal, decoration of the human body is. There *are* cultures in which clothing *per se* does not exist. There are no cultures in which some form of decoration does not exist. The logical conclusion is that decoration of the self is a basic human practice. Clothing the body may have grown out of this decoration of the self, and protection, modesty, and status may have been important motivations for the elaboration and development of complex forms of dress.

Functions of Dress

Throughout history clothing can and has served many purposes. It has served to differentiate between the sexes; designate age, marital and socio-economic status, occupation, group membership, and other special roles that individuals played.

DISTINGUISHING THE SEXES

In most societies it is customary for the dress of men and women to be different. For many hundreds of years in Western civilization, skirts were designated as feminine dress, breeches or trousers as male dress. In some Eastern countries, the reverse was true and skirts were the male costume, while bifurcated garment, a sort of "harem pants" belonged to women. The type of dress designated as appropriate for men and women was never universal, but the assignment of specific types of dress to each sex has been a long established custom.

DESIGNATION OF AGE

Sometimes clothing serves to mark age change. In Western Europe and North America at an early age boys and girls often were dressed alike, but once they reached a designated age, a distinction was made between the dress of boys and girls. In England during the Renaissance this stage was celebrated in a ritual called "breeching" when the five or six year old boy was given his first pair of breeches.

Age differentiation may, as in the preceding example, be an established procedure, but it is often less a ritual than an accepted part of the mores of a society. Children, for example, are rarely dressed in black in Western societies. Even in an era when mourning practices required the wearing of black, children were more likely to be dressed in white with touches of black. Young girls throughout the 19th century wore shorter costumes than their adolescent sisters. During the 1920's and 30's the wearing of knickers marked a stage of development between childhood and adult life for many young men.

DESIGNATION OF STATUS

Occupational status is frequently designated by a uniform or a particular style of dress. In England, even today, lawyers wear an established costume when they appear in court. The police, fire fighters, nurses, postal workers, and some of the clergy are but a few of those whose dress immediately identifies them as members of a particular profession. Sometimes the uniform worn also serves a practical function, as for example the fire fighter's waterproof coat and protective helmet or the construction worker's hard hat.

Dress designating occupational status is not limited to a "uniform." For many years, particularly during the 1950's and 60's, men employed by certain companies in the United States were required to wear white shirts with ties to work. Colored shirts were not permitted. Young lawyers who, on first entering the practice of law, go into a men's wear store and request "a lawyer's suit" will find salespersons know exactly what they want.

Marital status may be indicated by customs of dress. In Western society a wedding ring worn on a specific finger signifies marriage. Among the American religious group called the Amish, married men

2. L. Langner. *The Importance of Wearing Clothes.* New York: Hastings House, 1959, p. 6.

wear beards while unmarried men do not. It was customary for many centuries for married women to cover their hair, while unmarried women were permitted to go without head coverings. This practice is still followed among many orthodox Jewish groups.

In some cultures or during some historical periods certain types of clothing have been restricted to persons of a particular rank, social, and economic status. During the 14th century in England persons who worked as servants to "great men" were required to limit the cost of their clothing, nor were they permitted to wear any article of gold or silver, embroidery, or silk.[3]

In ancient Rome only the male Roman citizen was permitted to wear the costume called the *toga*. This distinguished his socio-political status.

IDENTIFYING GROUP MEMBERSHIP

Clothing is also used to identify an individual as belonging to a particular social group. The group identification may be in the form of a uniform or insignia adopted formally by that group and kept for its members alone, as in the uniforms of fraternal groups such as the Masons or Shriners, or religious groups such as the Amish of today or the Puritans of the 17th century. Or, on the other hand, the group identification may be an informal kind of uniform like those adopted by adolescents who belong to the same clique or "zoot suits," a style of dress affected by groups of young Blacks during World War II.

Cartoonists frequently make use of this practice of using clothing as a symbol of group identification. Helen Hoskins, a cartoonist of the post-World War II period, drew a "suburban matron" type who was readily identifiable by her flowered hats, dark suits, and furs.

CEREMONIAL USE OF CLOTHING

Ceremonies are an important part of the structure of most societies and social groups. Designated forms of dress are frequently an important part of any ceremony. Specific costumes exist in modern American society that are considered appropriate for weddings, baptisms, burials, to designate mourning, and for graduation. Most significant moments of life are accompanied by the wearing of ritual costume specified by custom in each culture.

ENHANCEMENT OF SEXUAL ATTRACTIVENESS

In many cultures clothing is considered to enhance the sexual attractiveness of individuals. In some cultures this is quite explicit, with clothing being designed to focus attention on the breasts of women or genitals of men. For example: In Europe in the 16th century the codpiece, a section of men's clothing which covered the genitals, was often padded and enlarged. In many periods women have padded dresses to make the bosom appear larger or have worn dresses with very low necklines designed to call attention to the breasts. At other times the waist, the hips, or the legs have been emphasized. James Laver, a well-known costume historian, believed that fashion changes in women's dress were a result of "shifting erogenous zones." His theory was that women uncovered different parts of the body selectively in order to attract men and that as men became used to seeing more of the breasts, this area lost its interest and power to excite and so that area was covered and another area, the hips, for example, was emphasized.[4]

Laver also suggested that sexual attractiveness might lie in other aspects of dress. Men in modern, Western society, he said, are considered attractive because they appear from their dress to be affluent and successful.[5]

Clothing as a Means of Communication

The foregoing discussion of the functions of clothing leads to the conclusion that clothing serves as a means of communication. To the person who is knowledgeable about a particular culture, clothing is a sort of silent language. Clothing tells the observer something about the organization of the society in which it is worn in that it discloses the social stratification of the society, reveals whether there are rigid delineations of social and economic class or a classless society. For example, the political leaders in the African Ashanti Tribe wore distinctive costumes marking their special status. Any subject who wore the same fabric pattern as the king would be put to death. In contrast, the costume of American political leaders does not differ from that of most of the rest of the population. The political

3. A. F. Scott. *Everyone a Witness: The Plantagenet Age.* New York: Thomas Crowell Company, 1976, p. 85.

4. J. Laver. *Dress.* London, Albemarle, 1950, p. 16.
5. *Ibid.*

distinctions between the two cultures—the one an absolute monarchy, the other a democracy—are mirrored in the clothing practices.

Other aspects of social organization may be manifest in clothing. The dress of religious leaders may distinguish them or may show no differentiation between the clergy and the worshiper. The roles of men and women may be distinctly identified by dress (as in Islamic tradition where women are veiled) or a blending of the roles of men and women may be reflected by a blurring of sharp distinctions in the customary dress of the sexes as has been true in Europe and North America since the 1920's when women have been free to wear trousers, a garment formerly reserved for men.

Clothing as an Art Form

Expression through the arts is rooted in a particular culture and historical period. Certain conventions or customs determine the form and content of art in any given period. Although the human impulse toward expressing feelings through art is universal, the specific expression of an era is determined by a complex mixture of social, psychological, and aesthetic factors often called the *zeitgeist* or spirit of the times.

All of the artists or designers of a given period are subjected to many of the same influences, therefore it is not surprising that even different art forms may display similar qualities, either in the decorative motifs that are used or in scale, form, color, proportion, and the feelings they evoke. This is certainly true of clothing, and similarities between dress and architectural forms, furnishings, and the other visual arts can often be identified.

At the same time, clothing offers the designer or the wearer a medium of expression with its own forms and techniques. The lines, textures, colors, proportions and scale of fabric designs and shapes of garments can and have been given variety, at different times and in different places throughout history. Ideals of human beauty change with changes in the *zeitgeist*. Often clothing is used by individuals as part of an attempt to conform to the physical ideal of human beauty at a particular time.

LIMITATIONS OF DRESS

As in any medium, there are limitations imposed on the design of clothing. Costume has some func-

tional aspects. Except for costumes that have only a ceremonial purpose, the wearer must be able to move, to carry the weight of the costume, and, often, to perform certain duties while wearing the garment. The duties assigned to an individual will have a direct influence on the kind of costume he or she can wear. Obviously the affluent women throughout history with servants to do the work of the household were able to dress in one way while the servants dressed in costumes more appropriate to the labors they were expected to perform.

There are other limitations as well. Although paint and ornaments can serve as the prescribed dress in some cultures, most societies evolved more complex clothing. Early peoples may have used skins. The draping qualities of skins are different from that of cloth, and would therefore impose certain limitations on the shapes of garments that could be constructed.

Once people learned to spin yarns and weave fabrics these were employed to make clothing. Before the advent of synthetic fibers in the 20th century only natural materials were available for use. Each of these had inherent qualities that affected the characteristics of fabrics that could be made. Some materials such as raffia, made of fibers from an African palm tree, are relatively stiff whereas fibers such as cotton, wool, or linen are more flexible.

Isolated regions were limited to the use of local materials. Trade between regions could bring materials from one part of the world to another. Silk was unknown in Europe until the Romans imported it from India and China about the beginning of the Christian era. Cotton does not grow in the cool Northern climate of Europe and so was unused in Medieval Europe until after the Crusaders imported the fabric from the Near East.

In order to devise a garment that fits the body, the people of different cultures have devised differing means of constructing clothing. Costume is generally either "draped" or "tailored." Draped costume is created by the arrangement around the body of pieces of fabric which are folded, pleated, pinned, and/or belted in different ways. Draped costume usually fits the body loosely.

Tailored costume, being cut and sewn to fit the body closely, provides greater warmth than draped garments and hence is more likely to be worn in cool climates. Draped costume is more characteristic of warm climates. Some costume combines elements of both draping and tailoring.

Technology has an important impact on costume. Some regions developed spinning and weaving skills to a far greater extent than others. Many of the changes in the form of costume that came about in Europe and North America after the 18th century can be directly or indirectly attributed to developments such as mechanized spinning and weaving, the sewing machine, development of the American ready-to-wear industry. The resulting mass production doubtlessly helped to simplify styles and speed-up fashion changes.

Costume is also limited by the mores and customs of the period. It is interesting to note that the word *costume* derives from the same root as the word *custom*. Those persons who deviate too radically from the customary dress of their culture or even from that of their socio-economic class are often considered to be asocial—perhaps even mad. George Sand, a French female writer of the 19th century who dressed in men's clothing was considered to be decidedly eccentric. Psychologists report that mental disturbance often first manifests itself in lack of attention to dress or in bizarre clothing behavior.

The study of costume, then, must take into account the socio-economic structure of a society, the customs relating to dress, the art of the period, and the technology available for the production of both fabrics and clothing itself. To obtain this information, the costume historian must utilize the evidence he or she can garner from a variety of sources.

Sources of Evidence for the Study of Historic Costume

The sources of evidence used by the costume historian are plentiful for some periods, relatively scarce for others. Obviously the further back one goes in history, the less clear and abundant is the historic record. For periods before the 16th century, the major sources of information are sculpture and painting, and, sometimes, written records. Rarely does fabric remain, although there are a few examples of fabrics or clothes from burial sites. Archeological evidence is usually limited to the unperishable: jewelry, buttons, pins, and/or decorations.

After the invention of printing in the 1500's, written and pictorial records of European costume became more abundant. Fabrics and individual items of costume have been preserved since the early Renaissance although the supply becomes plentiful

only around the 18th century. When photography was invented in the mid-19th century, a vast record of costume became available. Many items of dress from the early 19th century on have been preserved in museums and costume collections.

To obtain a complete picture of costume in a given era historians must assemble evidence from all of the sources available. These sources must be checked against other sources including written as well as pictorial records. Even so, the student of historic costume must be aware of some of the problems involved in obtaining accurate dates for particular styles.

Since many of the representations of costumes from the 18th century and earlier periods come from art works, one must be aware of the artistic conventions of a given period that may interfere with accurate representation of dress. For example, it is believed that Egyptian artists depicted women in tight-fitting garments that were probably actually worn in a less form-fitting version; and pre-Muslim Indian artists always depicted women without bodices covering their breasts, whereas written records contradict this, indicating women also wore garments that covered the entire body. Artists such as Gainsborough and Rembrandt enjoyed dressing the persons who were sitting for portraits in fanciful, imaginary costumes. Some paintings done at a later date of earlier historical scenes put the figures into costumes the artist imagined were those used at the time, as when French painters of about 1800 showed scenes from Greek and Roman history and dressed the figures in paintings in imagined Greek or Roman styles.

Sometimes the attribution of a painting to a particular country or date may be in error. Also, standards of modesty may preclude the depiction of certain items of costume, such as underclothing, leaving the costume historian without a record of the appearance of such garments.

Even when fashion magazines of the 19th or 20th centuries are consulted, one must remember "proposed" styles were often shown, and not necessarily those which were actually worn at the time. It is a fairly safe assumption that many women copied the fashion plates shown therein, and yet Elizabeth Ann Coleman, curator of Costumes and Textiles at the Brooklyn Museum points out that even though skirts with lavish panels of decoration are depicted in fashion magazines of the Crinoline period, few if any costumes in collections show this characteristic. Fashion magazines stress the "ideal" and not necessarily the "real."

Nor can written material always be so easily interpreted. Fashion terms that had one meaning at one time may have taken on a different meaning at a later time. The term "pelisse" when used before 1800 usually implied an outdoor garment with some fur trim or lining. In the 19th century, a pelisse was still an outdoor garment, but didn't necessarily have fur associated with it. The precise meaning of some terms is lost. The words "kalasiris" in Egypt and "cotehardie" in the Middle Ages are examples of words which have been given a number of different definitions by various costume historians. Colors and fabrics may have had names that are no longer understood.

The interpretation of written material cannot always be taken literally. This is particularly true of writing about sumptuary laws. These laws which restrict the use of certain luxury goods or spending on luxury items such as clothing were often passed, but were not always enforced. Although such laws may express a certain attitude toward social stratification, society was not always prepared to obey or enforce them.

Finally, one must even treat actual garments that remain with some degree of skepticism. Actual dating of some items may be inaccurate. The author once encountered an item from a collection that had been labeled as "time of George Washington" that was actually from the 1880's, a hundred years later. Persons who donate items to costume collections may give the date of an item on the basis of the ages of the owners during the last years of their lives rather than at the time garments were actually worn. Then, too, a garment may have been remodeled several times, thereby making it difficult to assign an accurate date.

The dating of historic costume, therefore, requires corroborative evidence from a variety of sources. For this reason, one may often encounter conflict between different writers about historic costume as to the precise practices in periods where evidence is scarce or fragmentary.

Summary

The reasons for which an individual student undertakes the study of historic costume vary. Some persons are interested in the practical application of information gained to some aspect of personal or professional activity. Fashion designers often draw on styles of the past for inspiration. Those persons employed in various aspects of the fashion industry will, likewise, find it useful to understand fashion and the development of the 20th century fashion industry.

Persons entering any of a number of fields related to the arts may wish to be familiar with styles in clothing and their historical development. Historical society and museum staff members may collect, catalog, and date historic costumes or materials depicting costume. Anthropologists, sociologists, social historians, and psychologists all have varying interests and viewpoints concerning the history of clothing. Teachers of art, home economics, and social studies will find the study of costume fascinates their students and adds a new dimension to the subject matter.

Other persons may choose to study costume for pleasure rather than for practical value. Clothing offers great opportunity for varied artistic expression and many persons respond to costume purely for its aesthetic value. Still others may find it satisfies curiosity about the past by bringing the people who lived in past times and other places closer to us today.

But whether one studies the past for pleasure or for practical value, one looks for understanding. This understanding comes from a view of clothing as a means of communicating personal and societal values within a context of a specific historical period of which the viewer must have some knowledge if his or her observation is to be an informed response. In the chapters that follow the authors hope they have provided a key to better understanding of the history of costume.

PART I

The Ancient World

C. 3000 B.C.–300 A.D.

The roots of Western Civilization are to be found in the area around the Mediterranean Sea, a region which gave rise to a series of civilizations which formed the artistic, religious, philosophical, and political basis of western culture. The valley of the Nile River and the land between the Tigris and the Euphrates rivers in Mesopotamia (today a part of Iraq) were the locations of some of the earliest agriculturally-based urban societies.

About 3500 years before Christ, a civilization flourished in Mesopotamia. The region became the home of a people called the Sumerians. Subsequently, over the next 2500 years the center of civilization and the site of political power in this area spread gradually north into Babylonia and Assyria.

Concurrently, about 3000 B.C., in the Nile River Valley the Egyptians were developing another center of culture, a civilization which endured for almost 3000 years. And also between 2000 and 1400 B.C., the island of Crete (the home of a people known as the Minoans) became the center of an important Mediterranean civilization. Minoan civilization was marked by a high standard of housing and material possessions, organized production of food, textiles, and other products, and by a vigorous trade with remote regions. The Minoans controlled not only Crete, but eventually extended their cultural influence to mainland Greece, including the town of Mycenae which gave its name to a civilization. After about 1400 B.C., the Mycenaeans, in a reversal of power, came to dominate Crete.

Soon after 1200 B.C., the Dorians, a wave of invaders from the north, overwhelmed the Mycenaean civilization, and Greece entered a Dark Age about which little is known. During the Archaic Age (eighth and seventh centuries B.C.) the period of the poet Homer, Greek colonists left their homes to found colonies in the Mediterranean area. The Classical Age of Greece, fifth and fourth centuries B.C., the period of the great philosophers and playwrights and Greek democracy, ended in the early 300's after Greeks led by Alexander the Great had conquered much of the eastern Mediterranean regions.

The westward colonization which extended Greek art and culture influenced the Etruscans, a people living in the Italian peninsula who dominated central Italy from 800 B.C. until absorbed by the Romans in the third century B.C. As the Etruscans were absorbed by the Romans, so were the other civilizations surrounding the Mediterranean. Eventually the Roman legions conquered not only North Africa and the Middle East but the lands extending as far north in the east to the Danube River and north-west into much of Britain.

Table I-1 compares the periods and durations of each of these civilizations. As the table shows, some of these peoples reached their peak of power and development at the same time. Others flowered,

Table I–1. Civilizations of the Ancient World

Time period B.C.	Mesopotamia	Egypt	Crete	Greece	Etruria	Rome
4000–3000	Sumerian Civilization	Unification of Egypt				
3000–2000		Old Kingdom				
2000–1000	Rise of Babylonia	Middle Kingdom New Kingdom	Minoan Civilization	Mycenaean Civilization		
1000–800	Rise of Assyria			Dark Age		
800–600		Decline of Native Eygptian Civilization		Homeric (archaic) Period	Rise of Etruscan Civilization	
600–500	Neo-Babylonia Period					Etruscan Kings of Rome
500–400	Persian conquests of Asia and Middle East			Golden Age		Roman Republic
400–300				Alexander, the Great		
300–200					End of Etruscan Confederations	
200–0 A.D.					Roman Empire	
0–300	Roman Domination	Roman Domination		Roman Domination		
C.400						Fall of Western Rome

then declined while new centers of influence were rising. Some cultures borrowed liberally from each other, like the Greeks, the Etruscans, and the Romans, while others like Egypt and Mesopotamia though in contact, evolved in separate directions. (Figure I-1 shows the locations of the most important of the civilizations of antiquity.)

In costume, as in other art forms, the different Mediterranean cultures showed both independent characteristics and similarities. The Mediterranean basin possesses a warm, and in some areas tropical climate. Although each culture had its own distinctive forms of various items of dress, certain basic garment forms can be identified that were common to most of these cultures. It may be useful to identify these, and define them before beginning the discus-

sion of the specific costumes of the different ancient civilizations of the Mediterranean world.

The garments of the civilizations of the ancient world were, with a few notable exceptions, draped. The basic form of much ancient clothing was a length of square, rectangular, or semicircular fabric, draped to create a variety of styles, each of which was distinctive and characteristic of the particular culture and/or period within that culture. These draped garments were fastened together, when fastening was required, with pins or by sewing. The general term used by archeologists for a pin that was used in holding a garment together is a Roman word, *fibula*.

The forms into which these draped garments were made can be further sub-divided, and included

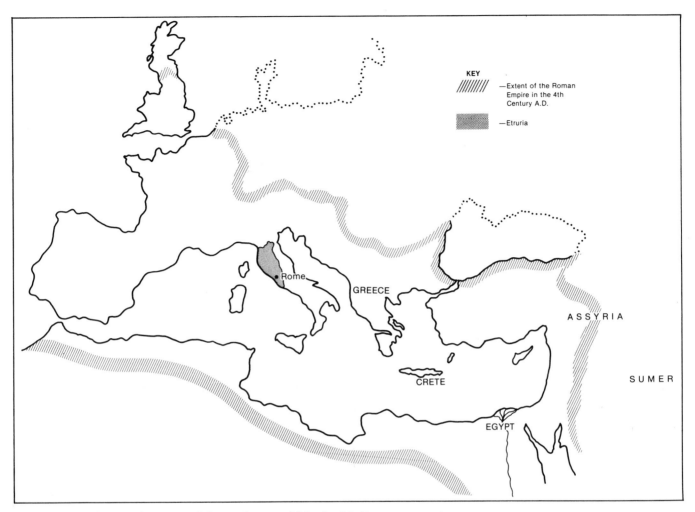

I.1 Locations of the civilizations of the ancient world in the Mediterranean region.

loin cloths, skirts, tunics, shawls, cloaks, and veils.[1] The skirt, in the ancient world, was a garment that began at the waist or slightly below and hung loosely around the body. Skirts were worn by both men and women and varied in length. The loin cloth was a length of cloth wrapped in any of several ways to cover the genitals. The tunic was a simple, one-piece, and often T-shaped garment, cut with an opening for the head and arms. Tunics were usually long enough to cover the trunk and were made in as many different lengths as skirts.

Rectangles, squares or ovals of fabric (which might be called shawls) were commonly combined with skirts or tunics. These ranged from pieces that covered only the upper body to larger squares that could be wrapped to make a complete garment. The veil was a smaller rectangle distinct from the body-covering shawl in that it covered the head and sometimes part of the body and was worn almost exclusively by women. A third large square of fabric, that for convenience will be called a cloak, was a cape-like outdoor garment tied or pinned around the shoulders.

1. Costume terminology from these periods can be confusing, as different authorities use different phonetic terms for words which modern people have never heard pronounced, and with which readers are unfamiliar. For this reason, descriptions of costume must rely upon using the closest modern equivalent for the costume, in order that the reader can relate the unfamiliar term to one which is more familiar. Sometimes modern costume terms have taken on connotations that are misleading or confusing when that term is applied to historic costume. For example, the term "skirt" is associated in modern usage with women's costume, whereas in the ancient world, men and women both wore "skirts." As a result, many costume sources will refer to the skirt as worn by men as a "kilt," even though "kilt" is actually a Scottish word for a specific skirt worn by men. For this reason the authors have chosen to use the nearest equivalent modern word that will be descriptive of the form of the ancient costume, except in those instances where an ancient word has come into modern usage, such as *toga* (from Latin) or *chiton* (from the Greek).

CHAPTER 2

The Ancient Middle East

C. 3500 B.C.–600 B.C.

Historical Background

MESOPOTAMIA

The first civilizations in the Middle East were located in Mesopotamia (the name means "between rivers"), the region between the Tigris and Euphrates Rivers. The area extended from the Persian Gulf to near the borders of modern Iraq and Turkey. Towns and cities developed in the southern parts of the region in the rich, fertile plains created by the deposits from the two rivers. Agriculture and herding produced sufficient food to enable the people to establish more permanent residences in towns and cities where they gradually developed an increasingly complex social organization.

The people who founded the first cities in southern Mesopotamia, called the Sumerians, entered the area from the northeast about 3500 B.C. The complexity of the Sumerian civilization (3500–2800 B.C.) led to the invention of a form of writing which enabled them to keep records of their activities, codify laws, and transmit knowledge. The Sumerians, however, never developed a strong political organization and remained only a loose confederation of city states. Sumer came under the domination of the northern neighbor, Akkad, led by Sargon (c. 2334–2279 B.C.), whose dynasty extended Akkadian influence into Asia Minor. Then new invaders from the west, the Amorites, conquered Sumer and

Akkad, and established a new empire with the capital at Babylon. The Babylonians created an autocratic state, extending their control northward during the reign of King Hammurabi (c. 1792–1750 B.C.). His famous law code, dealing with almost every facet of life, influenced later Middle Eastern law codes, including the Mosaic law.

After about 1700 B.C., Babylonian power declined as a series of invaders attacked the empire. Control of the region see-sawed back and forth among the invaders until after 1000 B.C. when a powerful Assyrian army from the upper Tigris River conquered Babylonia. The Assyrians, once the vassals of the Babylonians, developed the first great military machine with a large standing army armed with superior equipment, including iron swords. Their empire, the largest the Near East had seen, stretched into Syria, Palestine, and even Egypt. The cruelties of the Assyrian armies made them so hated and feared that their enemies, conspiring against them, eventually brought about their downfall. In 612 B.C. the armies of the Chaldeans, who now ruled Babylonia, destroyed Ninevah, the capital of Assyria, ending the Assyrian Empire. In turn Chaldean Babylon fell to a new and greater power, the Persians under Cyrus in 539 B.C.

Chaldean Babylon, notorious for its luxury and wealth, became the site of the hanging gardens, a terrace roof garden, considered one of the seven wonders of the ancient world. Motivated by their religion, the Chaldeans became the most competent astronomers in Mesopotamian history. Their records of the movements of the heavenly bodies were maintained for over 350 years.

EGYPT

At much the same period that the early Mesopotamian civilization was developing between the Tigris and Euphrates Rivers, another river, the Nile, became the site of the Egyptian civilization. The development of an advanced civilization in Egypt was aided by the deserts and the seas which helped protect the land from foreign invaders. In addition, agriculture flourished thanks to the annual flooding of the Nile which left behind a rich deposit of soil making fertilizers unnecessary.

The ancient Egyptian kingdoms have been dated from about 3100 B.C. to about 300 B.C. when Greeks led by Alexander the Great conquered Egypt. Historians have divided Egyptian history into six periods: the early dynastic period, the Old Kingdom, the first intermediate period, the Middle Kingdom, the second intermediate period, and the New Kingdom. Within each period are a number of dynasties or sequences of rule by members of the same family.

During the early dynastic period (c. 3200–2620 B.C.) two kingdoms, which had existed along the Nile, were united under the first pharaoh or king. The first pyramid, a step pyramid, was constructed. Pyramids were intended not only to be the tombs of the pharaohs but also a sign that the Egyptian state was indestructible. In addition to building the first pyramids, the needs of the newly unified state required the keeping of records and so the earliest form of Egyptian writing was invented.

By the time of the Old Kingdom (2620–2280 B.C.), the powers of the pharaohs had become unlimited, and pyramid building had become the chief activity of the monarchy. The pyramids were astounding feats of engineering dwarfing monuments from other eras. The great pyramid of Cheops, which reached the height of 481 feet, contained more than 2 million limestone blocks, some weighing more than 15 tons, fitted together with great precision. But pyramid building exhausted the government's revenues. Weak pharaohs lost control of the government, and local nobles, usurping power began to act like petty kings.

The succeeding first intermediate period (c. 2260–2134 B.C.) became a time of troubles, civil war, and disorder. Tombs of the pharaohs were looted while highwaymen robbed travelers, and desert tribes invaded Egypt.

Pharaohs of the 11th and 12th dynasties established the Middle Kingdom (c. 2134–1786 B.C.) and united the country after the period of anarchy. A stronger central government was restored; public works which benefited the population replaced pyramid building which lacked any practical use. Egyptian influence was extended into Palestine and south along the Nile. As prosperity returned, wealth became more widely spread among the Egyptian people. The period ended with the first serious threat from abroad.

Another time of troubles came in the second intermediate period (c. 1786–1575 B.C.) when the nobility again revolted and the pharaohs' power became weak. About 1750 B.C., a nomadic people from western Asia, the Hyksos, seized control of Egypt for much of this period. The Hyksos, who brought horse drawn chariots and new weapons, soon adopted Egyptian customs and ways, including the power and title of pharaoh.

Hated by Egyptians, the Hyksos stimulated them into launching a revolt under the leadership of the founder of the 18th dynasty who finally drove the Hyksos out of Egypt. In the period of the New Kingdom (1575–1087 B.C.) or the period of Empire, Egypt became a strong, military power under the pharaoh Thutmose III (1504–1450 B.C.). He expanded Egyptian rule eastward as far as the Euphrates in seventeen campaigns and made Egypt a powerful force in the eastern Mediterranean area. The new monarchy restored temples and built luxurious palaces. Art forms which had been formal, stylized, and monumental became more natural and realistic.

By the 12th century Egyptian power had declined; society had decayed; the empire was disappearing. Libyans occupied the throne of the pharaohs in the 10th century only to be followed by Nubian conquerors in the 8th century. In 670 B.C. Assyria conquered Egypt but remained only eight years. Regaining independence, Egypt enjoyed a national renaissance until the Persians invaded in 525 B.C. Egypt stagnated, its glory far in the past. In 332 B.C., Alexander the Great, a Greek from Macedonia, conquered Egypt, ending Persian rule. Successive periods of Egyptian history were marked by domination first by Greece and then by Rome. A truly native Egyptian civilization had been ended.

Details of the life and history of Egypt are more complete than those for Mesopotamia over the same period for a variety of reasons. Like the Mesopotamians, the Egyptians had a form of writing, known as hieroglyphic, that has been deciphered by historians. Written records provide an abundant source of information about Egyptian life and religion. The Egyptians not only believed in life after death but followed the practice of burying with the dead their personal possessions which they might need in the hereafter. These included tools, furniture, food and drink. The hot dry climate of the desert, where prominent Egyptians were buried, preserved these objects, often in excellent condition. Also many of the temples and tombs contained paintings and sculpture, but unlike the Mesopotamians whose art generally emphasized the ceremonial aspects of life, the Egyptians painted and sculpted individuals in a variety of daily tasks.

DIFFERENCES IN THE DEVELOPMENT OF EGYPTIAN AND MESOPOTAMIAN CIVILIZATION

One of the most outstanding aspects of Egyptian civilization was the relative slowness with which changes occurred. Indeed there were changes in the 3000 years during which this civilization existed, but they took place so gradually that they seemed almost imperceptible even over several hundred years. For almost 3000 years, Egyptian civilization existed, scarcely affected by foreign cultural and political influences. "Between the Egypt of the Pyramid Age and that of Cleopatra were many differences, but many of these seem superficial, for much of the hard core of Egyptian thought and institutions was comparatively unchanged after some twenty-five centuries."[1]

In contrast, the civilizations of Mesopotamia displayed greater diversity when viewed over a period of 3000 years. One of the reasons for these differences may have been the geographical unity of the landscape in Egypt in contrast to a variety of landscapes and types of terrain in Mesopotamia. Egypt was a narrow strip of land set in the valley of the Nile where annual floods maintained the fertility of the land. Deserts on either side provided security from invasion while throughout Egypt farmers carried on the ceaseless routine of agriculture in the same way. But in Mesopotamia, regions differed more. Each area supported specific crops and each crop required special skills and care. The required labor force, the investment of capital, the organization of agriculture were different in each region. For example, flocks had to be moved seasonally, but grain crops required long term storage and distribution throughout the year. Some crops required long-range planting and planning, while others could be sewn and harvested in a short time.

These differences also accounted for some differences between the costume of the two cultures. While the climate in Egypt was relatively warm and uniform throughout the year, Mesopotamia had a greater variety of climates, including areas at higher altitudes where warm clothing was required at some times of the year and other hot, desert areas.

Ecology, then, was a factor contributing to the differences between Egyptian and Mesopotamian civilizations. Another was the degree to which each culture was subjected to outside influences. Both traded abroad to obtain raw materials unavailable within the boundaries of the region. With trade came outside influences. Egypt, however, was subjected less to outside influences because of natural barriers, the sea and the desert, which provided security from foreigners. Because natural barriers to invasion were lacking, foreign invaders periodically entered Mesopotamia, some of whom came to dominate the region. These groups adopted many traditions of the native peoples so there was a continuity of tradition, but at the same time new ideas were also incorporated into the culture. Egypt maintained a continuity in political and religious tradition that until the close of its long history was seriously threatened from outside only once, by the Hyksos.

Mesopotamian Civilization

For the convenience in the study of costume the history of the Mesopotamians will be sub-divided into three periods: Early Sumerian (c. 3500–2500 B.C.) and Later Sumerian and Babylonian, (c. 3500–1000 B.C.) and Assyrian (c. 1000–600 B.C.). Of the earliest period of Sumerian history relatively little is known. During the latter part of the period the record is clearer and it is possible to obtain a better picture of some aspects of life in general and of costume in particular.

SOCIAL STRUCTURE

The Babylonian culture was based on the earlier Sumerian civilization and the social structure of the Babylonians was similar to that of the Sumerians. Social classes were clearly defined. Other than the nobility which stood far above all the rest of society, one can identify three major classes in Babylonian society: free men, an intermediate class which might be called "the poor" who were "worth

1. W. A. Fairservis, Jr. *The Ancient Kingdoms of the Nile.* New York: New American Library, 1962, pp. 84–85.

little," and the slaves who were "worth nothing." The free men made up a sort of middle class of artisans, tradesmen, lesser public officials, and laborers. Farmers were generally part of the "intermediate" or "poor" class. Slaves were relatively few in Sumer, but by the time of the Babylonians had grown in number as they became an increasingly necessary part of the work force. Slaves could be foreign captives, the children of slaves, or wives and/or children of free men sold into slavery to meet the debts of the father of the family. Adopted children who disgraced their adoptive parents could also be sold into slavery.[2]

THE FAMILY

The family was patriarchal in structure. Marriage was a contractual arrangement generally made to cement an economic alliance between two families. By this contract a man had a principal wife, but could, and usually did, keep one or more concubines as well. Divorce was easily obtained if the principal wife was unable to have children.

That the position of women was subordinate is reinforced by the art that remains from Sumer and Babylonia. Representations of men predominate, with illustrations of women being relatively rare, usually goddesses, priestesses, or queens. They were not completely without rights, however, as Babylonian law codes extended to women the right to testify in court cases and provided some degree of economic protection to women in the case of the death of a spouse.

Although children had no legal rights, letters written on clay tablets and sent from children of the upper classes to their parents reveal that they felt free to demand the clothing or jewelry which they considered appropriate to their rank. One boy wrote to his mother:

> From year to year the clothes of the young gentlemen here become better, but you let my clothes get worse from year to year. Indeed you persisted in making my clothes poorer and more scanty. At a time when in our house wool is used up like bread, you have made me poor clothes. The son of Adid-iddinam, whose father is only an assistant of my father has two new sets of clothes while you fuss even about a single set of clothes for me. In spite of the fact that you bore me and his mother only adopted him, his mother loves him, while you do not love me.[3]

Another boy wrote to his father:

> I have never before written to you for something precious I wanted. But if you want to be like a father to me, get me a fine string full of beads, to be worn around the head . . . It should be full (of beads) and it should be beautiful. If I see it and dislike it, I shall send it back! Also send the cloak, of which I spoke to you.[4]

FABRICS AND CLOTH MANUFACTURE

The cloak and the new sets of clothes for which these boys pleaded were most likely made of wool. The chief products of Mesopotamia are described as barley, wool, and oil. These fabrics were produced not just for domestic consumption, but were traded to other regions as well. Flax is occasionally mentioned in the ancient records, but although fragments of linen have been found in excavations and there were skilled linen weavers, linen was clearly less important than wool which is mentioned often along with quotes for current prices. Clothes, tapestries, and curtains were made of wool. One contract has been found which describes the period of apprenticeship for a weaver as five years, an exceptionally long period when compared with other artisans. However, the variety of fabrics and the decorations applied to them seem to have been quite complex, so the weaver may have had to master quite a complicated system of manufacture.[5]

Mesopotamian Costume: Sumer, (c. 3500–2500 B.C.)

SOURCES OF EVIDENCE FOR COSTUME

The evidence for details of the costume of Mesopotamia is largely derived from visual materials. Depictions of persons are found on seals (small engraved markers used to press an identification into clay and wax.) These seals had scenes of Sumerian mythology incised or cut into them. A few wall paintings survive, as do small statuettes of worshipers left at shrines as substitutes for the worshipers themselves, to provide a sort of perpetual presence of the individual at the temple. From these rather limited remains and the excavation of Sumerian tombs, some impressions of Sumerian dress can be gained.

2. G. Contenau. *Every Day Life in Babylon and Assyria*. London: Edward Arnold, 1954, p. 15 ff.

3. A. L. Oppenheim, *Letters from Mesopotamia*. Chicago: University of Chicago Press, 1967, p. 85.

4. Oppenheim, Ibid., p. 87.

5. A. Leix. "Babylon-Assur. Land of Wool." *CIBA Review*, # I, p. 406.

COSTUME FOR MEN AND WOMEN

Item / Description

skirt—Basic costume item for men and women, probably first made of sheepskin with the fleece still attached. Lengths varied: servants and soldiers wore shorter lengths; royalty and deities, longer lengths. Skirts apparently wrapped around the body. When fabric ends were long enough, the end of fabric was passed up, under a belt, and over one shoulder. (See Figure 2.1.)

NOTE OF SPECIAL INTEREST: Even after sheepskin had been supplemented by woven cloth, the cloth was fringed at the hem or constructed to simulate the tufts of wool on the fleece. A Greek word, *kaunakes*, has been attached to this fleece or fleece-like fabric. (See Figure 2.2.)

belt—worn at waist to hold skirts in place. Appears to be wide and padded.

cloak—covered upper part of body. Probably made from either animal skins, leather, or heavy, felted cloth.

hats and head dress—soldiers wore close-fitting helmets with pointed tops, perhaps made of leather.

Both men and women might pull their long hair into a bun or *chignon* which was held in place at the back of the head by a headband or *fillet*. Alternatively, they also wore the hair falling straight to the shoulders and held in place by a fillet.

Men are depicted both clean-shaven and bearded, sometimes with bald heads. (See Figures 2.1 and 2.2.)

NOTE: Shaving the head was a practice of several Mediterranean cultures, including the Egyptian, very likely as a means of discouraging vermin and for comfort in the hot, humid climate.

jewelry—From archeological evidence some royal women apparently wore elaborate gold jewelry.

NOTE: An excavation at Ur from just after 2800 B.C. unearthed a beautiful gold and jeweled crown, made with delicate leaves and flowers and massive gold necklaces and earrings. Comparable items have not been found for later periods, nor are they depicted in the art of the period. Fragments of cloth from this tomb showed that the Queen and her attendants wore a bright, red, heavy woolen fabric.

Mesopotamian Costume: Later Sumeria and the Babylonians (C. 2500–1000 B.C.)

Styles evolved slowly, and sharp distinctions cannot be made between costume of the later Sumerian and early Babylonian periods. Costume generally increased in complexity. Although men and women's dress continued to utilize similar elements, evidence indicates a trend toward greater distinctions in the clothing for each sex.

COSTUME FOR MEN (C. 2500–1000 B.C.)

Item / Description

MILITARY COSTUME

skirts—persisted in military dress, having fringed decoration around the lower edge; probably made of woven fabric.

shawls—worn with skirts, the center placed across the left shoulder, ends crossing the chest and carried back to be knotted over the right hip.

helmets—of leather or metal, sometimes with horn-shaped decorations.

sandals—worn when rough terrain made foot coverings necessary.

CIVILIAN DRESS

skirt, loin cloth and tunic—probably made up the most common items of dress for the poor.

draped garment—Nobility or mythological figures wore garment described by Houston on the basis of visual analysis and draping of similar styles as made from square of fabric about 118 inches wide and 56 inches long and draped as depicted in Figure 2.3.

NOTE: Sumerian and Babylonian art depicts these garments as smooth-surfaced, without draped folds, but this is probably an artistic convention. Not only do the woven fabrics appear to fall without folds, but even faces, skin, and arms have smooth planes and lack of detail. Fabrics are fringed and/or have woven or embroidered edgings.

head dress—Men before 2300 B.C. are shown both clean-shaven and with beards, but later only with beards.

2.1 Praying Figure. (*Left*) Mesopotamian, Sumerian, c. 2200 B.C. Sumerian man wearing *Kaunakes* garment in the form of a wrapped skirt. The end of the skirt is thrown over his left shoulder. Both men and women wore the same type of garment. His head is shaven. (*Photograph courtesy of the Metropolitan Museum of Art, Harris Brisbane Dick Fund, 1949.*)

2.2 Praying Figure. (*Below*) Mesopotamian, Sumerian, c. 3000 B.C. Bearded Sumerian man wears fringed skirt. (*Photograph courtesy of the Metropolitan Museum of Art, Fletcher Fund, 1940.*)

2.3 Standing Figure of Gudea. (*Above*) Mesopotamian, 22nd century, B.C. The garment shown here was probably made from a rectangular length of fabric wrapped around the body. The head from a similar figure in the background wears a close-fitting hat with a small brim or padded roll. (*Photograph courtesy of the Cleveland Museum of Art, purchase from the J. H. Wade Fund.*)

hats—turban-like, close-fitted at the crown with a small brim or padded roll at the edge. (See Figure 2.3.)

footwear—usually feet are bare or with sandals which provided adequate covering in rough terrain.

NOTE: A clay model of a leather shoe with a tongue, upward curve to the toe, and a pompom on the toe dating from about 2600 B.C. was found. Born suggests that such shoes may have originated in mountainous areas where there was snow, and that they may have been brought from there to Mesopotamia. This style of shoe seems to have taken on a ceremonial function, being reserved in sculpture for a hero-figure representing the king. "The peaked shoe with a pompom," says Born, "is probably to be regarded as a regal attribute."[6]

COSTUME FOR WOMEN (C. 2500–1000 B.C.)

Item / Description

kaunakes garment—persisted for a time for women, but gradually became associated with religious figures (goddesses, priestesses, or minor deities). In this period, garment was cut to cover entire body, not just one shoulder as in earlier period. Possible constructions were:
· skirt in combination with short cape cut with opening for the head, or
· tunic with openings for head and arms.
(Evidence is inadequate to be certain of specific construction.)

other garments—Figure 2.4, based on Houston's recreation, shows two additional women's garment forms utilizing a long piece of fabric wrapped around the body in slightly different ways.

head dress—continuation of the chignon held in place with fillet; in some representations hair appears to be confined in a net.

footwear—bare feet or sandals for the well-to-do

jewelry—that shown most often was tight-fitting, dog-collar type of necklace made from several rings of metal.

---

6. W. Born, "Footwear of the Ancient Orient," *CIBA Review*, # III, p. 1210.

COSTUME FOR CHILDREN

Sources do not provide any solid information either about underclothing for adults or children's clothing. Children occupied a subservient position in the family. The father of the family had the right to sell his children into slavery or leave them on deposit with a creditor as security for repayment of a loan! Their costume was probably minimal. When clothing was worn it may have consisted of the simplest of the adult garments: a loin cloth, a skirt, or a tunic. Children of the upper classes probably wore clothing like those of their parents.

Mesopotamian Costume: Later Babylonia and the Assyrians (C. 1000–600 B.C.)

The Assyrians adopted Babylonian costume and a clear break between the late Babylonian and early Assyrian styles cannot be seen. At some point the skirt and draped garments characteristic of the earlier Babylonian period were replaced by a tunic, a T-shaped garment with openings for the head and arms. Perhaps the tunic, a closely-fitting garment more suitable for cooler climates, was borrowed from nearby mountain peoples.

Although the Assyrian leaders adopted the styles of the Babylonians they added to their decoration. Woven or embroidered pattern is seen in great profusion on the costumes of the king and his chief officials. The Assyrians continued the tradition of wearing wool garments, but King Sennacherib (c. 700 B.C.) is said to have introduced cotton to Assyria, probably from India.[7]

COSTUME FOR MEN

Item / Description

tunic—ending above the knee. Worn with a belt and little decoration by the laboring classes, with armor by soldiers. *For royalty:* floor length tunic with several long, fringed shawls wrapped around the body. Draping of shawls juxtaposed horizontal, vertical, and diagonal arrangement of fringes and were sufficiently complex to inhibit movement, therefore it is likely that these costumes were for state occasions and everyday clothing even for royalty may have been simpler. In those

---

7. H. Wescher, "Cotton in the Ancient World," *CIBA Review*, #64, p. 2322.

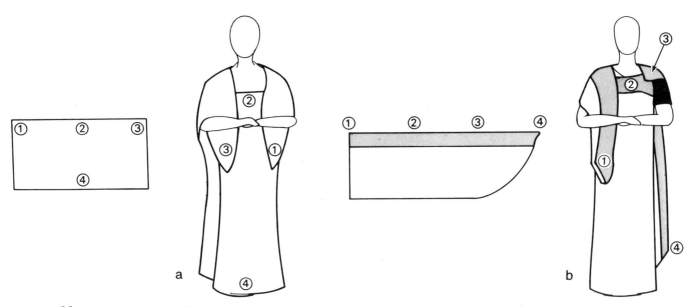

2.4 a and b. Houston suggests these reconstructions for Babylonian women's costume. (*Drawings adapted from M. G. Houston. Ancient Egyptian, Mesopotamian, and Persian Costume. New York: Barnes and Noble, 1964, Chapter 10.*)

a. Costume is draped from a rectangle of fabric. Point 2 is placed at center front, points 1 and 3 are drawn under the arms, segment 2–3 crossing over 1–2 in back. Points 1 and 3 are pulled over the shoulder to hang down at each side in front.

b. Costume is draped from rectangle with one end curved. A small fold of fabric, (shaded area) is made at the top. Square corner at point 1 is draped across the right shoulder to the back, across the back and under the left arm, across the front again, passing under the drape of point 1. Point 3 is pulled across the back again and pinned over the shoulder to point 2 in the front. Section 3–4 falls in a drape behind the shoulder to the ground.

scenes depicting hunting or warfare, the king's costume has less encumbering drapery.

NOTE: The dress of royal figures in any civilization is set apart by differences in style, more valuable materials, greater elaboration in its decoration, or by the emblems of power in the form of special head dress, a staff, or a scepter. Often the costume of royalty is specified by tradition and does not necessarily reflect current styles.

Mesopotamian artists depict the garments of the king as covered with what appears to be embroidery, although some authors suggest that these designs may have been woven. The specific garment worn by the king on any given day was determined by the priests. The Assyrians believed that some days were favorable and some unfavorable therefore the priest would prescribe the most auspicious garment, its color and fabric. On some unfavorable days the king was not permitted to change his clothing at all.

head dress—men were bearded, the hair and beard arranged in small curls achieved with the help of curling irons. The king's beard was longer than that of other men, and supplemented with a false

section. Lower class men had shorter beards and hair. (See Figure 2.5.)

hats—included a high brimless hat similar to the *fez or tarbush*, a modern-day, traditional Arab style worn in South West Asia or Northern Africa. This hat is sometimes depicted with broad bands of fabric hanging down the back. The king wore a higher, straighter version similar to hats worn in later centuries by Persian royalty and by Eastern Orthodox Christian priests in the 20th century.

footwear—sandals and, less commonly, closed shoes. Depending on whether they were to be given heavier or lighter use, soles of sandals were thicker or thinner. High boots are shown on horsemen, probably as protective footwear necessary for the aggressive Assyrian military forces. (See Figure 2.5.)

jewelry—earrings, bracelets, and armlets. Decorative motifs on jewelry often resemble those seen on patterned fabrics. (See Figure 2.5.)

2.5 Winged Genie (a mythological figure) from Mesopotamia, Assyrian Period, 8th century B.C. A short tunic over which a fringed shawl has been placed is worn by this figure. Other aspects of his costume that are characteristic of Assyrian dress are the sandals with wedge-shaped heels, jewelry including that worn on the arms and at the neck, earrings, a fillet on the hair, and elaborately-arranged curls in the hair and beard. (*Photograph courtesy of the Cleveland Museum of Art, purchase from the J. H. Wade Fund.*)

COSTUME FOR WOMEN (C. 1000–600 B.C.)

Few representations of women are found in Assyrian art. The status of women in Sumer and Babylon had been relatively low, but under late Babylonian law women had been given the right to testify in court. Under Assyrian law this right was taken away, and some of the protections extended to women in regard to property rights in Babylon were removed. Historians see this as evidence of a possible influx of new people whose customs differed from those of the native population.

Customs surrounding the wearing of veils by women may also be related to such population and attitude changes. References to the wearing of veils are found in Assyrian law codes. In Assyrian and late Babylonian times the veil was considered to be the distinguishing mark of a free, married woman; slaves and prostitutes were not permitted to wear veils, and a concubine could wear a veil only when she accompanied the principal wife. Some representations show the veil hanging over the hair on either side of the face, but apparently veils often covered the face in public. This custom persists today in some areas of the mid-East and although the reasons for veiling women are no longer related to marital status, one can see that wearing the veil is a Middle Eastern tradition of long duration.

Item / Description

tunic—generally cut with somewhat longer sleeves than those for men. Fabrics were elaborately patterned.

shawls—fringed and draped around the body

footwear—sandals and closed shoes

head dress—considerable variety: earlier styles are elaborately arranged; later styles simpler with curly, shoulder-length hair.

jewelry—necklaces, earrings, bracelets, and armlets.

military dress—consisted of short tunic, a corselet of mail, and a wide belt. The mail was probably made by sewing small metal plates onto leather or heavy cloth. In some representations mail covers only part of the body; in others the whole tunic. Helmets fit the head closely, came to a peaked point at the back of the head. Both sandals and high boots were worn.

Egyptian Civilization

Egyptian culture and dress developed in quite different ways from that of the Mesopotamian civilizations. Furthermore more evidence in the form of works of art, real objects, and written records is available to the student.

SOCIAL STRUCTURE

Egyptian society has been compared to the pyramids. The Pharaoh, or hereditary king, was at the apex of this pyramid. At the next level were his chief deputies and the high priests. Below them were a host of officials of lesser status who were associated either with the court or the administration of towns and cities.

Other important positions were occupied by the scribes, comparable to the "white collar" workers of today such as department managers, bookkeepers, accountants, clerks, and bureaucrats. They were attached to the courts, city administrations, religious organizations, and the military. These occupations provided an avenue of upward mobility within Egyptian society.

A step below the scribes were the artisans or craftsmen, a vast throng of skilled workers such as painters, sculptors, architects, furniture-makers, weavers, and jewelers. Servants and laborers and the huge number of peasants who tilled the land provided the agricultural base on which the upper levels of the social pyramid rested. Slavery existed. Slaves were foreign captives, not native Egyptians. Some, like the Hebrew slave Moses, were able to attain freedom and rise to relatively high station, but this was rare.

Costume served to delineate social class, even though much of Egyptian costume was relatively simple. The draping, the quality of the fabrics, and the addition of costly jewelry and belts distinguished the garments of the upper from those of the lower classes. Higher standards of grooming were expected of the upper classes. Workmen are shown in paintings with a stubbly growth of beard; upper class men are invariably clean-shaven.

THE FAMILY

Marriage was a civil contract; divorce was easy. Multiple marriages were not common, although many well-to-do men had a harem or at least several concubines. Wall paintings of family scenes present a of warm, close, family life. Fathers and mothers caress the young, and small children play happily with toys or pets.

Upper class families lived in luxuriously-furnished houses. By 20th century standards, the quantity of furniture was small, but pieces were decorated with beautiful inlays and worked metal. Homes were spacious with carefully-tended gardens.

Social gatherings during the New Kingdom are often painted. Men and women are dressed lavishly for these occasions, wearing long, full pleated gowns, vivid cosmetics, and brightly colored jewelry and head dress. Musicians, acrobats, and dancing girls entertain. Cones of scented wax are set on the heads of guests and as the evening progressed these would melt, run down over the wigs, and perfume the air.

The hot, humid climate made cleanliness essential for comfort and the upper class Egyptians had high standards of personal cleanliness, bathing two or more times each day. In some periods, heads were shaved and wigs worn possibly as a means of keeping the head clean and free from vermin.

THE SKILLS OF THE CRAFTSMAN

The workmanship of artisans was of exceptional quality. Of special interest to the study of historic costume are the weaving and jewelry-making crafts.

Thanks to the hot, dry climate of the burial places of Egyptian kings and nobles, actual pieces of fabric have been preserved. Linen was the fabric most used by Egyptians. Cotton and silk were not known until the periods when Egypt had come under Greek and Roman domination. Wool was considered ritually unclean, and was not worn in sanctuaries, by priests, or used for burial. Herodotus, a Greek historian of the 5th century B.C., who traveled in Egypt reports that wool was worn as an outer garment,[8] but linen clearly predominated. Fabrics were dyed, however linen is often seen in paintings in its natural color, creamy-white, or bleached to a pure white.

By the time of the New Kingdom, spinning and weaving techniques were highly developed. Some fine, closely-woven fabrics with thread counts as high as 160 threads in the lengthwise direction and 120 threads in the crosswise direction have been found.[9] The finest sheer organdies of the 19th and 20th centuries rarely have thread counts as high as 150 in the lengthwise and 100 in the crosswise directions.[10] The items excavated from the tomb of King Tutankhamen, a boy Pharaoh of the New Kingdom, included robes made of beaded fabric, others with woven and embroidered patterns and

8. Herodotus on Egypt, reprinted in *The World of the Past*, V. 1, J. Hawkes, Ed., New York: Knopf, 1963, p. 553.
9. L. Casson, *Daily Life in Ancient Egypt.* New York: American Heritage Publishing Company, Inc., 1975, p. 70.
10. *American Fabrics Encyclopedia of Textiles.* Englewood Cliffs, New Jersey: Prentice-Hall, Inc., 1972, p. 568.

still others with appliqué, revealing that the arts of fabric construction included skill in beading, pattern weaving, embroidery, and appliqué.

Gold jewelry was prized by the Egyptians, however silver was not found in Egypt and had to be imported so that its use was limited. The Egyptians did not make glass, but natural volcanic glass and imported glass were used in jewelry. Semi-precious and precious stones such as carnelian, lapis lazuli, feldspar, and turquoise were worked into large, multi-colored round collars, pectorals (decorative pendants), earrings, bracelets, armlets, and hair or head ornaments. Religious symbols appear often in jewelry, as well as in art. The Egyptians had an abiding belief in magic, and thought that by representing symbols of religious figures in jewelry the positive qualities of the deity would be transferred to the wearer. The scarab, a symbol representing the sun god and also rebirth, was a popular motif. The hawk appears often as another symbol of the sun god. The cobra (also called the *uraeus*) was the symbol of Lower Egypt, the vulture of Upper Egypt. Used together on royal head dress and in jewelry, the two symbolized the unification of Lower and Upper Egypt under the Pharaohs. The "eye of Horus," a stylized representation of the human eye symbolized the moon. The lotus blossom, papyrus blossom, and animal forms that were native to the area were also translated into decorative motifs.

EGYPTIAN ART

It is through the art of Egypt that most of the information about Egyptian costume has been gained. The artist probably did not always depict costume with absolute fidelity, but was guided by artistic convention. One of the basic costumes for women is a straight, fitted garment of tubular form. Paintings and statues show this garment as fitting so tightly around the body that the wearer would be virtually unable to walk. Woven fabrics do not cling so closely to the body, and so far as research can ascertain, the Egyptians had not developed techniques such as knitting which would permit so close a fit, so one may hypothesize that artistic convention required the garment be shown as exceptionally tight-fitting.

Egyptian tombs yielded items of dress which seem to have no counterpart in paintings or statuary, such as the multi-colored garments and elaborately decorated sandals found in the excavation of the tomb of Tutankhamen. These might have been ceremonial garments, special funeral garments, or actual items from the King's wardrobe.

During the periods of Greek and Roman dominance Pharaohs were represented in art as dressed in the styles of the Old Kingdom, and yet records indicate that the rulers of the period actually dressed in Greek and Roman styles.[11] In spite of the wealth of pictorial and other evidence available, our knowledge about the clothing of Egypt is still incomplete, as is true of other periods when conclusions must be based on interpretation of illustrations of costume without adequate written records and actual garments for confirmation.

Egyptian Costume

COSTUME FOR MEN

Costume may express the relationships between the individual and his or her natural and social environments. As the social structures of society evolved, dress was one means of manifesting visually one's personal power, dignity, or wealth. Throughout the 3000 years of Egyptian history, slaves, peasants and other lower class men wore only the simplest of garments: a manifestation of the insignificant social status they were assigned. The climate of Egypt did not require clothing for warmth. Lower class individuals were excluded from participation in religious ritual. Personal wealth, power and dignity were beyond their grasp. It is not surprising that clothing played a minimal role in their lives.

Item / Description

loin cloth—shaped and worn like a triangular diaper. Worn alone by lower class men or as an undergarment by higher class men. (See Figure 2.6.)

skirt—called by various costume historians either a *schenti, shent, skent, or schent,* this garment was a wrapped skirt, the length, width, and fit of which varied with different time periods and different social classes. (See Figures 2.6, 2.7, 2.8.)

For laborers, it ended at the knee or above. For upper class men these variations can be identified: *In the earliest periods:* generally knee-length or shorter; fitted closely around the hips. Decoration achieved by rounding one end of the fabric to form a diagonal line across the front

11. B. Mertz, *Red Land, Black Land.* New York: Coward-McCann, Inc., 1966.

2.6 (*Top*) Egyptian wall painting, c. 1415 B.C. Included are a variety of costume types: loin cloth (upper right corner), a number of different *schentis*, sheer tunic with *schenti* placed both over (top row) and under (bottom row) the tunic, and woman in a sheath dress with a single strap (upper right). Note also a naked child in the center of the upper row and children in *schentis* in the same row. (*Photograph courtesy of the Metropolitan Museum of Art.*)

2.7 (*Above left*) Apuy, a sculptor of the New Kingdom Period and his wife receiving an offering. Men and women wear sheer, pleated linen gowns with wide, bead collars. Man making the offering wears a leopard skin with a pleated, linen *schenti*. All wear wigs, those of the men are shorter than those of the women. A scented cone of wax is placed on their heads. The fingernails and toenails of both men and women are polished, their eyes outlined in *kohl*. The men wear sandals. (*Photograph courtesy of the Metropolitan Museum of Art, copy in tempera of wall paintings from a tomb.*)

2.8 (*Right*) Prince, son of Ramses II, wears a *schenti* and sleeveless corselet. His hair is cut in the "lock of youth" which is characteristic of the young, especially royal princes. (*Picture from New York City Public Library Picture Collection, redrawing by Champollion, 1844–1889.*)

or by pleating the end, or by placing decorative panels at the front.

Middle Kingdom styles show the skirt elongated, sometimes reaching to the ankle, with shorter versions for work, for soldiers, or for hunters. A double skirt, the under layer opaque and outer layer sheer, appears, continuing in use into the new kingdom.

New Kingdom styles have pleated skirts, both shorter examples which tend to fit more closely, and long skirts that are quite full. Large, triangular decorative panels located at the front of some skirts.

NOTE: By following the lines of pleats in garments shown on statues one can gain some understanding of how the fabrics were draped. In one version a length of fabric appeared to have been pleated along its long direction. The pleats were arranged horizontally across the back, then pulled up, diagonally, to the waistline in front where the ends were tied or passed over each other. They hung downward at center front to form a pleated panel.

upper body coverings—*animal skins*—In very early representations one may see the skin of a leopard or lion fastened across the shoulders.

In later periods fabric replaced skins for general garment construction and wearing of animal skins was reserved for the most powerful element in society: kings and priests. (See Figure 2.7.) Finally even the skins were no longer worn, but were replaced by ritual garments made from cloth but simulating animal skins.

NOTE: The Egyptian belief in magic seems to underlie this practice. The Egyptians believed that by wearing the skin of a fierce beast the powers of the animal were magically transferred to the wearer.

cape-like or shirt-like garment—*Middle Kingdom*—short fabric cape, fastening at center front or a short-sleeved very short tunic, lengths of which ranged from short enough to expose the midriff to long enough to be tucked into the skirt or belted. Fabrics often quite sheer.
corselet—sleeveless and probably a decorative form of armor; might be either strapless or suspended by small straps from the shoulders. (See Figure 2.8.)
wide necklace—made from concentric circles of precious or semi-precious stones this cape-like ornament might be worn alone, over a linen gown, over a short cape, or with the corselet. (See Figure 2.8.)

tunic—similar to the tunic of Mesopotamia, and appearing in Egypt about the time of the New Kingdom. Wall paintings show it with and without sleeves; often of sheer almost transparent linen, under which a loincloth or a short shirt might be worn, or over which a skirt could be wrapped. (See Figure 2.6.)

NOTE: During the New Kingdom a number of new elements entered dress, probably as a result of the contacts with the near East, the invasion of the Hyksos, and/or the expansion of the Egyptian empire into the area west of Egypt. Two new costume forms are particularly notable. Costume terminology tends to be somewhat confused when certain of the basic Egyptian costumes are discussed. Many of those who write about the costume of Egypt use the term *kalasiris* or *calasiris* to refer to close-fitting garments worn by women from the Old to the New Kingdoms. Others apply the term to a loose-fitting garment worn by both men and women. Herodotus says of the 5th century Egyptians, "The clothes they wear consist of a linen tunic with a fringe hanging around the legs (called in their language calasiris), and a white woolen garment on top of it." From the testimony of Herodotus it would seem that the Egyptian name for a tunic-like garment was *calasiris* and it is in this application that the term is used in this text.[12]

long draped robe—another New Kingdom innovation. Long, loose, flowing garment with variations achieved by arrangement of the sheer pleated linen fabric. Probably made from a full square of fabric with an opening for the head. (See Figure 2.7.) Variations:
  · sides seamed with openings left for arms, then worn loose and full.
  · fabric arranged so that pleats fall in different directions at different points on the body.

COSTUME FOR WOMEN

Item / Description

skirts—worn by lowerclass women at work; slaves and dancing girls are also depicted without clothes occasionally.

sheath—most common garment for women of all classes. Closely fitted (though probably not so close as depicted in art), appears to have been

12. Herodotus quoted in J. Hawkes, *op. cit.*

a tube of fabric held in place by one or two straps. (See Figure 2.9.) Sometimes these straps cover the nipple; in other versions straps are too narrow or placed so that the breast is exposed. A style with a long life, it is seen in all periods though with less frequency in the New Kingdom.

NOTE: Often made of elaborately patterned fabric, the techniques used are not known. Speculations range from appliquéd leather or feathers to beadwork or woven designs. From the evidence in the Tutankhamen tomb we know that skill in beadwork was well-developed, however in the same tomb was a pair of gloves of woven fabric with a design similar to those seen on many of the sheaths.

tunic or calasiris—for women of lower station, such as musicians, rather than by upper class women. (See Figure 2.10.)

long draped robe—though at first glance the sheer, pleated robes of men and women look alike, careful examination reveals that their draping and arrangement was different. Some women's styles cover the breasts, others leave them exposed. (See Figure 2.7.)

NOTE: Houston's reconstruction of Egyptian costume suggests several possible methods of construction. Briefly summarized they are: combination of a skirt with a short cape that covered the back and upper arms; placing a rectangle of fabric with a neck opening over the head and tying the back edges of the fabric over the front; and a number of complicated wrappings of a

2.9 (*Above*) Models of girls of the Middle Kingdom (XI Dynasty) bearing baskets of offerings for a funeral. Both wear closely-fitted sheath dresses and wide, faience collars. (*Photograph courtesy of the Metropolitan Museum of Art, Museum Excavations, 1919–1920; Rogers Fund, supplemented by contribution of Edward S. Harkness.*)

2.10 (*Right*) Wall painting of musicians from the New Kingdom (Dynasty VIII). Figures on the extreme left and right wear sheath dresses, and have cones of wax on their heads. The flute player wears a *kalasiris*. (*Photograph courtesy of the Metropolitan Museum of Art.*)

rectangle of fabric around the body, some of which appear to be similar to the draping of costume from Mesopotamia during the Babylonian period.[13]

OTHER COSTUME ITEMS WORN BY MEN AND WOMEN

Item / Description

head dress—men clean-shaven, during some periods they shaved their heads as well; less commonly so for women. Wigs worn over the shaved head or over the hair. Shape, length, arrangement of wigs varies from period to period. More expensive wigs are of human hair; cheaper ones of wool, flax, palm fiber, or felt. Most are black in color, though blue, brown, white or some gilded examples exist. Even when wigs were relatively short, women's tend to be longer than men's. Their styl-

ing ranged from simple, long flowing locks to complex braidings, curls, or twists of "hair." (See Figures 2.7 and 2.9.)

head coverings—of kings and queens symbolized their status.

· the *pschent*, or double crown of Egypt, a towering head covering made up of a combination of the crown of Lower Egypt and the crown of Upper Egypt, each of which could be worn alone.

· the falcon or vulture head covering shaped like a bird of prey with the wings falling down at the side of the head and framing the face was worn only by the queen.

· the *uraeus*, a head band with the sacred cobra at the center front was worn by kings and queens.

· So-called *Nemes* head covering, worn by rulers from the Old to the New Kingdom was a scarf-like construction, fitted across the temple, hanging down to the shoulder behind the ears, and with a long tail at center back. The head was completely covered; an extended section

2.11 Head of Queen Hatshepsut, Dynasty XVIII. The Queen wears the *Nemes* head dress and a false beard, symbol of maturity and authority. (*Photograph courtesy of the Metropolitan Museum of Art, Museum Excavations, 1922–23, 1926–28.*)

13. Houston, *op. cit.*, Chapter 7.

2.12 From left to right: Shawl, of linen, from the Late Period (Dynasty XXI); kerchief from the New Kingdom (Dynasty XVII); child's linen garment, made like the description by Herodotus of the *kalasiris*, from the Late Period; sandals for a child and for an adult from the New Kingdom, (Dynasty XVIII). (*Photograph courtesy of the Metropolitan Museum of Art.*)

in front reached to below the collar bone. The shape of the *Nemes* head covering is similar to a simple, scarf-like head covering owned by the Metropolitan Museum. (See Figures 2.11 and 2.12.)

· high brimless head covering depicted in a famous bust of Queen Nefertiti, a New Kingdom Queen, who, judging from the sculpture, shaved her head. Many other types of head dress for royalty and deities too numerous to detail clearly show the role of items of dress in communicating role and status to a non-reading public.

footwear—bare feet or sandals predominate in art. Sandals were made of rushes woven or twisted together. Other examples from royal burials are elaborately decorated. As with other basic costume items the status of the wearer was demonstrated by superior workmanship, increased decoration, and finer materials. (See Figures 2.7 and 2.12.)

jewelry—with New Kingdom gowns jewelry or jeweled belts were often the main sources of color in costume. Wide jeweled collars were depicted in art from the Old Kingdom, persisting until the end of the New Kingdom and beyond. Men and women wore pectorals (hanging pendants), bracelets and armlets.

earrings—possibly another of the contributions of the Hyksos to Egyptian styles, as they are a late addition to Egyptian jewelry. First worn by women, they seem eventually to have been used by men also.

NOTE: In the 1977–78 exhibit of artifacts from the tomb of Tutankhamen it was suggested that earrings may have been worn by young boys but abandoned in manhood.[14]

belts and decorated aprons—jewelry techniques, beads, leather work, appliqué, and woven designs could all be used to construct the highly ornate decorative belts and aprons that were an integral part of Egyptian costume.

cosmetics—worn by both men and women for the decoration of eyes, skin, lips, finger and toe nails. Eyes were outlined in black, possibly serving to cut the glare of the bright desert sunlight. Red color applied to lips and cheeks; nails of hands and feet polished and buffed. Scented ointments were applied to the body.

14. *Treasures of King Tutankhamen.* Catalog of the exhibition at the British Museum. London: British Museums, 1972, p. 39.

COSTUME FOR CHILDREN

The children who are depicted in Egyptian paintings are generally the offspring of wealthy or royal families. These representations and the numerous toys found in Egyptian tombs indicate that children were regarded with interest and warm affection. Education was provided for boys—the very rich had private tutors, the less affluent went to temple schools. Children of the lower classes were taught a trade or craft, while sons of peasants labored in the fields with their fathers.

Dress for the very young was minimal. Little boys are depicted as naked except for an occasional bracelet or amulet; little girls wear necklaces, armlets, bracelets, anklets, and sometimes earrings. Some pictures show girls wearing a belt at the waist. After beginning school, boys apparently were dressed in the schenti, or among the lower classes probably a loincloth. Girls apparently continued to go naked until close to the time they reached puberty when they were dressed like their mothers. (See Figure 2.10.)

Special hairstyles for children appear. In some representations, the head is completely shaved; in others part is left unshaven. The long locks of hair that grew in the unshaven part of the head were arranged in curls or braids. The sons of the Pharaoh wore a distinctive hair style called the lock of Horus or the lock of youth in which the head was shaven except for one lock of hair on the left side of the head. This lock was arranged carefully in braids over the ear. (See Figure 2.8.)

COSTUMES FOR SPECIALIZED OCCUPATIONS

Costume for specialized occupations showed some minor variations from the basic Egyptian styles.

Military Costume—The ordinary foot soldier of Ancient Egypt wore a short skirt, which in the New Kingdom representations had a stiffened triangular panel at the front possibly to protect the vulnerable genitals. A helmet, made of padded leather, covered the head. He carried weapons and a shield. In some instances a sleeveless armored corselet supported by straps was shown. This garment covered the chest and is thought to have been made of small plates of bone, metal, or leather sewn to a linen body. Many soldiers are depicted as barefooted; others are shown in sandals.

When the Pharaoh dressed for war, he wore the costume typical of his era plus the special insignia of his rank: a crown or other head dress and a false beard. The beard was a symbol of maturity and authority and was, as a consequence, worn—or at least depicted on paintings and sculpture—not only by adult male rulers but also by young kings and even Queen Hatshepsut who ruled around 1500 B.C. (See Figure 2.11.) When at war the king carried weapons. After the adoption of chariots for warfare the Pharaoh was often represented riding in a chariot while a servant preceded him, carrying his sandals.

Religious Costume—The costume of priests does not differ much from that of ordinary Egyptians. Priests were usually depicted with shaven heads, and one of the insignias of the priesthood was either a real or simulated leopard skin draped over the shoulders.

Gods and goddesses are shown in Egyptian art dressed as ordinary mortals, but wearing special head dresses or carrying symbols of their divinity. In the New Kingdoms, goddesses dressed in the older, fitted sheath style often appear alongside mortals dressed in the pleated robe. It may have been a convention to show these divinities in costumes that emphasized their timelessness. The Pharaoh, who was considered to be divine, frequently appears wearing the special headdress or insignia of the gods.

Musicians, Dancers, and Acrobats—Entertainers, such as dancers and acrobats, are often shown as naked or wearing only a band around the waist. Musicians, both male and female, dressed in the simpler costume forms of the period. During the New Kingdom this would have been a full, very sheer tunic or robe. (See Figure 2.10.)

Summary

Egyptian costume began with the simple loin cloth or skirt for men and a straight, form-fitting sheath or a skirt for women. Throughout the history of this civilization, although the forms of these costumes grew more elaborate and more decorative and although additional types of garments were added, the basic concept of clothing that complemented the natural lines of the body was retained. Linen, a fabric that was comfortable in the heat of a tropical climate and which could be made into soft, sheer, drapable, fabrics remained the primary material from which garments were made throughout the history of this civilization.

Mesopotamian costume, too, continued to utilize one fiber to a considerable extent: wool, which made a fabric of greater bulk and warmth than linen. (In the later periods, both cotton and linen seem also to have been added to the materials from which Mesopotamians made their clothes.) Throughout their history the Mesopotamians also retained a consistent approach to clothing. Mesopotamian clothing was designed not to compliment the body, but to cover it. The early Kaunakes skirts and full-length garments, the draped styles of the later Babylonians, and the shawls that wrapped the Assyrian kings covered the body with layers of fabric that obscured its natural lines. Such differences have been attributed not only to geographical difference between the two countries, but also to differences in standards of taste. Leix pointed out that Egyptians loved clarity of form in life and in art, while the Babylonians loved pomp and luxury. This latter preference is reflected in the heavy fabrics, rich patterns, and elaborate fringes of Mesopotamian styles. Furthermore, moral reasons, possibly expressed as different views of modesty in dress, may also have influenced styles. Mesopotamian religions show a greater pre-occupation with ethical problems than do those of Egypt.[15]

The decline of the Assyrian civilization did not totally obliterate all traces of Mesopotamian costume. At least one element of dress persisted in the region and, eventually, found its way into other parts of the world. The high crowned head dress worn by Assyrian kings was adopted by the Persians. From its use in Persia it eventually found its way into the costume of the Eastern Orthodox Christian priests.

Certain other aspects of Mesopotamian costume utilized not only by the Sumerian, Babylonian, or Assyrian peoples, but also more generally throughout the Near East have survived into more recent times. The practice of women to wear a veil outside of the home is one example. It has also been suggested (although it cannot be documented) that the kaunakes fabric in the form of a garment worn by shepherds and other rustic peoples may have come into European art to symbolize people from little known or distant lands of the Middle East.

Egyptian costume did not long survive the Greek and Roman domination of Egypt, although it was used for the formal portraits of the last Pharaohs and Queen Cleopatra. Instead the Egyptians adopted first Greek, then Roman styles. In several instances, however, ancient Egyptian fashions have

15. Leix, *op. cit.*, p. 407

influenced 20th century styles. The first was in 1920 when the discovery of the tomb of King Tutankhamen gave rise to a short-lived vogue for Egyptian-inspired fabrics, jewelry, and to a lesser extent, women's fashions. The exhibit of artifacts from this same tomb in 1977–78 also motivated fashion and jewelry designers to orchestrate a revival of Egyptian-inspired products. This, too, proved to be a short-term fashion. Dr. Mary Ellen Roach Higgins pointed out that one of the most interesting aspects of these revivals is that the Egyptian culture can be treated as an "exotic style," since so few Egyptian motifs and basic styles traveled to other cultures.[16]

Selected Readings

BOOKS CONTAINING ILLUSTRATIONS OF COSTUME OF THE PERIOD FROM ORIGINAL SOURCES

Mesopotamia

"Art of the Ancient Near East." New York: *Metropolitan Museum Bulletin*, April, 1960.

Lloyd, S. *The Art of the Ancient Near East.* New York: Frederick A. Praeger, 1961.

Parrot, A. *The Arts of Assyria.* New York: Golden Press, 1961.

Parrot, A. *The Dawn of Art (Sumer).* New York: Golden Press, 1961.

Stommenger, E. *5000 Years of the Art of Mesopotamia.* New York: Harry N. Abrams, Inc. N.D.

Wilkinson, C. K. *Egyptian Wall Paintings.* New York: Metropolitan Museum of Art, 1983.

Wooley, L. *The Art of the Middle East Including Persia, Mesopotamia, and Palestine.* New York: Crown Publishers, Inc., 1961.

Egypt

Egypt's Golden Age: The Art of Living in the New Kingdom, 1558–1085 B.C. Boston: Museum of Fine Arts, 1982.

Kirkbach, R. *The Fully Illustrated Book of Royal Members of the Ancient Aegyptian Dynasties.* Albuquerque, N.M.: Glouster Art, 1982.

Lange, K. and M. Hirmer. *Egypt: Architecture, Sculpture, Painting in Three Thousand Years.* London: Phaidon Publishers Inc., 1961.

Michalowski, K. *Art of Ancient Egypt.* New York: Harry N. Abrams, Inc., N.D.

Nims, C. F. *Thebes of the Pharoahs.* New York: Stein and Day, 1965.

16. In a reader's note to the author.

Poulsen, V. *Egyptian Art;* parts 1 and 2. Greenwich, Conn.: New York Graphic Society, Ltd., 1968.

Ross, E. D. *The Art of Egypt Through the Ages.* London: The Studio., 1931.

Westendorf, W. *Painting, Sculpture, Architecture of Ancient Egypt.* New York: Harry N. Abrams, Inc., 1968.

Yoyotte, J. *Treasure of the Pharaohs.* Geneva: Skira, 1968.

PERIODICAL ARTICLES

Barber, E. J. "New Kingdom Egyptian Textiles: Embroidery vs. Weaving." *American Journal of Archeology*, Vol. 86 No. 3, July, 1982.

Bass, G. F. "A Hoard of Trojan and Sumerian Jewelry." *American Journal of Archeology.* Vol. 74, No. 4, Oct. 1970, p. 335.

Cox, J. S. "The Construction of an Ancient Egyptian Wig (c. 1400 B.C.) in the British Museum." *Journal of Egyptian Archeology*, Vol. 63, 1977, p. 57.

Francis, M. "Form Follows Fashionable Function: The Look of the Egyptian XVIII Dynasty." *Dress*, 1978, p. 1.

Hall, R. and J. Barnett. "A Fifth Dynasty Funerary Dress in the Petrie Museum of Egyptian Archeology: its Discovery and Conservation." *Textile History*, Vol. 16, No. 1, 1985, p. 5.

Jastrow, M. "Veiling in Ancient Assyria." *Review of Archeology.* Vol. XIV., p. 209.

Larson, J. "The Het-sed Robe and the 'Ceremonial Robe' of Tutankamun." *Journal of Egyptian Archeology.* Vol. 67, 1981, p. 180.

Leix, A. "Ancient Egypt, the Land of Linen." *CIBA Review*, No. 1, p. 397.

Muscarella, O. W. "Fibulae Represented on Sculpture." *Journal of Near East Studies.* April, 1967, p. 82.

Reifstahl, E. "A Note on Ancient Fashions: Four Early Egyptian Dresses in the Museum of Fine Arts, Boston." *Boston Museum Bulletin.* Vol. 67 (354), 1970, p. 244.

DAILY LIFE

Mesopotamia

Contenau, G. *Everyday Life in Babylon and Assyria.* London: E. Arnold, 1964.

Oppenheim, A. L. *Ancient Mesopotamia.* Chicago: University of Chicago Press, 1967.

Oppenheim, A. L. *Letters from Mesopotamia.* Chicago: University of Chicago Press, 1967.

Seibnobos, C. *The World of Babylon.* New York: Leon Amier Publisher, 1975.

Egypt

Casson, L. *Daily Life in Ancient Egypt.* New York: American Heritage Publishing Co., Inc., 1975.

Champollion, J. *The World of the Egyptians.* Geneva: Minerva, 1971.

Cottrell, L. *Five Queens of Ancient Egypt.* Indianapolis: The Bobbs-Merrill Company, Inc., 1969.

Cottrell, L. *Life Under the Pharaohs.* New York: Holt, Rinehart, and Winston, 1963.

Erman, A. *Life in Ancient Egypt.* New York: Dover Press (reprint), 1971.

James, T. G. H. *Pharaoh's People.* Chicago: University of Chicago Press, 1984.

Mertz, B. *Red Land, Black Land.* New York: Coward McCann Inc., 1966.

Scott, N. *The Daily Life of the Ancient Egyptians.* New York: Metropolitan Museum of Art Bulletin, Vol. XXXI, No. 3, Spring 1973.

Sewell, B. *Egypt Under the Pharaohs.* New York: G. P. Putnam's Sons, 1968.

White, J. M. *Everyday Life in Ancient Egypt.* New York: Capricorn Books, 1963.

CHAPTER 3

Crete and Greece

c. 2900 B.C.–300 B.C.

Historical Background

On the narrow island of Crete in the eastern Mediterranean, over much the same time period as the Egyptian and Mesopotamian civilizations, a civilization developed named Minoan for its legendary king, Minos. The island enjoyed a peaceful growth from about 2900 B.C. to 1600 B.C. and developed an elegant culture. The Minoans were a prosperous, sea-faring people who carried on an active trade with Egypt, Syria, Sicily, and even Spain. The Minoan people are depicted in the wall paintings of Egypt; their pottery and other traces of their contacts with foreign lands have been discovered in Asia Minor, Greece, and islands in the Aegean Sea. Their cities had no fortifications because they depended on their fleet for protection. The pleasure loving secure life of the Minoan people has been caught by the Cretan artists in the delicate, brightly colored frescoes which have been found on the walls of the palaces in Crete. The crowning achievement of Crete was the palace of Knossos with so many rooms that it gave rise to the legend of the labyrinth.

Sir Arthur Evans, the English archeologist, who first revealed the rich civilization of Crete, divided Minoan history into three main periods: Early Minoan (c. 2900–2100 B.C.), Middle Minoan (c. 2100–1600 B.C.), and late Minoan (c. 1600–1150 B.C.). During most of the Middle Minoan period, Minoan civiliza-

tion dominated not only Crete but also mainland Greece. But there a Greek people, named for the most powerful city-state, Mycenae, grew stronger until about 1400 B.C. when they became able to control Crete and the Minoan people. By that time the cities of Crete had been wrecked by earthquakes and fires, and plundered by invaders from the mainland of Greece.

The Mycenaen civilization, unlike that of Crete, extended throughout Greece, centered in more than three hundred towns. The towns spread out around the palaces which each king tried to make as a monument to his power and glory. The palaces were decorated with magnificent frescoes of great artistic and technical quality. The remains of these towns reveal great works of architecture and large scale engineering projects which so astounded later generations of Greeks that they thought the walls of the Mycenaen cities and palaces had been built by giants. In addition to the ruins of the palaces and towns, as a source of information about the Mycenaens, there are many grave sites in which the artifacts of gold and silver reveal a civilization both wealthy and sophisticated.

At the end of the 13th century, the mysterious "Sea People" devastated the Eastern Mediterranean area and ruined trade in a series of piratical raids. Many Mycenaean cities and towns suffered. The people were driven within the city walls for safety while their houses outside the fortifications were destroyed. Mycenae survived another century before it too was destroyed, probably by the Dorians. Some settlements were abandoned because they had depended upon trade which no longer existed. Throughout Greece the population declined. Among the Mycenean cities, Athens survived although somewhat impoverished. At the beginning of the 12th century, Greece entered a Dark Age about which little is known; about the same time the Minoan civilization disappeared.

SOCIAL ORGANIZATION AND MATERIAL CULTURE

Evidence about the organization and structure of Minoan and Mycenaean society is fragmentary. Apparently the Minoans had a basically two-class society, with the ruling classes separated by a great gulf from the common people. No genuine middle class developed in ancient Greece.

Women occupied a higher place in society than in most early cultures. They enjoyed equality with men and they were not secluded in the household but participated with men in public festivals. They engaged in athletics, often joining men in a favorite Minoan sport, vaulting over bulls. The position of women in Minoan civilization was an exception in the ancient world. This may have been reflective of the importance of female deities in Minoan religion—the major figure was the "mother goddess." At the same time, unlike Egypt where Queens did rule as Pharaohs in some periods, the rulers of Crete were invariably men.

Standards of material comfort for the wealthy were high. Several palaces have been excavated and their remains reveal that the private apartments in the palace were well-lighted, decorated with wall paintings (frescos), and even had running water piped into bathrooms.

The Mycenaeans imitated many aspects of Minoan decoration and styles, but their social organization seems to have differed somewhat. Little is known of the manner of life of the ordinary citizen. Wealth apparently was concentrated in the king's court. There was a lesser nobility and a large group of lower class craftsmen, peasants, and shepherds.

ART AND TECHNOLOGY

As a result of the close contacts between Mycenaeans and Minoans, the styles of clothing utilized by both groups were essentially the same from the Middle Minoan period until the Later Minoan period. Most of the evidence for costume during the Minoan civilization comes from the statuary and wall paintings discovered in Crete. Some frescos and statuary of the period have also been found in mainland Greece.

The costume of the small statuettes of Minoan goddesses and priestesses is depicted in good detail. The dress of these statues has been taken to be characteristic of the dress of upper class women. Wall paintings of general scenes of Minoan life confirm these details. Men's costume is more often shown on wall paintings than in statuary. Many of the wall paintings have been restored, with details reconstructed from fragments of the original paintings, so that inaccuracies may have been incorporated into the restorations.

Archeological evidence shows that the textile industries were well-developed in Crete. Wool and linen were the fabrics used. Elaborate designs are shown on Minoan textiles which were probably made by embroidery, and decorative tapes appear that may have been made by weaving designs into the fabric. Color was used lavishly, and skill in dyeing textiles must have been well-developed.

Minoan Costume

In commenting on many of the objects from the early Greek civilizations that archeologists have found, a Greek archeologist George Mylonas said ". . . these may be likened to the illustrations of a picture book for which the scholar must provide the text. This text, however, can be widely divergent in its interpretations and highly subjective."[1] Precisely the same comment can be made about the representations of costume from the Minoan Period. The lack of any body of literature, legal texts, or religious writings and even the fragmentary nature of many of the paintings from this period leave the costume historian at a loss as to the precise function of many items of dress and the conclusions that are drawn are, therefore, somewhat tentative.

COSTUME FOR MEN AND WOMEN

Item / Description

loin cloth—Fitted garment, depicted as worn by men and by women athletes. Covers much the same area as a pair of modern athletic briefs. A

1. G. Mylonas. *Mycenae and the Mycenaean World*. Princeton: Princeton University Press, 1966, p. 136.

similar costume (in Greek, the *perizoma*) was worn by Greeks and Etruscans. (See Figure 4.2.)

NOTE OF SPECIAL INTEREST: When worn by athletes the loin cloth was re-inforced at the crotch to protect against the horns of bulls, over which the athletes performed athletic leaps.

skirts—Shown as men's garment in varying lengths:
  · short, ending at the thigh, apparently wrapped around the body generally ending in a point with a suspended, weighted, tassel at center front and/or center back and made of elaborately patterned fabric. (See Figure 3.1.)
  · longer lengths, ending below the knee or at the ankle.

poncho-like cape—On men, to cover upper part of body, usually worn in combination with a skirt, and appearing to consist of a rectangle of fabric, folded in half, with an opening cut for the head.

belt—Tight, rolled belt, apparently made from fabric or leather and decorated with metal, for men and boys from the earliest periods, but adopted by women during later Minoan period.

NOTE: Since Minoan men are shown with abnormally small waists (which may have been an artistic convention) some authorities speculate that these belts may have been placed on young boys

3.2 Redrawing of figures depicted on a sarcophagus from the 14th century B.C. at Hagia Triada, Crete showing a procession of two women and a man. The woman at the left wears a sheepskin skirt and a fitted bodice. The man and woman at the right are wearing long tunics decorated with trimming that may be woven braid.

from age twelve or fourteen and that belts constricted development of the waist.

tunic—Men and women wore T-shaped tunics with long or short sleeves and in long or short skirt lengths. Generally decorated with bands of woven tapes or embroidery at the hem, along the sides, and following the shoulder lines. (Figure 3.2.)

NOTE: Mycenean men are more likely to be depicted in tunics rather than skirts or loincloths.

capes or cloaks—Men and women wrapped shawl-like garments made from animal skins or heavy wool around the body in cold weather.

women's bodice—Smoothly-fitted and lacing or otherwise fastening beneath the breasts and leaving the breasts exposed. Sleeves fitted closely to the arm, though a few examples have small puffs at the shoulders.

NOTE: Since most depictions of this breast-exposing style are of priestesses some authorities believe ordinary women covered the breasts with sheer fabric.

women's skirts—Skirts were bell-shaped and had at least three different forms: (See Figure 3.3.)
  · smooth, bell-shape, fitted at waist and flaring gently to the ground.
  · series of ruffles, each successive ruffle wider in circumference than the one above it.

3.1 Egyptian wall painting c. 1450 B.C. of men from Crete who wear wrapped skirts with tassel at the front. A rolled belt is visible at the waist. (*Photograph courtesy of the Metropolitan Museum of Art.*)

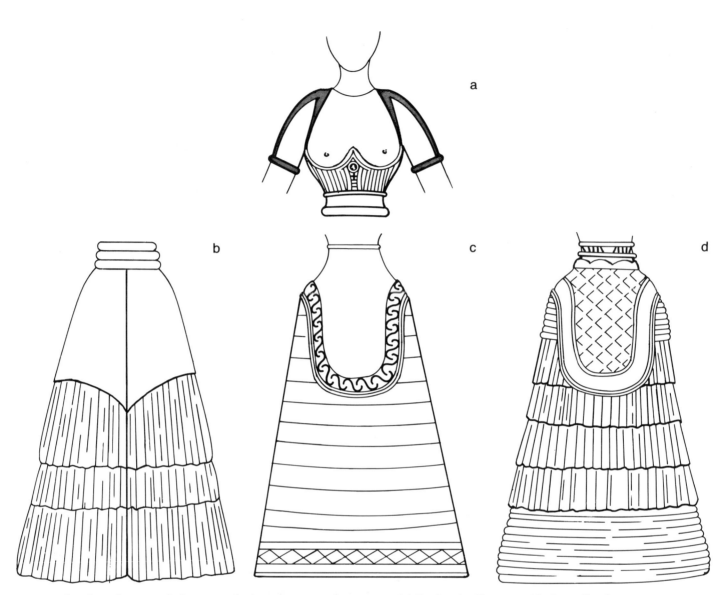

3.3a,b,c,d. Redrawing of elements of Minoan costume for women. (a) Depicts bodice cut with short, fitted sleeves, a tight bodice which is open to below the breasts, made from patterned fabric and trimmed with bands of braid or embroidery. Whether all women bared their breasts is not clear, but figurines showing either priestesses or goddesses are represented with this bodice style. (b) may have been made in the form of wide-legged trousers, although the exact construction is not clear. (c) is a flared skirt with decorative horizontal bands. (d) is apparently made from rows of ruffles. Both (c) and (d) are depicted with an apron-like covering that extended from below the waist to the hip area. All drawings show tightly-fitting wide belts.

· of uncertain cut: drawings and sculpture show a clear line down the center of garment which can be interpreted either as a culotte-like bifurcated garment or as V-shaped ruffles.

apron-like garment—worn over skirts by women, extending in front and back to about mid-thigh.

NOTE: Archeologist Arthur Evans believed this garment to be a ritual survival in religious costume for women of a primitive loin cloth worn originally by both sexes.[2]

hair and head dress—Men wore hair long and curly or short, cut close to the head and curly. Sometimes tied in a braid or lock at the back of the head, sometimes held in place with a fillet. Hat styles include elaborate, possibly ritual types: high, round and crown-like with a tall plume, turbans, small caps, and wide-brimmed.

Women had long, curly hair often held in place with a fillet or elaborate arrangement of plain or jeweled bands. Hats ranged from high, tiered, brimless styles to beret-like flat hats.

NOTE: Curly hair was apparently an ethnic characteristic. Probably much of the head dress had religious significance and may have served as symbol of priest or priestess status.

footwear—Men and women wore sandals or shoes with pointed toes that fitted the foot closely and ended at the ankle. Athletes (bull-leapers) wore a soft shoe with what appears to be a short sock or ankle-support.

NOTE: An example of how archeological evidence can contribute to conclusions about costume is seen in archeologists' findings that the floors of palaces show little wear from shoes, while entrance stairs are worn away from the passing of shod feet, leading to the conclusion that people went barefoot indoors but wore shoes out-of-doors.

jewelry—Men and women wore rings, bracelets, armlets. Women wore necklaces. Although earrings were found in Minoan graves, they are not generally depicted in the art.

cosmetics and grooming—Women shown with eye makeup and, probably, lip coloring. Men were clean-shaven.

2. A. Evans. "Scenes from Minoan Life." *The World of the Past.* Ed. J. Hawkes. New York: Knopf, 1963, p. 104.

COSTUME FOR CHILDREN

Little evidence exists for the costume of children. One statuary group from Mycenae shows a small boy—perhaps about three or four years of age—dressed in a floor-length skirt and wearing a necklace and a padded, rolled belt. Probably children wore simple costumes such as skirts or tunics. After puberty they undoubtedly assumed adult clothing.

SUMMARY

Parallels have been pointed out between the tiered skirts of Minoan women and the fringed kaunakes garments of Mesopotamia by some costume historians. Similarities also exist in language elements between Crete and the Middle East. Cretan traders traveled extensively throughout the Mediterranean area both to the East, and South to Egypt. Certainly the Cretan traders reached the areas of Asia Minor where the kaunakes garments were worn, but even if the origin of the tiered skirt for Minoan women was to be found in the Middle East, the forms that evolved during the height of Minoan civilization differed markedly from costume of Mesopotamia and Egypt during concurrent periods.

Sometime after the close of the Minoan-Mycenean period the fitted, full-skirted costume for women disappeared. Just how long it persisted after the beginning of the Dark Age and how it came to be supplanted by the later Greek styles is unknown. After a period of almost four hundred years mainland Greece emerged from the Dark Age into the Archaic Period. By this time costume in general and the costume of women in particular had altered dramatically.

Greece: Historical Background

Written records vanished during the Dark Age because Greek civilization had been shattered. The political history of the period does not exist. Intellectual achievements were limited to epic ballads, sung perhaps by wandering bards, which were eventually woven into a cycle familiar to modern readers from the poems *Iliad* and the *Odyssey* attributed to Homer. Although he related stories about the heroes of the Trojan War which occurred during the Mycenaen Period, his epic poems describe the life and customs of his own times.

As the Dark Ages ended and Greece entered the

Archaic Period, c. 800 to 500 B.C., the Greek people began to prosper as their culture revived. Village communities began to evolve into independent city states which would provide the first type of democratic government with elections, juries, and government by citizens of the city state.

In the Classical Age, c. 500 to 323 B.C., Greece enjoyed a golden age, one of the most creative eras in the history of western civilization. Greek philosophers—Socrates, Plato, and Aristotle—pondered the nature of the universe, the meaning of life, and ethical values. Tragic dramatists—Aeschylus, Sophocles, and Euripides—wrote dramas for the public dealing with the nature and fate of man. The Greeks developed a new literary form, history, which related and analyzed man's past experiences. Through sculpture the Greeks glorified the human body; through new techniques of using marble the Greeks created architectural masterpieces.

Even before the Classical Age, Greeks had for centuries been establishing colonies throughout the Mediterranean, first on the western coasts of present day Turkey which the Greeks called Ionia. Greek settlements had also been established in Sicily, throughout southern Italy, and as far west as southern France. These centers of Greek culture and trade helped to spread Greek culture. Etruscan costume (the Etruscans were a people living on the Italian peninsula whose civilization pre-dated the Roman) shows many resemblances to that of the Greeks, as do the later Roman styles. At the same time Greek costumes borrowed from the regions with which the Greeks came into contact, particularly from the Middle East.

Greek influence was spread also by the conquests of Alexander the Great of Macedonia (336–323 B.C.) whose father had brought Greece under his control. Alexander carved out an empire which stretched from Greece and Egypt in the west to the shores of the Indian Ocean in the east. After Alexander's death his empire fell apart; Greek influence waned while that of the Romans began to expand. Gradually the Romans supplanted the Greeks as the dominant force in the Mediterranean region, although the art and the wisdom of Greece continued to influence the world long after its political power was eclipsed.

SOCIAL ORGANIZATION

Society in the time of Homer was made up of nobility and commoners. Households were largely self-sufficient, each one producing its own food and textiles for clothing. A man's home was, quite literally, his

fortress, protected by walls against the raiders who frequently attacked the Greek settlements which were located near the sea.

By the Classical Age, a period for which written and art records abound, Greek communities had grown into city states, and had developed a far more sophisticated and urban organization. A quite detailed picture of daily life in ancient Greece can be painted. Athens, the most famous city state in Greece, was composed of a population of adult men, the active citizens; their dependant women and children; resident foreigners; and slaves.

An ordinary Athenian lived in a small, unpretentious house made of sun dried brick which lacked central heating and running water. When not engaged in work, he might attend the assembly or the law courts. "His recreation was found in the festivals and public facilities like gymnasiums which were provided by the city. Luxuries of diet, clothing, and furniture were for the very rich, although they, too, lived relatively simply. In democratic Athens extravagance and ostentation were quick to attract attention and draw censure."[3]

In Homeric times women occupied a subordinate position, but judging from the writings of Homer they had a rather open, companionable relationship with men. By the Classical Age all this had changed. Women of good families not only lacked political power, they quite literally had no control over their own destinies. From birth to death they were under the control of some man. Even widows or divorced women, although they retained title to their inherited property, had to be supervised by their nearest male relative. Marriages were arranged, and monogamy was the rule. Husbands did not consider their wives as equals, socially or intellectually, and did not appear with them in public. Secluded in the household, the wife oversaw the running of the home where she was responsible for the children, food and clothing. Through the spinning and weaving of fabrics and the making of clothing, she made a very real contribution to the economy of the household.

Women of the Classical Age were even required to be veiled-out-of-doors, this practice may have come to Greece from Ionia and the Near East about 530 B.C., along with such styles as the Ionic form of dress. This veiling symbolized the subjugation of women to their husbands. As evidence for this custom, a large number of statues of women have

3. Carl Roebuck. *The World of Ancient Times.* New York: Charles Scribner's Sons, 1966, p. 266.

been found in which veils are pulled down at least partially over the face.[4]

Clearly the activities of married and unmarried upper class women were restricted. They tended the house but did not participate in social activities with their husbands or their husbands' friends. They could participate in religious processions and festivals or, if appropriately veiled and accompanied by servants, go to market, attend tragic plays, or visit close friends. They were not allowed to attend comedies, however, perhaps because these tended to be bawdy.

There were exceptions to these strict regulations. In Sparta, the largest and the most militaristic Greek city state, women were less restricted, a state of affairs other Greeks found disquieting. The historian Plutarch described Spartan women as bold, masculine, and overbearing and seemed shocked at the notion that they spoke openly "even on the most important subjects."[5]

One group of women was not subject to these restrictions: the prostitutes. The lowest class of prostitutes lived in brothels, often in seaports. They dressed so lightly that literary references described them as "naked." Nudity for women was not socially acceptable. A slightly higher class of courtesans were the "flute girls" who entertained with music and dancing at the all-male parties that were customary. These women are often depicted on vase paintings where some are shown clad in ordinary dress, some in special short dancing costumes, and others in the nude. The highest class of courtesans were the *hetairi*, the literal translation of the word is "companions." These women moved freely among men. They were often better educated than ordinary women and some were known for their skill in philosophical disputation or for their literary efforts. A few became quite famous. Many dyed their hair blonde (the predominant hair color among Greek women was dark) and it appears that the law required them to wear specially decorated robes to distinguish them from respectable women.

In the period after 300 B.C.—the Hellenistic Period—the status of women seems to have risen somewhat. Female nudity in art increased (although it is not likely that women ever appeared nude), women were treated more openly and sympathetically in the drama, and, interestingly, the influence of the *hetairi* on Athenian life diminished.

FABRIC CONSTRUCTION

Spinning and weaving were considered fit occupations for queens and goddesses. In Homer's story of the Odyssey, Penelope, Ulysses faithful queen, promises to choose a new king for Ithaca after she has completed the weaving of a shroud or burial sheet. After each day of weaving she secretly, at night, unraveled the work that she had done on the previous day. In this way she avoided taking a new husband. Athena, goddess of wisdom, patroness of the city of Athens, and patroness of artisans is credited, in Greek mythology, as being the first woman to work with wool. As part of the religious ceremonies held in Athens every four years in honor of the goddess a magnificently embroidered garment, the sacred *peplos*, was carried in procession to the temple to be placed upon her statue. It had been woven by two women selected from those who participated in fertility rites associated with cult of Athena.

Sheep herding was practiced in the mountainous Greek peninsula, and from those sheep wool for weaving was obtained. The Greeks also used linen, particularly after the 6th century. Linen use seems to have come to Greece from Egypt by way of Asia minor, particularly from the Ionian region where many Greeks had settled. Most of the linen used in Greece was imported from the Middle East and Egypt. The island of Cos was known, in the late Greek period, for the production of silk, but scholars believe that the silk produced there was made by unraveling fabrics imported from China by way of Persia and re-weaving the fibers, often in combination with linen, in order to make the precious fiber go farther. Cotton fiber was apparently brought to Greece by the soldiers of Alexander the Great. It could not be grown there because of the climate. For the most part, however, Greek clothing was made from wool or from linen.[6]

Greek women were gifted weavers, and they were talented in embroidery. Fabrics had color applied by dyeing. Skill was developed in pleating fabrics and some sort of clothes press for smoothing and flattening fabrics and pressing in pleats existed. Fabrics were bleached with the fumes of a sulphur compound. Since Greek costume was draped, not cut and sewn, the fabric was probably woven to the correct size and did not require cutting. (See Figure 3.4.)

4. C. Galt, "Veiled Ladies." *American Journal of Archeology.* Vol. 35, No. 4. (1931) p. 373.

5. Will Durant, *The Life of Greece. The Story of Civilization* Vol. 2. New York: Simon and Schuster, 1966, p. 84.

6. Faber, G. A. "Dress and Dress Materials in Greece and Rome." *CIBA Review*, No. 1, p. 297.

ART

The sculpture and vase paintings of Greece provide evidence concerning the costume of ancient Greece. Records from the early Archaic period are unclear. The art of that time was highly stylized (it is called "Geometric art"), and provides little information about dress. The statuary of the 7th century B.C. begins to be sufficiently representational to permit some conclusions to be drawn about costume. The later periods, particularly the Classical Period, abound in representations of costume in sculpture and painting.

The Greek attitude toward nudity should be mentioned in this context. Nudity was not acceptable to the Minoans, the Myceneans, or the Homeric Greeks. Tradition records the date at which Greek men began to participate in athletic events in the nude as around 720 B.C.[7] Athletic games in Greece were part of religious ritual. The performing by athletes in the nude therefore had a religious context. Furthermore, the Greek ideal stressed not only perfection of the soul but perfection of the body as well. At about the same time that nudity came into athletics, artists began to make representations of the male nude.

Female nudity did not, however, follow. Except in Sparta women did not participate in athletics nor could they attend the games. Women dancers and acrobats wore, at the minimum, a perizoma and usually also a band covering the breasts. It is only after 400 B.C. when attitudes toward women seem to have become somewhat less restrictive that artists sculpted some of the now-famous nude or partially nude statues of women such as the Venus de Milo, although in earlier periods the ideal of the well-formed female body was clearly visible beneath the softly flowing draperies of the costume.

Costumes of the Greeks

The garment called the tunic heretofore was called a *chiton* by the Greeks. Although many of the earliest depictions of Greek chitons give the impression of a garment sewn together at the shoulders and under the arms, later versions were not necessarily sewn, but often were created by taking a single rectangle of fabric and wrapping it around the body, securing it at the shoulders with one or more pins.

Variations in the appearance of chitons were often

7. L. Bonfante. *Etruscan Dress.* Baltimore: Johns Hopkins Press. 1977, p. 20.

achieved by belting the chiton at any of several locations, by creating and manipulating an overfold at the top of the fabric, and by varying the placement of the pins at the shoulder.

Over the chiton Greek men and women placed shawls or cloaks. Some of the over-garments were decorative, others were utilitarian. The summary and illustrations that follow describe the major costume forms in use during the Archaic, Classical, and Helenic Periods of ancient Greek history. Various authors use conflicting terminology to identify different types of chitons. The terms used here are those which seemed to the authors to be most consistently used by reliable sources.

COSTUME FOR MEN AND FOR WOMEN

Item / Description

chiton—a tunic, having slightly different forms at varying periods, which were:

chitoniskos—short chiton, worn by men in the Archaic period and until about 550 B.C. Probably sewn closed at shoulders and under arms. Made of wool, fabric often patterned; shaped close to body.

Doric peplos—worn by women in the Archaic period and until about 550 B.C. Tube-shaped, upper section folded over to just above waist. Shoulders pinned together with large, straight pins with decorative heads. Belted at the waist. Of wool, usually patterned. (See Figure 3.4.)

NOTE: Greek author Herodotus claims Doric peplos style was abandoned because of an incident toward the beginning of the 6th century B.C. in which Athenian women supposedly used their dress pins to stab to death a messenger who brought the bad news of the almost total destruction of an Athenian military force in battle. According to Herodotus, the wearing of the Ionic chiton, which did not utilize these large, sharp pins was mandated as a result.

Ionic chiton—worn by men and women from 550 B.C. to 480 B.C., and less frequently from 480 B.C. to 300 B.C. Men wore either short or long versions; women, long styles. Garment had increased fullness, achieved by utilizing wider widths of fabric, and longer sleeves formed by placing a number of small pins at various points along the arm. Often finely pleated, seems to have been made of light-weight wool or linen. Over-folds at top of garment were rare. (See Figure 3.5.)

3.4 (*Above*) Athenian women working wool, weaving, and folding cloth, c. 560 B.C. These women are dressed in the form-fitting Dorian *peplos* of the Archaic Period. (*Photograph courtesy of the Metropolitan Museum of Art, Fletcher Fund, 1931.*)

3.5 (*Below*) Greek vase, c. 500–490 B.C. shows woman in Ionic *chiton* over which she wears a *chlamydon*. (*Photograph courtesy of the Cleveland Museum of Art, purchase, Leonard G. Hanna Jr. Bequest.*)

NOTE: Ionic chiton appears to have come to Greece from the Middle East by way of Greek settlements in Ionia, in Asia Minor.

> *Doric chiton*—worn by men in short version and by women in long version from about 450 B.C. to 300 B.C. Narrower than Ionic form, Doric form was pinned only once at the shoulder, often made with over-fold. Fabrics: wool, linen, or silk. (See Figure 3.6.)
>
> *Helenic chiton*—worn by women from about 300 B.C. to 100 B.C., this variation of the Doric chiton was narrower and often belted just below the bosom.

himation—A rectangle of fabric large enough to wrap around the body. Usually the upper corner covered the left shoulder, the bulk of the fabric wrapped across the back, passed under the right arm, and finished over the left shoulder or was carried across the left arm. Women wore this garment over a chiton; men wore it over a chiton or, at some periods, alone without a chiton beneath. (See Figures 3.7, 3.8.)

perizoma—A loin cloth, worn by men, either as an undergarment or for athletic contests. (See Figure 4.1.)

diplax—Small rectangle of fabric worn by women, especially over the Ionic chiton, draped in much the same way as the himation.

chlamydon—More complicated form of the diplax in which fabric was pleated into a fabric band. (See Figure 3.5.)

cloaks and capes—Various styles worn for cool weather. Most notable example was the *chlamys*, a rectangular cloak of leather or wool pinned over the left shoulder. Worn by men especially for traveling, it could be used as a blanket for sleeping at night. (See Figure 3.8.)

3.6 Redrawing of figure from a Greek vase by Thomas Hope (18th century). Woman fastens the shoulder of her Doric *chiton.* Notice the small weights at the end of the drapery that falls from her right shoulder.

3.7 Greek youth wearing *himation.* (*Photograph courtesy of Photo Arts Company.*)

3.8 5th century B.C. Greek vase shows (from left to right) a woman in an Ionic *chiton* with a shawl drawn over her head; a naked cupid; a goddess in a Doric *chiton;* a woman in an Ionic *chiton,* a veil over her head and a shawl—possibly an *himation*—over her shoulders; two men in *chlamys* and *petasos;* and a man in an *himation.* Older men are bearded, the youth is clean-shaven. (*Photograph courtesy of the Metropolitan Museum of Art, Rogers Fund, 1907.*)

hair and head dress—Men wore long or medium length hair and beards in the Archaic Period; young men, short hair and no beards and older men longer hair and beards in the Classical period. Hats for men included fitted caps and the *petasos*, usually worn with the chlamys. Its wide brim provided shade in summer, or kept rain off the head. Though not a Greek style, *Phrygian bonnets*, brimless caps with a high padded peak that fell forward, were often depicted in Greek art.

NOTE: Phrygian bonnets in Greek art identify wearers as foreigners from the Middle East. This style reappears in European styles in the Middle Ages.

The *pilos*, a narrow-brimmed or brimless hat with a pointed crown, was worn by both men and women.

Women wore hair long in curling tresses with small curls arranged around the face, in the Archaic Period; pulled into a knot or chignon at the back of the head in the Classical Period. Fillets, scarves, ribbons, and caps were used to confine the hair.

Veils on women worn over the head; occasionally pulled across, covering the face.

footwear—Sandals for men and women. For men, fitted shoes, ankle high or high mid-calf length leather boots that laced up the front for travel or warfare.

jewelry—Jewelry more often worn by women, consisting of necklaces, earrings, rings, decorative pins for fastening the chiton, brooches.

cosmetics—Statues and vase paintings do not reveal extent to which makeup was worn. Writings of the period record use of perfumes.

COSTUME FOR CHILDREN

infants—*swaddling clothes*—bands of fabric wrapped around the body, and a close-fitting, peaked cap.

NOTE: Swaddling of babies was a common practice throughout Europe until the 19th century and was thought to prevent deformity of children's limbs. As the Greeks emphasized bodily perfection it may be that they held similar beliefs. A few representations of infants, perhaps older ones, show them wrapped in loose cloth draperies rather than in swaddling bands.

older children—Sometimes small boys are depicted in the nude. School-age boys wore short belted or unbelted *chitons*. Girls' chitons were arranged much as those of older women and belted in a variety of ways. Boys and girls wore *himations*; girls over a chiton and boys either alone or over a chiton.

> *cloaks*—a small, rectangular cloak with a clasp on the right shoulder; or a long cape with a pointed hood that either closed in front or had an opening through which it could be slipped over the head.
> *hair styles*—for small children and boys, short; older girls dressed the hair as did women.
> *hats*—for girls: a high, peaked hat with a flat, stiff brim. For boys and girls: a flat-crowned hat with a heavy roll as a brim.
> *footwear*—sandals, closed shoes; often barefoot.
> *jewelry*—earrings, necklaces, bracelets, especially those in the form of a serpent.

SPECIALIZED COSTUME

Military Costume—Military costume during both the Archaic and Classical periods varied from one city-state to another, but usually included some form of protective clothing worn over a tunic.

> *Archaic Period*—*breastplate*—made from metal plates or disks mounted on a fabric corselet; held up by shoulder straps.
> *helmet*—made of either leather or bronze, had a chin strap and high crest intended to make the warrier look more fearsome.
> Other elements:
> *greaves*—shaped leather or metal protectors for lower legs; wide metal belts; shields.
> *cloak*—of rough wool.
> *Classical Period*—For common soldier: leather *cuirass* (close-fitting, shaped body armor), metal belt, greaves. For heavily-armed infantry: metal or leather cuirass with row of leather tabs hanging down from cuirass at waist to protect lower part of body. (See Figure 3.9.)
> *helmet*—became more protective, having extended pieces to cover the cheekbones, nose, jaws, and neck. Either with or without crests.
> *chlamys*—style cloak worn.
> *Both Periods*—barefoot or high boots.

Theatrical Costume—The theater was important in Greece and eventually acquired a traditional style of costume through which the theater-goer could immediately identify the characters. Male

3.9 Greek soldier wearing leather cuirass with suspended leather panels. Note that the cheek guards of the helmet are raised. When in use, these panels would fold down to protect the side of the face. The soldier wears *greaves* on his legs. (*Redrawing by Thomas Hope, 18th century, from a Greek vase.*)

actors played all of the parts in both comedies and tragedies. Tragic actors wore a tragic mask, either tall wigs or tufts of hair fastened to the mask, and thick-soled platform shoes. Kings, queens, gods, goddesses, happy characters, tragic figures, and slaves each had a specific style of dress, special insignia, or color that identified them. For those who are interested in a more lengthy exploration of Greek theatrical costume several references are listed in the bibliography for this chapter.

Summary

Some of the variations in the forms of the chiton serve to illustrate the way in which clothing styles may be affected by external events. The Ionic chiton was a style with non-Greek origins, most probably a Middle Eastern style adopted by Greeks in Ionia, a settlement at the far eastern end of the Mediterranean. From Ionia the style spread to the mainland where it supplanted the Doric peplos.

About 480 B.C., as a result of war with Persia, a period of intense interest in the Greek past and a denigration of oriental styles apparently led to a rejection of the Ionic chiton in favor of a new style, the Doric chiton, which represented a sort of revival of the older, native Dorian peplos.

But the travels of the chiton do not end with the decline of Greek power. The spread of Greek settlements and Greek culture throughout the Mediterranean world resulted in the adoption of many elements of Greek costume by Egyptians of the period, and in Italy first by the Etruscans, and later by the Romans.

By way of Roman costume, Greek costume can be said to have served as a basis for the costume of Romanized Europe for the six centuries following the downfall of Alexander the Great. It can even be argued that its influence in certain aspects of dress can be felt until the latter part of the Middle Ages. Moreover, Greek influence on dress was not limited to the civilizations that co-existed with Classical Greece. Elements of classical art have been revived during the Renaissance (15th and 16th centuries), the Neo-classical Period (18th century), and the Empire Period (early 1800's.) In this latter period a method of belting the dress high, under the bust-line, was copied from Helenistic chiton styles. Called the "empire waistline," this Greek-inspired style is revived periodically by fashion designers of the 20th century, many of whom look to historic periods for design inspiration. The soft, flowing lines of the Greek styles seem to appeal particularly to lingerie designers and designers of evening dress.

Selected Readings

BOOKS CONTAINING ILLUSTRATIONS OF COSTUME OF THE PERIOD FROM ORIGINAL SOURCES

Charbonneaux, J., R. Martin, and F. Villard. *Classical Greek Art*. New York: George Braziller, 1972.

Charbonneaux, J., R. Martin, and F. Villard. *Helenistic Art*. New York: George Braziller, 1973.

Hale, W. H. *The Horizon Book of Ancient Greece*. New York: American Heritage Publishing Company, Inc., 1965.

Higgins, R. *Minoan and Mycenaen Art*. New York: Thames and Hudson, 1985.

Klein, A. E. *Child Life in Greek Art*. New York: Columbia University Press, 1932.

Mylonas, G. *Mycenae and the Mycenaean Age.* Princeton: Princeton University Press, 1966.

Richter, G. *A Handbook of Greek Art.* New York: Phaidon, 1974.

Ruskin, A. and M. Batterberry. *Greek and Roman Art.* New York: McGraw-Hill Book Company, 1964.

PERIODICAL ARTICLES

Alexander, S. M. (Editor). "Information on Historical Techniques, Textiles: 1. The Classical Period." *Art and Archeology Technical Abstracts.* Vol. 15, No. 2, 1978.

Born, W. "Footwear in Greece and Rome." *CIBA Review.* No. 3, p. 1217.

Faber, G. A. "Dress and Dress Materials in Greece and Rome." *CIBA Review.* Vol. 1, p. 296.

Galt, C. "Veiled Ladies." *American Journal of Archeology.* Vol. 35 (1935), p. 373.

Peterson, S. "A Costuming Scene from the Room of the Ladies on Thera." *American Journal of Archeology,* Vol. 85 (2) April 1981, p. 211.

DAILY LIFE

Browning, R. (Editor). *The Greek World.* New York: Thames and Hudson, 1985.

Chadwick, J. *The Mycenaean World.* New York: Cambridge University Press, 1984.

Durant, W. *The Life of Greece. The Story of Civilization, Vol. 2.* New York: Simon and Schuster, 1966.

Flaceliere, R. *Daily Life in Greece at the Time of Pericles.* New York: MacMillan Company, 1965.

* Hawkes, J. *Dawn of the Gods.* New York: Random House, 1968.

Robinson, C. E. *Everyday Life in Ancient Greece.* Oxford: Clarendon Press, 1933.

*Vaughan, A. C. *The House of the Double Ax.* Garden City, N.Y.: Doubleday Company, Inc., 1959.

Webster, T. B. L. *Athenian Culture and Society.* Berkley, CA: University of California Press, 1973.

Willets, R. *Everyday Life in Ancient Crete.* New York: G. P. Putnam's Sons, 1969.

GREEK THEATER COSTUME

Simon, E. *The Ancient Theatre.* New York: Methuen, 1982.

Stone, L. M. *Costume in Aristophanic Comedy.* Salem, N.H.: Ayer Company, Publishers, 1981.

* Books dealing with Minoan Civilization.

CHAPTER 4

Etruria and Rome

c. 800 B.C.–400 A.D.

Since men and women first appeared in Europe, the Italian peninsula has been the home of many peoples. They migrated to Italy from Africa, Sicily, Spain, France, the Danube Valley, and Switzerland. Because they left no written records, they are known only through archeological remains. They were pastoral people who tilled the soil, wove clothing, and made pottery and bronze implements. Among the pre-Roman peoples who migrated into Italy, none left a deeper impression than the Etruscans.

In certain areas of the Italian peninsula by about 800 B.C., a culture had been developed superior in skills and artistic production, and more complex in organization than the culture of the neighboring tribes. The people who created this culture the Romans called Etruscans. Eventually their territory stretched as far north as the region near the present-day city of Venice, but the most important settlements in Etruria were concentrated in the western area which today is bounded on the north by Florence and on the south by Rome, known today as Tuscany.

Another group of immigrants entered Italy. By the latter part of the 8th century, Greek colonies had been established in Sicily and in southern Italy. By the 6th century the Greeks reached the northern limits of their colonization, the southern boundary of Etruria. (It was the Greeks who gave the name "Italy" to the region, naming it after an early king of one of the native tribes.)

In addition to the Etruscans and the Greeks, other native tribes populated the Italian peninsula. One

of these, the Latins, lived in an area near the mouth of the Tiber River. At some point, possibly in the 8th century, on one of the hills near the river, a colony of these people established a settlement on the Palatine Hill that grew into the city of Rome. But the Romans, as these people were to be known to history, did not become an important political force in the Mediterranean until about the 3rd century B.C. when they subjugated the Etruscans.

The Etruscans: Historical Background

The origins of the Etruscans are shrouded in mystery. They may have immigrated from Asia Minor, or they may have been an indigenous people, native to the Italian peninsula. Because of their superiority in arms and fighting ability, they were able to seize strategic points along the coast. From there they pushed inland, seized strategic sites from which they could control the local population. Eighteen fortified cities have been found. The twelve most important cities ruled by kings and nobles, formed a loose confederation. The Etruscans were in the minority—a dominant, military, aristocracy.

The Etruscans left abundant records of their lives in wall paintings, statues, and in the objects which they placed in their elaborate necropoli or grave cities. Although they had a written language, using a Greek alphabet, unlike the languages of the Egyptians, the Mesopotamians, and the Greeks, it is not fully understood today. Almost 10,000 inscriptions have been found, some words and phrases are known, but full texts cannot yet be read. Consequently, terms related to Etruscan costume will be given in Greek or Latin-based words.

The chief Etruscan towns had been founded by the middle of the 7th century B.C. Not only did the Etruscans improve the arable land, plant vineyards and olive groves, they mined and smelted iron ore, exploited deposits of copper, traded throughout the Mediterranean area, and amassed great wealth. In building their cities, they utilized a form of city planning. When a new site for a city was selected, they laid out the towns in a checkerboard pattern with two main streets intersecting at right angles.

SOCIAL LIFE

Of family life we know relatively little. Women seem to have occupied a position of greater importance in Etruscan society than that of either Greek or Roman women. Roman writers frequently sneered about the foolishness of the Etruscans in granting their women such privileged status. Many of the funerary statues and paintings show men and women reclining together on couches at banquets in attitudes and with expressions of warm affection. When family groups are shown they are depicted in relaxed, informal poses. Some recently excavated terra cotta statues of children are among the most delightfully realistic statues from antiquity of infants and small children.

ART AND TRADE

The art of the Etruscans showed strong Greek influences, particularly during the 6th and 5th centuries when Greek colonies were well-established in southern Italy, and reflects an active and close trading relationship with Greece. The scenes depicted by the Etruscans of daily life, however, were scenes of daily life among the Etruscans, not in Greece. This is indicated not only by the inclusion of some dress styles and conventions that are peculiar to the Etruscans but also by the way in which respectable women are depicted as dining and appearing with men in public. The Etruscan tomb paintings were done in color so the observer can see the characteristic use of vivid color and pattern in clothing. While much of the art of Etruria was of local production, rich Etruscans also purchased imported *objets d'art* from abroad, especially from Greece, and many of these objects were placed in the tombs with their owners.

Etruscan Costume

COSTUME FOR MEN AND WOMEN

Item / Description

perizoma—Loin cloth (like that worn by Minoans and Greeks) worn alone, especially by laborers; with a short, shirt-like chiton; or under a slightly longer chiton. (See Figure 4.1.)

NOTE: Greek acceptance of male nudity was apparently not shared by the Etruscans.

4.1 Figure from the island of Cyprus, c. 7th-6th centuries, B.C. wears a *perizoma* (loin cloth) of the type worn by both the Greeks and the Etruscans. (*Photograph courtesy of the Metropolitan Museum of Art, The Cesnola Collection, purchased by subscriptions, 1874–76.*)

chiton—Tunic worn by men and women. Etruscan versions were essentially the same as those worn by Greeks. Most common length for men was to the thighs, but longer versions were also depicted. The *Doric peplos* was made in woven plaid or decorated with what may be embroidery. (See Figure 3.4.) Subsequently a chiton cut fuller than the Doric peplos and with pleats appears in Etruscan art.

NOTE: Bonfante suggests this may be a forerunner of the later Ionic chiton, noting that the Ionic chiton appeared in Etruria slightly earlier than in mainland Greece and suggesting that both Greece and Etruria may have adopted the style independently from a third source: the Ionian region of the Near East.[1]

Both Ionic and Doric chitons were worn between 580 B.C. and the beginning of the Roman period, around 300 B.C. Although Greek and Etruscan chitons are often difficult to tell apart, Etruscan chitons consistently tend to be shorter, less voluminous than Greek. (See Figure 4.2.) Some appear to have sleeves cut and sewn into the garment, giving garments a closer fit and less draped appearance. (See Figure 4.3.) During the Classical Period upper class Etruscan ladies wore a badge of status consisting of a fringe or tassel that hung down at the front and back of each shoulder.

mantles—Wraps for the body; among the most distinctive styles developed by Etruscans. Varieties included a heavy woolen cloak for men, similar to Greek chlamys, fastening at one shoulder; the

4.2 (*Above*) Reclining Etruscan figure dressed in Doric *chiton* with shawl draped around her body, over her shoulders, and drawn over her hair. She wears a small fillet in her hair. (*Photograph courtesy of Photo Arts Company.*)

4.3 (*Right*) Dancing maenad (a mythological figure in the form of a young girl), Etruscan, late 6th century, B.C. Etruscan garments such as this one often show more shaping in the cut of the sleeves and a more fitted line through the body than Greek costume of a comparable period. This figure also wears characteristic Etruscan pointed-toed shoes and the *tutulus*, a high-crowned, small-brimmed hat. (*Photograph courtesy of the Cleveland Museum of Art, purchase from the J. H. Wade Fund.*)

1. L. Bonfante. *Etruscan Dress.* Baltimore: Johns Hopkins Press, 1975, p. 38.

himation, adopted after it first appeared among the Greeks. The *tebenna*, a rounded mantle worn by men and women, seemingly woven with curved edges in a roughly semicircular or elliptical form, and draped in various ways: like a chlamys, or worn back-to-front with the curved edge hanging down in front and the two ends thrown back over the shoulder, or like an himation. (See Figure 4.4.)

NOTE: Tebenna is a Greek rendering of what was probably an Etruscan word. This garment is thought to have been a forerunner of the Roman *toga*, a semicircular draped garment symbolizing Roman citizenship.

hair and head dress—Men in the Archaic period wore medium-length hair and pointed beards; in post-Archaic period hair was short, faces were clean-shaven. During the Archaic period women arranged their hair in a single braid at the back or in long, flowing tresses. In post-Archaic periods women's hair styles were like those of Greek women.

Hat styles included wide-brimmed hats similar to the petasos for men, fillets to confine the hair for men and women. On festive occasions men and women wore a crown-like head piece. Both wore high-crowned brimless hats; men's styles often peaked while women wore the *tutulus*, with a rounded crown.

footwear—Sandals for men and women, together with a style covering the foot up to the ankle and with an elongated toe that curled upward, often red in color.

NOTE: Bonfante suggests this style may have survived from Myceneae and come by some unknown route to Etruria from Greece in the 6th century when they first appear.

jewelry—More often worn by women: necklaces, earrings, decorative brooches, fibulae both of local origin and imported from abroad.

COSTUME FOR CHILDREN

So far as one can tell there were no specialized costumes for children. Small children went naked in warm weather. Young boys dressed in short tunics. (Figure 4.5.) Specific evidence of the dress of young girls is lacking, but probably they wore chitons similar to those of Greek girl children.

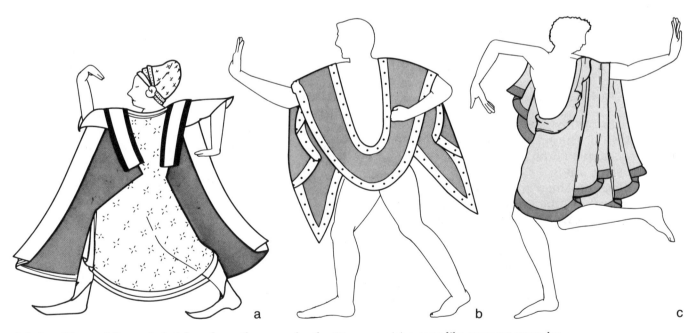

a b c

4.4a,b,c. Three of the varied styles of mantles worn by the Etruscans (a) a cape-like garment worn by women that had long tabs hanging down in the front. (b) a *tebenna*, worn with the curved edge hanging down in the front and the two ends thrown over the shoulders. (c) a *tebenna*, draped over one shoulder, in a manner much like the *himation*. Compare the draping of 4.4c to that of the *toga* in figure 4.6. The *tebenna* is thought to have been the precourser of the *toga*.

4.5 Etruscan statue of boy wearing *chiton* (tunic). This tunic is seamed at the shoulders and carries a band of decoration down either side at the front. These decorations were called *clavi* by the Romans. (*Photograph courtesy of Photo Arts Company.*)

Rome: Historical Background

Early Roman history was closely intertwined with that of Etruria. During the early years of Roman history, kings ruled Rome. Several of the early kings were Etruscan, but in 509 B.C. revolution ended the reign of Etruscan kings in Rome. Following the revolt, Etruscans and the Romans battled each other until, one by one, the Etrurian cities became a part of the growing Roman cofederation, losing their independence and becoming another of the many ethnic strands woven into Roman Italy.

The Roman Republic, founded about 509 B.C., had a conservative government with two consuls elected annually who exercised the executive powers and in time of war commanded the armies. In addition, Rome had a senate and a popular assembly.

Under this form of government, Rome fought a series of wars which expanded Roman control over all of Italy. A quarrel over Sicily between Rome and Carthage, whose empire stretched across North Af-

rica, led to the first wars of conquest which produced the Roman Empire. Ultimately under the Republic, the empire included much of North Africa, large areas of the Middle East, eastern Europe up to the Danube River, and most of continental Europe.

Rome became a wealthy, complex society. However, the strain of the war on the society and the economy, the resulting social strife, the rivalries of ambitious generals led to civil war and to a dictator for life, Julius Caesar.

After Caesar's assassination in 44 B.C., Augustus, his grandnephew and adopted son, won out over all rivals in a struggle for power and became emperor in 27 B.C. Augustus laid the foundations for an empire that would give the Mediterranean world two hundred years of prosperity and peace, the *Pax Romana*, (Roman Peace). Augustus and his successors added territory to the Empire in Arabia, Africa, Germany east of the Danube, and in Britain. But not until the third century A.D. would decline set in, culminating in the fall of the Roman Empire. Among the causes for the decline of the Roman Empire were the quality and competence of the emperors, the military anarchy and civil wars, the failure of the economy, and the collapse of Roman society. A major cause for the fall of the Roman Empire was the migration of the German tribes into the empire in search of land and provisions.

The construction of a new capital in the eastern portion of the empire, Constantinople (now called Istanbul), by the Emperor Constantine about 325 A.D. signalled the decline of the western empire. In 395 A.D., the naming of two Roman emperors, one for the east and one for the West, in effect split the Empire; each portion became involved in separate struggles for survival. In the west, where German chieftans had begun to establish Germanic kingdoms, a barbarian chieftan deposed the last emperor in the west in 476. The Eastern Roman Empire, wealthy and secure, grew into the powerful and influential Byzantine Empire.

SOCIAL LIFE DURING THE ROMAN EMPIRE

During the early imperial period the population of the city of Rome is estimated to have been more than a million people: Roman citizens (only men were citizens, but citizens could be rich, middle class, or poor), their families, their slaves, and foreigners.[2] By the second century A.D. perhaps 90 percent of the residents of Rome were of foreign

2. Friedlander. *Roman Life and Manners Under the Early Empire.* Vol. 1, New York: E. P. Dutton and Company, 1936, p. 17.

extraction, however many foreigners were provincials to whom citizenship had been extended.[3]

The well-to-do population lived in town houses built around a sunny courtyard and decorated with colorful frescos, or in large, comfortable apartments located on the ground floor of apartment buildings that rose from four to nine storeys high. The less affluent and the poor lived in these tenements on the higher floors, sometimes under crowded conditions, with poor lighting, bad ventilation, and the constant threat of disastrous fires.

Heading every Roman family was the oldest male member, the *paterfamilias*. The paterfamilias was the sole owner of family possessions, including not only those of his children but also of his grandchildren. He decided whom his children would marry. If a marriage was not a success, it could be dissolved very easily. Married women of middle class or higher status supervised the household and the children, the size and complexity of which depended upon her socio-economic status. Members of the aristocracy lived in large households composed of relatives, servants who were often freed slaves, and household slaves.

In spite of socio-economic differences among Romans, the primary distinction made in Roman society was between the citizen and the non-citizen. This status was clearly marked by dress. The male citizen was entitled to wear the *toga*, a draped, eliptically-shaped mantle that probably had evolved from the Etruscan tabenna. Slaves, foreigners, and adult women were prohibited from wearing this costume.

The Emperor and the imperial court were at the very top of Roman society, and the upper classes more or less faithfully mirrored the manners and customs of the court of the day. Upper class men generally belonged to one of the civil and military orders, the most important of these were the senators and the second in importance, the knights. Beginning in Republican times, senators were distinguished by their dress. Their tunics (and those of the Emperor) had broad purple bands that extended from hem to hem across the shoulders. These bands were called *clavi* (plural) or *clavus* (singular). Furthermore, they wore shoes with laces that wrapped around the leg half way to the knee. The tunics of knights had slightly narrower purple bands and they wore a gold ring that signified their rank. After the end of the 1st century A.D., however, it became customary for all male members of the nobility to wear clavii on the tunic.

The remainder of the citizenry had no special insignia aside from the toga, although there were a number of special types of togas worn for certain occasions or to designate particular roles. (See page 50.) Foreigners wore the costume of their native land, and slaves wore tunics.

SOURCES OF COSTUME INFORMATION

Many details about dress are provided through archeology, Roman writings, and remarkable artifacts and works of art preserved by the burial of two cities, Pompeii and Herculaneum following the eruption of the volcano, Mt. Vesuvius, around 79 A.D.

Roman art shows strong Greek influences. Greek artists were brought to Rome to work as slaves. Often Roman statues are copies of sculptures created by earlier Greek artists, however Roman portrait sculpture (many executed by Greek sculptors) emphasized a realism not to be found in some of the more idealized copies of Greek work. Many of these statues are portraits of individuals which provide an excellent idea of the appearance, coiffures, and garb of upper class Romans.

Painting techniques developed to a very high level. Frescos have been found that provide some indication of the range of colors used in Roman costume and further insight into clothing practices.

CLOTHING PRODUCTION

The textile industry was not a home craft, as it had been in Greece, although many Roman women did weave cloth for their families. Weaving, dyeing, and finishing were carried out in business establishments that might employ as many as 50 or 100 people. These "factories" were located in many towns in all parts of the Empire. Some cities were especially well known for making certain types of cloth or items of clothing. A cloak from Modena was considered superior to one from Laodicia or a tunic from Scythia better than one from Alexandria.[4] Both fabrics and garments were imported to Rome from all parts of the Empire, and beyond. By the year 1 A.D. Rome had established a lively silk trade with China. Cotton was imported from India. Wool and linen were used more extensively than either of these relatively more scarce imports, however.

Wealthy families probably had their clothing

3. L. Casson. *Daily Life in Ancient Rome*. New York: Heritage Publishing Company, Inc., 1975, p. 12.

4. A. H. M. Jones. "The Cloth Industry under the Roman Empire." *Economic History Review*. Vol. 8, No. 2, 1960 p. 185.

needs provided by the slaves of the household, but evidence concerning trades in Roman times indicates that there was also a thriving "ready-to-wear" business. A dialog in a Greek-Latin book reflects the nature of bargaining that went on in these shops:

"I am going to the tailor."

"How much does this pair cost?"

"One hundred denarii."

"How much is the waterproof?"

"Two hundred denarii."

"That is too dear; take a hundred."[5]

Tailors are accused of adjusting their prices for winter garments according to the severity of the season.

Specialization among shoemakers was apparently sufficiently great that differentiation was made between shoemakers, bootmakers, sandal makers, slipper makers, and ladies' shoemakers. Jewelry crafts members included workers in pearls and diamonds, gold and silversmiths, and ringmakers. Each craft was concentrated in a different district of the city.

Roman Costume

The basic form of the chiton, called "tunic" by the Romans, was adopted from the Greeks possibly by way of Etruscan dress. The most distinctive Roman costume form, the *toga*, was apparently Etruscan in origin. These adopted costumes, however, took on Latin names and characteristics that reflected the Roman character.

In describing clothing the Romans made a distinction between garments that were "put on" (*indutus*) and garments that were "wrapped around" (*amictus*). Indutus was worn underneath or closest to the skin (as was the tunic, for example), and amictus might be considered outer wear (for example, the toga or the himation).

THE TOGA

Over his tunic the male Roman citizen wore his toga. Each variety of toga had distinguishing characteristics in shape, mode of decoration, color, or form of draping. The earliest toga, the basis of later styles, was draped from a length of roughly semi-circular white wool fabric with a band of color around the curved edge. Wilson, in a lengthy study of the Roman toga, determined that the early toga was shaped as depicted in Figure 4.6a.[6]

5. L. Friedlander, *op. cit.*, p. 148.

6. L. M. Wilson. *The Roman Toga.* Baltimore, MD: Johns Hopkins Press, 1924, p. 33.

By the Imperial period the shape of the toga had evolved to that shown in Figure 4.6b and 4.7 and its draping had become more complicated. A *sinus*, a sort of pocket, in the drapery at the front, served to hold paper scrolls. The over-fold of fabric was sometimes pulled up and over the head at the back to form a sort of hood.

It required care to apportion the folds of a toga properly and to balance the bulk of the fabric. Carcopino comments:

> the toga was a garment worthy of the masters of the world, flowing, solemn, eloquent, but with over-much complication in its arrangement and a little too much emphatic affectation in the self-conscious tumult of its folds. It required real skill to drape it artfully . . . It required unremitting attention if the balance of the toga were to be preserved in walking, in the heat of a discourse, or amid the jostlings of a crowd.[7]

One variant which developed by the time of the late Empire (after the 2nd century A.D.) was known as the "toga with the folded bands." The over-fold was folded back-and-forth upon itself until a folded band of fabric was formed at the top of the semi-circle and probably held in place by stitching or pinning. When draped around the body, the folds created a smooth, diagonal band across the breast to the shoulder. (See Figure 4.8.)

The toga was required dress during most of the Imperial period for audiences with the Emperor, at the spectacles that were staged in the Roman arena, and for any event where a citizen appeared in an official capacity. The heavy garment was probably uncomfortably hot in summer. To keep it white required frequent cleaning which must have caused the toga to wear out quickly. Martial, a satirical poet, is constantly complaining about having a threadbare toga that he must replace. It is not surprising, then, to learn that Romans of the later Empire, when etiquette grew more lax, preferred the Greek himation (called in Latin, *pallium*) to the toga and wore their togas only when they could not avoid it.

Each different type of toga had a particular function and style. Togas were male garments with the exception of the *toga praetexta* which was worn by girls from noble families until they married, a practice which could be a survival from Etruscan times when women as well as men wore the tabenna.

7. J. Carcopino. *Daily Life in Ancient Rome.* New Haven: Yale University Press, 1940, p. 155.

4.6a The Toga. (*Drawing adapted from L. M. Wilson.* The Roman Toga. *Baltimore, MD: Johns Hopkins Press, 1924.*)

Steps in draping the early form of the *toga,* seen below.

Step 1: The *toga* is placed over the shoulder with point 1 below the knee.

Step 2: Point 3 is drawn across the back, under the right arm and up to the left shoulder.

Step 3: Point 3 is thrown across the left shoulder and arm to hang down in back of the left shoulder. Point 1 is obscured by draping the bulk of the toga across the front of the body.

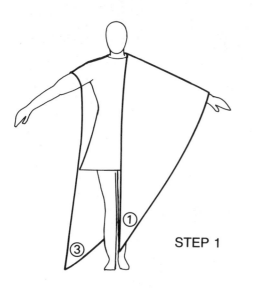

STEP 1

The Early Toga

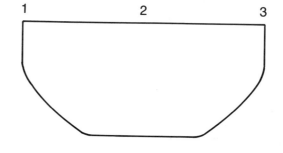

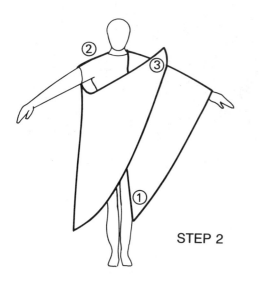

STEP 2

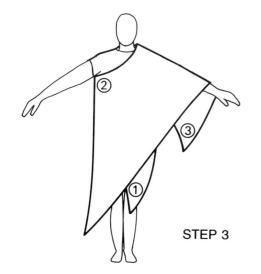

STEP 3

Imperial Toga, full size

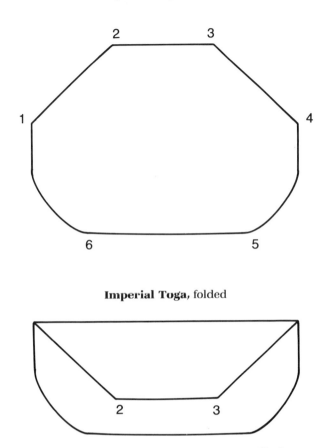

Imperial Toga, folded

4.6b The Imperial *toga* was draped in essentially the same way, except that the extra fold created an extra drapery at the front of the body. The fold and the *sinus* (a pocket formed by pulling part of the side fold to the front) can be seen in Figure 4.7. (*Drawings adapted from drawings and photographs in L. M. Wilson,* The Roman Toga. *Baltimore MD: Johns Hopkins Press, 1938.*)

ROMAN COSTUME FOR MEN

Item / Description

loin cloth—in Latin, *subligar*, comparable to the Greek perizoma and serving as an undergarment for middle and upper class men; a working garment for slaves.

tunic—ending around the knee; short-sleeved; T-shaped. Served as underclothing or a night shirt for upper class men. Belted tunics, the usual street costume for poor men. By the first century of the Empire these variations are noted: tunics cut shorter in front than back; shorter versions for manual laborers and military. Several layers worn in cold weather, one as an undergarment (interior tunic) and one as an outer garment (su-

4.7 Roman wearing the Imperial *toga* over a tunic. The draped pouch at the front is the *sinus*. (*Photograph courtesy of Photo Arts Company.*)

perior tunic). Those sensitive to cold wore two undertunics.

NOTE: The Emperor Augustus is said to have worn four layers! Personal style also affected wearing of the tunic. Horace, a Roman writer, describes two extremes: "Maltinus minces about with his tunic trailing low, another has it hoisted obscenely up his crotch."[8]

toga—(See page 47.) Among the types of togas identified by Wilson were these:

toga pura or toga virilis—Plain white, undecorated wool toga worn after the age of sixteen by the ordinary male Roman citizen. Candidates for office lightened this toga to an exceptional white, and it was called a *toga candida* from which the word "candidate" is derived.

toga praetexta—with purple border, worn by the young sons and daughters of the nobility (until age sixteen) and also by certain adult magistrates.

8. N. Rudd, translator. *The Satires of Horace and Persius.* Baltimore: Penguin Books, 1973, p. 33.

toga pulla—black or dark-colored toga said to have been worn for mourning.

toga picta—purple, with gold embroidery, assigned on special occasions to victorious generals or other persons who distinguished themselves in some way.

toga trabea—apparently multi-colored, striped toga which was assigned to augurs (religious officials who prophesied the future) or important officials.

cloaks and capes—Outdoor garments for cold weather with or without hoods. The most important of these, cited by various sources:

paenula—a heavy wool cloak, semicircular in shape, closed at the front, with a hood.

lacerna—rectangular, with rounded corners and a hood.

laena—a circle of cloth folded to a semicircle which was thrown over the shoulders and pinned at the front.

birrus or burrus—resembling a modern, hooded poncho, cut full and with an opening through which the head was slipped.

paludamentum—a large white or purple cloak similar to the Greek chlamys, worn by emperors or generals.

4.8 *Toga* with the folded bands. (*Redrawn by Thomas Hope from the Arch of Constantine.*)

military cloaks—including: the *abolla*, a folded rectangle fastening on the right shoulder and worn by officers; the *sagum*, like the abolla generally red, a single layer of thick wool worn by ordinary soldiers and, in time of war, by Roman citizens. The phrase "to put on the sagum" was synonymous with saying "to go to war." Generals leaving the city of Rome for a military campaign donned a purple rectangular cloak, larger and thicker than the cloaks of either officers or common soldiers.

ROMAN COSTUME FOR WOMEN

Item / Description

loin cloth—(subligar) together with the *mamillare*, a band of soft fabric or leather which supported the breasts, comprise undermost garments.

NOTE: A mosaic in Sicily shows female athletes in what looks like a two-piece, modern bathing suit. It is thought these are the subligar and the mamillare.

4.9 Woman wearing the *stolla* and, draped over it, a *palla*. Her hair is dressed in the simple style of the Republican period. In her hand she carries a folded linen handkerchief, a symbol of rank. (*Photograph courtesy of Photo Arts Company.*)

interior tunic—Served as night dress and worn alone in the privacy of the home.

stola—an outer tunic (counterpart to the Greek chiton) worn for out-of-doors and more formal occasions. (See Figure 4.9.)

palla—A draped shawl (counterpart of the Greek himation), placed over the stola. (See Figure 4.9.) The interior tunic, or the stola, or both usually had sleeves. The stola usually bordered in a color contrasting with the rest of the garment. In some depictions a ruffle, the *institia*, borders the hem of the stola.

NOTE: The institia seems to have been a mark of status, identifying married, upper class women. Horace differentiates between a respectable married woman and a prostitute by saying of the former that "their feet are concealed by a flounce sewn on their dress."[9]

Pallas are depicted as draped in these ways: similarly to the toga; casually pulled across the shoulder; pulled over the head like a veil.

cloaks—for outdoor wear, including the paenula when traveling in bad weather.

COSTUME FOR MEN AND WOMEN

Item / Description

hair and head dress—Women in the Republican period had softly-waved hair. By the end of the 1st century, complex almost architectural forms built of curls, braids, and artificial hair, if needed. Blonde hair fashionable, achieved through bleaching or wearing wigs made from the hair of Northern European blonde captives. (See Figure 4.10.)

NOTE: Roman writers ridiculed the custom of elaborately dressing the hair, saying: "So numerous are the tiers and stories piled one upon another on her head: in front you would take her for an Andromache; she is not so tall behind; you would not think it was the same person."[10]

During the later Empire, hair styles simplified with braids or locks doubled up in back and pinned to the top of the head.

Men's hair was cut short, arranged by a barber. Sometimes straight hair was favored; other times,

9. Horace, *op. cit.*, p. 33.
10. Juvenal, quoted in Carcopino, *op. cit.*, p. 167.

Roman Women's Hairstyles

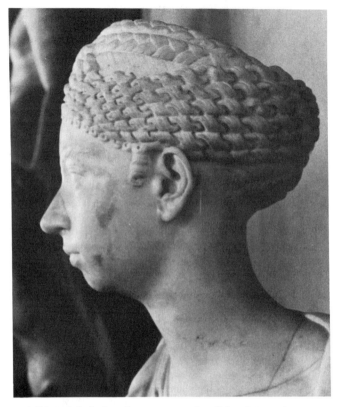

4.10 Women's hairstyles: *top*, a style of the 1st century A.D.; *bottom*, a style of the 2nd century. (*Photograph courtesy of Photo Arts Company.*)

curls. Men who wished to appear more youthful dyed their hair. Beards predominated in the Republican years; clean-shaven faces during the Empire until the reign of Hadrian (c. 120 A.D.), an Emperor who was bearded.

NOTE: Without sharp-edged steel razors, shaving was a painful and sometimes dangerous experience. Penalties were established for barbers who scarred their clients; a really good barber could become very prosperous. At least one barber was commemorated for his skill by a Roman poet. A man's first shave was a rite of passage, celebrated with a religious ceremony. The shaven hairs were deposited in a special container and sacrificed to the gods at a festival to which family and friends were invited.[11]

Few hats worn by women. Instead the palla or a scarf were pulled over the head; fillets and coronets were worn.

Men's hat styles similar to Greek petasos; or hoods; rounded or pointed caps.

footwear—sandals for men and women (in Latin, *solae* or *sandalis*) and also boots and a slipper-like shoe reaching to the ankle (*soccus*).

jewelry—Beautifully crafted rings, bracelets, necklaces, armlets, earrings, diadems, as well as less costly versions. Of these only rings were worn by men.

cosmetics—According to the satirists cosmetics were used lavishly by both men and women. Practices reported for women: whitening the skin with lead, tinting the lips red, darkening eyebrows.

NOTE: One disgruntled lover makes this charge about his mistress, "You lie stored away in a hundred caskets; and your face does not sleep with you."[12]

Appearance-conscious men were said to use makeup cream on the cheeks and to paste small circles of cloth over skin flaws. Both sexes used perfume.

grooming—Large public baths were frequented not only for cleanliness and exercise, but also as a place to socialize and do business. In some periods baths were segrated by sex; in others men and women bathed together.

11. Carcopino, *op. cit.*, p. 160.
12. Carcopino, *op. cit.*, p. 169.

accessories of dress—Women carried fans and handbags. Sunshades were needed for the games held in the arenas—either wide hats or parasols were used.

A white linen handkerchief and its variants had differing names and uses:
  sudarium—wiped off perspiration, veiled the face, or was held in front of the mouth to protect against disease.
  mappa—a table napkin. (Guests brought their own napkins.)
  orarium—slightly larger version of the sudarium, which became a symbol of rank and in the late Empire was worn by upper class women neatly pleated across the left shoulder or forearm.

COSTUME FOR CHILDREN

Except for the wearing of the toga praetexta by sons and daughters of the nobility, Roman children dressed as did their elders. Noble Roman girls ceased wearing the toga praetexta when they married or reached age 16. At age 16, noble Roman boys gave up the praetexta in favor of the toga pura, which was also worn by freeborn Roman boys.

Infants were swaddled. At the time a free-born child was named, a locket made of gold or leather and containing charms against the evil eye was placed around the infant's neck. This was worn throughout childhood.

MILITARY COSTUME

Item / Description

body armor—worn over the tunic. Variations included leather bands or corselets of metal plates or disks mounted on fabric or leather; or large metal plates hinged at the shoulders and molded to fit the body. A wide band of leather rectangles might be suspended from the waist to cover the lower torso. *Greaves* protected the legs; *helmets* protected the head.

footwear—boots that laced up the front, covering the leg to above the ankle; sandals; open-toed shoes; or closed-toed shoes.

NOTE: During the imperial period Roman soldiers adopted knee-length trousers placed under the tunic in cold weather. These garments were similar to those worn by the Gauls, a northern European tribe.

COSTUME FOR SPECIAL EVENTS

The Synthesis—The synthesis was a garment worn by men at dinner parties, the precise form of which is a matter of debate. After a careful analysis of the Latin texts, McDaniel concluded that the synthesis was a lightweight garment worn instead of the toga for dining because the toga was too heavy and cumbersome to wear when the Romans reclined to eat. The texts that refer to the synthesis imply that the garment had two parts, and McDaniel suggested that these two parts probably consisted of a tunic plus a shoulder garment, such as the pallium or other drapery. Latin authors speak of the synthesis as bright and colorful.[13]

NOTE: The synthesis was never seen outside of the home except during the Saturnalia, a public festival in December. One of the characteristics of the Saturnalia was that everything was turned "upside down." For example, masters waited upon their slaves, gambling games that were normally forbidden were allowed. The wearing of the synthesis out-of-doors may be another example of the upsetting of tradition that was part of the Saturnalia.

Bridal Costume—Roman bridal costume for women introduced certain elements that have continued to have traditional association with weddings even until the present day: the veil and orange blossoms. Bridal costume consisted of a tunic woven in a traditional way, and tied around the waist with a knotted belt of wool; a saffron-colored palla and matching shoes; and a metal collar. The bride's hair was arranged with six pads of artificial hair, each separated by narrow bands and over this a veil of bright orange (the *flammeum*). The veil covered the upper part of her face. On top of the veil a wreath made of myrtle and orange blossoms was placed.

RELIGIOUS GARB

Religious garb differed little from the costume of ordinary persons. Vestal virgins, a group of unmarried women assigned to guard the sacred flame kept burning in the temple of Vesta, wore veils that fastened under the chin and six pads of artificial hair separated by bands like those worn by brides. Augurs wore the multicolored, striped toga trabea.

13. W. B. McDaniel, "Roman Dinner Garments." *Classical Philology*. Vol. 20, 1925, p. 268.

COSTUME OF THE LATE EMPIRE

In the closing century of the Roman Empire, the toga became less and less favored. After the fall of the Empire it survived in modified form as draped shawl worn over the tunic during the Byzantine Empire and the early Middle Ages in Europe. This garment was perhaps more like a Greek himation in form than a toga.

A late variant of the tunic was the *dalmatic*, a fuller T-shaped tunic with long sleeves of considerable width.

Throughout the Imperial period articles of local, non-Roman dress had tended to survive or be incorporated into Roman clothing in outlying regions. The Gallic cloak; a loose-fitting, unbelted tunic worn in Roman Gaul (now France); and trousers, worn by Northern barbarian tribes provide examples of this tendency. As Roman control over the outer limits of the Empire eroded, local styles and Roman costume tended to merge even more. When the Western Roman Empire fell, at the close of the 4th century, the focus of Roman styles shifted eastward, to the court in Constantinople where elements of Roman style blended with influences from the East to produce Byzantine styles.

Summary

Much of what was originally Greek clothing styles came to the Romans by way of the Etruscans. Comparisons of Greek, Etruscan, and Roman styles may serve not only to summarize the material in Chapters 3 and 4, but also to point up differences in these three cultures that are reflected in their costume.

Most Greek garments are based on rectangular forms. Roman and Etruscan styles used a greater variety of shapes, with particular emphasis on rounded or eliptical forms. (In this context it is interesting to note that the Etruscans are thought to have originated the round arch, now called the "Roman arch," whereas the Greeks used the rectangular post-and-lintel construction in their buildings.) Both Roman and Etruscan styles rely less than Greek styles on the draping of a single piece of fabric and make greater use of cutting and sewing, although draped elements are also present in the styles of the Italian region. This and the tendency of the Romans in particular to use wool fabrics in preference to linen helps to account for the difference in appearance between the free flow of Greek clothing and the heavier draperies of Etruscan and Roman clothes.

Both the Etruscans and Romans used more ornamentation and accessories, and in general they also wore more clothing. The climate may have been a factor (the climate of Northern Italy is cooler than that of Greece), but it also reflects a cultural attitude. The Etruscans and Romans did not share the Greek appreciation of nudity or the lightly clad human body.

The most significant difference between Greek and Etruscan and Roman dress seems to be in the assignment of the function of distinguishing status to clothing. Age differences were reflected in dress: young boys wore the toga praetexta, men wore the toga pura or virilis; girls wore a toga, women did not. Neither the Greek nor the Etruscan costumes carried any such as significance. Nor did their costume differentiate between citizen and non-citizen, as did the Romans. Throughout Roman costume one finds more evidence of the use of costume to set the individual or the occasion apart. One thinks in this context of the special garment for dining, the synthesis; the special costume of senators and of knights; the variety of togas and the significance of each. While Romans took the tunic (the chiton) from the Greeks and the toga (the tabenna) from the Etruscans, they "selected superficial characteristics like dress, yet always preserved their religion and their attitudes—in short their distinct identities."[14]

Selected Bibliography

BOOKS CONTAINING ILLUSTRATIONS OF COSTUME OF THE PERIOD FROM ORIGINAL SOURCES

Becatti, G. *The Art of Ancient Rome and Greece*. New York: Harry N. Abrams, Inc., 1967.

Bonfante, L. *Etruscan Dress*. Baltimore, MD: Johns Hopkins University Press, 1975.

Heintze, H. *Roman Art*. London: Phaidon Press, 1974.

Kraus, T. *Pompeii and Herculaneum*. New York: Harry N. Abrams, Inc., 1975.

L'Orange, H. P. *The Roman Empire*. New York: Rizzoli, 1985.

Pallotino, M. *The Art of the Etruscans*. New York: Vangard Press, 1955.

Strong, D. and D. Brown. *Roman Crafts*. New York: New York University Press, 1976.

Von Matt. *The Art of the Etruscans*. New York: Harry N. Abrams, Inc., 1970.

PERIODICAL ARTICLES

Bonfante, L. "Etruscan Dress as an Historical Source." *American Journal of Archeology*. July, 1971, p. 277.

Bonfante, L. The Language of Dress: Etruscan Influences." *Archeology*. Jan./Feb., 1978, p. 14.

Braun-Ronsdorf, M. "The Sudarium and Orarium of the Romans." *CIBA Review*, No. 89, p. 3298.

Jones, A. H. M. "Cloth Industry Under the Roman Empire." *Economic History Review*. December, 1960, p. 183.

Wild, J. P. "Byrrus Britannicus." *Antiquity*, September 1963, p. 193.

Wild, J. P. Chapter 13: "Textiles" in *Roman Crafts*, Editors: D. Strong and D. Brown. New York: New York University Press, 1976.

DAILY LIFE

Balsdon, J. V. D. *Life and Leisure in Ancient Rome*. New York: McGraw-Hill Book Company, 1969.

Bonfante, L. *Etruscan Life and Afterlife*. Detroit: Wayne State University Press, N.D.

Brilliant, R. *Visual Narratives: Storytelling in Etruscan and Roman Art*. Ithaca: Cornell University Press, 1984.

Carcopino, J. *Daily Life in Ancient Rome*. New Haven, Conn.: Yale University Press, 1940.

Casson, L. *Daily Life in Ancient Rome*. New York: American Heritage Publishing Company, Inc., 1975.

Cowell, F. R. *Everyday Life in Ancient Rome*. New York: G. P. Putnam's Sons, 1961.

Friedlander, L. *Roman Life and Manners Under the Early Empire*. Vols. 1–4. New York: E. P. Dutton and Company, 1936.

Giannelli, G. *The World of Ancient Rome*. New York: G. P. Putnam's Sons, 1967.

Grant, M. *The Etruscans*, New York: Scribners, 1981.

Heurgon, J. *Daily Life of the Etruscans*. New York: Macmillan Company, 1964.

Liversidge, J. *Everyday Life in the Roman Empire*. New York: G. P. Putnam's Sons, 1976.

Nichols, R. and K. McLeish. *Through Roman Eyes*. New York: Cambridge University Press, 1976.

Paoli, U. E. *Rome, Its People, Life, and Customs*. New York: David McKay Company, Inc., 1964.

Strong, D. *The Early Etruscans*. New York: G. P. Putnam's Sons, 1968.

14. L. Bonfante. "The Language of Dress: Etruscan influences." *Archeology*, Jan./Feb. 1978, p. 26.

PART II

The Middle Ages

c. 300–1500

The founding of Constantinople, the new capital of the Roman Empire, signalled the decline of Rome and the western portion of the empire. It also meant two cultures would develop in the empire, in addition to two imperial lines of emperors. The advantage belonged to the wealthier, more populous eastern Empire whose capital, Constantinople, was well situated to defend the eastern empire and to dominate the eastern economy. The western empire, ruled from Rome, was overwhelmed by the mass migration of German tribes which began at the close of the 4th century and continued on throughout the 5th century.

Because of its geographical location, the city of Rome was sacked in 410 A.D. and several times later in the century. The western emperors, however, moved the capital of the western Empire from Rome to Ravenna in 403 A.D., hoping that this city on the Adriatic coast, south of Venice, would be less easily attacked than Rome. In 476 when Odovacar, king of an obscure German tribe deposed the emperor of the west, Roman power disappeared from Italy.

Certain elements that had been part of Roman civilization and culture survived. The Christian church, which had endured persecution, eventually became the official state church of the Empire in the 4th century, exercising a unifying force in western Europe and converting the barbarians to Christianity. The church had continued to function be-cause its organization paralleled that of the Roman Empire. The head of the church was not the emperor (as in the Byzantine Empire) but the bishop of Rome, the Pope. In each important city across Europe, bishops loyal to the pope administered the affairs of the church. Over the bishops in each capital city of the province were archbishops (metropolitans in the Eastern Empire) who corresponded to the governors over the Imperial Roman provinces.

After Christianity became the official state religion some Christians sought a more ascetic form of Christianity; they found satisfaction in monasticism. Originating in the east, it became the way of life for those who wanted only to seek salvation for their souls. Because the monks had to be occupied with some form of work, the copying of books by hand became an appropriate form of labor for them. Through the centuries monastery libraries would preserve not only Christian but also earlier Greek and Roman classical literature which otherwise would have been lost forever.

The early Middle Ages, from the fall of the Roman Empire until the 9th century, have often been called the Dark Ages because of the decline in cultural standards as people lost command of the Latin language. Education for the laymen disappeared, producing generations who could neither read or write. In much of the period depopulation, poverty, and isolation affected many areas of Europe; the quality of life declined seriously. A major cause for the decline in Roman civilization was the decay of the cities and towns which had been the centers of Roman culture. Written records from the period are often sparse, leaving gaps which cannot be filled. Records of costumes are especially scarce. With the decline in living standards and the decrease in wealth, works of art were rarely commissioned except for those intended for the church. Literary production decreased as well because of illiteracy. Nevertheless enough evidence remains to construct a general, if not too detailed picture of life in the early Medieval period.

Throughout the Middle Ages, the Eastern Roman Empire, or the Byzantine Empire as it is more often called, survived, helping to preserve ancient Greek thought and creating magnificent works of art. The survival of the Byzantine Empire was based on an efficient bureaucracy and a sound economy. While trade and urban life almost ended in the west, cities and commerce flourished in the Byzantine Empire. With money obtained from trade, the Byzantine officials recruited, trained, and equipped armies that held off one attacker after another. A period of expansion ended in the 7th century when Arab armies invaded Byzantine territories.

A new religion, Islam, founded by Mohammed in Mecca in the early 7th century, inspired the Arab armies. Mohammed's successors united the Bedouin tribes in Arabia into a military force that soon swept across the Middle East. Arab armies, seeking booty and land, inspired by their new faith, conquered Iraq, Syria, Palestine and pressed on to seize territories as far to the east as India. On more than one occasion their armies beseiged Constantinople. After conquering North Africa, they moved northward through Spain and into southern France where their expansion was halted at the battle of Tours, 732.

Throughout its history, the Byzantine Empire was menaced by attacks from both the East and West. In spite of constant pressure from hostile forces, the Empire survived until 1453 when the city of Constantinople and the remains of a once powerful empire fell to a conquering force of Ottoman Turks. In its history of more than a thousand years, the Byzantine Empire developed an artistic and intellectual atmosphere in which styles and ideas of both East and West were merged. Records and traditions from Greek and Roman antiquity were preserved in the libraries and in the Byzantine art collections, although the Turks destroyed many of the manuscripts and works of art.

In the western Roman empire, Roman government disappeared by the end of the 5th century to be replaced by Germanic kingdoms. These helped to fuse Roman and Germanic cultures into a new civilization. One of the Germanic kingdoms which retained its political identity was the kingdom of the Franks. In the year 800, the pope crowned the king of the Franks, Charlemagne, emperor of the Romans. The ceremony symbolized a declaration of independence from the Byzantine Empire and a revival of the Roman Empire, but it was in fact more German than Roman. After his death in 814, Charlemagne's empire, which extended over much of western Europe, disintegrated under the impact of new and more destructive invasions. From the wreckage of the Carolingian Empire emerged a feudal society in which petty, local lords controlled small areas. These leaders pledged their personal loyalty to more powerful lords in return for their protection, and above them all was the supreme overlord, the king.

Under feudal monarchies, Europe revived so much so that by the 11th century a great military expedition, the first crusade, was launched to regain the Holy Land from the Moslems. Originally preached by Pope Urban II, it was a call for the unruly feudal knights to do battle for a righteous cause. Thousands of people, both knights and poor people, responded to the pope's call. For centuries Christians had done penance for their sins by going on pilgrimages to holy places. Now the crusade became a super-pilgrimage. Jerusalem was captured by the crusaders in 1099 and the inhabitants slaughtered. The crusaders established feudal states which were soon under attack from the Moslems prompting a series of crusades continuing for two hundred years until the crusading spirit vanished. From the Middle East the crusaders returned to Europe bringing back new products: spices, fabrics, perfumes, jewelry and new ideas.

By the 12th century, trade among the nations of Europe again flourished, and their once-stagnant economies experienced a remarkable revitalization. By the 1400's the arts, the intellectual life, and the social structure of Europe had been virtually reformed. During this transformation of society a change had come about in the speed with which clothing styles changed. Many costume historians and social scientists believe that the phenomenon of "fashion" in dress in Western society began during the Middle Ages.

Fashion has been defined as "a pattern of change in which certain social forms enjoy temporary acceptance and respectability only to be replaced by others . . ."[1]

Bell[2] pointed out that the increasingly rapid change of dress styles characteristic of Europe after the Middle Ages contrasts with the more static nature of clothing in earlier and non-Western civilizations. *The Dictionary of Social Sciences* describes fashion as "a recurring cultural pattern, found in societies having open-ended class systems . . ." and notes that "fashion becomes a matter of imitation of higher by lower classes in the common scramble for unstable and superficial status symbols."[3]

These two elements, an open-ended class system and the imitation of higher classes by lower classes, are both facets of Medieval life in the 13th through the 15th centuries. Peasants who moved from rural areas to cities often became part of the growing middle class. A wealthy merchant, Jacques Coeur, adviser to the king of France in the 1400's, was made a nobleman by that king to reward his service. The passage of sumptuary laws regulating dress and other luxuries in the 13th to the 15th centuries is good evidence of the vain attempts of the nobility to prevent the increasingly affluent commoners from usurping those status symbols the nobility considered to be their own.[4]

Two other conditions contributed to the spread of fashion. In order to imitate those of higher status, the imitator must have sufficient means to afford the latest fashions; and for fashions to be more than a merely local style, fashion information must be carried from one place to another. The late Middle Ages satisfied the aforementioned conditions. A newly affluent middle class, largely merchants and artisans, was emerging and provided not only social mobility but also increased affluence for a substantially larger proportion of the population, while increased trade and travel provided for a constant flow of fashion information.

As the Middle Ages drew to a close the phenomenon called fashion was firmly established and the duration of the periods that fashionable styles endured grew shorter and shorter. No longer can one speak of styles, like those of the Egyptians, which lasted for thousands of years. Instead, by the close of the Medieval period one speaks of fashions that lasted less than a century.

1. H. Blumer. "Fashion." *International Encyclopedia of the Social Sciences*, V. New York: Macmillan Company, p. 342.

2. Q. Bell. *On Human Finery*. London: Hogarth Press, 1948, p. 41.

3. R. L. Gold. "Fashion" in the *Dictionary of the Social Sciences*. New York: Free Press, 1964, p. 262.

4. D. Nicholas. "Patterns of Social Mobility" in *One Thousand Years: Western Europe in the Middle Ages*. New York: Houghton-Mifflin, 1974, p. 45.

CHAPTER 5

The Byzantine Empire and the Early Middle Ages

c. 300–1400

The first section of this chapter will deal with the Byzantine Empire which lasted from 330 to 1453 A.D. The latter section will deal with Europe during the period sometimes referred to as the "Dark Ages" or the "Early Middle Ages" and focuses on the years between the fall of Rome (c. 400) to 900 A.D.

In the years between 400 and 900 styles of the Byzantine Empire influenced all of Europe. Byzantium was the greatest cultural center of the period, while in the remainder of Europe literacy was barely kept alive in the monasteries. After the 10th century, however, Europe began an economic recovery and Byzantine influences became somewhat less important. The development of European life and styles in the period after 900 requires a separate discussion which will be provided in Chapter 6.

The Byzantine Period (c. 330– 1453): Historical Background

The capital of the Byzantine Empire was Constantinople, a Greek city that had been selected by the Roman Emperor Constantine in 330 to be the capital of the Eastern part of the Roman Empire. Located at the entrance of the Black Sea, the city and its surrounding territories commanded both land and

sea trade routes between the West and Central Asia, Russia, and the Far East. At the same time, the city was protected by the rugged Balkan mountains from the invading barbarians who over ran Rome and the Italian peninsula.

As a result, Constantinople was the metropolis of the Mediterranean economy until 1200. But while the location of the capital insured its survival, it also altered its character. Situated at the literal crossroads between East and West, the city and the Empire of which it was capital, became a rich amalgam of Eastern and Western art and culture. In costume one sees this reflected in a gradual evolution of Roman styles as they added increasingly ornate Eastern elements.

By the year 565 the Byzantine Empire had stretched north through the Balkans to the Danube, East into Asia Minor, Syria, and Palestine; West into Egypt and North Africa, Italy and Southern Spain. (See Figure 5.1.) During the 7th and 8th centuries its size was reduced, and by the mid-9th century it comprised only the Greek peninsula, and much of modern-day Turkey. This diminished empire was separated from the rest of Europe to such an extent that the Latin language was replaced by Greek, and Middle Eastern influences on life and styles became pronounced.

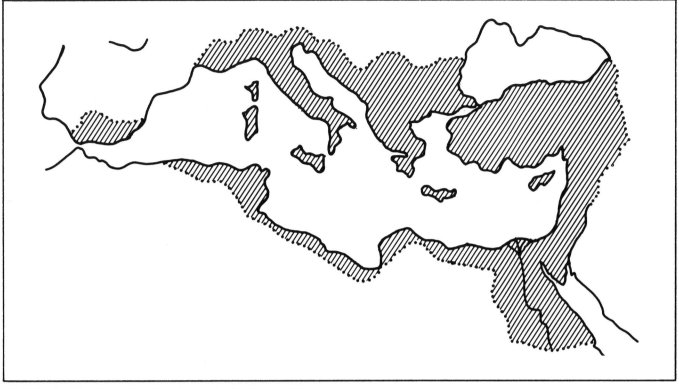

5.1 Extent of the Byzantine Empire under Justinian, 6th century A.D.

Throughout its history, Byzantium was constantly at war with a series of enemies: the Persians, Arabs, Bulgars, Avars, Seljuq Turks, and at the end, the Ottoman Turks. Even the Crusaders became enemies. On the Fourth Crusade, the Crusaders were unable to pay the price Venetians charged to transport them to the Holy Land. After more bargaining, the Crusaders agreed to capture the city of Zara for the Venetians, but after taking Zara the Crusaders were still short of cash to pay for the passage to Jerusalem. Urged on by the Venetians, the Crusaders accepted the offer of a pretender to the throne of the Byzantine Empire to supply the necessary cash if they helped him take Constantinople. The crusaders obliged but when he reneged on the bargain, in 1204 they seized Constantinople, sacked the city, destroying manuscripts and priceless works of art and made a crusader emperor. In 1261 a Byzantine emperor retook Constantinople but the once great empire had vanished. Byzantium was reduced to little more than a Balkan state. The artistic and intellectual life of the city revived, but the menace of invasion by the Turks continued. Finally, in 1453, the Ottoman Turks captured Constantinople, destroying the empire.

SOCIAL ORGANIZATION

At the head of the Byzantine state was the Emperor who was not only the absolute ruler who could make law as he wished, but also the head of the Eastern church, which separated from the Christian church in the west in 1054. The emperor lived with the empress in an elaborate palace in Constantinople. But the finest example of Byzantine architecture was to be found in the church of Santa Sophia (Holy Wisdom) constructed by the emperor Justinian (527–565). The interior was decorated with gold leaf, colored marble, bits of tints of glass, and colored mosaics. Similar motifs and decorative elements appear in Byzantine costume. A landed nobility made up an important element in the provincial economic life and the government of the empire. A well developed civil service helped the imperial administration function as long as it did, collecting taxes, administering justice, raising armies, and putting them into the field. The aristocracy was one of wealth, rather than blood line so ambitious young men could rise from one social group to the next, unlike the process in western society.

Education was important to wealthy families.

Most had tutors for their sons, there were schools in some provincial areas and Constantinople had a well-known university.

The status of women was rather advanced, although more so in the earlier Empire than in the late phase when ideas from the Near East predominated. Empresses were known to reign alone or as regents for minor sons, and a number of them exercised great power.

At the other end of the social scale were the slaves, both foreign captives and the poor who sold themselves into slavery in order to survive.

CULTURE, ART AND TECHNOLOGY

Throughout its history the city of Constantinople saw itself as a center for the preservation of the "antique" (i.e., Greek and Roman) culture. Writings and works of art were consciously preserved. Many of these treasures were destroyed in the sacks of the city by the crusaders and the Turks, however others were saved or were carried away by raiders to other places where they were preserved.

The art of the Byzantine Empire provides the major record from which costume information comes. Artists decorated churches with mosaics (pictures or designs made from small, colored stones) many of which still exist. Other special skills included carving of ivory, and illumination (hand-painting and lettering) of manuscripts. Byzantine art displays a blending of classical and middle eastern motifs and forms of decoration.

Fine textiles were woven by the Byzantines. From the 4th to the 6th centuries linen and wool predominated in use. Production of silk fabrics had been a secret process held first by the Chinese and later by the Japanese. Gradually knowledge of how silk was produced spread westward. Trade routes had brought silk fabrics and possibly some raw silk fiber to Greece and Rome as early as the 1st century B.C., but silk production had been possible only on a very limited scale. It is reported by Byzantine historians that in the 6th century a pair of monks brought the secret of sericulture (silk production) to the Byzantine Emperor. Not only did they learn how the silkworm was bred and raised and fed, but it was reported that they smuggled a number of silkworm eggs out of China in a hollow bamboo pole.[1]

1. F. M. Heichelheim. "Byzantine Silk Fabrics." *CIBA Review.* 1975, p. 2761.

From this point until the 9th century when Greeks in Sicily also began to produce silk, the Byzantines produced silk for all of the Western world. The emperor exploited his monopoly by charging enormous prices for the fabrics, and therefore only the wealthiest Europeans could afford the fabric. Brocades woven in Byzantinum were especially desirable. Often the designs used in these fabrics were Persian in origin. Christian subjects were also depicted in complex woven patterns. When made into garments or wall hangings, these luxurious fabrics might be adorned with precious and semi-precious stones, small medallions of enamel, with embroidery, and/or appliqués.

Byzantine Costume

Early Byzantine and late Roman costume are virtually indistinguishable. When the Emperor Constantine moved his capital to Constantinople, the Roman administrators carried with them Roman costumes and customs. With time, Roman influences eroded and Oriental influences gained. The evolution of the toga is an example of this process. The toga, diminishing in use by Romans from the 3rd century on, was by the 4th century used only for ceremonial occasions by the Emperor and the Consuls, important state officials. Finally only a vestige of the toga remained, a narrow band of folded fabric which wrapped around the body in the same way as the toga. Eventually even this was transformed into the Emperor's narrow, jeweled scarf.

BYZANTINE COSTUME FOR MEN

Item / Description

tunic—Basic garment, (See Figure 5.2.) with these decorative elements:
>*clavi*—by now these stripes on either side of the tunic had become ornamental rather than indicative of wearer's status.
>*segmentae*—square or round decorative medallions placed in different areas of the tunic.

Tunic lengths varied, Byzantine art showing these differences:
>· 6th Century: Emperor Justinian depicted in a short tunic.
>· Later centuries: emperors and important court officials wear full-length tunics; less important persons wear short, knee-length tunics.

5.2 Tunic from the Byzantine Period in Egypt, c. 5th–6th centuries. Careful examination of the tunic reveals narrow *clavi* over the shoulders and *segmentae* on the lower left of the skirt and at the upper left over the shoulder. *(Photograph courtesy of the Metropolitan Museum of Art, gift of George F. Baker, 1980.)*

• Long tunics—either cut with sleeves fitted to the wrist or an under tunic with long, close-fitting sleeves was placed beneath an outer tunic (*dalmatic*) with shorter, fuller sleeves. Tunics generally belted.

• Short tunics—usually with long sleeves, wider at the top and tapering to fit closely at the wrists. Working men frequently caught-up the hem of the tunic and fastened it to the belt at a point just over each leg in order to make movement easier.

NOTE: Tunics of the wealthy were decorated with vertical and horizontal bands elaborately patterned with embroidery, appliqué, precious stones, or woven designs. In the early part of the Empire fabrics were usually plain in color and decoration achieved by use of clavi, segmentae, and banding but as Oriental influences gained, fabrics developed overall patterning.

hose—Worn with short tunic. Some with horizontal bands of geometric patterns.

cloaks—*Paludamentum:* fastening over the right shoulder with a jeweled brooch; this cloak distinguished by a large square decoration (*the tablion*) in contrasting color and fabric located at open edge over breast. (See Figure 5.6.) For upper class men and, among women, only the Empress. For common people and women, a simple, square cloak replaced the hooded paenula of Roman times for general wear. After the 7th and 8th centuries a semi-circular cloak pinned at the shoulder or at center front came into general use.

pallium or lorum—A long, narrow, heavily jeweled scarf possibly evolved from the toga with the folded bands, became part of official insignia of the Emperor. Initially draped up center front, around shoulders, across the front of the body and carried over one arm, it eventually became a simpler panel of fabric with an opening for the head, sometimes with a round collar-like construction at the head opening. (See Figure 5.3.)

AFTER THE 11TH CENTURY

Item / Description

tunic—More closely fitted to the body. Under tunics had fitted sleeves, outer tunics had wide sleeves and were shorter than undertunics. When belted, some of fabric of tunic was bloused out, over the belt. Fabrics had overall patterns and bands of jeweled decoration placed at hem and on sleeves, with a wide, decorative yoke at the neck. (See Figure 5.4.)

cloaks—Semi-circular cloak fastened at center front replaced paludamentum for out-of-doors.

5.3 Enameled picture of Archangel Michael, in the Byzantine style, c. 10th–12th centuries or later. The Archangel wears a jeweled *lorum* or *pallium* over an ankle-length tunic. (*Photograph courtesy of the Metropolitan Museum of Art, gift of the estate of Mrs. Otto H. Kahn, 1952.*)

5.4 Byzantine man's costume end of the 11th century and after. (*19th century redrawing by Jacquemin. New York City Public Library Picture Collection.*)

BYZANTINE COSTUME FOR WOMEN

Item / Description

tunics—Earliest styles continue use of stola and palla of Romans. Gradually, dalmatic decorated with clavi and segmentae replaced stola and was worn over an under tunic with closely fitted sleeves, while the palla was replaced initially by a simple veil worn over the head, then returned to use in a modified form that wrapped around the body and covered the upper part of the skirt, the bodice, and either one or both shoulders. (See Figure 5.5.) By the 7th century: although an occasional outer garment with long fitted sleeves is depicted in art, for the most part women wear double-layered tunics, the under tunic with long fitted sleeves and the outer tunic with full, open sleeves cut short enough to display the sleeve of the under tunic. (See Figure 5.6.)

fabrics—Elaborately patterned, often jeweled. Jeweled belts and collars also worn by the nobility and wealthy.

cloaks—Square or semi-circular cloaks fastened either at one shoulder or at the center. Empresses were the only women permitted to wear the paludamentum and items of Imperial insignia such as the lorum or pallium. (See Figure 5.6.)

LATE EMPIRE STYLES

style changes—Increased ornamentation. Variations in sleeve styles, including wide, hanging sleeves or sleeves with long bands of fabric forming a sort of pendant cuff. Occasional depictions of what appears to be a skirt and long, knee-length over-blouse, though this may be just an especially short outer tunic.

5.5 Women (mosaic from the church of St. Apollinarius in Ravenna) who each wear a white under tunic and patterned outer tunic or *stola* of the 6th century. A white *palla* is draped across the shoulders. (*Photograph courtesy of Edizione Alinari.*)

5.6 The Empress Theodora and her retinue, 6th century. Each man to the left of the Empress wears a *paludamentum*. Her women attendants wear mantles over richly-patterned tunics over which are placed wide, jeweled collars. All of the women completely cover their hair with turban-like hats. (*Mosaic from the Basilica of St. Vitale, Ravenna, Italy. Photograph courtesy of Edizione Alinari.*)

Item / Description

hair and head dress—4th to 10th centuries men tend to be clean-shaven. (See Figure 5.6.) Later, men more likely to have beards. Emperors wear jeweled crowns, often with strings of pearls suspended. Other head coverings include a Phrygian bonnet-like style (a high-crowned, soft hat in which the crown falls forward) shown in a mosaic depicting the Magi, and several versions of a high hat with an upstanding brim surrounding either a high-crowned turban, a smooth, close-fitting crown or a soft crown with a tassel at the back.

Women: Some early representations of women with hair parted in the center, soft waves framing the face, and the bulk of the hair pulled to the back or knotted on top of the head. Otherwise, women's hair is usually covered. Characteristic hair coverings included veils, turban-like hats which appear from the 4th century to the 12th century. This latter style has been described as looking like a cap surrounded by a small tire. (See Figure 5.7.) It evolved from having a fairly large crown with a smaller roll surrounding it to a smaller crown with a much larger roll. The hat itself might be trimmed with jewels. Empresses set their crowns on top of the hat. Crowns were heavily jeweled diadems with pendant strings of pearls. (See Figure 5.6.) Very late representations of Empresses may show them wearing a crown over their own hair which is dressed close to the face.

footwear—shoes with decorations cut out of the material and quite open in construction, made of cloth (including silk) or leather. Some tied, others buckled at the ankle. Many ornamented with stones, pearls, enameled metal, embroidery, appliqué, and cutwork. Red apparently a favored color for Empresses. Hose were worn under shoes.

Boots generally ended just below the calf, although a few are depicted as high at the front and lower behind the knee. Some decorated styles for the wealthy. Military figures from early Byzantine Empire wear Roman-like, open-toed boots; later a closed boot was worn. Boots seem to be worn by men, not women.

jewelry—Not only accessories, but also an integral part of costume; especially wide, jeweled collars worn by Empresses over the paludamentum or at the neck of the dress. Also worn: pins, earrings,

5.7 Byzantine sculpture, 2nd half of the 5th century. Marble bust of a lady of rank who wears a large, turban-like haircovering. (*Photograph courtesy of the Metropolitan Museum of Art, the Cloisters Collection, purchase, 1966.*)

bracelets, rings, and other types of necklaces made by jewelers skilled in techniques of working gold, setting precious stones, enameling, and making mosaics.

Western Europe From the Fall of the Roman Empire to 900 A.D.: Historical Background

Even though Constantinople was nominally the capital of the Eastern and Western sections of the Roman Empire when Constantine moved the capital there in 300 A.D., events soon caused each part of the empire to develop along separate lines. For centuries the Germans had been filtering into the Roman Empire in search of land. Many enlisted in the Roman armies, rising to high rank, often commanding Roman armies. Eventually entire German tribes migrated into western Europe and North Africa. The tribes were on the move because those in the north had been attracted by the Roman standard of living and those from east of the Danube sought new homelands. The tribes from the east were on the move because they had been dispossessed by the Huns, fierce, nomadic warriors who had pushed westward from their Asiatic homeland, driving Germanic tribes into the Roman Empire. One group, the Visigoths, were admitted into the empire in 376, but after being mistreated by corrupt Roman officials, they rebelled, and in 378 defeated a Roman army and killed the emperor in the battle of Arianople. The defeat shattered the prestige of the hitherto invincible Roman armies. After wandering through the eastern Roman empire, the Visigoths invaded Italy and sacked Rome in 410, an event that shocked the entire empire. Elsewhere other tribes entered the Empire and finally settled down to live alongside the Romans. They intermarried with the Romans, adopting many of their customs, converted to Christianity, and established German kingdoms in the lands once ruled by Augustus. The fusion of Roman and Germanic cultures would make up medieval civilization. After the establishment of Germanic kingdoms in the west and the end of any semblance of a Roman Empire, the eastern and western sections drifted farther apart, divided by religion, culture, and political systems.

During the reign of the Emperor Justinian (527–565) Byzantium gained control over Italy and southern Spain at enormous expense, all part of Justinian's dream of restoring the Roman Empire to its former greatness. His dream was doomed to failure, but he left behind an important legacy: the codification of the Roman law which became the basis of civil law in European countries. After Justinian's death, the Byzantine Empire suffered a series of losses as a result of attacks by barbarians and the Moslems reducing the empire to a small territory in Europe and in Asia, centering on Constantinople.

In the west the early Germanic kingdoms were soon destroyed, but one of these survived, the Franks. Their kingdom was founded by the brutal Clovis (481–511) who conquered most of modern France and Belgium, and founded the Merovingian dynasty. Eventually the Merovingian line degenerated into "do-nothing" kings who allowed the chief minister, titled "mayor of the palace" actual rule. In 751 a mayor of the palace, Pepin the Short, de-posed the Merovingian king with the blessing of the pope and himself became king.

King Pepin was succeeded by his son, Charles the Great, known to history as Charlemagne (768–814), who expanded the kingdom into central Europe and southward into central Italy. He became the dominant figure in western Europe; his contemporaries compared him to the ancient Roman emperors. His greatest achievement was encouraging the establishment of schools to teach reading and writing. He founded a palace school to which he invited scholars from all over Europe. The climax of his reign came with his coronation on Christmas Day 800 when the pope crowned him emperor of the Romans. For a time Charlemagne hoped to arrange a marriage between himself and a Byzantine empress and to unite the Eastern and Western Empires, but he failed. Nevertheless, throughout this period, contacts between the Eastern and Western Empire continued, with Byzantine styles exercising a strong influence on European dress.

Charlemagne's success in uniting the Western European empire lasted for only a little while after his death in 814. His successors were not strong enough to hold Charlemagne's empire together and the empire was once again divided.

Costume in the Western World

During the Roman era the people residing in the provinces had become Romanized in their dress, and tunics for men and stolla and palla for women had become primary garments. Costumes that developed after the fall of Rome were based on these costumes in combination with those of the barbarian tribes that moved west and who brought with them their own clothing practices. They, too, utilized a tunic cut to the knee, and with it a type of trousers. Coming as they did from colder climates, they used more fur, often as a sleeveless vest worn over the tunic. Gartered hose, which became part of western, medieval dress, were derived from barbarian costume.

THE MEROVINGIAN PERIOD

Clovis, the first of the Merovingian kings of Northern France, was crowned in 493. He married a Christian, converted to Christianity, and adopted Byzantine style dress for his court as a symbol of his change from the status of tribal chief to Christian king. He wore a short tunic, decorated with bands of embroidery or woven design, but without the lavish jeweled decoration of the Byzantine emperors, together with hose tied close to the leg with garters. The paludamentum and a crown completed his regalia. He retained one earlier Frankish practice. The king wore his hair long as a symbol of his rank, while the rest of the men in his court and other subjects cut their hair short.

COSTUME ITEMS

Item / Description

men's costume—*tunic*—similar to that described for the king, but less elaborate. (See Figure 5.8.)
gartered hose.
cloak—similar to chlamys, fastening over one shoulder or a hooded cape, possible descendant of the paenula.
boots or shoes.

women's costume—*tunic*—(presumably; evidence is sparse)—loose-fitting
shawl—or palla-like drapery placed over tunic.

NOTE: Archeological excavations of a tomb in Paris have brought to light a burial of a Merovingian queen of the 6th century. Enough clothing remained to permit determination of the various layers of her costume and their general form. These were:
· Closest to the body—a linen shift or chemise.
· Over this, a knee-length under tunic of violet silk, belted with a richly-jeweled belt.
· Cross-gartered linen stockings.
· A long, outer tunic of dark red silk, opening at the front and closed with richly-jeweled pins.
· Red silk veil on her head.
· Thin leather slippers on her feet.
· Jewelry, including earrings, brooches, silver belt ends and buckles, a long gold pin, and a signet ring identifying her as Arnegunde, a queen known to have lived about 550 A.D.[2]

fabrics—From the foregoing description it is clear royal families were importing silk from Byzantium. Common people would have worn linen, which grew well in damp Northern climates, and wool from local sheep herds. Cotton was not yet imported into Europe.

jewelry—Techniques and styles influenced by Byzantine jewelry. Mountings of large stones and fine enamel were common.

2. D. T. Rice, Editor. *The Dawn of European Civilization.* New York: McGraw-Hill Company, Inc., 1965.

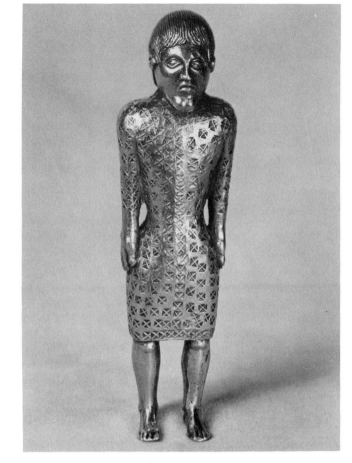

5.8 Statuette of a man from the region of Gaul that dates from the late 4th or early 5th century. He wears a knee-length tunic that has an overall pattern of decoration and what appears to be a braid decoration at the neck, the hem, and down the center front. (*Photograph courtesy of the Dumbarton Oaks Collection, Washington, D.C.*)

CAROLINGIAN PERIOD (C. 750–900)

Little difference from costume of the Merovingian period, as elements of Byzantine influence continue to be apparent in dress of the powerful and wealthy.

COSTUME ITEMS

Item / Description

men's costume—*tunics*—short except for ceremonial occasions. Decorations included clavii, ornamental bands around neckline, and sleeve edges. Shape seems to have narrowed through the body and widened in the skirt.

belts—worn over tunics.

hair—no longer worn long by king, all men cut hair below the ear and adult men wore beards.

boots—ending below the calf or shoes.

women's costume—Also strong Byzantine influences.

undertunic—with fitted sleeves.

outertunic—often with wider sleeves; bands of ornamentation. Garments cut full.

palla-like shawl—sometimes draped over tunics.

veil—or shawl placed over the head, hair generally covered.

CLERICAL COSTUME

Much of the clerical costume that was to become traditional for the Roman Catholic priests, monks, and nuns originated during the early Middle Ages. Both the priesthood, with its ceremonial costume, and the monks and nuns who separated themselves from the world, evolved a distinctive garb which changed relatively little over later centuries until the mid-20th century.

Ecclesiastical costume worn by priests and higher church officials developed gradually from the 4th century to the 9th century. Before the 4th century priests wore no special costume. Throughout the Medieval Period the parish priest who lived in the community was more clearly distinguished by his tonsure (hair cut) than by his every day costume. Either of two distinctive hair cuts were adopted. In one the top of the head was shaved and a fringe of hair grew around the shaved area. In the other, the forehead was shaved from ear to ear.

Higher-ranking prelates wore more distinctive costume on ceremonial occasions or during church services. By the 9th century a number of items had been established as part of the liturgical costume of the Roman Catholic church. Briefly summarized these were:

Item / Description

amice—strip of linen placed around the shoulders and tied in position to form a collar. Worn by priests saying mass.

alb—long white tunic with narrow sleeves and a slit for the head, tied with a belt. Name derived from Roman *tunica alba* (white tunic.)

chausuble—an evolved form of the paenulla, the round Roman cape which after being given up

by the laity continued to be worn by clergy in a form with sides cut shorter to allow movement of the arms.

stole—Long, narrow strip of material worn over the shoulder during the mass.

pallium—a narrow band of white wool worn by popes and archbishops.

NOTE: This band evolved from the Greek himation, losing its shawl-like form and becoming a narrow band that in Roman and then Byzantine styles was a symbol of learning. Prelates wore the band with one end falling to the front and the other to the back.

cope—a voluminous cape, worn for processions.

Other refinements of costume specific to particular clerical rank or ceremonies such as colors or garments assigned to certain days within the liturgical year were made at different periods of the history of the Catholic church. For those interested in a more detailed exploration of clerical costume some references are included at the end of this chapter.

MONASTIC DRESS

The practice of leaving the world to devote oneself to prayer and self-denial began early in the history of the Christian church. After the 4th century entire communities were formed, often around the person of a particularly holy man or woman. These monasteries or convents did not require specialized costume, but rather dressed in the ordinary costume of the poor. In time, however, although the costume of most people changed, the monks and nuns retained their original dress thereby distinguishing them from the "worldly." Both men and women wore a loose-fitting tunic with long, fairly wide sleeves that reached to the ground and was belted. Specific colors and cut showed some variations from order to order, but the usual colors employed were brown, white, black, or grey.

Monk's costume included a cowl, a hood which was either attached to the tunic or a separate garment. Nuns covered their heads with veils. On first entering convents, women cropped their hair closely. Members of some orders went barefoot; most wore sandals. Over time the distinctions among the various orders became quite pronounced and the order with which the individual was associated was evident to even the most casual observer.

Summary

During the early Middle Ages styles might be characterized as Roman forms in combination with local forms. In Byzantium the non-Roman elements came from the Middle East whereas in Europe the non-Roman elements came from Barbarian dress. In both cases, however, the chief components of dress were layered tunics combined with a mantle of some sort.

Byzantine styles influenced European styles among the upper classes. Byzantine silks were purchased and Byzantine styles were adopted by rulers in Europe. These men aped the Byzantine styles in order to bring to their courts a reflection of the wealth and status associated with the court at Constantinople which had become the most cultured center of the period.

Except for the introduction of sericulture into the West by way of the Byzantine Empire neither technology for the production of cloth nor basic styles took any great leaps forward in Europe during the period before 900. The major changes of the Middle Ages in Western Europe were yet to come.

Selected Readings

BOOKS CONTAINING ILLUSTRATIONS OF COSTUME OF THE PERIOD FROM ORIGINAL SOURCES

Backhouse, J. et al (Editors). *The Golden Age of Anglo-Saxon Art. 966 to 1066.* Bloomington, IN: Indiana University Press, 1985.

Beckwith, J. *Early Christian and Byzantine Art.* New York: Viking, 1980.

Bon, A. *Byzantium.* Geneva: Nagel Publishers, 1972.

Grabar, A. *The Golden Age of Justinian.* New York: Odessey Press, 1967.

Hollander, H. *Early Medieval Art.* New York: Universe Books, 1974.

Kessler, H. L. and M. S. Simpson (Editors). *Pictoral Narrative in Antiquity and the Middle Ages.* Washington, D.C.: National Gallery of Art, 1985.

Mutherich, F. and J. E. Graehde. *Carolingian Painting.* New York: Braziller, 1977.

Sherrard, P. *Byzantium.* New York: Time Inc., 1966.

PERIODICAL ARTICLES

Cameron, A. "A Byzantine Imperial Coronation of the Sixth Century." *Costume*, 1973, p. 4.

Herchelheim, F. M. "Byzantine Silk Fabrics." *CIBA Review*, No. 75, p. 8761.

Sencer, Y. J. "Threads of History" (Woolen textiles in ancient Ireland). *The F.I.T. Review*, Vol. 2, No. 1, Oct. 1985, p. 5.

"Symbolism of Imperial Costume as Displayed on Byzantine Coins." *Numismatic Society Museum Notes.* 1954, p. 24.

DAILY LIFE

Hussey, J. *The Byzantine World.* London Hutchinson, 1961.

Quennel, M. C. and C. H. B. Quennel. *Everyday Life in Roman and Anglo-Saxon Times.* London: Batsford, 1959.

Rice, D. T. (Editor). *The Dawn of European Civilization.* New York: McGraw-Hill Company, Inc., 1965.

Riché, P. *Daily Life in the World of Charlemagne.* Philadelphia: University of Pennsylvania Press, 1984.

Todd, M. *Everyday Life of the Barbarians, Goths, Franks and Vandals.* New York: G. P. Putnam's Sons, 1972.

ECCLESIASTICAL DRESS

Butler, J. T. "Ecclesiastical Vestments of the Middle Ages." *Connoisseur*, Vol. 177 (714), August 1971, p. 297.

Davenport, M. "The Roman Catholic Church" in *The Book of Costume.* Vol. 1, New York: Crown Publishers, 1972, p. 93.

Mayo, J. *A History of Ecclesiastical Dress.* New York: Holmes and Meier, 1984.

CHAPTER 6

The High Middle Ages

c. 900–1300

Historical Background

Charlemagne's successors were not only incapable but unable to maintain the unity of his empire which was too large for effective government in view of the inadequate communications system. No single power emerged to replace the ineffective Carolingian kings. The last was deposed in 888. The remnants of Carolingian rule gradually collapsed under the impact of new and more destructive invasions. From the east, hordes of Magyar horsemen devastated the eastern lands of the Carolingian Empire. From the south came the Saracens, Arab raiders, who plundered southern France and coastal Italy. The most destructive of the invaders, the Northmen or Vikings, came from Scandinavia, attracted by the wealth of the Christian churches and the monasteries, they looted and burned, killing their victims ruthlessly. Britain and France suffered the worst spoilation, but about the middle of the 9th century the annual expeditions in search of plunder gradually ended.

Many areas in the west were depopulated and ruined. However, a new Europe began to appear. Commerce and town life began to revive; improvements in agriculture helped produce an increase in population. The Carolingian Empire was followed by feudal monarchies, the nations of the future.

Society was feudal, a system which developed out of the need for protection as the Carolingian Empire collapsed under the attacks of the Vikings, Magyars, and the Saracens. Central government vanished; law and order disappeared. Security could be found only in military might. Leaders gathered around them trained fighting men, much as chiefs in the Germanic tribes assembled their warriors in war-bands. Then a new invention, the stirrup, revolutionized warfare by combining human and animal power to produce mounted warriors with sword and lance capable of shock combat. The warriors became the armored knights on horseback. But knights, who were professional warriors, needed years of training to learn how to handle the horse and the weapons. Training began in youth, and it was not cheap. The knight needed not just one horse, but a number especially trained and bred for warfare. There must be someone to look after the horses for the knights. So knights become elite, professional fighters.

Knights were also vassals of a lord, sworn military retainers just like the warriors in the German warband who swore to be faithful to their chief. The word "vassal" came from a Celtic word meaning "one who serves." To maintain his vassals, a lord granted each of them land, a fief (*feudum*), in exchange for military services. The knight lived on his fief when he was not off fighting on behalf of his lord. Along with the fief came serfs, who worked the land for the lords and knights. Serfs had lost their freedom years before when an ancestor surrendered his freedom and that of his family to a lord in return for protection.

In theory, the feudal king was the supreme lord and theoretical owner of all the land within his kingdom. His great vassals owed him allegiance but, if a powerful independent vassal challenged him, the monarch could only call on his vassals to assemble their knights to help discipline the unruly noble. If they chose to be disloyal, he had no national army that could be mobilized. On the local level, whatever law and order existed, it was enforced by the lord and his vassals who were undoubtedly illiterate.

The feudal lords not only fought invaders but they went to war with other feudal nobles. Fighting, however, was not so dangerous as in modern warfare. The armored knight more often then not was liable to be captured and held for ransom. The serfs and peasants suffered more because their lives, homes, and crops could be destroyed in a battle.

Feudal lords and knights built castles on their lands to serve as places of protection. At first these castles were rude structures of wood intended only for defense, but by the 12th century they had become very elaborate. Not only were castles defensive structures, but they were also homes for the lord and his family. They were uncomfortable, cold, damp, dark, and very windy because the windows in the outer walls were slits without glass.

Feudalism took various forms in different parts of Europe because it developed from local practices and customs. Originating in northern France, it spread from there into southern France, Germany, and into northern Italy. England did not develop feudal organization until after Duke William of Normandy invaded England in 1066 and became king of England.

Political developments in Europe over the period from 900–1300 were far too complex to describe in detail in this survey. The reader may be best served by a brief note of some of the more important developments in the difference areas of Europe.

In Germany, after the German line of the Carolingian emperors had died out, a new dynasty emerged from the duchy of Saxony. Otto I (936–973) halted the Magyar threat to Europe, forcing them to settle in Hungary. He spent years battling rebellious dukes, while making alliances with archbishops and bishops whom he chose and to whom he granted large estates making them his vassals. After invading Italy, he proclaimed himself king and had the pope crown him Holy Roman Emperor in 962. Although the empire was thoroughly German, it was considered to be a continuation of the ancient Roman Empire. Otto's heirs encountered opposition from later popes who sought independence from the emperors. After Otto's line ended in 1125, the Hohenstaufen emperors ruled until the last one was executed in 1268. The task of trying to rule Germany, Italy and Sicily while at the same time fighting off rebellious dukes and hostile popes had proved too much for the Hohenstaufen dynasty. When the nobles elected the first Hapsburg emperor in 1273, Germany had become a collection of semi-independent principalities instead of a united empire.

After the Roman legions had been withdrawn, from northwestern Germany, Angles, Saxons, and Jutes invaded Britain in the 5th century, driving the original Britons, the Celts, westward into Wales, Devon, Cornwall and north into Scotland. The Anglo-Saxons settled down, intermarried, converted to Christianity and established seven Anglo-Saxon kingdoms. In the 9th century, the Anglo-Saxons suffered an invasion by the Danes (Vikings), who came to plunder and settle. The Anglo-Saxon king, Alfred the Great (871–899) halted the Danes; his dynasty united Britain under one king. When the Alfred's line died out in 1066, William the Conqueror, Duke of Normandy, claiming the throne, invaded England and defeated the Anglo-Saxon claimant to the throne in the battle of Hastings. William I established feudalism in England, but it was better organized and more centralized than on the Continent of Europe. Under Henry II (1154–1189) one of the greatest of English kings, whose mother was a granddaughter of William I and whose father was of the Plantagenet family, England laid claim to large areas of France. These claims were based on the fact that William the Conqueror had ruled Normandy and Henry II had married Eleanor of Acquitaine, an heiress who controlled a large area of southwestern France. For many years thereafter France and England battled over these claims; the struggle climaxed in the Hundred Years War (1337–1453) which ended with the English driven from France except for a foothold in Calais. The Plantagenet family ruled over England until 1399. It was followed by the Houses of Lancaster and York.

In France, after the death of Charlemagne, the title of king carried with it little actual wealth or power. The kings were often less powerful than their feudal vassals. The election of Hugh Capet (987–969) as king marked the beginning of the famous Capetian dynasty which ruled France for more than 300 years. But not until the 1100's would the French kings begin to increase the power and wealth of the monarchy and to weaken their mighty vassals. By the time that the Capetian line died out in 1328, the French king had become a genuine force in European power politics by consolidating his holdings, subjugating the powerful dukes, and replacing provincialism with unifying national patriotism. (See Figure 6.1.)

Factors Related to Developments in Costume

Political, social, and economic events may have both direct and indirect influence on clothing styles. The availability of the raw materials from which costumes are made, the social stage on which they are worn, and even the practical needs which they must satisfy will each play a part in their development.

THE CRUSADES

In the 11th century under the urging of Pope Urban II, the European powers launched the first of seven

6.1 Major political divisions of Europe in the mid-14th century.

crusades against the Moslems. Ostensibly intended to free the holy places of Christendom from the Moslems who now controlled them, the actual motivations for each of the crusades varied from genuine religious fervor to outright mercenary designs for accumulating wealth and power.

By the end of the crusades in the 13th century, many new products had been imported to Europe. New foods, spices, drugs, works of art and, especially relevant to developments in costume, fabrics were brought back by the crusaders. New fabrics such as muslin, dimity, and silk damask came into use as did a new fiber, cotton. Many crusaders stopped in Constantinople on their way to and from the wars, resulting in a continuation of the strong Byzantine influences on the costume of the nobility of Western Europe.

MEDIEVAL CASTLES AND COURTS

The feudal lord and his family had private quarters in large, fortified dwellings called castles. Rooms were poorly ventilated. In winter only a large fireplace provided heat. Woolen garments were desirable not only in winter to combat the cold, but also in summer when castles continued to be damp and chilly. By modern standards furnishings were simple and not very comfortable, however more luxurious furnishings such as carpets, wall hangings, and cushions were brought back from the East as a result of the crusades. In spite of these improvements, multiple layers of clothing provided the most practical way of dressing for comfort.

The institution of knighthood and chivalry, the system for training the young knight required that he learn not only the arts of war, but also the manners and customs of the upper classes. Generally to do this he had to leave his home and reside in the castle of a powerful lord. These courts, especially those of the dukes and kings, attracted artists, poets, troubadours or wandering singers, musicians, and other entertainers. The courts of southern France were especially noted as centers of artistic, musical, and literary expression. Moreover, they provided a stage for the display of fashion.

TOWN LIFE

After the fall of Rome many formerly thriving urban centers had been severely depopulated. During the 10th and 11th centuries urban life revived. By the 12th and 13th centuries an economic upturn in agriculture, manufacturing of goods, and trade made many cities lively centers that attracted an increased population. Among those residing in towns were wealthy merchants whose affluence was such that they could dress themselves in clothing styled after that worn by the nobility. The clergy disapproved of this blurring of class distinctions, saying that "Jesus Christ and his blessed mother, of royal blood though they were, never thought of wearing the belts of silk, gold, and silver that are fashionable among wealthy women."[1]

FABRIC MANUFACTURE

By the 12th century European craftsmen had established a number of centers for the manufacture of cloth for export. Trade guilds had first been established in the 11th century when they were organizations of merchants designed to prevent the importation of competing goods. By the 12th century the craftsmen had begun to form their own guilds. Only by apprenticing himself to a guild could a young boy become a practitioner of a craft, so that guilds were able to regulate the number of artisans and to set quality standards, rates of pay, and regulate working conditions.

Textile trade guild members were permitted to hire their wives and daughters to spin and weave. The widow of a guild member could, herself, become owner of her late husband's business and a member of the guild, however pay scales for women were consistently lower than those for men.

Wool was an especially important fiber in the European textile trade. Wool grown in England was considered to be the finest. Much English wool was exported to Flanders where skilled weavers made it into high quality cloth. But cloth merchants were by no means limited to wool cloth. Linen was grown throughout Europe and used for household textiles and for clothing. Silk was, by the mid-1200's a major industry in Italy, Sicily, and Spain. Cotton, at first imported from India, was introduced into Spain by the Moors, and it, too, was available for spinning.

The merchant purchased the raw fiber. After cleaning, carding, and combing it, he sold it to the weaver. The weaver's wife spun the yarn with spindle and distaff (spinning wheels had not yet been introduced to Europe), and the weaver created the cloth on a hand loom. Some finishing steps were given to the fabric, and if color had not been added to either the fiber or the yarn, the fabric might be dyed. In some cases, the fabric was sold undyed to skilled dyers from Italy who added the color.

1. J. Gies and F. Gies. *Life in a Medieval Castle.* New York: Thomas Y. Crowell Company, 1974, p. 47.

Art of the Period as a Source of Evidence About Costume

As Europe experienced this economic awakening, it also underwent marked changes in the arts. Most of the art produced was intended not solely as decoration, but told the generally unlettered population the stories of the Christian faith. The artists dressed biblical or other religious figures in the costume of the artist's own time or, sometimes, in costumes based on imagination or on the reports of costume brought back by the returning crusaders. It is from these works of art that most of the visual evidence of 12th and 13th century costume comes.

Important art forms included manuscript illumination and the carving of miniatures in ivory and wood. Tenth and 11th century Romanesque architecture, characterized by rounded arches and massive, well-proportioned buildings utilized the work of sculptors as an important element of decoration. After the 1150's Romanesque architecture was superceded by the Gothic style, predominant until the end of the 1400's. Gothic churches with their pointed arches and soaring, graceful structures used not only sculpture but also beautiful stained glass windows to tell stories to the faithful.

10th and 11th Centuries

COSTUME FOR MEN

Item / Description

underclothing—undershirt (or chemise)—short-sleeved, linen garment; underdrawers (or *braies*)—loose-fitting, linen breeches, fastened at the waist with a belt (See Figure 6.7); knee-length or in longer, ankle-length variations which were wrapped close to the leg with gartering.

tunics—*undertunic*—same length or slightly longer than outer tunic.
    short outer tunics—almost always with close-fitting sleeves, sometimes cut so that they extended over the hand with the excess fabric pushed up into folds above the wrist. (See Figure 6.2.)
    long outer tunics—either fitted sleeves, or (more often) wide, full sleeves beneath which the sleeve of the under tunic showed.
    necklines—round or square.
    belting—usually belted at the waist.

NOTE: Social class distinctions are evident in length of tunic and its decoration. Outer tunics of wealthy were decorated with bands of silk embroidery at neck, sleeves, and hem. Long flowing robes were worn by nobility for ceremonial occasions and by clergy. For hunting and warfare all classes wore more practical short tunics, as did working class men.

    fabrics—linen and wool most widely used. The poor wore wool almost exclusively. Silk imported by very well-to-do.

cloaks or mantles—*open mantles*—made from one piece of fabric which fastened on one shoulder. (See Figure 6.2.)
    closed mantles—made with a slit through which the head could be slipped. (See Figure 6.3.)
    10th century mantles—usually square.
    11th century mantles—begin to see semicircular mantles. Mantles draped much like Greek himation worn by persons of importance at ceremonial events.

footwear and leg coverings—When braies extending to the ankle were not worn, men wore either:
    • *hose*—made of woven fabric, cut and sewn to fit the leg, ending either at knee or thigh, (See Figure 6.2) or

6.2 Page from a manuscript c. 1050 B.C. Men at left wear short tunics with gaitered hose, over which they wear cloaks. The long sleeves of their tunics are pushed up into folds above the wrist. Their hats are in the Phrygian bonnet style. Women on the page wear long tunics and cover their hair with veils. (*Photograph courtesy of the Morgan Library.*)

- *leg bandages*—strips of linen or wool wrapped closely around the leg to the knee and worn either over the hose or alone.

  socks—brightly colored, some with decorative figures around the upper edges might be placed over the end of the braies, over hose, or worn with leg bandages.

  boots—frequently decorated. Either short to the ankle or longer, reaching to mid-calf.

  flat shoes—(raised heels were not used during the Middle Ages)—cut with a slight point at the front opposite the big toe. Closely fitted, shoes generally ended at the ankle, fastening when necessary with thongs of leather or fabric. (See Figure 6.2.)

  Byzantine-style slippers—cut low over the instep, were worn by some clergy.

hair and head dress—*hair*—parted in the middle, falling naturally either straight or in waves at the side of the face to the nape of the neck or below. Young men clean-shaven; older men bearded. (See Figure 6.2.)

  hair coverings—except for helmets worn in war predominating styles were hoods and Phrygian bonnet styles. Hats with small round brims and peaked crowns were often used in paintings to identify the wearer as being Jewish.

COSTUME FOR WOMEN

Costume of men and women showed relatively few differences during the 10th and 11th centuries.

Item / Description

undergarments—consisted of a loose-fitting, linen garment (in French, a *chemise*) cut much as the man's under shirt, though somewhat longer.

tunics—*under tunic*—often with close-fitting sleeves and an embroidered border at neck, hem, and sleeves. Floor length.

  outer tunic—also floor length. When made with wide sleeves, the sleeves of the under tunic were visible. Usually the outer tunic was pulled up and bloused over a belt to display the decorative border of the under tunic. (See Figure 6.3.)

cloaks or mantles—Both open and closed styles. *Double mantles*—lined in contrasting colors. Winter mantles could be fur-lined. (See Figure 6.6.)

footwear and leg coverings—*hose*—(stockings) tied into place around the knee.

  shoes—similar to those of men and also open slippers with bands across the ankle like those worn by some clergymen.

  wooden clogs—placed on top of leather shoes to raise them out of the water, mud, or snow.

hair and head dress—For young girls—loose, flowing and uncovered. *Married (and older) women*—hair covered by a veil, which was pulled around the face, under the chin; or open, hanging close to the sides of the face and ending about mid-chest. (See Figure 6.3.) The rich had silk or fine linen veils; the lower class used coarser linen or wool.

jewelry—rarely depicted on paintings and sculpture of the period, however written records indicate that wealthy women wore head bands (circlets) of gold; neckbands or beads; bracelets; rings; earrings. Jeweled belts (often called *girdles*) are sometimes depicted in art.

12th Century

COSTUMES FOR MEN

Both the under tunic and outer tunic continue as the basic elements of dress for men, although on some representations no evidence can be seen of an undertunic and probably in some instances only a single tunic was worn.

Item / Description

tunics—An alteration in cut produced a closer fit of the tunic. Heretofore tunics were cut in one piece from shoulder to hem. For the changed style a separate section cut to fit the upper part of the body and lacing shut at the sides was joined to a fuller skirt. The joining of skirt and bodice came below the anatomical waistline, over the hips. (See Figures 6.4, 6.5 and 6.6.)

  Sleeve constructions grew more varied, including:
  - close-fitting sleeve with a decorative, turned back cuff.
  - elbow-length, full sleeve on the outer tunic revealing a fitted sleeve on the tunic underneath.
  - a sleeve cut fairly close at the shoulder and widening to a full bell at the end.

6.3 (*Above left*) 12th century manuscript illustration depicts woman in closed mantle with a light-colored veil over her head. The outer tunic has been raised up to display the under tunic which is of a contrasting lighter color. The garb of the angel is similar, except that he wears an open mantle. (*Photograph courtesy of the Morgan Library.*)

6.4 (*Above center*) First half of the 12th century. Fashionable tunics, both short and long, are more closely fitted through the torso in the 12th century, whereas the monk's costume retains the fit and characteristics of an earlier period. With their short tunics, the servants wear hose, over which they place short striped stockings, and shoes that end at the ankle. (*Photograph courtesy of the Morgan Library.*)

6.5 (*Above right*) French sculpture, 12th century. This *bliaut* worn by a figure representing a king, is fitted through the waist to the hip where a finely pleated skirt joins the top. The sleeves are slightly pendant. Both sleeves and neckline are edged in decorative fabric. (*Photograph courtesy of the Metropolitan Museum of Art, purchase, 1920, Joseph Pulitzer Bequest.*)

6.6 (*Left*) Manuscript illustration for a Bible from before 1185 depicts a variety of costume, including woman (at left) with wide, pendant cuffs on the outer tunic. The sleeves of the undertunic are visible at the wrist. One woman wears a closed, one an open, mantle. The mantle of the man in the center panel is lined with fur. (*Photograph courtesy of the Morgan Library.*)

The High Middle Ages **77**

COSTUMES FOR WOMEN

While costume for lower class women changed very little, upper class women's costume underwent changes in fit that correspond to those described for men's costume. The chemise, the under tunic, and the outer tunic all fitted the body more closely. To achieve the closer fit, garments laced shut at the sides. Some sculpted representations of styles of this period show fabric that looks as if it may have been smocked or crinkled.

Item / Description

women's outer garments—Sleeves of women's dresses were even longer and more exaggerated in their cut than those of men. Some illustrations show closely-fitting sleeves ending in a long, pendant cuff or band that hangs all the way to the floor. If both under and outer tunics were worn, the sleeves of the under tunic were usually long and fitted while the outer tunic had either pendant cuffs, wide cuffs with decorative banding, or sleeves narrow at the top and flaring gradually to end in a bell shape. (See Figure 6.6.)

NOTE: This elaborate, closely-fitted garment was limited in its use to upper class men and women, and French writers of the period call it a *bliaut*. (See Figure 6.5.) Made of costly fabrics such as silk, satin or velvet and embroidered with gold thread and decorated with precious stones, the cut of the bliaut shows the progress in clothing construction that had taken place during the 12th century. Not only were the bodice and skirt sewn together, but an inset bias (diagonal) fabric piece seems to have been used to assure better fit at the hips. Seams were concealed by applied pieces of decorative tape. There is no evidence, however, that sleeves were set in.

Yet another distinctive feature of the bliaut demonstrating radical changes in attitudes toward modesty was the method of its closing. Both the bliaut and the chemise laced shut. These lacings sometimes fell one above the other, revealing the bare flesh beneath.

The *chainse* was another distinctive type of garment for upper class women. Made of washable material, probably linen, it was long and seems to have been pleated. (See Figure 6.7.)

NOTE: Many costume historians have confused the terms *chainse and chemise*, however Goddard in a study of costume terminology for women's styles of the 11th and 12th centuries found that contemporary texts state clearly that the chainse

6.7 Garment (possibly a *chainse*) of crinkled fabric (German manuscript, c. 1200) shows a row of lacing up the side, under the arm. (*Photograph courtesy of the Morgan Library.*)

was worn over the chemise and that it was definitely a separate garment.[2] The chainse seems to have been worn alone, without an outer tunic as a "house dress" and seems to have been especially used in the late 12th century. It is possible that it may have been a summer garment, since it was washable and made of lightweight fabric.

cloaks or mantles—Worn out-of-doors. The old French word *mantel* (from which the English word "mantle" derives) was originally applied to cloaks worn by upper class women; long, cape-like garments that opened down the front and fastened with a long ribbon attached to clasps placed on either side of the front.

NOTE: some of these *mantels* were exceedingly luxurious. One is described as being made of rose

2. E. R. Goddard, *Women's Costume in French Texts of the 11th and 12th Centuries.* Baltimore: Johns Hopkins, 1927, p. 87.

and white cloth from India, woven or embroidered with figures of animals and flowers; cut in one piece, and lined with scented fur. It had a collar and a border spotted with dark blue and yellow and fastened with jeweled clasps on the shoulder that were made from two rubies.[3]

Some cloaks were fur lined or decorated with fur. *Pelicon* or *pelice* are terms applied to any of a number of fur-trimmed garments including outer wraps, under tunics and outer tunics.

hair and head dress—Women of the highest classes adopted a style in which hair was arranged in two long plaits which hung down on either side of the face. Decorative bands of ribbon might be intertwined in the braids or the end of the braid held in a jeweled clasp. Over this a loose veil was placed, however the hair was quite visible.

veils—covering the hair entirely and wrapped so closely that only the face showed, were still worn by most women. New head dress developments included:

· *barbette*—a linen band passed from one temple, down, under the chin and up to the other temple. Worn with:

· a *fillet*—a standing linen band, rather like a crown. (See Figure 6.11.) (Over these a veil might be draped.)

· *wimple*—a fine white linen or silk scarf that covered the neck, the center placed under the chin and each end pulled up and fastened above the ear or at the temple. Generally worn in combination with a veil. (See Figure 6.8.)

NOTE: Wimples were worn until the 1960's by many orders of Catholic nuns.

6.8 Manuscript of about 1240–1260. Lower left panel shows three men harvesting wheat. The man on the right wears only his *braies* and a small, white *coif* on his head. His fellow workers wear short tunics or *cotes*, the man on the left has tucked his into his belt, thereby revealing his *braies* and the tops of his hose, which fasten to the top of his *braies*. Women in the upper panel wear (from left to right) a *cote*; a *cote* with a sideless *surcote* (which is lifted up to reveal her patterned stockings); *cotes* and mantles. The woman at the far right is wearing a fur-lined mantle. (*Photograph courtesy of the Morgan Library.*)

3. Poet of the *Roman de Troie* quoted in Goddard, *op. cit.*, p. 164.

13th Century

PROBLEMS OF COSTUME TERMINOLOGY

The history of costume of the later Middle Ages is marked by increasing variety in types of dress. This tendency which began to accelerate in the 13th century presents the costume historian with difficulties in terminology. The written records of the period abound in descriptions of items of luxurious dress, but these descriptions are not accompanied by illustrations of the garments or accessories that they describe. The application of these terms to costume leaves the reader with a maze of terms in several languages that cannot be attached to particular garments with complete accuracy. For this reason textbooks, costume histories, and journal articles dealing with costume may be in conflict as to the names applied to particular items or the definition of terms. Furthermore, modern English words frequently derive from the early names for costume items, but the modern usage of the term is often markedly different from its original use.

The following table is presented in an effort to clarify the meaning of some of the terms which the student may encounter and also to point out some of the modern English words that derive from the old English and French words. The table is restricted to English and French as these are the languages most often utilized in writing about historic costume in English.

Table 6–1: Old English and French Costume Terms

Type of garment	Definition	Old French term	Old English term	Modern English term derived from:
Underwear:	undergarment for men, worn next to the skin and covering the lower part of the torso and upper legs. (See Figure 6.8.)	braies	brech	breeches
	undergarment for both men and women worn next to the body and cut as loose, linen garment with sleeves. (See Figure 7.4.)	chemise	shirt	shirt chemise
Under tunic:	under tunic worn by both men and women and placed over chemise or shirt (See Figure 6.8.)	cotte	cote	coat* petticoat**
Outer tunic:	top most garment (excluding garments worn for out-of-doors to protect against weather). Worn either over or under tunic or when no under tunic is worn, worn over chemise or shirt. (See Figure 6.9.)	sorcot	surcote	overcoat**
		rogue	roc	frock
		sorquenie	sukkenie	smock
		bliaud	bliaut	blouse**
		cuertel	kirtel or kirtle	none currently in use
		cotte-hardie cotardie	cotehardie	none currently in use
		gonele*	goune or gowne or gonne*	gown
Outdoor garments:	cloak or cape designating high rank. (See Figure 6.9.)	mantel	mantel	mantle
	wide cape with hood	chape	cope	cape
	hood, cut and sewed to a *chape* (See Figure 7.3.)	chaperon	chaperon	chaperon***
	long cloak with cape-like sleeves	garnache or gamache or ganache	garnache	none currently in use
	cloak with long, wide sleeves having a slit below the shoulder through which the arm could be slipped, leaving the long, full sleeve hanging behind. (See Figure 6.11.)	herigaut	herigaut	none currently in use
		gardecorps	gardcors	none currently in use
Sets of garments:	a set of garments consisting generally of under tunic, outer tunic, and mantel, however, the same term is also used to refer to a single garment.	robe	robe	robe

* Seems to have first been applied to the dress of elderly priests and to that of nuns.
** Modern term differs markedly from term of origin but is a clothing term.
*** No longer a clothing term, but is applied to another item altogether.

Type of garment	Definition	Old French term	Old English term	Modern English term derived from:
Head coverings or parts of head coverings	hood	coul	couel	cowl**
	veil worn around the side of the face and under the chin. (See Figure 6.10.)	guimpe	wimpel or wimple	none currently in use
	circlet worn around head	chapel or chapelet	chapelet	chaplet
	small white cap that tied under the chin. (See Figures 6.8, 6.10.)	coif	coif	coif**
	long tube of fabric hanging down from the back of a hood (See Figure 7.3.)	cornette	liripipe	none
Leg coverings:	Garment that fits the foot and leg up to the knee or thigh (See Figure 6.2.)	chasusses	hose	hose
Other terms:	fur-trimmed garment	pelicon	pellison	pelisse (19th century)
	narrow band of cloth attached to hood, head dress, or sleeve. (See Figure 7.3.)	coudieres	tippet	none

** Modern term differs markedly from term of origin but is a clothing term.

COSTUME FOR MEN

Throughout the 13th century men would have dressed in garments of similar functions as those described previously, however the terminology used to describe this clothing underwent some changes. In summary, then, a man would wear knee-length or shorter braies (breeches) and a linen chemise (under shirt.) Over this he placed a *cote* (under tunic) and over the cote, a *surcote* (outer tunic.) In cold weather or for protection out of doors he added yet another garment, some form of cloak with a more or less fitted cut.

NOTE: An emphasis on greater modesty in court dress came at the time that Louis IX was King of France. Louis, a very pious man, was the only French king ever to be declared a saint by the Catholic Church. During his reign, court dress became more austere and luxurious display was discouraged.

Item / Description

cote—*under tunic*—worn long by upper classes, short by working class men. Two types of sleeves appear most frequently:
 · long and tightly fitted (See Figure 6.10.)
 · cut very full under the arm, tapering to a close fit at the wrist. (Some costume references call this a *magyar* sleeve.) (See Figure 6.9.)

surcote—*outer tunic*—had these variations in cut:
 · sleeveless with a round or wide, horizontal neckline and wide armholes, the garment sewn closed under the wide armhole. (See Figure 6.9.)
 · with sleeves to the elbow or three-quarters of the way down the arm. (See Figure 6.9.)
 · with long sleeves cut full and wide under the arm, tapering to the wrist (as described for the cote.)

6.9 (*Left*) Manuscript page from the first half of the 13th century shows, on the upper panel, a king and queen. The queen, Blanche of France, wears a *cote*, cut full under the arm and over it a fur-lined mantle. The king who is her son, St. Louis IX, wears a *cote* with long, fitted sleeves and a *surcote* that ends below the elbow with wider sleeves. His mantle closes at the front with a decorative brooch. The author of the book and scribe on the lower panel each wear sideless *surcotes*. (*Photograph courtesy of the Morgan Library.*)

6.10 (*Right*) Manuscript of about 1240–1260 shows a variety of costumes including a *garnache*, a cloak with wide, cape-like sleeves depicted both in the lower left panel and the upper right-hand panel. (*Photograph courtesy of the Morgan Library.*)

NOTE: Long surcotes were often slit to the waist to make riding and other movement easier. Even short surcotes and cotes worn without a surcote sometimes had these slits at the front. (See Figure 6.10.)

outdoor garments—Distinctions between the surcote and some of the cloaks and mantles worn out-of-doors blur. With some outdoor garments no surcote was worn. Major items of outdoor wear included:

· Open or closed cloaks or mantles. Mantles placed over the shoulders and fastening across the front with a chain or ribbon remained a symbol of high rank or status.

· the *garnache*—a long cloak with cape-like sleeves, often lined or collared with fur, this garment was open at the sides under the arms. (See Figure 6.10.)

· the *herigaut*—a full garment with long, wide sleeves and a slit below the shoulder in front through which the arm could be slipped, leaving the long, full sleeve hanging behind. In some instances the top of the sleeve was pleated or tucked to add fullness to the sleeve. (See Figure

6.11.) (From descriptions, the *gardcors* or *gardecorps* seems to have been the same kind of garment.)

· the *tabard*—originally a short, loose garment with short or no sleeves worn by monks and lower class men. In some instances it fastened for only a short distance under the arms either by seaming or with fabric tabs. In later centuries the garment became part of military dress or the dress of servants in lordly households. (See Figure 6.12.) Decorations were applied to the tabard that identified the lord to whom the wearer owed allegiance. Slits or *fitchets* that look to the modern eye like pockets were made in some of the more voluminous outdoor gar-

6.11 Manuscript illuminated after 1262 depicts Virgin and Christ child, along with donors of the manuscript each shown wearing an *herigaut*. The woman on the right has her hair enclosed in a net, a *barbette* around her chin, and a *fillet* around her head. (*Photograph courtesy of the Morgan Library.*)

6.12 Kneeling monk (14th century) wearing a *tabard* which closes with cloth tabs under the arm. (*Photograph courtesy of the Cleveland Museum of Art, John L. Severance Fund.*)

ments so that one could put his hands inside for warmth or to reach a purse hung from the belt around the waist of the garment beneath.

***footwear*—**Closed shoes that buckled or laced, open slippers, shoes open over the top of the foot and having a high tab behind the ankle, and loose-fitting boots rarely above calf-height. (See Figure 6.10.) Both long hose and short stockings. Footed hose increased in use.

hair and head dress*—hair*—worn parted in the center, moderate length. Younger men wore shorter hair than older. If beards were worn, they were short, however many men were beardless because a new, closed military helmet, that completely covered the face, was uncomfortable if worn over a beard.

head coverings—the coif and hoods. (See Figure

6.10.) Some hoods no longer had attached capes. By the end of the 13th century, hoods fitted the head more closely and some were made with a long, hanging tube of fabric at the back. The French called this a *cornette*; the English, a *liripipe*.

COSTUME FOR WOMEN

While women did not wear braies, the other garments in their wardrobes corresponded to those of men, i.e.: a chemise, cote, surcote, and out-of-doors a mantle or cloak.

Item / Description

***cotes and surcotes*—**Cotes had either fitted sleeves or sleeves cut full under the arm; surcotes were either sleeved or sleeveless. Sleeves of surcotes ended somewhere between the elbow and the wrist and were generally quite wide and full. Sleeveless surcotes were cut with wide armholes through which the cote beneath was visible. (See Figure 6.8.) The loose, enveloping garments considered proper during the time of Saint Louis were replaced by more fitted styles toward the end of the 13th century.

NOTE: In warm summer months some women wore the surcote over the chemise, but this was considered daring and immoral behavior. Some women laced the cote (under tunic) tightly to emphasize their figures which were visible through the wide armholes of the surcote.

outdoor garments—The ceremonial open mantle worn by women of high rank was worn indoors as well as outside. (See Figure 6.9.) Cloaks like those of the 11th and 12th centuries continued in use, some of them hooded for cold weather. Women occasionally wore the herigaut and less often the garnache which was for the most part a man's garment. (See Figure 6.11.)

footwear—underwent no major changes from the preceding century.

hair and head dress—The practice of young girls wearing uncovered hair and adult women covering the head persisted. Long braids (like those of the 12th century) were no longer seen. Veils and hair nets covered the hair. Barbettes, fillets, and wimples continued in use, although sometimes they were placed over a hair net instead of a veil. (See Figure 6.11.)

Accessories of Dress for Men and Women—The High Middle Ages

Item / Description

accessories—limited to jewelry, wallets, purses, or other devices for carrying valuables, and gloves.
  gloves—according to Cunnington, worn only by the nobility and the clergy until the 13th century. Kings are sometimes represented wearing jeweled gloves. By the close of the 13th century, gloves seem to have been used more commonly by both men and women. Some were elbow-length, others wrist-length. Some women were said to have worn linen gloves to protect their hands from sunburn.
  purses, pouches or wallets—suspended from belts (and rarely, from the shoulder), sometimes worn underneath and reached through an opening or slit in outer garments.
  jewelry—rarely visible in pictures or statuary, but described in literary sources. Most impor-

tant were rings, belts, clasps used to hold the ribbon that fastened the mantle, and a round brooch (*fermail* or *afiche*) used to close the top of the outer tunic, bliaut, or surcote.

cosmetics—After the Crusades, perfumes and ointments imported from the Middle East came into general use.

NOTE: Cunnington says Englishwomen of higher ranks used rouge in the 12th century. If it was imported for use in England where the nobility retained close ties to France and to English territories on the continent, one can be sure it was used on the continent as well. The same source mentions hair dyes and face creams.[4]

Military Costume

Entire books have been devoted to the subject of military costume and armor. The discussion which follows touches upon only the highlights of this topic. For those interested in more detailed information about military costume a section of the bibliography at the end of this chapter provides several specific references.

Blair, an authority on armor, suggests that armor be divided according to types of construction: (1) soft armor, made of quilted fabric or leather that has not been subjected to any special hardening process; (2) mail, made of interlocked metal rings; and (3) plates of metal, hardened leather, whalebone, or horn. The third category can also be divided into large plates that completely cover areas of the body and are flexible only where necessary for movement of the body; or small plates fastened together to provide more flexible covering.[5]

In the Greek and Roman armies all three of these forms were utilized. During the early Middle Ages in Europe the plate type of armor seems not to have been used. Blair, in a lengthy study of European armor, says that although some forms of small plate armor were used by the Franks and the Vikings, "it is probably safe to say that during the period c. 600–1250 when anything other than soft armor was worn it was in ninetynine cases out of a hundred made of mail." (See Figure 6.13.) Mail in Medieval Europe was made of circular rings, each ring having four other rings hooked through it.

4. C. & P. Cunnington. *Handbook of Medieval Costume.* London: Faber and Faber, Ltd., 1952, p. 41.

5. Blair. *European Armour.* London: B. T. Batsford, 1972, p. 19.

6.13 Mail shirt, 15th century. This shirt typifies the construction of chain mail garments which were the major form of armor in the early Middle Ages and continued to be used in conjunction with plate armor in the later Middle Ages as well. (*Photograph courtesy of the Metropolitan Museum of Art, Bashford Dean Memorial Collection, gift of Edward S. Harkness, 1929.*)

The Bayeux Tapestry is one of the earliest and most important sources of information about the appearance of Medieval armor. Dated from the second half of the 11th century, or slightly later, the tapestry depicts the events leading to and the actual battle of Hastings which took place in 1066. In the tapestry many figures wear knee-length shirts of mail which are split in front for riding. This mail shirt was called a *hauberk* or *byrnie*. A hood of mail was worn to protect the neck and head. This may have been a separate piece, but in most later armor the hood is made in one with the body of the hauberk for maximum protection of the neck. Some figures also wore leg-protectors of mail, or *chausses*. Some chausses merely covered the front of the leg while others were more like hose and fitted all around. On the head and over the mail hood the warrior placed a cone-shaped helmet which had a bar-like extension covering the nose.

In the mid-12th century men began wearing a surcote over the armor. (Figure 16.14.) Possibly the practice originated during the crusades in an attempt to protect the metal armor from the heat of the Mediterranean sun, a custom which may have been copied from Moslem soldiers. In later periods soldiers wore surcotes decorated with a coat of

6.14 Soldiers in chain mail with colorful *surcotes* placed over the mail. The mail covers all parts of the body except the face. (*Photograph courtesy of the Metropolitan Museum of Art, the Cloisters Collection, purchase, 1968.*)

arms that identified the force to which they belonged, a necessary step when faces were covered by helmets.

In the 12th and 13th centuries, armor consisted of a coat of mail—some times quite long, other times shorter—hose and shoes of mail. The sleeves reached over the hands to form a sort of mail mitten. The whole outfit weighed from 25 to 30 pounds and was worn over a padded garment. In the early 13th century, a closed form of helmet developed. Blair compares it to a modern welder's helmet, except that it was closed in the back, with eyeslits and breathing holes, sort of like wearing a large, inverted can over the head. Placed over the chain mail coif and a small padded skull cap that protected the head from the ridges of the mail, the helmet was worn only for combat as it was too uncomfortable for general wear. In the last half of the 13th Century, large crests in animal or bird-like shapes were placed on top of the helmet so as to identify the knight.

The use of closed helmets brought about changes in hair styles. Men wore their hair shorter and were clean-shaven in order to avoid the heat and discomfort that came from wearing a closed helmet over a full beard or long hair.

Common foot soldiers were not equipped with chain mail. Their protection was most likely limited to reinforced, quilted coats like those worn under the armor to which they might add quilted leg guards.

By the end of the 13th century, a change from mail to plate armor had begun. This development will be discussed in Chapter 7.

Summary

In the years between 900 and 1300, costume had evolved gradually from loosely-fitted, T-shaped tunics and mantles to more closely fitted styles of a more complex cut. As Medieval courts became the center of fashionable life, a special court dress developed. Made of more costly materials, clothing was often so extreme in cut that it demonstrated clearly that the wearer belonged to a more leisured class. As the economy improved, the manufacture and distribution of fabrics increased, and new types of cloth became available. With a gradually increasing merchant class in the towns, fashionable dress was adopted not only by the nobility but also by the bourgeoisie.

Even so the changes in styles that were seen in the High Middle Ages were gradual. A young woman of modest means might be married and, many years later, buried in the same dress, or she might pass it to her daughter in her will. After the end of the 13th century, this was less likely for fashion with its rapid changes was becoming an important aspect of dress, and styles began to change at what must have seemed like a dizzying pace. No wonder that a writer of 1350 was to look back on the styles at the end of the 1200's and lament that "Once upon a time women wore white wimples, surcoats with hanging sleeves, long full skirts, and decent hoods of cloth or silk. A woman had only three dresses. One for weddings and great feasts, one for Sundays and holidays, and one for every day. Narrow laced shoes and buttoned sleeves were for courtesans; decent women tied their bodices with ribbons and sewed their sleeves, wore their belts high and plaited their hair round their heads."[6]

Selected Readings

BOOKS CONTAINING ILLUSTRATIONS OF COSTUME OF THE PERIOD FROM ORIGINAL SOURCES

Aubert, M. *Le Cathedral de Chartres.* France: B. Arthaud, N.D.

Bertrand, S. *Tapisserie de Bayeux.* Bayeux, France: Heimdal, N.D.

Harksen, S. *Women of the Middle Ages.* New York: Alsner Schram, 1975.

Jantzen, H. *High Gothic.* New York: Pantheon Books, 1962.

Lucas, D. *A Gallery of Great Paintings.* New York: Hamblyn, 1975.

Martindale, A. *Gothic Art.* New York: Oxford University Press, 1967.

Sronkova, O. *Gothic Women's Fashion.* Prague: Artia, 1954.

PERIODICAL ARTICLES

Alexander, S. M. "Information on Historical Techniques. Textiles, 2: The Medieval Period. *Art and Archeology Technical Abstracts.* Vol. 16, No. 1, 1979, p. 198.

6. Evans, op. cit., p. 24–25.

Backhouse, J. "Manuscript Sources for the History of Medieval Costume." *Costume*, No. 2, 1968, p. 3.

"Faldying and Medlee." *Journal of English and German Philology.* January, 1935, p. 39.

Hughes, M. J. "Marco Polo and Medieval Silk." *Textile History.* 1975, p. 119.

Robbert, L. "Twelfth Century Italian Prices." *Social Science History*, Vol. 7 (4), Fall 1983, p. 381.

"Wife of Bath's Hat." *Modern Language Notes.* June, 1948, p. 381.

DAILY LIFE

Altschul, M. *A Baronial Family in Medieval England.* Baltimore: Johns Hopkins University Press, 1965.

Coulton, G. G. *Medieval Panorama.* New York: Macmillan Company, 1944.

Davis, W. S. *Life in Medieval Barony.* New York: Harper and Brothers Publishers, 1923.

Gies, F. and J. Gies. *Women in the Middle Ages.* New York: Barnes and Noble, 1978.

Gies, J. and F. Gies. *Life in a Medieval Castle.* New York: Thomas Crowell Company, 1974.

Holmes, V. T. Jr. *Daily Living in the 12th Century.* Madison, Wisconsin: The University of Wisconsin Press, 1952.

Howarth, D. *1066: the Year of the Conquest.* New York: Viking, 1978.

Kendall, A. *Medieval Pilgrims.* New York: G. P. Putnam's Sons, 1970.

Kraus, H. *The Living Theatre of Medieval Art.* Philadelphia: University of Pennsylvania Press, 1967.

Labarge, M. *A Baronial Household of the Thirteenth Century.* London: Eyre and Spottiswoods, 1965.

Labarge, M. *Court, Church and Castle.* Ottawa: The National Gallery of Canada, 1972.

McLanathan, R. *The Pageant of Medieval Art and Life.* Philadelphia: The Westminster Press, 1966.

Rowling, M. *Everyday Life in Medieval Times.* New York: G. P. Putnam's Sons, 1968.

Stuard, S. M. *Women in Medieval Society.* Philadelphia: University of Pennsylvania Press, Inc., 1976.

CHAPTER 7

The Late Middle Ages

c. 1300–1500

Historical Background

As medieval monarchs centralized the government, the power of nobles and knights declined. Feudalism began to wane before the 14th century because kings found new sources of revenue by taxing cities and towns and the income gained enabled them to hire knights who fought as long as they were paid. Monarchs had learned that a paid army was more dependable than feudal nobles who, under the usual feudal practice, were expected to serve only forty days once a year at their own expense.

Changes in warfare hastened the decline of the armored knight on horseback. In the Hundred Years War the English longbow decimated the French knights. In the 15th century, the introduction of gunpowder and cannon gave an even greater advantage to the infantry over the armored knight on horseback. Gunpowder also ended the security of medieval castles.

As kings brought law and order to their realms, the revival of trade, commerce and industry that had begun in the 12th century continued. Although the towns lost some independence as the royal government grew stronger, kings had to protect the cities since they were centers of trade and commerce, a most important source of taxes. Within the cities, as commerce became more capitalistic, the medieval guilds which had apportioned business among the members of the guild declined in importance. The merchant class, however, became more influential, turning to new fields of commerce, particularly banking which made them welcomed by their rulers. In France, Jacques Coeur, son of a lowly artisan, made his fortune through investing in commerce and mining, became treasurer to Charles VII, who later had him imprisoned and confiscated his wealth. In the late 15th century, the Fugger family of Ausgburg built a vast financial empire based on silver, copper, and iron mines. They became papal bankers as well as bankers to the Emperor Charles V to whom they lent money enabling him to bribe the electors and win election as Holy Roman Emperor.

Serfs gradually disappeared except in parts of Germany and France where they were in a minority. They were replaced by free peasants who no longer owed their lord services in return for the use of his land. Instead their services were commuted to money payments: rent. With the funds gained, the lord could hire landless peasants to work the land. The vast majority of the population consisted of peasants. They were the farmers, day laborers, millers, bakers, cattle dealers, and domestic servants. In time of war they were the foot soldiers of the king.

As free men they were more mobile, too. Increased commercial activity in the towns drew people from the countryside in search of work and higher salaries. These new townspeople could, if they had the talent and the opportunity, move up in social status. As a result the population of the rural areas declined after the middle of the 14th century while some towns and cities continued to grow.

Another reason for the increase in urban population was the flight of peasants from the countryside because of a series of famines resulting from poor harvests in the early years of the 14th century. Heavy rainstorms and cold weather ruined the crops on which people and cattle depended. The result was catastrophe: famine and starvation.

A population already weakened by famine suffered another scourge, the Black Death, a plague which struck Europe in 1347 and repeatedly throughout the 14th and 15th centuries. As late as 1665 London was devastated by an outbreak of the plague. The Black Death was probably a combination of bubonic and pneumatic plague. This devastating disease killed a third of the population in the regions which it struck. The densely populated Italian cities suffered heavy losses. But as a result of this depopulation labor became scarce and a vacuum was created in many areas. Aspiring workers from the lower classes were, thereby, afforded opportunities for advancement that had not existed before the Black Death.[1]

Wages rose sharply. Landlords and merchants had to grant concessions to peasants and workers. But when they tried to restrict wages and raise rents, social unrest and popular insurrections followed, lasting throughout the century.

Late medieval society can be divided into three classes: the nobility, the bourgeoisie, and the peasants. The clergy are excepted from this division as they were regarded as a separate class. (An early medieval bishop once said that society was divided into those who prayed, the clergy; those who fought, the nobles; and the rest of society, which labored.[2])

1. D. Herlihy. "Ecological Conditions and Demographic Change," *One Thousand Years: Western Europe in the Middle Ages.* ed. De Molen. Boston: Houghton-Mifflin Company. 1974, p. 34 ff.

2. D. Nicholas. "Patterns of Social Mobility." De Molen, ed., *op. cit.*, p. 45.

7.1 Upper class men look on while peasants harvest grain. Illumination from a book depicting agricultural techniques, French, c. 1470. (*Photograph courtesy of the Morgan Library.*)

THE PEASANT

The rural peasant is frequently depicted at his labors in the Books of Hours painted during the Middle Ages. These prayer books illustrated by the artists of the day show the farmer and his wife at work. (See Figure 7.1.) Men and women worked side by side on the land, planting, harvesting, clipping the fleece from sheep. Women tended their children and prepared simple food in a house of two or three rooms, furnished with utilitarian tables, benches or stools, chests or cupboards and beds.

Every day clothing for the peasant was plain and serviceable, and very like that of the earlier medieval period for men: a homespun tunic, belted at the waist, with stockings for cold weather and a cloak. Wooden clogs or heavy boots (for muddy weather), a hat to keep off the sun in summer or a hood against the cold in winter completed his workaday wardrobe. His wife wore a gown with a close-fitting bodice and a skirt with moderate fullness. When the task required or to protect the garment beneath, an apron was placed over the dress. If she worked in the field where her long skirts hampered her movement, the skirt was tucked up into the belt and the chemise underneath exposed.

Although many of the peasants were very poor and lived a hand-to-mouth existence, others were better off and some even reasonably affluent. The poorest were, of course, able to clothe themselves in only coarse, undyed cloth. The more affluent were not unaware of current fashions and for festive occasions their dress reflected somewhat the fashionable lines of upper class dress.

THE NOBILITY

If one were to judge from the painted miniatures, the life of the nobles was an endless round of entertainment: riding and hunting, feasting and talking, music and dancing. (And, of course, warfare.) The 1300's was also marked by intermittent fighting in France between the French and English, as the Hundred Years War continued off-and-on between 1337 and 1453.

Entertainment among the nobility provided a stage for the display of fashion. Wealthy noblemen and women dressed in rich silk brocades and velvets trimmed with fur. The Court of Burgundy was especially notable for luxurious dress during the 14th and 15th centuries. The kingdom of France did not then control all of the regions that are part of the present country of France. Sections such as Brittany to the Northwest and Burgundy to the Northeast were governed by powerful, autonomous dukes who sometimes allied themselves with and sometimes against France.

The court of the Dukes of Burgundy was renown for its splendid costume. The garments worn by the dukes, their families, and members of the court have been described at length in the chronicles of the period and painted by artists of the time. Some of the costumes of Philip the Bold, Duke from 1363 to 1404, indicate the costliness of Burgundian dress. One of his doublets was described as scarlet, embroidered in pearls in a design of 40 lambs and swans. The lambs had little gold bells around their necks and the swans held bells in their beaks.[3]

The fabrics of which Burgundian clothing was made were imported from all over Europe. Inventories list silk from Italy, wool from Flanders, and felt from Germany.

Headgear of men and women could be quite extreme. An inventory made in 1420 of the clothing of Philip the Good mentions a silk hat with peacock and other feathers, flowers, and gold spangles. At the close of the 14th century Burgundian women adopted an exaggerated hat style, the hennin. Hennins were tall, pointed, steeple-shaped headdresses. Sumptuary laws regulated the size of these hats.

3. H. Wescher. "Fashion and Elegance at the Court of Burgundy." *CIBA Review* No. 5, p. 1842.

Princesses could wear hennins of a yard in height, while noble ladies were permitted hennins of no more than 24 inches. The word hennin derives from an old French word meaning "to inconvenience," and certainly a tall, peaked hennin a yard high must have been a considerable inconvenience.

The Dukes of Burgundy and their retinues traveled to other parts of Europe for royal weddings, funerals, councils, and other events where the styles they affected were copied by others.

Much of the color and pageantry of costume of this period derives not only from the dress of royalty with its vivid colors and fanciful headdresses, but also from the costume of the dependent nobles and servants. Kings, dukes, and feudal lords had established the practice of presenting robes or sets of clothing to men and women of their household. The French word for "to distribute" is *livraison* and the items distributed became known as the *liveree* or in English, *livery*. Eventually the word livery came to mean special uniforms for servants, however during the 14th and 15th centuries livery was worn not just by servants, but also by officials of the court and ladies-in-waiting to queens or duchesses. Although subject to the wishes of the queen or duchess, a lady-in-waiting was not a servant, but a wellborn woman who lived and took part in the life of the court as part of the queen's retinue.

The garments which were distributed were decorated with special devices or symbols associated with the noble or his family. Finding unique patterns had led to the practice of coloring one part of a garment in one color and other parts in another color- or *parti-coloring*. Some examples of parti-colored hose show as many as four different colors in a single pair of hose. Parti-colored effects were utilized in both men's and women's costume.

THE BOURGOISIE

Merchants were part of a kind of "middle class," not of the nobility and yet far wealthier than the peasant. Some of these men like the previously discussed Jacques Coeur, became rich and powerful and achieved high offices under kings whom they helped to finance.

By far the larger number of merchants, however, were men of more modest incomes who lived in the towns and who achieved the means to live comfortably in houses which were furnished with well-crafted furniture, linen, and china. They lacked none of the necessities and had the means to obtain some of the luxuries of the period. These homes were run with efficiency by the wives of the merchants.

The wife of the merchant supervised the running of the household, but did not do the housework herself. If she lived up to the standards of behavior for a woman of her class, she conducted herself discreetly and modestly. If her dress followed the ideal expressed by churchmen and by others such as the "Goodman of Paris" it was free from extravagance. The "Goodman of Paris" was an elderly husband of a very much younger wife. This gentleman wrote out a book of instructions for his sixteen-year old wife on how to conduct herself in every aspect of management of the home. He even included some recipes for her. In his advice as to her dress and comportment when out-of-doors, he wrote:

> Have a care that you be honestly clad, without new devices and without too much or too little frippery. And before you leave your chamber and house, take care first that the collar of your shift (chemise), and of your blanchet, cotte, and surcotte, do not hang out one over the other . . . have a care that your hair, wimple, kerchief and hood and all the rest of your attire be well arranged and decently ordered that none who see you can mock at you, but that all the others may find in you an example of fair and simple and decent array.[4]

Not all merchants, however, agreed with the "Good-man" of Paris. Some merchants demonstrated their affluence through lavish dress for themselves and their wives. The passage of numerous sumptuary laws during this period testifies to the growing tendency of well-to-do burghers to imitate the nobility. For example, one set of sumptuary laws from the time of Edward IV of England (c.1450) was entitled "For the Outrageous and Excessive Apparel of Divers (different) People, against their Estate and Degree (status) to the Great Destruction and Impoverishment of All the Land."

FABRICS AND TAILORS

The technology and organization of cloth manufacture underwent no major changes, although the spinning wheel (brought to Europe from India) gradually replaced the distaff and spindle for the making of yarn. Tailors underwent a lengthy and rigorous apprenticeship which made them skilled in the construction of clothing. Different items of dress were made by different craftsmen, e.g., tailors for making garments, professional lingerie makers for making

wimples and veils, bootmakers, or shoemakers.[5]

The variety of materials and colors was considerable. Fabrics were traded all over Europe, and imported from Turkey and Palestine. Furs were used both as trimmings and linings. One king of France, Phillippe le Long, who was described as "anything but extravagant" used 6,364 skins of grey squirrel in three months just to fur his own robes.[6]

SOURCES OF COSTUME INFORMATION

The variety of sources of information available to the costume historian for this period are considerably greater than for the earlier periods. Secular romances and religious works such as Bibles and prayer books were hand-lettered and illustrated with vividly-colored, painted miniatures. These miniatures depicted scenes from the romances, from the Bible, or from church history in terms of every day medieval life. Stone sculpture from the facades of Gothic cathedrals, the tombs of the rich and high-born, and painted wooden statues for churches show the three-dimensional form of costume. Only a few individual items of dress from the period have survived, such as a *pourpoint* (a sort of man's jacket) worn in the second half of the 14th century by a French noble, Charles of Blois, or a jacket worn by the Burgundian, Charles the Bold, around 1477. In France and England, annual inventories were kept of the clothing given to or purchased by the royal families and these inventories not only described fabrics from which clothing was made but also gave their cost. Often the introduction of a style can be dated quite precisely from these lists. Even so, many terms from these two centuries are still in doubt as to their precise meaning. Apparently, too, similar terms were applied to different items in each country or region.

14th Century

COSTUME FOR MEN

For the first forty years of the century, styles for men continued to be much the same as those of the previous century, i.e., the cote worn with a sur-

---

4. E. Power, *Medieval People*. New York: Barnes and Noble 1968. p. 102.

5. The word lingerie which will be encountered frequently in subsequent chapters derives from the French and originally meant "makers of linen cloth." Over the years this meaning has altered and the term is now applied to women's underclothing, an application made because until the 19th century linen was the fabric most often used for women's underwear.

6. Evans, *op. cit.*, p.26.

cote. About 1340 styles for men changed markedly. Short skirts, always a part of peasant dress, returned to fashion for men of all classes. A number of new garments come into use, along with modifications of earlier forms. These are:

Item / Description

pourpoint (or doublet)—Originating in military dress—from the turn of the century men wore this close-fitting, sleeveless garment with a padded front over their armor. About 1340 they began wearing the pourpoint (also called a *gipon*) for civilian dress, together with a pair of long hose. Worn over the undershirt, cut to fit the body closely, it fastened down the front, closing with laces or closely-placed buttons. Neckline was round; sleeves fitted the arm, fastening with buttons at the wrist. (See Figure 7.2.) Initially pourpoints were usually worn unbelted beneath another garment, but after about 1350 they were often the outermost garment, and were belted. Those seen in the second half of the century become increasingly shorter, barely covering the hips. Some have sleeves extending below the wrist in a point as far as the knuckles. In English usage the term *doublet* replaced the word pourpoint after 1400.

hose—Both footed hose with leather soles and hose cut with a strap under the instep and meant to be worn with shoes or boots. Strings sewn to the underside of the pourpoint skirt below the waist allowed attachment of hose to the pourpoint rather than to the waistband of the braies.

NOTE: This mode of attachment of hose gave the pourpoint its name. *Points* were the laces or ties which ended in small, metal tips or "points" and the garment was "pour les points" or "for the points."

surcote—When worn over the pourpoint, surcotes were shaped close to the body, short in length, and either sleeveless or with sleeves.

cote-hardie—A new term coming into usage, generally thought to have been a variant of the surcote or outer tunic.

NOTE: This term provides a good illustration of the differences in usage of the same term from one country to another and of the variation in definition of terms that are encountered from one costume historian to another. Evans, a specialist in French medieval history, says that in France the cote-hardie was always a sleeved gar-

ment for outdoor wear first worn by the lower classes and later becoming a more elegant, often fur-trimmed or fur-lined, garment.[7] Boucher, a French costume historian, notes the confusion surrounding the terminology, and suggests that the term seems to have been applied variously to the first short outer garments for men, and to a gown, and to a surcote for men that was open in front and which buttoned at the sides.[8] The Cunningtons, who have compiled a handbook of English medieval costume, identified the cote-hardie in England as a very specific garment which replaced the older form of surcote for use over the pourpoint.[9]

The Cunnington's provide quite a complete description of the English cote-hardie which included these features in the first half of the 1300's: fitted through the waist where it buttoned; flaring to a full skirt that was open at the front and, usually, knee-length. The sleeves, apparently its major distinguishing feature, ended at the elbow in front while in back hanging down as a short tongue or longer flap, although in some versions both the sleeve and the flaps were absent. The English belted the cote-hardie low, on the hip. For the lower classes a variation is described: looser, not buttoned but slipping on over the head; its skirt and sleeves like the more fashionable garment; either unbelted, belted at the waist, or belted at the hip. (See Figure 7.3.)

In the second half of the 14th century these changes: buttons extended from neck to hem, instead of from neck to waist; hanging flaps at the elbows became longer and narrower; the length grew shorter; edges of skirts and hanging sleeve flaps were often decorated with *dagging*, a form of decoration in which edges of the garment were cut into pointed or squared scallops.

belts—Those worn with a cote-hardie might be long, with hanging ends, or short, made of metal placques with an ornamental buckle. Placement at hip level was usual.

houppelande—First mentioned in French royal inventories in 1359, this important garment seems to have come to England slightly later. Apparently originating as a man's house coat worn over the pourpoint, the garment was fitted over the shoul-

7. Evans, *op. cit.*, p. 25.

8. F. Boucher. *20,000 Years of Fashion.* New York: Harry N. Abrams, Inc. N.D., p. 428.

9. C. W. and P. Cunnington. *Handbook of Medieval Costume.* London: Faber and Faber, Ltd., 1952, p. 55 ff.

7.2 Short doublet or *pourpoint* is depicted in panels showing "Scenes from the Passion" from Austria, c. 1400. The laces that close the doublet are visible on the second figure, upper left, who also wears parti-colored clothes. The hose of one man in the same panel have been undone, revealing his *braies.* His doublet is unbuttoned. (*Photograph courtesy of the Cleveland Museum of Art, purchase, Mr. and Mrs. William H. Marlatt Fund.*)

7.3 Man on stilts wears a *cote-hardie,* and over his head a *chaperon* with a long, *liripipe* hanging down the back. The pages of manuscripts were often decorated with playful figures in scenes from games or other aspects of life like this one. (*Photograph from an illuminated manuscript, c. 1350, courtesy of the Morgan Library.*)

der, then widened below into deep, tubular folds or pleats, which were held in place by a belt.

construction—four long pieces, sewn together at the sides, center front, and center back, requiring that it be put on over the head. Sometimes seams were left open at the bottom for a short distance to form vents.

length—short to the thighs; long for ceremonial occasions; in the 1400's a mid-calf version appeared.

neckline—most commonly had a high, standing collar that encircled the neck. Collar edges might be dagged or the collar lined in contrasting color.

sleeves—at first funnel-shaped, with the upper edge ending at the wrist and the lower edge extending, in the most extreme versions, as far

as the ground. Sleeve edges also dagged; or sleeves lined in contrasting color.

fabrics—suited especially to heavy fabrics such as velvet, satin, damasks and brocades, and wool. Often fur-trimmed. (See Figure 7.4.)

outdoor garments—Garnache, herigaut, and varied capes and cloaks continue, new forms appear also:

houce or *housse*—in French accounts described as a wide-skirted over-coat with winged cape sleeves and two, flat, tongue-shaped lapels at the neck. From descriptions this appears to be a French variation of the garnache, which also had these tongue-shaped tabs. (See Figure 7.5.)

corset—or round cape, buttoned on the right shoulder, leaving the right arm free or closing at center with a chain or ribbon, ranging in length from full-length to mid-thigh. Some capes button to close down the front. Short, shoulder-length capes; after mid-century many finished at the edge with dagging.

7.4 Two older, more conservative kings on the left from a French manuscript of about 1420 wear fur-lined mantles. A third, younger and more fashionable, king at the right wears a *houppelande a mi jambe* (mid-calf) with wide, funnel sleeves, parti-colored hose, and a short, "bowl crop" haircut. (*Photograph courtesy of the Morgan Library.*)

7.5 Man at right wears a *garnache* or *houce*, with two, flat, tongue-shaped lapels at the neck. Man at the left wears a *cote-hardie* with a *chaperon*. (*Photograph from a manuscript c. 1360, courtesy of the Morgan Library.*)

7.6 Shoe of the type called *poulaine* or *crackowe* from the 15th century. (*Photograph courtesy of the Victoria and Albert Museum.*)

footwear—*stockings*—reaching to the knee or just below the calf, especially for lower class men.

long hose—often in colors contrasting with rest of costume, or *parti-colored*, each leg made of a different color.

shoes—cover the foot entirely or cut away, closing with a strap over the ankle. Points at toes grow increasingly longer. (See Figure 7.6.)

NOTE: the *poulaine* or *crackowe*, an elongated, exaggeratedly pointed-toed shoe developed toward the end of the century. The name derived in French (poulaine) from the word for Poland and in English (crackowe) from the name of the capital city of Poland, Krakow. It has been suggested that the style for pointed-toed shoes had first appeared in the 10th century, traveled to Poland where they continued in use while the style was abandoned in the rest of Europe, then returned to Western Europe from Poland about 1360.[10] Although the toes of all shoes of this period were pointed, the extreme forms were worn only by nobles and the rich. As one writer put it, "The crackowe was a badge of rank; it was the characteristic of a man whose mode of life did not require him to perform physical labor."[11] The style was followed in France, in England, in Portugal, and in Spain but never took hold in Italy to any great extent. By 1410 poulaines were out of fashion, but experienced a revival later in the 15th century.

boots—ankle length; calf-length; for riding: thigh length. Both fitted and loose styles.

clogs—worn by working class men for muddy weather.

hair and head dress—Faces most often clean-shaven.

hair—cut moderately short, below the ears.

hats—in the first half of the century, little change from coifs, berets, caped hoods with liripipes; and the addition of a hat with a low, round crown and elongated, pointed brim at the front and one with a high, domed crown and small rolled or turned-up brim. In the second half of the century styles grew more varied and fanciful through the use of plumes and colorful hat bands and decorative brocades. Hoods were transformed into turban-like styles by varying the way they were worn: the face-opening was placed around the head, the cape extending on one side and the liripipe on the other, both of which could be draped or tied into various positions.

accessories—belts, as mentioned previously, including some with suspended daggers or pouches for carrying valuables.

gloves—now worn by all classes, usually cuffed; more elaborate styles embroidered.

COSTUME FOR WOMEN

Item / Description

gowns—In English the term *cote* is superceded by the term *gown*. Changes in the first half of the 1300's mostly confined to alterations of fit:

10. A. Chevalier. "The Most Important Articles of Dress in the Middle Ages." *CIBA Review*, # V, p. 2078.

11. W. Born. "The Development of European Footwear from the Fall of Rome to the Renaissance." *CIBA Review*, # III, p. 1229.

the gown conformed closely to the body through the torso and flared out to a full skirt below.

surcote—worn over the gown, made with or without sleeves, and also following body contours.

NOTE: By the second half of the century a traditional form of dress for French royal women had evolved. From this point on to the end of the Middle Ages this garment in painting or sculpture marked the wearer as a French queen or princess. Its major features were:

gown—fitting smoothly through the body and with tight-fitting, long sleeves.

surcote—sideless, with a low decolletage (neckline) giving the appearance of straps across the shoulders. A stiffened panel with a rounded lower edge (in French, the *plastron* and in English, the *placard*) extended to the hip where it joined a wide band encircling the hips to which the skirt was attached.

skirt—so long and so full that it had to be lifted when walking. A vertical line of decorative brooches was placed on the front of the placard. (See Figure 7.7.)

houppelande—Adopted for wear by women only after 1387, but its fuller development for women came in the 1400's.

cote-hardie—The English version of the cote-hardie for women had a low, round neckline and sleeves ending at the elbow, with a dangling lappet falling from behind the elbow. (See Figure 7.8.) French styles of this garment are unclear, although it appears to have been a garment for out-doors. The Italian form seems to have been like that of the English. (Pistolese and Horsting claim that the cote-hardie originated in Italy.[12])

outdoor garments—Ceremonial mantles, open and clasped across the front, together with a matching gown, worn by royal women for state occasions. Capes, cloaks, and the herigaut worn for warmth. Fur linings common for winter, although sumptuary laws attempted to regulate the type of fur that could be used for lining or trimming according to social status.

footwear—*stockings*—ended at the knee and tied in place.

shoes—similar to those of men, however the toes of women's shoes never elongated to the same extent as those of men.

12. R. Pistolese and R. Horsting. *History of Fashions.* New York: John Wiley and Sons, Inc., 1970, p. 148.

hair and head dress—*hair*—still confined, hidden under a veil or held inside hair nets for adult women. Hair dressing and head coverings all emphasized width. If visible, hair was plaited, and either coiled around the ears (first half of the century) or arranged parallel to the vertical direction of the face. (See Figure 7.9.) The barbette with the fillet in use during the first part of the century gradually went out of use. The wimple continued in use somewhat longer, but by the end of the century was worn only by widows and members of religious orders. A narrower fillet was worn over a net or *fret*.

veils—often held in place by a fillet or *chaplet*, were not so closely wrapped as in earlier periods. A specialized veil style seemingly confined to England pleated the section of the veil closest to the face forming a frame for the top and both sides of the face. (See Figure 7.10.) Fillets of metal, for royal ladies in the form of a small crown or coronet, were important accessories. (The inventory of belongings of a French queen of 1372 included 60 such chaplets.) With the ceremonial placarded surcote royal women arranged the hair in a jeweled net over the ears; a coronet set on the head over the net. For bad weather—hoods or wide-brimmed hats.

accessories—*jewelry:* necklaces, bracelets, earrings, rings, decorative brooches; jeweled belts and buttons and clasps for mantles. Gloves.

cosmetics and grooming—Late in the 1300's it became fashionable to have a broad-looking, high forehead, achieved by plucking the hair growing around the face on the forehead. Eyebrows were also plucked. Although not common practices, dyeing the hair, especially to a blonde shade, and "face painting" were occasionally reported.

Costume of the 15th Century

The styles of the 1400's described in the following section are those of Northern Europe, especially France and England. Italian styles of the 15th century will be examined in Chapter 8 which deals with the Italian Renaissance which began in Italy and spread slowly Northward.

Variations also existed between styles worn in France and those worn in England, differences which have been attributed not only to the less

7.7 Queen Isabelle of England at the center of a manuscript illumination of 1388 wears traditional dress of queens: a sideless *surcote* over a closely fitted *cote*. The bodice has a *plastron* or *placard* decorated with a vertical row of decorative brooches. King Richard II is shown receiving a copy of a manuscript of Froisart's chronicles from the author. King Charles VI of France, brother of Isabelle greets her and Prince Edward whom she holds by the hand. Other men in the illustration wear a variety of doublets and robes. (*Photograph courtesy of the Morgan Library.*)

7.8 (*Left*) Three women in *cote-hardies* with sleeves that end in long, hanging lappets. Second quarter of the 15th century. (*Photograph courtesy of the Morgan Library.*)

7.9 (*Right*) Hair plaited, coiled over the ears and a fillet (originally jeweled) worn over the hair. (Bust of a Lady of Rank, France, 14th–15th centuries. *Photograph courtesy of the Metropolitan Museum of Art, gift of George Blumenthal, 1941.*)

7.10 Scenes from the life of Alexander the Great from a manuscript of the 14th century depict woman in a pleated veil. The man wears a closely fitted doublet and the pointed-toed shoes called *poulaines* or *crackowes*. (*Photograph courtesy of the Morgan Library.*)

abundant supply of rich fabrics in England, but also to differences in social organization in these two countries. The French court and the nearby court of Burgundy provided a stage for the display of costume that was not equaled in England. Evans pointed out:

England had a lower standard of luxury, and the life of its upper classes was based rather on the castles and manors of the countryside than on Windsor or Westminister. Fashions were less splendid and changed less rapidly.[13]

13. Evans, *op cit.*, p. 79.

COSTUME FOR MEN

Item / Description

pourpoint or doublet—Short, barely reaching to the thighs, and in some cases extending only a little below the waist. Worn as an underlayer after the first decade of the century and placed over the under shirt and beneath the jacket.

  sleeves and collars—often the only sections visible, therefore some doublets were made with decorative fabrics in collar and sleeves and plain, less expensive fabrics in the body of the garment. Detachable sleeves appeared at the close of the 15th century.

hose—Exposed for almost their whole length; constructed in a new form, a sort of combination of braies and hose into one garment comparable to modern tights. The *codpiece*—a pouch of fabric cut to accommodate the genitals and tied shut with laces was placed at the front. Hose laced to doublets by means of a series of small eyelets around the lower edge of the doublet and the upper edges of the hose. *Points*—laces made of leather and with plain or decorated metal tips connected the eyelets.

houpplelande—important as a garment for men for the first two-thirds of the 15th century. After mid-century it is called a *gown* or *robe* in England. The term does not appear in royal accounts in France after 1470, although it appears often in the reign of Charles VII who died in 1461. (See Figure 7.11.)

  Structure of the garment: fitted across the shoulders, full from that point. From 1410–1440, fullness arranged all around the body with an equal number of pleats (often two) spaced at the front, back, and each side. After 1440, fullness concentrated at front and back; smooth at the sides. Closing down the front, though often the fastening was not visible.
  Sleeves—open or closed at the cuff:
  Open styles:
  · wide funnel (stylish until 1450)
  · plain cylinder, often lined in contrasting colored fabric and turned back at the wrist.
  Closed style:
  · "bagpipe" shape (exceedingly popular after 1410)—widened from shoulder to form a full, hanging pouch below a tight cuff.
  After 1445, these changes:
  · Sleeve cap given increased height by small pleats.

7.11 Men and women in a tapestry dated from 1435–40. Short versions of the *houppelande* worn by men show a variety of sleeve constructions and include those with slits through which the arm could be placed, leaving the sleeve hanging behind. Women's gowns have V-shaped revers. Elaborately patterned fabrics are used for both men's and women's styles. (*Photograph courtesy of the Metropolitan Museum of Art, Rogers Fund, 1909.*)

· Sleeves narrowed somewhat, tapering to the wrist.
· Hanging sleeves were either open or closed at the wrist and provided an opening above the elbow for the arm; the rest of the sleeve then hung down, behind the arm.
Other features:
· In winter, fur linings.
· Decorations—ranging from dagging to embroidery or construction from colorful, woven, patterned fabrics.
· Shorter versions worn, lengths ranging from mid-leg (*houppelande a mi-jambe*) to hip length, though the short styles were less common than longer ones.

jacket—During the early part of the 15th century the cote-hardie was gradually replaced not only by the shorter houppelande but also by an alternative style called the jacket. (See Figure 7.12.) For the first part of the century in England the terms jacket and cote-hardie may be used interchangeably; after 1450 "cote-hardie" is no longer used. In France, the term pourpoint is still applied to what the English call the jacket.

> *jacket structure*—similar in appearance to the short houppelande, but constructed differently having a seam at the waist to join bodice and skirt, the skirt flaring out sharply from the hip. Most popular lengths barely covered the hips; in other versions, skirts reached mid-thigh. Whereas short houppelandes went out of fashion, jackets continued to be important garments. Some elements included:
> · vertical pleats at front and back.
> · shoulders built up over pads to produce a broad, full, sleeve cap.
> · usually collarless with round neck shaping to V at front and back; or a deep V to the waist held together with lacings.
> *Sleeves:*
> · full shoulder narrowing to wrists.
> · full sleeves gathered to small wrist bands.
> · tube shapes with wide, turned-back cuffs.
> · hanging sleeves. (Toward the end of the century slashes were made in parts of the sleeves through which the undersleeves of doublet or shirt were visible.)

outdoor garments—Cloaks or full capes with hoods—chief outdoor garment for working men. *Huke* (French, *huque*)—worn by upper class men. Like the cote and surcote originating as a covering for armor, hukes were shaped much like tabards, being closed over the shoulders and open at the sides, and having in short versions a slit at the front for ease when riding. In longer versions for walking, made without the slit. Worn unbelted, belted, or with the belt passed across the front while the back hung free, hukes were more fashionable in the first half of the century than the second. (See Figure 7.13.) Shoulder capes and a variety of short capes about the same length as the jacket.

footwear—Stockings of knee or mid-calf length—worn by lower class men.

> *hose*—the preferred leg covering. Joined hose predominated, although separate hose continued in use. Joined hose made with leather soles

were worn without other shoes both indoors and out. Bright colors, usually, many parti-colored.

NOTE: Even though paintings may show hose as fitting the leg quite closely, hose of this period were still cut on the bias for greater stretch and seamed together up the back. Wool was the most common fabric. Knitted hose did not take the place of woven cloth stockings until the 16th century. The date at which the art of knitting became a widespread craft is uncertain, but knitted stockings are listed in the records of the English city of Nottingham as early as 1519 and the oldest guild of stocking knitters was not founded until 1527 in Paris.[14]

Shoes and footed hose were pointed, some with exaggerated or *piked* toes, the length waxing and waning over the century. For the first ten years the shape, while pointed, was relatively short; after mid-century the piked poulaines were revived, persisting in use until about 1480 when shoe forms became more rounded. Very long points were stuffed and stiffened, some even rolled up. As in the 14th century, the extremes of this style were limited to the affluent.

> *shoes*—laced or buckled at the side to fit the foot closely.
> *pattens*—raised wooden platforms (or sometimes leather for the upper classes) fastened over the shoe with a strap for protection during bad weather.
> *boots*—close-fitting, short to the calf and closed with laces or buckles. Long, thigh-length boots with a turned-down cuff at the top worn for riding in the first half of the century became fashionable for general pedestrian wear in the second half.

hair and head dress—*hair*—at the beginning of the century a new style frequently called the "bowl crop" as it gives the appearance of an inverted bowl around the top of the head. Below the cut hair the neck was shaved. (See Figure 7.13.) After mid-century the shortness of the cut modified somewhat, to be replaced after 1465 by longer styles similar to what in modern terminology would be called a "page boy" cut. Faces were generally clean-shaven.

> *head coverings*—enormous variety, many quite fanciful. To describe them all is not possible, however see Figures 7.11, 7.12, and 7.13 for ex-

14. "The Knitted Stocking," *CIBA Review*, No. 106, p. 3800 ff.

7.12 Men of all classes, including criminals, are depicted in this scene from a French manuscript of 1480. Fighting men at lower left seem to be wearing padded jackets. Criminals are executed in their *chemises* or undergarments. Fashionable gentlemen looking on wear robes and jackets cut in many styles. (*Photograph courtesy of the Morgan Library.*)

7.13 Man at far right wears a *huke*, open at the sides under the arm. The man at the center wears a *houppelande* with bagpipe sleeves. The seated figure, a king, wears a robe and mantle. (*Manuscript of 1438, photograph courtesy of the Morgan Library.*)

7.14 Tapestry of the third quarter of the 15th century has a rare depiction of woman and a man clad in *chemises*. Woman's *chemise* is embroidered at the neck and armscye. Man's garment has embroidery at the armscye. Other figures wear rich brocades. The man at the center of the right-hand panel wears a belted *huke*. (*Photograph courtesy of the Metropolitan Museum of Art, gift of J. Pierpont Morgan, 1907.*)

amples of some of the most popular styles.

the coif—gradually disappeared except in the dress of clergy and professions such as medicine. Caped hoods went out of style except for country folk, although a number of the hats that developed were derived from hoods.

accessories—Jeweled collars, daggers, pouches or purses, gloves and decorative girdles. (In the first half of the 1400's a man's belt was one of his most important possessions, and to deprive a man of his belt was a symbol of degradation. In the second half of the century belts became a less essential part of the costume.)

COSTUME FOR WOMEN

Terminology tends to become somewhat confusing as styles become more varied and as the same garments are called by different names in different countries. As before, women tended to wear linen undergarments and one or two layers of outer garments.

Item / Description

chemise—woman's undermost garment called a *smock* or a *shift* in English. (See Figure 7.14.)

gowns—The English use the term "gown;" the French "cote" or "cotte." Style variations included:

· two layers of gowns

· a gown plus a sideless surcote

· cote-hardie with hanging tippets in England where styles generally were less revealing than in France.

· a gown for upper class women in France, cut with a low neck, closely-fitted bodice which emphasized the breasts, and a full, long skirt. (See Figure 7.15.) Sleeve variations:

· close-fitting shoulder to wrist

· wide, full, funnel-shapes

· hanging sleeves

houppelandes for women—always long and belted slightly above the anatomical waistline, soft, natural shoulder line, but otherwise simi-

lar in cut to those of men. Collar variations:
· high standing collar, usually open at the front to form a sort of winged effect. (See Figure 7.16.)
· flat, turned-down around a round or V-shaped neckline. Sleeve variations:
· huge funnel shapes, lined in contrasting colors or fur and reaching to the ground
· bagpipe sleeves
· plain tubular sleeves turned back at the end to show contrasting cuffs
· hanging sleeves, usually tubular in shape.

Gown styles developed in the second half of the century. Its evolution proceeded in this way—rigid, tube-shaped pleats disappeared from women's dresses, being replaced by soft, gathered fullness. The bodice developed a deep V, sometimes reaching all the way to the waist, and sometimes shallower. The edges of the V were turned back into revers,

which were generally lined in a contrasting color or in fur. The skirt was long and trained, usually so long that it had to be lifted up in front to avoid treading on it when one walked. Often the skirt was bordered in the fabric from which the revers were made. The deepness of the V generally required that a modesty piece or filler be placed across the bodice. A wide, stiff belt was placed at the waist.

In the earliest of these styles, the cut of the bodice was soft with fullness caught in by the belt. (See Figure 7.11.) As the style evolved, the cut became more tailored and the bodice fitted the body more closely. (See Figure 7.17.) When the V-shaped revers were set further out on the shoulders, women wore a transparent linen fabric piece pinned to the garment at the neckline, shoulders, and back to secure it in place. (If one looks very closely at some of the Flemish portraits of the period, one can see that artists often give a hint of this fabric and sometimes depict the pins at the front of the bodices.)

7.15 Gown of 1400 shows the low-necked, close-fitting style worn in France at the period. Over it is placed an open mantle. (*Photograph courtesy of the Metropolitan Museum of Art, gift of J. Pierpont Morgan, 1916.*)

7.16 Woman's *houppelande* with fur trimming at the hem. (About 1430.) (*Photograph courtesy of the Morgan Library.*)

7.17 Women dressed in a variety of styles from the second half of the 15th century, including the full gown that appears often in Flemish or German painting. Two of the figures have raised the skirts of their gown's so that the under-dress in a contrasting fabric is visible. (*Photograph courtesy of the Morgan Library.*)

loose-fitting gown—a style that appears infrequently, seemingly most often in Flemish and German paintings, in which the bodice is cut with a round neckline from which a cascade of gathers or pleats falls at the very center of the front and back. Unbelted and made in soft fabric, the dress falls loose and unfitted to the ground. Sleeves were long and fitted or short and when sleeves were short, the gown was worn over a long-sleeved under dress. (See Figure 7.17.)

outdoor garments—Hooded cloaks for bad weather. Open mantles, worn over matching gowns, and fastened with chains at the front remained unchanged.

footwear—*stockings*—ending at the knee where they tied around the leg.

    shoes—although toes were pointed and somewhat elongated, women never adopted the exaggeratedly piked cut characteristic of some men's shoes. Shoes fitted the foot closely.

    wooden pattens—worn in bad weather.

hair and head dress—*Uncovered hair for unmarried girls, brides, and queens* at their coronations; all other respectable adult women placed some covering over the hair. High, smooth foreheads, achieved through plucking out the hair remained fashionable, therefore little or no hair is visible around the edges of the fanciful head dress that became fashionable.

• For the first half of the century: Fullness concentrated from side to side. If head dress did not fully cover the hair, the hair was generally placed in a net. Various structural forms were placed on the head, often veils were draped over the entire structure.

• In the second half of the century: Head dress grew taller, ranging from a flat-toped toque (a high-crowned, brimless hat) four or five inches high to the pointed French *hennin*, an enormous cone-shaped, peaked hat that was as much as a yard high. This latter style was limited in use to France and Burgundy. (See Figure 7.18.) Veils, ideally of exquisite fineness, sheer, and gossamer-like, were pinned and draped over the head dresses.

accessories—Jewelry, gloves, pouches or purses, girdles (belts), and with lower necklines, necklaces became more important.

COSTUME FOR CHILDREN

Throughout the Middle Ages what evidence is available shows that except during infancy children were dressed in the same fashions as adults. The infant was swaddled, wrapped in bands of linen from head to foot. It was believed that swaddling prevented deformity when the child grew older. There is no clear evidence as to how long infants were swaddled, but apparently the swaddling grew looser as the child grew older, and by the time he or she became more active, the practice was discontinued.

During the first four or five years, both boys and girls dressed in loose gowns. Those of royal children were of rich fabrics, elaborately trimmed. When chil-dren were old enough to take part in the work or other activities of the family and to leave the nursery, they were dressed as miniature adults. (See Figure 7.7.) Boys' tunics were generally somewhat shorter than those of adult men, except of course in periods when the male jacket became extremely short. Girls always wore long gowns.

The major difference in the dress of girls and women was in the hairdressing. Young girls went about with their hair uncovered until they married.

MOURNING COSTUME

Special costume practices during the mourning period after the death of an individual were not well-established until the close of the 15th century when the etiquette of mourning became more fixed and elaborated. By the mid-1300's black had been recognized in Northern Europe as a symbol for grief.

7.18 Fragment of a tapestry depicts head dress of men and women of the second half of the 15th century. Woman at center wears a tall, pointed *hennin.* Man to the right, wears a "sugar loaf" hat. (*Photograph courtesy of the Metropolitan Museum of Art, bequest of George Blumenthal, 1941.*)

Previously a dark drab-colored garment worn with an enveloping dark hood and placed over ordinary colored clothing was all that was required. Nor did the mourner have to give up color for a long period of time. A mother of the 1300's is cited as wearing black on the death of her son in the Fall, but by the following Spring she was dressing in colors again.

The dress of widows, however, was more fixed by tradition. After the wimple was given up by women in general in the 1400's, it was traditional for widows to wear this veil. Bereaved wives also avoided bright hues, often wearing shades like violet and grey for the rest of their lives.

It was not considered fitting for men to wear the short pourpoint or jacket during the mourning period. Robes had to be long and black. In France the long, hooded cloak was worn by both sexes for mourning. Servants of great men were issued these black garments upon the deaths of their masters.

OCCUPATIONAL COSTUME

Student Costume—

Toward the close of the Middle Ages, certain items of dress that had once been part of "fashionable" dress but had since gone out of style, became traditional for particular professions or categories of persons. During the 1400's students retained the cote and surcote after it had been abandoned for general wear. A variant of this long robe has been passed down over the intervening years and is still part of official academic dress, worn by students and faculty at the time of graduation.

Military Dress—

During the 14th and 15th centuries the chain mail armor that had characterized the armor of the earlier medieval periods was gradually replaced by armor made from large, rigid plates. The first step in this direction came with the development of solid metal defenses for the legs, elbows and knees. By the third decade of the 14th century, these were universally adopted. Subsequently solid armor for the trunk developed. This was first a cloth or leather garment lined with metal plates, called a coat of plates.

About 1350, the following would have been the form of armor worn by a knight. He would first don a close-fitting shirt, braies, and hose. His arms and legs would be covered with metal protectors. Then a padded undercoat, called a gambeson, over

this his hauberk (or the shorter coat of mail called the haubergeon) and over this a coat of plates, and over all a surcote, often belted, and a sword belt. When going into action, he added his helmet, and a pair of metal gloves or gauntlets.

By 1400 the shape of the helmet had become more rounded. It still covered the entire face, but usually had a hinged visor, a face-guard that could be opened. Craftsmen skilled in making armor varied this construction and shape of helmets according to their individual techniques, and local differences are also evident in sizes, shapes, and con-

7.19 Complete suit of armor, Italian, 15th century. Mail protection is visible at those areas not covered by the plate armor. (*Photograph courtesy of the Metropolitan Museum of Art, Bashford Dean Memorial Collection, gift of Edward S. Harkness, 1929.*)

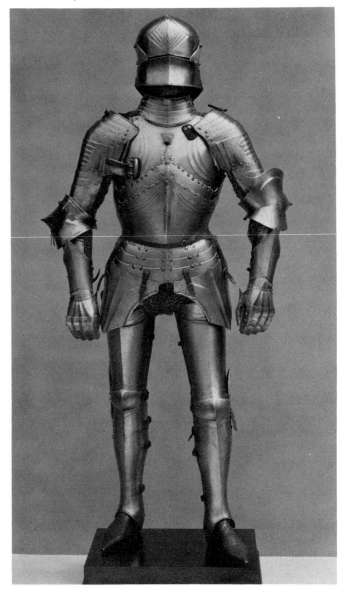

struction of all parts of the suit of armor. (See Figure 7.19.)

The breast plate and back plate were constructed to protect these areas, and it was a logical step from this point to the complete suit of armor that could be constructed to protect all areas of the body. The armor was worn over a haubergon until the second half of the 1400's when the coat of mail was replaced by an arming coat, a padded coat made with mail in those areas not protected by the armor.

Until about 1420 a padded jacket, often sleeveless, was worn over the armor, but after this date "white" armor, or highly polished metal armor, was rarely covered except by a tabard or huke which served to identify the wearer by its colors or decoration.

The forms of armor that developed were many and were varied in their specific construction. For persons interested in further exploration of this topic there are several extensive and particular studies of armor cited in the bibliography.

Summary

The 14th and 15th centuries are marked by rapid fashion change, new costume forms for both men and women, and more distinctions between dress for men and dress for women. At the beginning of the 14th century both men and women wore cotes and surcotes which though different in fit were not especially different in their basic construction. By the second half of the century men had adopted short styles: the pourpoint and hose. These styles which came to men from military dress when contrasted with the long, flowing gowns of women served to dramatize the difference between the active life of men and the passive lives of the women. Many historians have pointed out that women of the later Middle Ages had lost many of the economic and social privileges they had in the High Middle Ages. David Herlihy suggests that it was because the life expectancy of women increased in the 14th and 15th centuries. In the earlier periods because many women died young, the value to society of a young woman of child-bearing age was very much greater.[15]

The increased emphasis on fashionable dress was seen in the accession to popularity for men of first the cote and surcote, then the cote-hardie or pourpoint, followed by the long and short houppelande, and finally giving way to the jacket. For women

15. D. Herlihy. "The Natural History of Medieval Women." *Natural History*. March, 1978, p. 56 ff.

comparable changes in fashion were demonstrated by the popularity of the gown and sideless surcote, the cote-hardie or fitted gown, the houppelande, and finally the high-belted fitted gown of the second half of the 1400's, together with a multitude of changes in headdress styles.

Economic changes of the late Middle Ages were in large part responsible for an increased interest in fashionable dress. Greater prosperity had brought fashionable clothing within the reach of an enlarging middle class, especially the merchant class. The nobility, wanting to set themselves apart from the newly rich and lower classes passed sumptuary laws to restrict luxurious dress, but historians tell us that these laws were generally ignored. Increased trade was one of the reasons for the greater prosperity of the period, and trade also brought a wide variety of fabrics from all over the world to the population centers of Western Europe. The availability of these fabrics made possible the construction of colorful and elaborate garments characteristic of upper class dress of this period.

These relatively rapid fashion changes that began in the 14th and 15th centuries became a fixed aspect of all subsequent periods in Western costume history.

Fashion change not only continues, but it accelerates. As a result subsequent chapters in this book will be dealing with increasingly short periods of time.

Selected Readings

BOOKS CONTAINING ILLUSTRATIONS OF COSTUME OF THE PERIOD FROM ORIGINAL SOURCES

The Art of Chivalry. New York: Metropolitan Museum of Art, N. D.

Avril, F. *Manuscript Painting at the Court of France.* New York: George Braziller, 1978.

Evans, J. (Ed.) *The Flowering of the Middle Ages.* New York: McGraw-Hill Book Company, 1966.

Evans, J. *Dress in Medieval France.* Oxford: Clarendon Press, 1952.

Newton, S. M. *Costume in the Age of the Black Prince.* Totowa, N.J.: Rowan and Littlefield, 1980.

Scott, M. *Late Gothic Europe, 1400–1500.* Atlantic Highlands, N.J.: Humanities Press, 1980.

See also reproductions of Books of Hours such as:
Tres Riche Heures of the Duc de Berry,
Tres Belle Heures of the Duc de Berry,
King Rene's Book of Love,
The Hours of Anne of Cleves

PERIODICAL ARTICLES

Bell, C. R. and E. Ruse. "Sumptuary Legislation and English Costume: an Attempt to Assess the Effect of an Act of 1337. *Costume*, 1972, p. 22.

Bridgeman, J. "The Palermo 'Triumph of Death.'" *The Burlington Magazine*, CXVIII, No. 868, 1975, p.480.

Hawkins, C. "A Fifteenth Century Pattern for Chausses." *Costume*, 1972, p. 84.

Nevinson, J. L. "Costume in Castile." *Connoisseur*, September 1960, p. 10.

Parker, L. "Burgundian Court Costume from a Norwich Tapestry." *Costume*, No. 5, 1971, p. 14.

Staniland, K. "Medieval Courtly Splendor." *Costume*. No. 14, 1980, p. 7.

Sutton, A. F. "George Lovelyn, Tailor to Three Kings of England: 1470–1504." *Costume*. No. 15, 1981, p. 1.

DAILY LIFE

Chadwick. *Social Life in the Days of Piers Plowman.* Cambridge: The University Press, 1922.

Coulton, C. G. *The Medieval Scene.* Cambridge: Cambridge University Press, 1967.

Evans, J. *Life in Medieval France.* London: Phaidon, 1969.

Huizinga, J. *The Waning of the Middle Ages.* New York: Doubleday Books, 1954.

Lacroix, P. *France in the Middle Ages.* New York: Frederick Unger Publishing Company, 1963.

Loomis, R. S. *A Mirror of Chaucer's World.* Princeton, N.J.: Princeton University Press, 1965.

Marques, A. H. de O. *Daily Life in Portugal in the Late Middle Ages.* Madison, WI: University of Wisconsin Press, 1971.

Rowling, M. *Everyday Life of Medieval Travelers.* New York: G. P. Putnam's Sons, 1971.

Scott, A. F. *The Plantagenet Age.* New York: Thomas Crowell Company, 1975.

The Secular Spirit Life and Art at the End of the Middle Ages. New York: E. P. Dutton and Company, 1975.

Tuchman, B. *A Distant Mirror.* New York: Alfred Knopf, 1978.

PART III

The Renaissance

c. 1400–1600

Exciting cultural changes began in Italy about mid-14th century when sculptors, painters, and writers began to identify with the ancient civilizations of Greece and Rome. These Italians believed that 1000 years of darkness and ignorance separated them from the Roman era and their times. They believed that there had been a "re-birth" of classical arts and learning, a "Renaissance," a term derived from the Italian word *"renascere"* meaning to be re-born. Modern historians in general do not consider that there was "re-birth" of the arts, but that rather Europe underwent a chaotic change, a period of profound transition as medieval institutions crumbled and a new society and culture began to appear. The Renaissance could be viewed as a time of transition from medieval to modern view of man and the world.

The Renaissance began around the middle of the 14th century in Italy and lasted until the end of the 16th century. Dates assigned to artistic and to costume periods are of necessity arbitrary. In this book, the dates assigned to Renaissance costume style of 1400–1600, while a useful device for separating one period from another, do not take into account that the intellectual and artistic trends leading to the development of the Renaissance style in Italy, where it had its first flowering, actually appeared before 1400 during the late Middle Ages.

In the preceding chapter, the costume styles of the 15th century in northern Europe have already been discussed as part of the medieval styles. For not only do costume and artistic periods fail to fit into neat, clearly-defined time periods, they also begin and end at different times in different parts of the world. While the rest of Europe was following a line of political, economic, and artistic development that was an extension of trends begun during the Middle Ages, a new perception of life had begun to emerge in Italy in the 15th century and from there spread to the rest of Europe.

Even during the Medieval period between 400–1300 Italy was in some ways different from the rest of Europe. Its ties with the Byzantine Empire were closer than those of northern Europe. Until the 11th century, Northwestern Italy and Sicily were part of the Byzantine Empire. During the Middle Ages before the economic revival in Europe, urban life in most of northern Europe was severely disrupted, but in Italy urban centers remained more vigorous. Moreover, feudalism had relatively shallow roots in Italy because it flourished best in a more rural society. Italian feudal lords seldom exercised the independent powers of the great barons of France, England, and the Holy Roman Empire. Italian seaports, which declined to some extent during the early Middle Ages, nevertheless continued to carry on overseas trade, thanks to Italy's geographical position in the Mediterranean Sea. Consequently in much of Italy throughout the early Middle Ages, the people enjoyed a higher standard of living, thanks to a more thriving economy, than did the men and women living in the more depressed northern lands where cities had declined, international trade had slowed to a trickle, and literacy was preserved only in the monastaries.

When the European economic revival began in the 11th century, Italy benefited first. By the 12th century, city-states such as Venice and Genoa with large seaports carried on a large volume of trade with the Middle East and with northern Europe. Crusaders bought provisions for their expeditions and sailed from Italian ports for the Near East. In addition, improvements in ship construction allowed the Venetians and Genoese to carry more cargo, and even to sail into the stormy Atlantic Ocean. The money generated by this trade enriched the merchants and rulers of these states with enormous profits. The Italian merchants became financiers and bankers as well as traders, chiefly in textiles.

Not only merchandise but also ideas traveled the routes of trade, and the 12th and 13th centuries in Italy witnessed an intellectual ferment that radically altered philosophy, literature, and art in the 14th and 15th centuries. By the 15th century a fresh vitality in the arts and a new attitude toward man and his place in the world had emerged: the Renaissance.

At the same time, Europe also experienced a revival of interest in studying and reading the Greek and Roman classics. The learning, the arts, and the philosophy of the Romans and the Greeks had not been lost during the Middle Ages because medieval scholars had continued to study and to read the ancient writers in order that they might know God. Medieval Christianity had emphasized the spiritual, the need for man to prepare himself for the next world. When Renaissance scholars turned to the writings of Greek and Roman philosophers, many of which had been preserved in the monastary libraries, they focused on the humanistic aspect of classical thought which emphasized the interests, achievements, and capabilities of human beings. From the spirituality of the Middle Ages, artists and scholars turned toward a more secular emphasis on man, his abilities, and his place in the world. Even within the Roman Catholic church, St. Francis of Assisi and his followers brought a new spirit of emphasis on human and earthly problems.

In the Renaissance, there was a strong sense of individualism unlike the Middle Ages when people thought of themselves as part of a social or religious group. Italians with unusual talents were not afraid of being unique. There was a stress on the fullest development of a person's potential whether painter, writer, scholar, or sculptor.

During the 14th and 15th centuries the Renaissance was largely confined to Italy. But the increasing growth of international trade throughout Europe along with contacts between nations that came through warfare promoted the exchange of ideas. Students from northern Europe flocked to Italy to imbibe the learning of the Renaissance and to carry it back to their countries. Kings and wealthy nobles brought back Italian scholars and artists, and many Italians were given prominent positions at court and in the church. Consequently during the 15th century the Renaissance in the arts and learning spread into northern Europe. There the new Renaissance learning would strongly influence the challenge to the established religious beliefs which produced the Protestant Reformation.

And it was during the Renaissance that the configuration of present-day Europe as characterized by a number of independent nations gradually became established. During the Medieval period strong nations with distinct national identities and strong hereditary monarchies such as France, England, and Spain had emerged. By the close of the Renaissance in 1600 the general outlines of European nations had begun to emerge. In Germany, however, there was a great variety of separate states owing little allegiance to the Holy Roman emperor who by this time was always the head of the Austrian house of Hapsburg. Italy remained a set of independent city states or territories, which were often under the domination of one or the other of the great European powers.

The styles that developed during the Renaissance in art and architecture, textiles, clothing, music, literature, and philosophy continued to influence western culture. The artistic, literary, and philosophical works of the Renaissance are studied in colleges and universities of the 20th century. The plays of William Shakespeare and Christopher Marlowe are still performed, museums contain large numbers of Renaissance paintings, Renaissance music is performed in concerts, and Renaissance textile designs are often reproduced in fabrics for drapery or upholstery materials or copied for wall paper designs. Renaissance furniture and architectural styles experienced a number of revivals in the centuries that followed the close of the Renaissance. The term "a Renaissance Man" is still applied to the ideal of the cultured, learned person of many talents.

Moreover some of the discoveries and inventions

of the Renaissance had a profound impact on the history of subsequent periods. Among the most important of these was the discovery of America by Christopher Columbus in 1492. His discovery opened up new areas of the world for expansion and colonization by European peoples and shifted the center of European economic power away from Italy and the Mediterranean to the Atlantic. The discoveries also opened up new opportunities to make fortunes. In addition during the Renaissance there was a revolution in science. One of the most revolutionary developments was the theory developed by Copernicus that the earth revolved around the sun.

Another invention, with far reaching historical consequences was Johann Gutenberg's invention of printing from moveable type. Heretofore all books had to be hand-lettered or hand printed by a laborious, expensive process. The new method of printing reduced substantially the cost of books thus making them more readily available and consequently enabling more people to read them.

Although the Chinese, the Hindus, the Greeks, the Arabs, the English and the Germans all claim to have invented gunpowder, it was only during the Renaissance that it was used as a propellent first in guns and then in cannons, thus helping to end feudalism and begin a revolution in warfare.

CHAPTER 8

The Italian Renaissance

c. 1400–1600

Historical Background

Italy had been the center of the largest and most influential of the civilizations of classical antiquity. All around the Italians were imposing ruins, physical reminders of the grandeur of ancient Rome. Roman and Greek manuscripts had been copied by monks and priests and thereby preserved in the libraries of the monastaries and churches.

The actual cause of a renewed interest in the writings of the classical period seems to have come from the work of the lawyers and notaries in Italian city-states who looked to Roman law for justification of the independence of these territories. Many of the earliest Renaissance writers, such as Petrarch, a gifted Italian writer who lived from 1304 to 1374, were trained in the law. Petrarch contrasted the humanistic approach of the classics with what he saw as a narrow, academic philosophy in the Medieval universities. Others followed Petrarch's lead, and by the early years of the 15th century a revival of interest in the classics in literature and the arts was under way.[1]

1. W. L. Gundersheimer. *The Italian Renaissance.* Englewood Cliffs, New Jersey: Prentice-Hall, Inc. p. 6.

ITALY—THE POLITICAL ORGANIZATION

At the time of the Renaissance the word Italy referred not to a country but to a geographic area made up of a number of small city-states, each ruled by a powerful prince. These princes were sometimes members of ancient noble families, sometimes *condottieri* or hired military commanders who had taken over the reins of government in the states that they were hired to defend, and sometimes wealthy merchant families that had come to political as well as financial leadership.

Many of these princes were violent men; oppressive and cruel to their subjects. Others were more benevolent. Fortunately for the progress of art, many of them used the acquisition of art to display their wealth. They dressed lavishly in expensive clothing, and the artists who painted or sculpted their portraits depict these garments in considerable detail.

Even the most benevolent of the princes were often engaged in warfare with other princes. And it was this failure to unify under a single leader as had France, Spain, and England that resulted in the loss of large parts of Italy to these other nations. From 1494 to 1549 the countryside was the scene of the "Italian Wars," a series of wars for control of large segments of Italy by the Northern powers.

At the same time, the occupation of Italy by the Northern countries had the effect of spreading the Renaissance more quickly through the rest of Europe, and it is from the beginning of the 16th century that the Northern Renaissance is generally dated.

LIFE IN RENAISSANCE ITALY

The population of Renaissance Italy was roughly divided among the aristocracy, the merchant class, artisans and artists, the town laborers, and the peasants of the countryside. Some families owned slaves from Mongolia, Turkey, or Russia. Most of these were women who served as domestic help.

The ruling class structure in most Italian city-states was composed of men of aristocratic or noble families. In some areas, however, merchants had gained great power and political control. These men generally sought to become more respectable by marrying into the noble families. In wealthy or noble families sons inherited the family wealth. Girls could take only a small portion of the family holdings even if they had no brothers. The family estate passed to the brother of the man who left no male heirs. Much of the family wealth had to be invested in equipping a marriageable daughter with a sufficiently large dowry to enable her to marry well. When a family had been blessed with too many daughters, some of them were packed off to convents where no dowry was required. A woman such as Caterina Sforza who ruled and defended the town of Forli against the assassins of her husband and later against other attacking forces was an exception and "existed outside of the general social framework of the Renaissance."[2]

The merchants, although often the wealthiest members of the city population, were considered of lower status than the aristocracy in some towns. Not so in Florence and Genoa, however, where the ruling families came out of merchant backgrounds. The sons of the merchant families were educated to succeed their fathers in running the family business. Most major businesses were in some way related to the textile industry—weaving, dyeing, finishing, or trading cloth. Even bankers had first been traders in cloth.

Skilled artisans could do well and were more fortunate than unskilled laborers who often had difficulty managing to feed and clothe themselves and their families. The attitude of those who were better off toward these people was expressed by one Matteo Palmieri, a rich merchant who said ". . . If the lowest order of society earn enough food to keep them going from day to day, then they have enough."[3]

At the very bottom of the social scale were the peasants who farmed the land, working on a share-cropping basis with the land owner. Not only were they dependent on the vagaries of the weather, but their lives were disrupted by the armies that constantly ravaged the countryside fighting for one city or another.

In spite of the economic difficulties involved, many of those from lower levels of society tried to imitate the upper classes in their dress. Records indicate that an enormous number of sumptuary laws regulating dress were passed during this period. The Renaissance author of a book outlining the appropriate conduct for gentlemen put the prevailing attitude of the authorities this way: "Everyone should dress well, according to his age and his position in society. If he does not, it will be taken as a mark of contempt for other people."[4]

The sumptuary laws that can be found in all Italian cities whose archives have survived, regulated the numbers of items of clothing an individual could acquire. The *guardaroba* was a set of clothing (the term is comparable to the word *robe* in medieval France) which was made up of three garments: two layers of indoor clothing and a mantle for outdoors. In middle class Italian families, one new set of clothing was ordered each year. Discarded clothing was then passed along to the poor either by outright donation or by sale through second-hand clothing dealers.[5]

The head of a household had the responsibility for clothing the members of the household which was usually made up of knights and squires committed to fight for him, pages, grooms and valets. The mistress of the household had to supply the clothing for her lady attendants.

THE CLOTH INDUSTRIES

The technology for making cloth did not change much from the Middle Ages to the Renaissance.

2. J. Gage. *Life in Italy at the Time of the Medici.* New York: G. P. Putnam's Sons. 1968, p. 179.

3. quoted in Gage, *op.cit.,* p. 100.

4. Della Casa, *Galateo,* quoted in Gage, p. 195.

5. E. Birbari, *Dress in Italian Painting 1460–1500.* London: John Murray, p. 15.

The spinning wheel had been well established in Europe by this time. Leonardo Da Vinci invented a bobbin-and-flyer mechanism for the spinning wheel that, had it been put into use, would have speeded up the process of spinning enormously. It did away with the necessity of stopping to wind up the yarn after each length was spun. Unfortunately, like so many of Da Vinci's inventions, it remained for a German inventor to actually put it into use in the mid-1500's.

Wool and silk were the primary fabrics loomed in Italy. Many of the wool fabrics were made from imported fiber, but the silk was cultivated locally. Renaissance painters depict many of these luxurious fabrics so realistically that one can identify them as satins, cut velvets, plain velvets, or brocades, simply by looking at the pictures. These fabrics were especially suited to the almost sculptural lines of fashions of the Renaissance in Italy. Birbari pointed out the superiority of Italian textiles and notes that Italy was the center of the most important and luxurious textile manufacture in all of Europe. "Her woolen cloth was unsurpassed for quality; her woven silks were unique in their splendor."[6]

SOURCES OF INFORMATION ABOUT COSTUME

The Renaissance artist painted realistically, and this realistic approach extended into the representation of clothing. Not only are the external folds and draping of the garment shown, but the artist depicts gussets, eyelets for laces, and even the wrinkles on a pair of ill-fitting hose.[7]

In addition to the representations of costume, some actual items of dress remain as do written documents such as letters, diaries, and inventories of personal possessions that shed some light on the quantity as well as the variety of garments commonly owned. The first of a number of books about costume were printed in the 16th century. Several books by Venetian authors depict authentic contemporary dress along with some historic and foreign costumes that scholars have found to be at the best inaccurate and at the worst, imaginary.

A caution should perhaps be made about the costumes on certain of the religious figures depicted by Renaissance artists. The Virgin Mary is almost always dressed more conservatively and less fashionably than other women. Her hair is usually covered by a veil. Angels are dressed atypically, and figures from classical mythology are sometimes garbed as the Renaissance artist believed ancient Greeks and Romans dressed. Furthermore, Newton's extensive study of Renaissance theatrical costume explores certain conventions of presenting figures such as the wise men in the Christmas story in the kinds of clothing worn by actors in religious pageants, rather than in realistic costume of the time.[8]

Italian Costume 1400–1450

Italian costume of the first half of the 15th century had many of the characteristics described in Chapter 7 for the rest of Europe. (See Figure 8.1.) These differences may be noted.

COSTUME FOR MEN

Item / Description

garments—*doublets*—knee-length, worn with hose. *houppelandes*—long or short, most with either wide, funnel-shaped or hanging sleeves. *hukes*—placed over doublets.

shoes—pointed, but without the extreme piking seen in other parts of Europe.

hair—Cut short, but the bowl cut does not seem to have been adopted in Italy.

COSTUME FOR WOMEN

Item / Description

garments—*houppelandes*—many with imaginatively-cut sleeves.

hair and head dress—Foreheads bare and fashionably high, as in the rest of Europe. Italian women covered their hair less completely than women elsewhere. Head-coverings more turban-like, possibly a reflection of closer contacts with the Middle East. In the second quarter of the century, large, round, beehive shaped hats.

6. Birbari, *op.cit.*, p. 7.

7. See E. Birbari, *op.cit.* for a fully-developed discussion of realism in Italian Renaissance paintings.

8. S. M. Newton. *Renaissance Theatre Costume.* New York: Theatre Arts Books, 1975.

8.1 Costume of men and women in Italy in the first half of the 15th century. Female figures at the lower left hand corner of the painting are wearing *houppelande*-style gowns with long, full sleeves. The edges of the sleeves are finished in dagging. The sleeves are lined in a contrasting fabric. They wear the high, round, beehive-shaped head dress favored by Italian women of the second quarter of the century. Just above and to the right are two men wearing knee-length jackets with full, hanging sleeves. Their hose are slightly piked. Men in fashionable dress in the rest of the picture wear variations of the same style in jackets; and a variety of fashionable hats. Monks, priests, and nuns are dressed in typical religious garb of the period. (Paradise, *by Giovanni de Paolo; photograph courtesy of the Metropolitan Museum of Art, Rogers Fund, 1906.*)

Italian Costume 1440–1500

About the beginning of the second half of the century Italian costume and that of Northern Europe diverged, with distinct differences evident until the early 1500's. Neither the V-necked gown with wide revers nor the tall hennin with which it was so often worn in France and Flanders spread to Italy. The houppelande was supplanted by new and distinctly Italian styles, although even within the Italian styles, regional variations, especially those of Venice, were evident.

COSTUME FOR MEN

The basic elements of men's costume of the Renaissance were not new. In addition to short linen breeches, men wore an undershirt called the *camicia*, over this a doublet to which hose were attached by lacing, and an outer jacket.

Item / Description

shirt or camicia—Worn next to skin as undergarment which was visible at edges or openings of outermost garments. Lower class men sometimes wore only the shirt for hard labor; for them, the camicia was made of coarse, heavy linen; for the upper classes: finer, softer linen. *Cut:* sleeve and body cut in one piece with a gusset inset under the sleeve to permit ease of movement. *Length:* variable, ranging from between waist and hip to above the knees. (See Figure 8.2.)

doublet—*Length:* varied from waist-length to below the hip. *Cut:* In longer lengths, sometimes cut with a small skirt. Four seams, front, back and both sides provided close-fitting shape. (See Figures 8.2 and 8.3.) *Neckline finish:* often made with a distinctive finish displaying the high level of skill of Italian tailors. At the front, doublet appears to have collarless neckline, but the back neck piece was cut with a deep U-shape at the base where it joined the back of the doublet. The top edge was straight, but stood away from the neck, the effect being to provide a smooth, unwrinkled line to the back of the doublet from waist to neck without using darts or gathers.

hose—Attached to doublet. Cut either as two separate pieces or seamed together at the crotch.

NOTE: Doublet and hose were worn for labor and warfare by men except for those of the uppermost classes, however by the end of the century fash-

8.2 Workman. This laborer wears his jacket open and detached from his hose in order to allow him to move freely. Under his jacket one can see his *camicia*, and at the hip, under his *camicia*, one gets a slight glimpse of his short drawers. The loosened hose are rolled below the knee and over the hose he wears shoes, probably leather, that come to the ankle. (*Photograph courtesy of Edizione Alinari.*)

ionable young men took to wearing the doublet and hose without an outer jacket. Most hose were still apparently cut from bias-direction, woven fabric. Tightness of lacing of hose to doublet helped attain a smooth fit, but hampered physical activity. Renaissance painters frequently depict men involved in physical activity with their laces untied and their hose hanging loosely at the back. (See Figure 8.2.)

jackets—Outermost garments worn by men (corresponded to the Medieval "outer tunic.") Differing forms included:

· about mid-century: smoothly fitted through the torso with a flared skirt attached at the waist and ending below the hip.

· in the last half of the 1400's: fitted over the shoulders and upper chest, then falling in full pleats from a sort of yoke with fullness belted in at the waistline.

· in the latter part of the century, alternative style: sleeveless, looking much like the *huke*, seamed at the shoulder and open under the arms. Full and pleated, it was worn belted or unbelted. (See Figure 8.3.)

sleeves—construction could be quite complex as they tended to become more fitted in second half of the century. Identifiable types seem to show a sort of evolution:

· earliest form—cut in two sections, one full and somewhat puffed from shoulder to elbow and the other fitted from elbow to wrist. (See Figures 8.2 and 8.3.)

· slightly later—a one-piece sleeve full at the shoulder and tapering gradually to the wrist. (See Figure 8.3.)

· even later—narrowing to fit smoothly for the length of the arm, but when so tight as to prohibit easy movement an opening was left at some point through which the long-white shirt-sleeve could be seen. Some ways of permitting this ease included leaving seams open at various places and closing them with laces, making a horizontal seam at the elbow and leaving it open at the back where the elbow bends. (See Figure 8.3.)

sleeve attachment—either sewn into the body of doublet or jacket or laced into the armhole, and the fabric of the camicia pulled through the openings between the laces to form decorative puffs. If laced, sleeves were interchangeable from one garment to another. Hanging sleeves, generally non-functional, purely decorative, and attached to the jacket while the fitted sleeve of the doublet covered the arm were still seen, though mostly in costume for ceremonial occasions. (See Figure 8.3.)

8.3 A variety of different jacket, doublet, and sleeve styles. Figure on the left wears a dark red doublet with fitted sleeves under a jacket of green with hanging sleeves. The doublet sleeve is slit at the back seam and the edges of the split tied together with laces. A thin line of white from his *camicia* shows at the opening. The figure behind him wears a doublet of dark blue with a huke-like jacket that is belted. The sleeve of the doublet is full to the elbow where it gathers to fit the tight lower portion of the sleeve which closes with a row of small buttons. The man emerging from the well wears a jacket with a full sleeve gathered to fit the armscye then narrowing gradually to the wrist. The standing figure wears the huke-like jacket over a green doublet. His flat, round hat is typical of the period as are the hair styles of all of the men. (*Photograph courtesy of Edizione Alinari.*)

ceremonial robes—usually full-length gowns, worn by state officials and lawyers, and worn over doublet and hose and jacket as a third, outermost layer, often with the aforementioned hanging sleeves.

outdoor garments—Open and closed capes, varying in length as the jacket varied, but always covering the jacket completely. Often trimmed in fur or lined in contrasting colors. (See Figure 8.4.)

hair and head dress—For younger men hair cut in medium to longer lengths tapering gradually from below the ears in front to about the shoulders in the back, often curly. Older men cut their hair shorter. Men were generally clean-shaven. A variety of hat styles including turban-like styles, brimless "pillbox" styles, high toques either soft or rigid, hats with soft crowns and upturned brims or round crowns and narrow brims.

footwear—pointed toes begin to round off at the front toward the end of the century. Leather-soled, footed hose by far the most popular footwear for men. When worn, shoes fitted closely, were cut high across the instep, and below the anklebone.

> **boots**—for out-of-doors in bad weather or for riding usually had a turned-down cuff and ended at mid-calf.

COSTUME FOR WOMEN

The most usual combination of garments for women during the Italian Renaissance was a chemise (*camicia*) under a dress or gown (these were called by different names at different times), and an overdress, however there are also a number of examples of women's dress in which only the chemise and an outerdress are worn.

Item / Description

camicia—made of linen, the quality varying with the status of the wearer. *Cut:* full-length, the fullness related to the weight of the fabric; the sheerer the fabric the fuller the cut. *Sleeves* generally long, some cut in raglan style (i.e., seams running from below the arm at front and back to the neck rather than being set into the armhole.) In the last part of the century, large sections of the neckline of the camicia were displayed at the neckline of gowns and fine embroidery, bindings, smocking, or edgings were added. (See Figure 8.9.)

NOTE: Although the camicia was an undergarment, peasant women are shown in some paintings wearing camicie to work in the fields and apparently during hot weather the garment was worn alone by women in the privacy of their own quarters.

dresses—The garment worn over the camicia was generally either:

· one piece from shoulder to hem, cut similarly to men's jacket styles in which a smooth-fitting, yoke-like construction over the shoulder enlarged into full pleats or gathers over the bustline. These full gowns were generally belted.

· two piece, with bodice joined to a full gathered or pleated skirt. These dresses usually closed by lacing up the front and sometimes also at the side. Their *necklines* varied:

· at mid-century necklines were usually rounded but cut relatively high.

· toward the end of the century, necklines were lower, some more square than round, or with deep V's held together by lacing that showed-off the upper part of the chemise.

two-layered dresses—underdresses usually cut with bodice and skirt joined, a fairly close fit, and visible at the neckline, sleeves and/or under the arm of the outer dress. Outerdresses often cut like the man's huke, i.e. sleeveless, seamed at the shoulders, and open under the arm to display the underdress. (See Figure 8.5.)

sleeves—similar to those described for men: two-piece with full, puff-like construction at the top; or closely-fitted with openings to display the sleeves of the camicia; some hanging sleeves.

NOTE: Lavish use of opulent fabrics for the dress of upper class women gave garments of relatively straight cut a splendid appearance. By carefully manipulating the layers of camicia, dress, and overdress and choosing contrasting fabrics for each layer, rich decorative effects were achieved.

outdoor garments—Open and closed mantles or capes, often lined in contrasting fabric and sometimes matching the dresses with which they were worn. A purely decorative cape, fastening to the dress at the shoulder but not covering the shoulder or upper arms, and extending into a long train at the back was also used.

hair and head dress—A major distinction is seen between Italian hair dressing and that of Northern Europe: while Northern European women covered the hair, Italian women dressed the hair elaborately, wearing a "token" head cover in the form of a small jeweled net set at the back of the head or a sheer, small veil. (See Figure 8.6.) Young girls dressed hair simply, curled into long tresses. Women arranged a loose, curling tress on either side of the face and pulled the rest into a bun or a long braid or made more elaborate

8.4 Saint Anthony distributing his wealth to the poor, painted by Sassetta, second quarter of the 15th century. This painting contrasts the ragged, torn clothing of the poor, dressed in long gowns with the fashionable, fur-trimmed costume of the Saint. Children are dressed as the adults, except that the skirt of the boy's garment is short. (*Photograph courtesy of the National Gallery of Art, Samuel H. Kress Collection, 1952.*)

8.5 Domestic scene following the birth of a child shows women dressed in a variety of costumes. To the far right are two women, one an older woman in a simple dress and mantle with a white veil over her head. To her left a fashionable matron in a brocade outer gown worn over a gold gown which can be seen at the neckline and at the end of the sleeves of the outer gown. The third figure to the left, a young woman, wears a fashionable under gown of blue brocade with red flowers. At the elbow of the sleeve and down the lower part of the arm her *camicia* is visible through the slits in the sleeve. Her sleeveless outer gown is of pink brocade and open at the sides. She carries a handkerchief. Her hair, which is uncovered, is of the fashionable blond shade. Other women in the room all wear two-layered gowns except for the mother whose *camicia* is visible at the neckline of her simple blue gown. The dress of the wet nurse, seated at the center, opens down the front so she can suckle the baby. The laces which close the dress of the seated figure at far left are visible under the arm. She, too, wears a split sleeve with her *camicia* bloused through below the elbow. Her mantle, the lining of which matches the sleeves of her under gown, has slipped off her shoulders and fallen to the ground. She wears a small, sheer cap denoting her status as a young matron. (*Photograph courtesy of Edizione Alinari.*)

8.6 *Portrait of Bianca Maria Sforza,* painted about 1493 by Ambrogio de Predis. The jeweled haircovering reveals more of the hair than was customary in Northern Europe. Puffed areas of a white *camicia* show through the openings where the sleeve and the bodice lace together and at the back where the two sides of the close-fitting sleeve are laced together. A fine black line running from behind the neck to under the neckline probably marks the edge of the sheer fabric of the *camicia* which is so fine that it seems to be transparent. (*Courtesy of the National Gallery of Art, Washington, D.C., the Widener Collection.*)

arrangements that combined braids, loops of hair, and curls.

footwear—rarely seen in paintings, but appear to have been cut along the same lines as those of men.

jewelry—Highly skilled jewelers created masterpieces from precious stones, pearls, gold and silver, making necklaces, earrings, brooches, interesting hair ornaments. One of the latter that became especially popular was a chain of metal or pearls worn across the forehead with a jeweled decoration located over the center of the forehead. This chain was called a *ferrioniere.*

REGIONAL DISTINCTIONS

Basic clothing forms (i.e., layers worn, construction techniques, etc.) similar but clearest and most distinctive differences are evident between costumes of Venice and those of other parts of Italy, particularly those of areas under Florentine influence.

Venetian dress for women—Waistline located just below bustline, producing a softer line. Fabrics utilized appear to have been less heavy and rigid, also.

for men—Waistline located at anatomical waist or slightly below at back, v-shaped in front. Long outer tunics were favored over jackets, although jackets were also worn.

for officials—The *Doge,* the highest official in Venice, together with an hereditary ruling class of nobles wore costume long-established: long robes with wide sleeves; the wider the sleeve, the more important the rank. Colors varied according to rank and office. The Doge's head dress was worn over a coif and had something of the shape of a Phrygian bonnet, the point at the back stiffened and rigid. (See Figure 8.7.)

NOTE: These costumes were not given up by Venetian nobility until the 18th century.

Italian Costume 16th Century

The distinctiveness of Italian costume persisted until about mid-way through the 16th century, after which, except for Venice, styles became subject to Spanish and French influences as a result of the occupation of large areas of Italy by these two powers. Venice remained independent, and Venetians continued to wear styles that had some unique qualities.

8.7 Costume of the Doge of Venice. Drawing was made in the 16th century, but the style of the garments is of much earlier origin. (*Reproduced from* Vecellio's Renaissance Costume Book, *first published in 1598 and reprinted by Dover Publications, Inc., 1977.*)

8.8 *Portrait of Ludovico Capponi* by Agnolo Bronzino, middle of the 16th century. A row of buttons closes the closely-fitted black jacket. The jacket sleeves end just below the shoulder, so that the slashed sleeves of the doublet are visible. At the wrists and around the neck the edges of the *camicia* are visible. A prominent *codpiece* is seen at the top of the paned trunkhose. (*Photograph courtesy of the Frick Collection.*)

COSTUME FOR MEN

Item / Description

camicia—White linen, necklines and cuffs often embroidered, especially with "black work," a black-on-white Spanish embroidery.

doublet—Close-fitting, sometimes worn without a jacket to create an extremely narrow silhouette, this style lasting only until shortly after the end of the first decade after which styles became fuller, though never so full as in France, England, or the German lands. Some had deep, square necklines to show off embroidered camicie. Decorative slashing, sometimes with puffs of contrasting fabric pulled through the slits, was more restrained than in other parts of Europe. (See Figure 8.8.)

hose—Attached to doublet had a distinct, usually padded, *codpiece*.

jackets—Some styles had short sleeves, ending just below the shoulder line, which allowed a contrast between the jacket and the sleeve of the doublet.

hair—Beards began to be worn again.

COSTUME FOR WOMEN

Item / Description

camicia—Sometimes cut high, to show above the gown neckline, sometimes just high enough to form a small border at the edge of the neckline. Often embroidered or otherwise decorated, and sometimes finished with a small neckline ruffle.

gowns—Grew wider and fuller.

necklines—tended to be square, wide and low.

sleeves—wider; often with a full, wide puff at the top, then more closely fitted from above the elbow to the wrist. Much decoration with puffs and slashes.

waistline—at first straight, but gradually adopting the Spanish-influenced V-shape in front. (See Figure 8.9.)

DISTINCTIVE VENETIAN STYLES

Item / Description

gowns—typically with a normal waistline in back, and dipping to a deep U-shape in front, especially toward the close of the century.

hair—Arranged in little, twin "horns" at the front. Although this style also appears in other parts of Europe, it seems to have been most extreme in Venice, as were shoes.

shoes—*Chopines*, a platform shoe worn throughout Italy and in Northern Europe.

NOTE: A Frenchman, Villemont, visiting Venice toward the close of the 16th century described the exaggerated forms of these styles worn by Venetian women: "They have their blonde hair for the most part hanging nicely and arranged at the forehead in the shape of two horns half a foot high, without any iron mounting or any other thing to hold them up, unless it were the charming braiding which they do themselves . . . They appear a foot taller than the men because they are mounted on patens of wood covered with leather, which are at least a foot high so that they are obliged to have a woman to aid them walk, and another to carry their train . . . But the Romans, Milanese, Neapolitans, Florentines, Ferrarans and other ladies of Italy are more modest, for their patens are not so high, and also they do not bare their breasts."[9]

CHILDREN'S CLOTHING

Once out of swaddling clothes, children's clothing was not distinctive from that of adults. The paintings of the Madonna and infant Jesus, which are numerous, confirm this. In some paintings the Christ child wears a camicia, in others a loose-fitting under tunic

9. quoted by H. K. Morse. *Elizabethan Pagentry.* New York: The Studio Publications, Inc., 1934, p. 19.

8.9 A young woman and her little boy by Agnolo Bronzino, first half of the 16th century. The woman's decoratively embroidered *camicia* extends well beyond the neckline of her red brocade dress, and the ends of the *camicia* sleeve can be seen at her wrist. The turban-like head dress was especially popular at this time. She carries a pair of gloves in her hand which at this period were often perfumed. (*Photograph courtesy of National Gallery of Art, Widener Collection, 1942.*)

and an over tunic. Boys of nursery years wear skirts, other boys wore doublets, jackets, and hose. Little girls wear dresses like those of older women. (See Figure 8.10.)

Summary

The styles in Italy during the last half of the 15th century differed markedly from styles in Northern Europe. The distinctions were evident in the cut of clothing and in the types of fabrics used. Elaborate brocades, attractive cut velvets, and other sumptuously decorated fabrics used in the clothing of the well-to-do were produced by Italian weavers. Paint-

8.10 Child in costume of the early 16th century. Compare this satin dress with the dress worn by the woman in Figure 8.9 in order to see how similar were the costumes of adults and children. The full, puffed sleeve at the shoulder joined to a section that fits the rest of the arm. The edge of her *camicia* is just barely visible around the square neck of the dress. Even the type of jewelry she wears is similar in its type and arrangement to that of the adult woman. (*Photograph courtesy of Photo Arts Company.*)

ers depicted the details of costume so clearly, that often even the type of fabric can be identified and the seams, layers, and closings of the costume are readily visible.

These costumes developed at a time when a new and independent spirit in the arts, literature, and philosophy was abroad in Italy. When Italy was overpowered by the Spanish, the French, and the Austrians in the 16th century, this period of innovation in dress ended. Foreign influences came to dominate the Italian city states. After 1500 fashions took on a more international cast. This was not only a result of the imposition of foreign rule on most parts of Italy, but also because of the increasing movement among peoples and the improvements in communications that took place throughout Europe in the 16th century.

Selected Readings

BOOKS CONTAINING ILLUSTRATIONS OF COSTUME OF THE PERIOD FROM ORIGINAL SOURCES

Baccheschi, E. *Bronzino.* Milano: Rizzoli Editore, 1973.

Bestetti, C. *Abbligliamento E Costume Nella Pittura Italiana-Renasciamento.* Rome: Carlo Bestetti, Edizone d' Arte, 1962.

Birbari, E. *Dress in Italian Painting, 1460–1500.* London: John Murray, 1975.

Christiansen, K. *Early Renaissance Narrative Painting in Italy.* New York: Metropolitan Museum Bulletin, Vol. XLI, No. 2, 1983.

Hay, D. (Editor) *The Age of the Renaissance.* New York: McGraw Hill Book Company, 1967.

Herald, J. *Renaissance Dress in Italy, 1400–1500*. New York: Humanities Press, 1981.

Ketchum, et al. *The Horizon Book of the Renaissance*. New York: American Heritage Publishing Company, Inc., 1961.

Murray, P. and P. de Vecchi. *Complete Paintings of Piero Della Francesca*. New York: Harry N. Abrams, Inc., 1961.

Sidonia, E. *Pisanello*. New York: Harry N. Abrams, Inc., 1961.

Standen, E. A. *Italian Painting*. Greenwich, Conn.: New York Graphic Society, 1956.

Toesca, E. B. *Benozzo Gozzoli, Gli Affreschi della Capella Medicea*. (text in English). Milano: Silvana Editoriale de' Arte, 1969.

Venturi, L. *Italian Painting*. (Volumes 1 and 2). Geneva: Skira, 1950.

PERIODICAL ARTICLES

Deruisseau, L. G. "Extravagances in Renaissance Dress." *CIBA Review*, No. 2, p. 604.

Deruisseau, L. G. "Velvet and Silk in the Italian Renaissance." *CIBA Review*, No. 2, p. 595.

Newton, S. M. "Homage to a Poet." *Metropolitan Museum of Art Bulletin*. August/September, 1971, p. 33. (This article is an analysis of the costume in a painting by a Renaissance artist in order to determine whether the painting was done by a follower of the master Giorgione.)

DAILY LIFE

Alexander, S. *Lions and Foxes. Men and Ideas of the Italian Renaissance*. New York: Macmillan Publishing Company, 1974.

Chamberlin, E. R. *Everyday Life in Renaissance Times*. New York: G. P. Putnam's Sons, 1965.

Gage, J. *Life in Italy at the Time of the Medici*. New York: G. P. Putnam's Sons, 1968.

Lucas-Dubreton, J. *Daily Life in Florence at the Time of the Medici*. New York: Macmillan Publishing Company, 1967.

Mee, C. L. Jr. *Daily Life in Renaissance Italy*. New York: American Heritage Publishing Company, Inc., 1975.

Origo, I. *The Merchant of Prato*. New York: Alfred Knopf, 1957.

CHAPTER 9

The Northern Renaissance

c. 1500–1600

Historical Background

By the beginning of the 16th century, northern Europe had experienced a gradual transition to participation in the new spirit of the Renaissance. Along with these changes in arts and letters came profound changes in religious attitudes which culminated in a revolution against the Roman Catholic church. This revolution, the Protestant Reformation, had a major impact on the European nations and split Europe into two hostile religious camps. It began in the German states of the Holy Roman Empire.

At the beginning of the 16th century, the Hapsburg territories, the Low Countries, and Spain came under the rule of one man, the Emperor Charles V. From his grandparents he inherited a vast array of lands and claims. From his paternal grandfather, Emperor Maximilian, he inherited the Hapsburg lands, including Austria, and from his grandmother Mary the Bugundian lands, including the Low Countries. From his maternal grandparents, Ferdinand of Aragon and Isabella of Castile, he received Spain and the Spanish empire in America as well as the kingdoms of Sicily, Naples, and Sardinia. In 1519 after having inherited all of these lands and kingdoms, Charles V was elected Holy Roman Em-

peror and thus gained imperial rights over all of Germany and northern Italy. At the age of nineteen, he ruled over a larger territory than any ruler had ever attempted to govern.

Obviously so vast a territory made up of such a variety of peoples and lacking geographical unity would be difficult to rule effectively. Moreover, the extent of Charles's empire meant that he would be continually involved in wars with rival monarchs who feared Hapsburg domination of Europe. Eventually Charles found his burden so heavy that in 1556 he abdicated, dividing his territories between his brother Ferdinand, who received Austria and the Holy Roman Empire, and his son Philip, who inherited Spain, the Low Countries and the New World.

DEVELOPMENTS IN GERMANY AND AUSTRIA

German artists, rejecting the Gothic style of the Medieval period, adopted the new Renaissance forms. Scholars turned toward an interest in science, philosophy, and morality. However, the artistic and intellectual ferment of the Renaissance in Germany coincided with an increasing dissatisfaction on the part of many people with certain practices within the Roman Catholic Church which culminated in the Protestant Reformation.

Among the major causes of the Reformation in Germany were Papal financial abuses (profiting financially from religion); corruption and moral laxity among some of the clergy and religious orders; the secular spirit of the Renaissance; dissatisfaction with medieval Catholic theology growing out of the study of the Bible from the original sources; and a growing nationalism which rejected the political influence of the Papacy. The printing press played a major role in the Reformation because it became easier to publish and disseminate the arguments of the reformers, including the first translation of the New Testament into German.

The translator was Martin Luther (1483–1546), a priest and university professor, who became the spokesman and theorist for the dissenters. Luther would not have succeeded without the support of local political leaders who saw in religious dissent an opportunity to break away from the control of Charles V, who was Catholic. The leaders also recognized the opportunity to confiscate the great wealth of the Christian church in Germany. Luther's argument with the Church began in 1517; it soon spread throughout much of Europe. And with it, often enough, came war and revolution.

SPAIN

Areas of Spain, which had been under control of the Moors from northern Africa until late into the 15th century, were finally united in the late 1400's under Ferdinand and Isabella. (She is famous to Americans as the patroness of Columbus's voyage to the New World.) Charles V had inherited the Spanish throne in 1506.

As a result of its exploitation of the American territories which Spanish explorers had conquered, Spain became incredibly wealthy, thanks to the influx of gold and silver from Mexico and Peru. Because Charles V had political interests in so much of Europe and with the wealth acquired through trade in goods from the Americas, Spain dominated Europe. The 16th century could well be called "The Golden Age of Spain." But the wealth proved a curse. There was so much gold that Spain suffered inflation, and the gold was spent on the expensive foreign wars of Charles V. When the wealth was exhausted, there was nothing left for the Spanish people.

Charles was a devout Catholic, and Spain the most orthodox nation in Europe. Consequently the Reformation had little effect on Spain. Nevertheless

it prevented Charles from maintaining control over the Holy Roman Empire and preserving the unity of the Christian faith in Europe. The strain of attempting to maintain the empire, led Charles V to abdicate the throne of Spain and the Low Countries in favor of his son, Phillip II. A fervent Catholic, who bore proudly the traditional title of the Spanish monarch, "The Most Catholic King," Philip II antagonized the seventeen prosperous provinces that made up the Low Countries by levying high taxes, by the appointment of haughty Spanish administrators. Moreover, he stationed Spanish troops among them, and attempted to repress Protestantism which had made deep inroads among the people of the Low Countries. In 1568 revolution had broken out, and by the end of the century, Philip had lost the seven northern provinces who formed the Dutch Republic or Holland. Again Phillip failed in 1588 when he dispatched the ill-fated Armada of 130 ships to conquer England and restore the land to the Roman Catholic faith. His intervention in the French religious wars also failed. The increasing decline in Spanish political influence helped to contribute to the end of the "Golden Age" of Spain.

ENGLAND

The 16th century in England was divided between the great Tudor monarchs Henry VIII (1509–1547) and his daughter, Elizabeth I (1558–1603). Henry broke with the church of Rome over the Pope's refusal to permit him to divorce his Spanish Queen Catherine of Aragon to whom he had been married for eighteen years. Henry had sought the divorce in order that he might remarry and father a male heir to preserve the Tudor line because Henry and Catherine had only one sickly, daughter, Mary. As a result, Henry established a national church of England, independent of Rome, but he maintained the basic beliefs of the Roman Catholic faith. During his son's reign, Edward VI (1547–1553), England became Protestant. Mary Tudor (1553–1558) tried and failed to restore England to the church of Rome.

Henry's reign saw the climax of the Gothic style in England and the beginning of the English Renaissance. During the Elizabethan era England enjoyed a literary Renaissance chiefly in dramatic poetry. Edmund Spenser's great epic poem, *Faerie Queene*, filled with national feeling, praised Elizabeth. English theater was born in the Renaissance thanks to dramatists which included William Shakespeare, Christopher Marlowe, and Ben Jonson. Shakespeare surpassed his contemporaries with the vast range of his plays—comedies, lyrical dramas, histories, profound tragedies—and filled them with characters that became immortal. Elizabethan music profited from the genius of Thomas Tallis and William Byrd.

Both Henry and Elizabeth brought painters and sculptors to England from other parts of Europe to decorate their palaces. Elizabeth, who was well educated and enjoyed reading Latin verse, patronized the arts, and music and literary productions were also stimulated as a result.

FRANCE

During the first half of the 16th century, the French Renaissance in the arts began under the monarch Francis I (1495–1542). From Italy he brought artists and artisans—including Leonardo da Vinci and Benvenuto Cellini—to the French court to work. His son, Henry II married an Italian, Catherine de Medici, who brought her Italian tailors and dressmakers, perfumers, cooks, and other craftsmen to France where they found ample opportunity to employ their talents. The French perfume industry is said to have been started by Catherine's Italian perfumers.

After her husband's sudden death in 1559, and the death of her son Francis II, in 1560, Catherine became the regent for her weak son, Charles IX, remaining the power behind the throne until 1589. In the reign of Charles IX, France was wracked by religious civil war as powerful Protestant and Catholic noble families struggled for political control. Catherine helped create a climate of revolt and political dissension for most of the rest of the century by throwing the royal support behind the Catholic faction.

The accession of the Protestant Bourbon Henry IV (1589–1610) brought an end to religious persecution of the French Protestants. To appease the Roman Catholics who were in the majority, Henry IV converted to Roman Catholicism and settled the religious problem by issuing the Edict of Nantes guaranteeing freedom of conscience and full political rights to all Protestants. In the economic sphere, Henry encouraged French industry, and the cloth industries especially benefited. French linen rivaled that of Holland and her silk weaving industry challenged what had formerly been an Italian monopoly on the manufacture of silk.

ROYAL WEDDINGS

One of the factors in the spread of fashion information from one part of Europe to another was the intermarriage of the royal families from different countries. These marriages were usually arranged to cement alliances between two powers, and the brides were sent from their own countries to their new homes, equipped not only with a substantial dowry, but also a trousseau of the latest fashions and accompanied by a group of fashionably-gowned ladies-in-waiting.

The following chart of intermarriages between royal families during the 1600's will illustrate the cross-influences of styles that accompanied such weddings.

The intermarriage of members of royal families from one country with those of another was only one of the ways that fashion information could be spread from one locality to another. Other sources of fashion information included imported fabrics and garments, books dealing with costume, and travelers who brought back information about and examples of foreign styles. Peasants tended to use regional rather than fashionable dress, but among the upper classes a more or less internationalization of styles occurred in which the predominant silhouettes and features had substantial similarities. At the same time, distinctive local styles often traveled abroad, as this 16th century poem attests:

Behold a most accomplished cavalier,
That the world's ape of Fashion doth appear.
Walking the streets his humours to disclose,
In the *French* doublet and the *German* hose,
The muff, cloak, *Spanish* hat, *Toledo* blade,
Italian ruff, a shoe right *Flemish* made.[1]

DECORATIVE TECHNIQUES

The 16th century brought new techniques for decorating fabrics into style. Embroidered decorations were applied not only to outer garments, but also to visible neck and sleeve edges of undergarments such as shirts and chemises. Spanish work, an especially fashionable embroidery, originated in Spain and spread throughout the rest of Europe. This embroidery consisted of delicate black silk figures worked on fine, white linen, often being applied to the neckband and wrists of men's shirts and women's chemises. (See Figures 9.1 and 9.10.)

A variety of Italian drawn and cut-work techniques were also employed. Threads were removed from the fabric and embroidery applied to the now-open areas. Cutwork was created by embroidering designs on solid cloth, then cutting away sections of the cloth between the decorations. In another

1. Quoted in E. R. Chamberlin. *Everyday Life in Renaissance Times.* New York: G. P. Putnam's Sons, New York, 1969, p. 54.

England and Scotland	France	Spain	Austria Germany	Italy
Henry VIII		Katherine of Aragon		
Henry VIII			Ann of Cleves	
	Henry II			Catherine de Medici
Mary, Queen of Scots	Francis II			
Mary I (of England)		Philip II		
	Henry IV			Marie de Medici

9.1 Woman's chemise from the late 16th century, probably from Venice. The white linen garment is embroidered with lavender floss silk and gold thread. Notice that the placement of embroidered designs on this chemise is similar to those on the neck and sleeves of the chemise in Figure 9.10. (*Photograph courtesy of the Metropolitan Museum of Art, gift of Mrs. Edwin O. Holtzer, 1941.*)

decorative technique called *filet* or *lacis* the artisan embroidered patterns on a net background. Both cutwork and filet are considered to have been forerunners of lace.

Lace-making probably began in Europe just before the beginning of the 16th century. Lace differs from either cut-work or filet in that it is constructed entirely from threads, dispensing with any backing fabric. Two types of lace were made: needlepoint lace, which seems to have originated in Italy, and bobbin lace, which may have originated in the Low Countries. Needlepoint lace is made by embroidering over base threads arranged in a pattern, and connecting these base threads with a series of small intricate stitches. Bobbin lace (also called pillow lace) was made by twisting or knotting together a series of threads held on bobbins into a complex pattern. These laces could be made of any fine thread—linen or silk or cotton. During the last half of the 16th Century the use of lace to decorate garments of both men and women was almost universal. (See Figures 9.3, 9.12 and 9.15.)

16th Century Costume

Costume of men and women in the 16th century can be said to have gone through three different phases in which styles differed quite markedly from the preceding phase. The general dates of these phases, however, are not the same for styles of women and men. Moreover, styles of accessory items and underclothing did not necessarily vary in the same way as the overall silhouette. For these reasons the summary of details of costume in this chapter is organized as follows: costume for each different phase will be discussed first for men, then for women, and finally a century-long overview will be given of accessory items for men and women.

COSTUME FOR MEN

The three phases seen in men's styles might be described as consisting of an early phase in which a transition was made from Medieval styles to the styles of the Renaissance; a second phase concentrated in the second to the fourth decades of the century in which marked German influence can be seen; and a final phase in which Spanish influences were strong.

Throughout the century men wore an evolved form of the earlier braies, which the English tended to refer to as *drawers*.

1500–1515

Item / Description

shirts—made of white linen, cut full, having long, raglan sleeves, and gathered into a round or square neckline, that neckline often being decorated with embroidery or cutwork. (See Figure 9.16.)

doublet and hose—laced together, the doublet being only waist-length. Hose seamed into one garment with a codpiece at the front. In one version the doublet (also called a *paltock* in England) was cut with a deep V at the front, which sometimes had a filler (or *stomacher*) of contrasting color inserted under the V. (See Figure 9.2.) Laces held the open area together and also held the sleeves in place. As in the Italian style, the sleeve of the shirt was bloused through openings in the sleeves.

9.2 *Lady with Three Suitors*, France, c. 1500. The two more visible suitors wear, respectively, a short, skirted jacket with wide lapels, and a long robe. Both dress their hair in the predominant straight-cut style and wear French bonnets. Their shoes have broad, rounded toes. The lady wears a wide-sleeved gown with a typically square-cut neckline. Her head dress is a *coif* with lappets hanging down on either side of the face. (*Photograph courtesy of the Cleveland Museum of Art.*)

jacket or jerkin—Sometimes worn over a doublet; cut the same length as the doublet; similar in shaping; and made with or without sleeves. Often it is difficult to make out from period illustrations whether men are wearing doublets or jackets as the outermost garment.

bases—separate, short skirts worn with a jacket or doublet for civil dress; over armor for military dress. Made from a series of lined and stiffened gores (wedge-shaped pieces), bases persisted in civilian dress until well into the mid-century, and over armor for even longer. (See Figure 9.2.)

NOTE: the metal skirts of some suits of armor are made to simulate bases.

robes or gowns—Long, full garments with huge funnel-shaped or large hanging sleeves. Gowns opened down the front, the front facings were made of contrasting fabric or fur and turned back to form wide, decorative revers. Younger and more fashionable men wore shorter gowns, ending below the hips. Gowns were worn over doublets or jackets. (See Figure 9.2.)

NOTE: This garment seems to have been distinctively Northern European and had no counterpart in Italian styles.

other outdoor garments—Circular cloaks, open at the front and with a slit up the back to facilitate horseback riding—worn over doublet and hose.

1515–1550

Whereas the earlier styles had relatively slender silhouettes, the second phase emphasized fullness in the construction of the costume with large, bulky, puffed areas; ornamented with decorative slashings or panes (narrow strips of fabric) under which contrasting linings were placed.

NOTE: A story is told of the origins of these slashes. A ragged but victorious Swiss army was said to have stuffed the colorful silk fabrics they had looted from the enemy camp under their badly torn clothes for warmth. This impromptu fashion was supposedly picked up and imitated by the general population. Whether the style actually had its origin in this way or not, it is true that the Swiss and German soldiers' uniforms were made with multi-colored fabrics decorated with a variety of cuts and slashes, panings, and layers. These same features were evident in men's costume almost everywhere, although German influences were more muted in Italy. (See Figure 9.3.)

9.3 The *Landsknect* (*opposite page*) and the *Lady Holding Pansies* (*left*) by Lucas Cranach, early 16th century. The knight on the left wears the decoratively-slashed costume of the German soldier. His hat is an exaggeration by the artist of the military head dress of the period. The lady wears typical German dress with sleeves made in alternately wider and narrower sections and having an extended V-shaped cuff that covers the back of the hand. Her head dress is also a fanciful exaggeration by the artist. (*Photograph courtesy of the Metropolitan Museum of Art, Harris Brisbane Dick Fund, 1926.*)

Item / Description

shirts, doublets, jackets—Continued much as before, with marked increases in aforementioned slashed decoration.

bases—Instead of separate bases, some doublets and jackets were cut with gored skirts; some having no sleeves; some with wide U or V-shaped necklines. Beneath the wide neck, the jacket and part of the skirt is often visible. Bases were still worn with armor. Sleeves of jackets or doublets, whichever was outermost, were cut very full often with a puff from armhole to elbow and a closer fit from elbow to wrist. (See Figure 9.4.)

hose—Laced to doublets. Some were divided into two sections, *upper stocks* and *nether stocks*, which were sewn together. (See Figure 9.3.) *Codpiece*, the pouch of fabric for the genitals sewn at the front of the upper stocks, was sometimes padded for emphasis. (See Figures 9.3 and 9.7.) Although upper stocks and nether stocks remained attached, upper stocks (also called breeches) took on the appearance of a separate garment, and were cut somewhat fuller than the lower section. *Variations:* long, fitting the leg closely and ending at the knee; or ending at the hip and more rounded. All types were often paned, with contrasting fabric beneath.

robes or gowns—Slight alterations in cut and trimming made for increased width. The wide revers extended into a wide collar and these sleeve types developed:
  · sleeveless but with wide, over-long armholes lined in contrasting fabric and turned back upon themselves to show off the lining.
  · short, very full, puffed-and-slashed or paned sleeves. (See Figure 9.4.)
  · long hanging sleeves.

1550–1600

By mid-century the width had narrowed somewhat and during the remainder of the century one can see gradual decreases in the width of the shoulders

9.4 In this miniature of 1520, François I of France and his courtiers wear skirted jackets cut with differing necklines, short robes, wide duck-billed shoes, and a variety of plumed hats. (*Photograph courtesy of the Morgan Library.*)

and gradual increases in the width of the hip area. By the beginning of the third phase a new combination of garments had evolved, and men no longer appeared in short jackets or long-skirted jackets and hose. Instead the upper hose and nether hose had evolved into a large, padded breech (called *trunk hose*) which was joined to nether or lower stocks. (See Figure 9.7.) Alternatively, separate breeches were worn with hose kept in place by garters. The codpiece gradually went out of style after mid-century.

Item / Description

shirts—*collars, ruffs:* around mid-century men displayed the small, square collar of the shirt at the neck edge of the doublet. Next the collar of the shirt became a small ruffle, and in the final

stage of evolution the ruff developed as a separate item of costume, separate from the shirt. Very wide, often of lace, and stiffly starched, the ruff became one of the most characteristic features of costume during the second half of the 16th century and persisted into the first decades of the 17th century as well. (See Figures 9.7 and 9.8.)

doublet—The neck was cut high; its shape and finish varied. Doublets were made with a row of small, square flaps called *pecadils* just below the waist. (See Figure 9.7.) Sleeves, though padded, followed the shape of the arm and narrowed as the century progressed until by 1600 sleeves were unpadded and closely fitted. Waistlines followed the natural waist at the back, but dipped to a point at the front, where padding emphasized the shape. By 1570 the padding increased in quantity and the point of the doublet became so pronounced that it was called a *peascod belly* as it resembled the puffed-out chest of a peacock. (See Figures 9.5 and 9.7.)

jacket or jerkin—Worn over the doublet; similar in shaping, but as it usually had short puffed sleeves or pecadils at the arm and no sleeve, the sleeve of the doublet beneath became the outermost sleeve.

breeches—Separate garments worn with stockings. Often called *Venetians*, the styles varied from skin-tight versions, those wide at the top and tapering to the knee; and those wide and full throughout. (See Figure 9.6.)

trunk-hose—Made in several shapes:
· melon-shaped; usually paned, heavily padded and ending at the hip or somewhat below; approximately the shape of a pumpkin. (See Figure 9.7.)
· sloping gradually from a narrow waist to fullness concentrated about mid-thigh where they ended. (See Figure 9.6.)
· a short section, not much more than a pad around the hips, worn with very tight-fitting hose. This form had limited use outside of very fashionable court circles. (See Figure 9.5.)

NOTE: Doublets, to a lesser extent, and trunk hose were heavily padded with *bombast*, a stuffing made of wool, horsehair, short linen fibers called

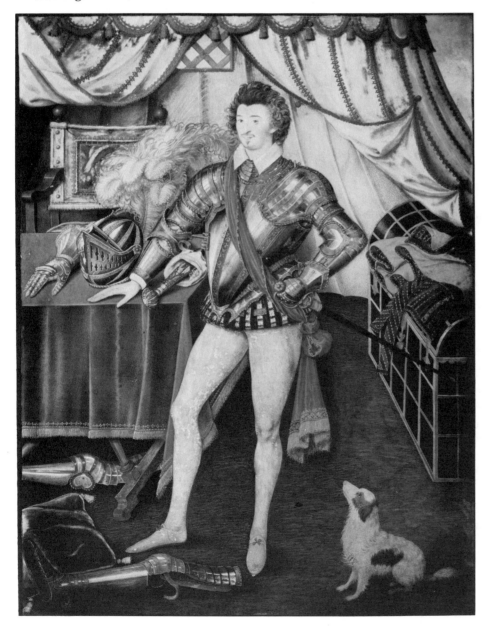

9.5 *Sir Anthony Mildmay* by Nicholas Hilliard. English, second half of the 16th century. The shaping of armor took on the peascod belly shape. Padded jackets worn underneath the plate armor helped to protect the body. Other elements of armor are shown scattered around the room. Sir Anthony wears trunk hose, the upper section of which is barely more than a pad around the waist. (*Photograph courtesy of the Cleveland Museum of Art, J. H. Wade Collection.*)

9.6 Close-up photograph of slashed satin breeches of about 1600 shows the way in which this garment was constructed. (*Photograph courtesy of the Victoria and Albert Museum.*)

tow, or bran. Excessive use of bombast led one chronicler to suggest that a man was carrying the whole contents of his bed and his table linen as stuffing in his trunk-hose, and it was said that the English parliament house had to be enlarged to accommodate the bulky trunks of the members.[2]

canions—an extension from the end of the trunk hose to the knee or slightly below; either made in the same color or a contrasting color to trunk-hose, canions were fastened to separate stockings at the bottom. (See Figure 9.8.)

hose and stockings—With trunk hose and canions, stockings were more used than the long, joined hose. Stockings and hose were either cut and sewn or knitted. References to knitting begin to appear around 1530 and in 1589 an English inventor made a machine for knitting stockings.

outdoor garments—Gowns were largely replaced by shorter and longer capes after the middle of the century. Short capes were cut very full, flaring out sharply from the shoulder. (See Figure 9.8.)

COSTUME FOR WOMEN

Before commencing a summary of costumes for women in the 16th century, a few comments should be made about changes in the function of undergarments, changes which had their beginnings in previous centuries, but which became especially obvious during the 1500's.

2. H. Wescher. "Dress and Fashion at the Court of Queen Elizabeth." *CIBA Review*, No. 78, p. 2846.

9.7 *Prince Hercule-François*, Duc d'Alençon, 1572. The Duke wears wide, somewhat melon-shaped, paned trunkhose. His jacket with its high collar surrounded by a small ruff has the fashionable *peascod* belly shape, and finishes below the waistline in a row of *pecadils*. His hat is in the *capotain* shape, decorated with a jeweled band and a plume. The short cape is fur-lined. (*Photograph courtesy of the National Gallery of Art, Samuel H. Kress Collection, 1961.*)

During the Medieval and Classical periods, undergarments helped provide warmth and both protected the skin from the garments worn above them and the clothing from being soiled by perspiration. Just when undergarments took on the function of shaping the body is not entirely clear. Ewing sees the forerunner of the corset in the tightly-laced cote of the Medieval Period and cites evidence of a linen

9.8 Group of gentlemen, second half of the 16th century. These gentlemen of the court of Queen Elizabeth I of England wear trunkhose with *canions*. Both ruffs and a square collar are visible. Short, round capes are decorated with braid and several appear to have contrasting linings. (*Photograph of illustration from Stubbes,* Anatomy of Abuses, *Queens College Library.*)

under-bodice made from two layers of fabric stiffened with glue. By the 17th century this garment, had taken on the name *stays* in English. Earlier it had been known as "a pair of bodys" as it was cut into two sections and fastened at the front and back with laces or tapes. This garment appears not only as an undergarment, but occasionally as an outer garment as well.[3]

A few examples of steel or iron "corsets" dating from the 16th century can be found in museums. These are regarded as either orthopedic garments or later, fanciful reconstructions. There is no evidence that these iron corsets were worn as fashionable dress. The stays that were worn seem to have followed the pattern described above: made of cloth,

3. E. Ewing. *Dress and Undress.* New York: Drama Books, 1981, p. 21 ff.

shaped as an under-bodice and laced together at front, back, or both. The stiffening was provided by a *busk*, a new device made from a flat, long piece of wood or whalebone that was sewn into a casing (or casings) provided in the stays.

Yet another function of undergarments, the shaping and support of the outergarment, is a particularly important element in women's clothing of the 1500's. Beginning with the *verdugale*, continuing with the "bum roll" and culminating in the huge *wheel farthingale*, undergarments henceforth are important elements in the shape of Western costume.

1500–1530

This first phase was a transition from the styles of the Medieval period. Gowns were fairly plain, somber colors predominated. Bodices were fitted, skirts long and full, flaring gently from the waistline to the floor in the front and trailing into long trains at the back. (See Figure 9.2.)

Item / Description

chemise—Undermost garment, worn beneath one or two over-dresses.

dresses—When two were worn, the underdress was closely fitted and the outermost had large, full, funnel-shaped sleeves. The skirt might be looped up in front to display the contrasting skirt of the under layer. Trained outer gowns often were made with a decorative underlining for the train which was buttoned or pinned to the waist at the back in order to show the lining fabric.
  necklines—usually square, with the edge of the chemise visible or cut with smaller or larger V-shaped openings at front or both front and back. Lacings held the V-together.
  sleeves—smooth-fitting narrow sleeves with decorative cuffs; wide, funnel shapes with contrasting linings; hanging sleeves.

outdoor garments—except for ceremonial occasions when the open mantle fastening with a chain or braid at the front was still worn, women wore long, full cloaks.

1530–1575

This second phase of costume for women was marked by Spanish influence, whereas men's styles of this period were more directly influenced by German styles until the second half of the century when Spanish influence was evident in men's clothing.

One important aspect of the Spanish influence was in a tendency to emphasize dark colors, especially black. German women's styles of this period are quite distinctive, and easily differentiated from those of French, Spanish, and English women. The following is a brief summary of the major features of German women's dress in the first half of the 16th century. (See Figure 9.3.)

GERMAN WOMEN'S COSTUME

Item / Description

bodice—closely fitted; necklines low and square or rounded. The neckline was usually filled in, probably by the chemise. Across the bosom bodices were often elaborately decorated or embroidered.

sleeves—close-fitting, with tight horizontal bands alternating with somewhat enlarged, puffed areas. The cuff extended into a point beneath the wrist. (This sleeve style does enter international fashion.)

skirt—softly gathered to the bodice.

hair—often held in a net, over which was placed a wide-brimmed hat trimmed with plumes.

OTHER NORTHERN EUROPEAN WOMEN'S STYLES

Changes, which represent a gradual evolution in style not a sudden radical change, were these (See Figure 9.9.):

silhouette—Rather like an hourglass, the bodice narrowing to a small waistline then a gradually-expanding cone-shaped skirt.

    bodice—narrowed and flattened, becoming quite rigid. The waist dipped to an elongated V at the front. A rich, jeweled belt outlined the waistline and at the V in front its long end fell down the center front of the costume almost to the floor.

    skirt—also more rigid, with many dresses untrained and ending at the floor all around.

    construction—Significant changes took place. Instead of an underdress and an outer dress women wore a petticoat and an over dress.

    • *petticoat*—cut from rich, decorative fabric (often brocade or cut-velvet). Apparently only the front of the skirt was made in expensive fabric, while the invisible back was made of lighter weight, less expensive fabric.

9.9 Dress in the style that developed after the third decade of the 16th century. The ruffled cuff of the chemise is visible at the end of the sleeve. Large, detachable undersleeves match the fabric of the petticoat. The flared skirt was supported underneath by a hoop called a *verdugale* or Spanish *farthingale*. The painting by an unknown artist is of Queen Elizabeth I as a princess. (*Photograph provided and printed by the gracious permission of Her Majesty the Queen Elizabeth II. Copyright reserved.*)

    • *dress*—made with bodice and skirt sewn together, the skirt having an inverted V-shaped opening in front through which the front of the petticoat was visible. (See Figure 9.9.)

neckline—at first square, but later a variety of more closed styles including:

    • a high, closed neckline with a standing, wing collar

    • neck fillers, part of the chemise, were closed up to the throat and ended in a small ruffle.

    • ruffs, of moderate size at this phase of their development, worn with high, fitted collars.

sleeves—Many variations. The first changes in style came early in the period when German and Italian style sleeves were adopted. Subsequently the following styles developed:

· narrow at the shoulder and expanding to a huge, wide square cuff that turned back upon itself. Often made of fur or of heavy brocade to match the petticoat. A detachable, false sleeve decorated with panes and slashes through which the linen of the chemise was visible might be sewn to the underside of the cuff or, if the chemise were richly decorated, the sleeve of the chemise might be seen below the cuff. (See Figures 9.9 and 9.10.)

· made with a puff at the shoulder and a close-fitting, long extension of the sleeve to the wrist. Though worn elsewhere as well, this style was especially popular in France.

· full from shoulder to wrist where they were caught into a cuff.

· wider at the top, narrower at the bottom.

· some remarkably complex, especially those worn at the Spanish court, utilizing combinations of fitted, full, and hanging sleeves.

Sleeve decorations included cutting and paning with decorative fabrics, fastening the panes with *aiguillettes* (small, jeweled metal points.) Padded rolls of fabric were sometimes located at the joining of bodice and sleeve and these served to hide the laces fastening separate sleeves to bodices.

supporting garments—The flared, cone-shaped skirt required support to achieve the desired rigidity of line. Support was provided by a Spanish device called the *verdugale or Spanish farthingale,* a construction of hoops graduated in size from

9.10 *Portrait of a Young Lady,* Flemish, c. 1535. The elaborately embroidered chemise worn by the young lady shows clearly at the neck and below the sleeves of her gown. Her sleeves, fitted at the shoulder, widen at the bottom. The small *coif* is decorated with jewels. The hair is enclosed in a dark, possibly velvet, hood at the back. (*Photograph courtesy of the Metropolitan Museum of Art, the Jules S. Bache Collection, 1949.*)

the waist to the floor and sewn into a petticoat or underskirt.

NOTE: Formerly a visible part of the construction of traditional Spanish dress of the region of Catalonia, the hoops were at first sewn into the dress itself. English chroniclers report that Katharine of Aragon, the first wife of King Henry the Eighth, wore such a skirt in the early part of the century when she came to England from Spain, however at the time it was noted as a foreign and atypical style.

ropa—A Spanish style of outer gown or surcote made either sleeveless, with a short puffed sleeve, or with a long sleeve, puffed at the top and fitted for the rest of the arm's length. It fell from the shoulders, unbelted in an A-line to the floor. Some versions closed in front, but most were open to display the dress beneath. (See Figure 9.11.)

1575–1600

The first changes in the last quarter of the century came in the shape of the skirt. (See Figure 9.12.)

Item / Description

farthingale—Instead of the cone-shaped Spanish farthingale, a padded roll was placed around the waist in order to give skirts greater width below the waist. The English called these pads *bum rolls*, "bum" being English slang for buttocks. For better support of dresses than these rolls provided and to attain greater width, a modification of the farthingale was made. Instead of using graduated circles of whalebone, cane or steel sewn into a canvas skirt, the circles were the same diameter throughout. Steel or cane spokes fastened the topmost hoop to a waistband. It was called the *wheel, drum,* or *French farthingale.* (See Figures 9.12 and 9.14.)

NOTE: This style was not used in Italy or, to any great extent, in Spain at this period where the older, hour glass shape of the Spanish farthingale with a slightly padded roll at the waist predominated. It was essentially a Northern European style, however it was not the only style worn by these women who also continued to wear Spanish farthingales, dresses widened slightly at the waist with bum rolls, or small, wheeled farthingales.

dresses—Those worn over wheel farthingales had enormous skirts which were either cut and sewn into one continuous circle all around or open at the front or sides over a matching underskirt.

9.11 *Margaretta of Parma* (incorrectly titled) by Anthonis Mor, second half of the 16th century. This lady wears a Spanish-style, sleeveless *ropa*. Small ruffles, probably on her chemise, extend above the high collar and below the ends of her sleeves. Her *coif* dips slightly at the front. (*Photograph courtesy of the Philadelphia Museum of Art, John G. Johnson Collection.*)

A ruffle the width of the flat shelf-like section of the farthingale was sometimes attached to the skirt. To avoid having the body appear disproportionately short in contrast with the width of the skirt, sleeves were made fuller and with very high sleeve caps and the front of the bodice was elongated, ending in a deep V at the waist. A number of high standing collars were used, and the hair was dressed high on the head.

ruffs—these grew to enormous widths. Made of sheer linen or of lace they had to be supported by a frame called the *supportasse* (See Figure 9.13.) or by starching. Constructions included:
- gathering one edge of a band of fabric to the size of the neck to form a frill of deep folds.

9.12 (*Top*) *Portrait of a Young Lady* by Marcus Gheeraerts the Younger, c. 1600. The lady wears a wheel *farthingale*. The skirt of the *farthingale* opens at the front, but the petticoat beneath it is not visible. Around the waist is placed a ruffle the width of the *farthingale*. She wears a lace "Medici" ruff at the neck. Her hair is dressed high with jeweled decorations. (*Photograph courtesy of the Metropolitan Museum of Art, gift of Kate T. Davidson, in memory of her husband, Henry Pomeroy Davidson, 1951.*)

9.13 (*Bottom*) Drawing shows a ruff "underpropped with a *supportasse*," a frame which holds the ruff in place. (*Photograph of drawing from Phillip Stubbes,* Anatomy of Abuses, *Queens College Library Collection.*)

- round, flat lace pieces without depth or folds like a wide collar.
- several layers of lace rounds placed one over the other.
- open ruffs, almost a cross between a collar and a ruff, high behind the head and fastened in front into a wide, square neckline. (See Figures 9.13 and 9.14.)

NOTE: During the 18th and 19th centuries revivals of this style were called *Medici* collars after Catharine de Medici, Queen of France during the period that this style was popular.

conch—or in French, *conque*—was a sheer, gauze-like veil so fine that in some portraits it can just barely be seen, was cut the full length of the body from shoulder to floor and worn cape-like over the shoulders. At the back of the neck it was attached to a wing-like construction that stood up like a high collar behind the head. Some references consider the conch to have had some significance as a widow's costume, and this may be true in France however in England it seems to have been more widely worn by women, such as Queen Elizabeth, who were never widowed. (See Figure 9.14.)

COSTUME FOR MEN AND WOMEN

Item / Description

hair and head dress—*Women*—The custom of having married and adult women cover the hair continued. Among the variety of head coverings, these were the most important:

- *coif*—a cap of white linen or more decorative fabric, usually with long lappets or short square or pointed extensions below the ears that covered the side of the face. Coif shapes ranged from round to heart-shaped or "gabled," an English style shaped like a pointed arch. (See Figure 9.2.)

9.14 *Portrait of a Lady*, c. 1600, by an unknown British painter. Over a farthingale-style dress, the lady wears a sheer, pearl-edged *conch* which is the cape with wired projections standing behind her shoulders. On her head is a sheer head dress made of the same fabric and decorated with the same jewels. Her lace ruff is in the open style. In her right hand she holds a feathered fan. Her brocade dress is decorated with jeweled rosettes. (*Photograph courtesy of the Metropolitan Museum of Art, gift of J. Pierpont Morgan, 1911.*)

· over the coif, a long band about 40 inches long and 4 inches wide was pinned. The ends either hung down at either side of the face or were arranged in decorative folds.

· some bands had a hood of semi-circular fabric attached at the back.

As the century progressed, the coif was set further back on the head, allowing more hair to show. Decorative overcaps might be placed on top of the coif, some trimmed with jeweling or metallic netting. (See Figures 9.9, 9.10 and 9.11.) In the last two-thirds of the century with more hair visible, the hair was combed back from the forehead, puffed up slightly around the face, then pulled into a coil at the back of the head. Local differences arose: the French combed the hair up, over small pads on either side to form a heart-shaped frame for the face; the English imitated the hair color of the Queen, which was red, so that among ladies of the court red, auburn, and varying shades of blonde hair were fashionable. (Toward the end of her reign Queen Elizabeth's hair had become so thin that she generally wore a red wig.) With the wheeled farthingale, extra height was gained by dressing the hair high and decorating it with jeweled ornaments. (See Figures 9.12 and 9.14.)

Other hats popular toward the end of the century were generally small, with high crowns and narrow brims and trimmed with feathers; jeweled nets and caps were also worn.

Men—Hair dressing at the beginning of the century: cut straight across the back in a length anywhere from below the ears to the shoulder together with a fringe of bangs across the forehead. (See Figure 9.2.)

· *Hats*—a pill-box like shape with turned-up brim that might have decorative cut-out sections in the brim-sometimes referred to as a "French bonnet." (See Figure 9.2.)

· a skull cap or hair net holding the hair close to the head topped by a hat with a basin-shaped crown and wide brim, the brim turned up at one point. Many hats were decorated with feathers.

· *After 1530:* beards became fashionable, and the hair was cut short. (See Figure 9.4.) *Hats for this period:* a moderately-sized, flat crowned hat with a small brim and a feather plume; beret-like styles with feather plumes. (See Figure 9.4.)

· After mid-century hair grew longer again; beards and moustaches remained popular. (See Figures 9.6 and 9.8.) *Hat styles:* marked by increasingly high crowns; some with soft shapes but others with stiffer outlines. Brims tended to be narrow. The high-crowned, narrow-brimmed hat was called a *capotain* and this style remained popular until well into the 17th Century. (See Figure 9.5.) Trimmings for hats included feathers, braid, and jewels.

footwear—Shoes had square toes, the shape becoming more exaggerated as the period progressed, especially for men's shoes. By mid-century, when Mary the First was Queen of England, shoes had become so wide that a law was passed limiting the width to six inches. During the second half of the century toes remained square, but width decreased and shoes conformed more closely to the shape of the foot. Decoration included slashing with puffs of fabric pulled through the openings (first half of the century) or slashes with a contrasting lining underneath which showed when the foot was bent (second half of the century.) (See Figure 9.15.) Some types of shoes:

· *mules*—backless shoes.
· Shoes with a tongue, tying with laces (*latchets*) that crossed the tongue from either side.
· *for women*—a low-cut slipper with a strap across the ankle.
· *boots*—worn for riding.
· High-heeled shoes for men and women first appeared sometime during the 70's; the heels about one and a half inches high; sometimes ribbon rosettes might be placed at the front of the shoe or decorative stones set into them.
· *chopines*—high, platform-soled shoes originating in Italy, and spreading to other parts of Europe.

jewelry—lavishly used by royalty and the wealthy. Among the items of jewelry most often worn were:

· *neck ornaments*—for men, wide jeweled collars that were not a part of the garment but a separate circular piece made of ornamental plates joined together; for men and women, neck chains of gold or other precious metals that were wrapped several times around the neck; for women, pendant necklaces.
· *brooches*—pinned to hats, hoods, and various parts of the clothing.
· *aiglettes*—small jeweled points mounted on laces which served to hold panes or slashes together, were placed on hats. Sleeve clasps, small jeweled pins, were also used to hold together paned segments of sleeves.

Bracelets were obscured by the large sleeves, and so were not much worn. Earrings were popular in

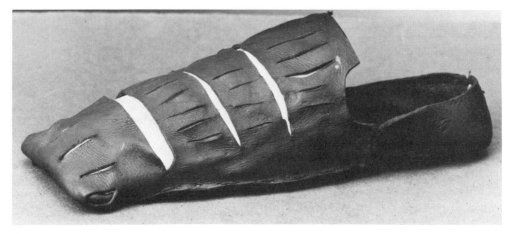

9.15 Slashed leather shoe from England, dated at between 1509 to 1547. (*Photograph courtesy of the Victoria and Albert Museum.*)

countries and periods when the hair or head dress did not cover the ears. Ferrioneres were worn in France, but not especially popular in England. Rings were worn everywhere. Jeweled belts with long cords hanging down the front became popular for women after the second decade. On the cord were mounted such things as a jeweled tassel, a perfume holder (*pomander*), a purse or a mirror. Jeweled decorations were applied to almost any part of the costume. During the time when large, lacy ruffs were worn, some of which looked somewhat like a spider web, women wore jeweled pins made in the shape of spiders among the folds of the ruff.

accessories—included:

purses—often suspended from belts and carried by men and women. Simple, leather pouches were carried by middle and lower class persons; those of the wealthy were ornamented with embroidery, beading, metalwork, jewels.

fans—Earliest form was a square of embroidered fabric mounted on a stick; later forms included ostrich or peacock feathers mounted on ornamental sticks and circular folding fans.

gloves—often had decorated cuffs.

handkerchiefs—were carried by both men and women.

masks—worn by women out-of-doors when riding to protect the complexion against the sun, and by amateur performers in theatrical productions. Reference is occasionally made to the wearing of masks by persons who want to remain disguised.

cosmetics—Many made from potentially dangerous chemicals such as mercuric salts, were used to whiten the complexion.

hair coloring—especially lightening or bleaching.

red coloring—applied to lips and cheeks.

perfumes.

NOTE: Puritans railed against these "evil practices," predicting that men and women would pay dearly for their concessions to vanity when they reached the after-world. "It must be granted that the dyeing and coloring of faces with artificial colors, and unnatural ointments is most offensive to God and derogatory to his Majesty. . . . And what are they [artificial colors] else than the Devil's intentions, to intangle poor fools in the nets of perdition."[4]

CHILDREN'S COSTUME

The pattern of dressing children in the same kind of costume as their elders continued during the 16th century. Small children, both boys and girls, were dressed in skirts until they passed the age of five or six, and then boys donned doublet and hose and whatever other garments were fashionable for men at the time. They did not escape even the large ruffs which must have been especially awkward and ungainly for active children. Royal children wore elaborate, costly silks made into heavy velvets and brocades. (See Figure 9.16.) Children of the poor and middle class dressed more simply, only because the lower and middle class adults dressed more simply than the wealthy.

4. P. Stubbes. *Anatomy of Abuses in England in Shakespeare's Youth A.D. 1583.* London: New Shakespeare Society, 1877, p. 66. (put into modern English by the author.)

PARVVLE PATRISSA, PATRIÆ VIRTVTIS ET HÆRES
ESTO, NIHIL MAIVS MAXIMVS ORBIS HABET.
GNATVM VIX POSSVNT COELVM ET NATVRA DEDISSE,
HVIVS QVEM PATRIS, VICTVS HONORET HONOS.
ÆQVATO TANTVM, TANTI TV FACTA PARENTIS,
VOTA HOMINVM, VIX QVO PROGREDIANTVR, HABENT
VINCITO, VICISTI, QVOT REGES PRISCVS ADORAT
ORBIS, NEC TE QVI VINCERE POSSIT, ERIT.

9.16 *Edward VI* (son of Henry VIII) as a child by Hans Holbein, the Younger, c. 1540. The young prince is dressed in a miniature version of adult styles of the time, including an embroidered shirt which is visible at the neck and sleeves. Both his hat and sleeves are decorated with *aiglettes*. Although the lower half of his garment is not visible, it is likely that at this early age the Prince would have been wearing long skirts. (*Photograph courtesy of the National Gallery of Art, Andrew Mellon Collection, 1937.*)

Summary

Clothing styles of the 16th century took on an increasingly international flavor. Although peasants continued to wear regional costume, the dress of the upper classes was likely to include elements introduced from abroad as well as maintaining some regional distinctions. The major influences in dress during the 16th century came from Germany, Italy, and Spain in the first half of the century; and chiefly from Spain in the second half. The rise and fall of fashion leadership by the Spanish closely parallels gains and losses of Spanish international prestige during the century. By the end of the century Spanish fashion influence decreased just as Spanish political power was also waning.

Selected Readings

BOOKS CONTAINING ILLUSTRATIONS OF COSTUME OF THE PERIOD FROM ORIGINAL SOURCES

Gersberg, M. *The German Single Leaf Woodcut: 1500–1550.* 4 Volumes. New York: Hacker Books, Inc., 1974.

Hay, D. *The Age of the Renaissance.* New York: McGraw-Hill Book Company, 1967.

Mellon, P. *Jean Clouet.* New York: Phaidon, 1971.

Morse, H. K. *Elizabethan Pageantry.* London: The Art Book Company, 1980 (reprint of 1934 Edition).

Plumb, J. H. and H. Weldon. *Royal Heritage: The Treasures of the Royal Crown.* New York: Harcourt, Jovanovitch, 1977.

Seward, D. *Prince of the Renaissance*. Great Britain: Constable and Company, Ltd., 1973.

Strauss, L. *The German Single Leaf Woodcut: 1550–1600*. 3 Volumes. New York: Abaris Books Inc., 1975.

Strong, R. *The Elizabethan Icon: Elizabethan and Jacobean Portraiture*. London: Her Majesty's Stationery Office, 1969.

Strong, R. *Tudor and Jacobean Portraits*. London: Her Majesty's Stationery Office, 1969.

Wolf, R. E. and R. Miller. *Renaissance and Mannerist Art*. New York: Harry N. Abrams, Inc., 1968.

PERIODICAL ARTICLES

Acton, B. "Portrait of a Swaddled Baby—16th Century." *Costume Society of Scotland Bulletin*, No. 17, Autumn 1976, p. 13.

Arnold, J. "Decorative Features: Pinking, Snipping, and Slashing." *Costume*, No. 9, 1975, p. 22.

Cocks, A. S. "Princely Magnificence: Jewellery at the Renaissance Court." *Connoisseur*, Vol. 205 (825), Nov. 1980, p. 210.

Marshall, R. K. "'Hir Rob Ryall': The Costume of Mary of Guise." *Costume*, No. 12, 1978, p. 1.

Nevinson, J. L. "Prince Edward's Clothes." *Costume*, 1968, p. 3.

Nevinson, J. L. "Shakespeare's Dress in His Portraits." *Shakespeare Quarterly*, Spring 1967, p. 101.

Olian, J. "Sixteenth Century Costume Books." *Dress*, Vol. 3, 1977, p. 20.

Wescher, H. "French Fashions in the Sixteenth Century." *CIBA Review*, No. 69, p. 2552.

DAILY LIFE

Braudel, F. *The Structure of Everyday Life. The Limits of the Possible. Civilization and Capitalism, 15th-18th Centuries*. New York: Harper and Row, 1981.

Burton, E. *Pageant of Tudor England: 1485–1558*. New York: Charles Scribner's Sons, 1976.

Dodd, A. H. *Life in Elizabethan England*. New York: G. P. Putnam's Sons, 1961.

Febvre, L. *Life in Renaissance France*. Cambridge, MA: Harvard University Press, 1977.

Hale, J. R. *Renaissance Europe: The Individual and Society, 1480–1520*. Berkeley, CA: University of California Press, 1978.

Rowse, A. L. *The Elizabethan Renaissance*. New York: Charles Scribner's Sons, 1971.

Smith, P. *The Social Background of the Reformation*. New York: Collier Books, 1967.

Williams, P. *Life in Tudor England*. New York: G. P. Putnam's Sons, 1965.

PART IV

Baroque and Rococo

c. 1600–1800

During the 17th century Europe endured a crisis—a series of social and political upheavals involving civil war, revolts, peasant uprisings, and a rebellion of the nobility. This European-wide crisis so shook Europe that a form of stronger government became necessary and to overcome the crisis, absolute monarchy developed. By the 18th century, absolute monarchy had been generally accepted except in Great Britain where the monarch's power had been limited thanks to the Glorious Revolution of 1688.

During the 18th century, nearly every year there was either a war in progress or a rumor of an impending war. European wars had also become global with fighting even in India and on the continent of North America. The century ended with an era of revolution, commencing with the American Revolution and ending with the cataclysm of the French Revolution.

The Reformation had ended, but religious strife continued in some areas. Late in the 1500's the Roman Catholic church mounted a Counter-Reformation which halted the spread of Protestantism. In many areas Protestantism was firmly established and from this point on Catholics and Protestants co-existed more or less peaceably. France and Spain were the major Roman Catholic powers; Britain,

northern Germany, Scandanavia, and Holland remained Protestant.

Religious toleration had been established in France in 1598 with the Edict of Nantes which ended a series of religious wars. However, in 1685, Louis XIV revoked the Edict of Nantes and resumed the persecution of French Protestants. Many of these people, called Huguenots, fled from France to other European countries or to America. Large numbers of them were concentrated in the textile trades, especially the silk industry, and their exodus had drastic effects on the French economy.

In England, a branch of Protestantism appeared which opposed the Church of England and sought to cleanse the Church of England by purifying it from rituals that were "Roman." Nicknamed, "Puritans," they became the leading faction in opposing the Stuart kings of England. Eventually Puritans would settle in New England.

Germany had become a patchwork of small principalities after the Thirty Years War, 1618–1648. The war began as a conflict between Lutherans and Roman Catholics but before it ended all of the great powers of Europe had become involved. As a result of the Peace of Westphalia which ended the terrible struggle, each German state had the right to determine its own religion.

The Arts

The Baroque style, generally dated from the end of the 16th century to the middle of the 18th century, is the name given to the artistic style that developed during this period. The Baroque style emphasized lavish ornamentation, free and flowing lines, full and curved forms. It was massive rather than delicate. The patrons for this art form included both the Catholic and Protestant churches, the aristocracy, and the affluent bourgeoisie. Since the courts of Europe were the center for royal patronage, artists and artisans often clustered around these centers.

Clothing styles were affected by these changes in the arts and one can see in the lines of garments, particularly those of the first half of the 1600's, reflections of the Baroque emphases on curvilinear forms. Squire speaks of artists who drew fashion plates in which they "caught the characteristic manner of bunching up the skirt when walking, to emphasize that exuberant ballooning drapery so beloved of artists like Bernini far away in Rome. Such a gesture was surely not accidental, but the unconscious spirit of an age working to achieve a recognizable style in every aspect of life."[1]

Of the second half of the Century, and its stylistic changes, Squire continues, "The fashionable dress of men and women in the second half of the seventeenth century interpreted the regimented ceremonial, the disciplined restraint and the academic precision of French modifications of an earlier exuberant Baroque."[2]

From about 1720 to 1770, the Rococo style supplanted the Baroque. Rococo is considered by art historians to be a trend within the overall classification of Baroque, a refinement of the heavier, more vigorous Baroque expression. Rococo styles were marked by "S" and "C" curves, tracery, scroll-work, and fanciful adaptions of Chinese, classical, and even Gothic lines, and was smaller and more delicate in scale. It, too, found a reflection in the fashions of the times: in the curving lines of the hoop-supported skirts, the delicate lace and flower decorations of dresses, and the pastel shades favored by women as well as in the men's waistcoats ornamented with delicate, Rococo embroideries.

1. G. Squire. *Dress and Society: 1560–1970.* New York: Viking Press. 1974. p. 86
2. *Ibid.,* p. 96

The final phase of the 18th century was marked by a revival of interest in classical styles. While this neo-classical art was expressed in architecture, painting, sculpture, interior design, and furnishings during the second half of the 18th century, its influence in costume was not really felt strongly until the last decade of the century during the *Directoire* period.

The Industrial Revolution

The Industrial Revolution began in England partly as a result of attempts to improve production of English cottons to compete with cheaper imports from India that were threatening English industry. Although it had its first stages during the 18th century and before, the most far-reaching effects of the changes resulting from industrialization were not felt until the following century. Its full impact on the textile industry was, however, a significant factor influencing textiles of the 1700's.

Technological innovations and industrial capitalism developed together in the textile industry, largely as a result of the high cost of some of the innovative machinery. For centuries weaving had been a cottage industry. The weaver, often a man, owned his own loom and worked at home. As more complex looms were made the weaver could no longer afford to buy his own machine. Instead, the industrialist purchased a number of looms, placed them together in one, long room, then hired people to come in to work. Gradually something close to factory organization developed in which the loom house was placed beside a bleaching and dyeing operation. As water power was utilized to operate looms in the silk industry, this led to increased production of silk, and silk looms which were expensive required outside capitalization.

But the true transformation of the clothing industry depended on an increase in and efficiency of carding and spinning, and in the perfection of a completely mechanically-operated loom. The former, in the form of the spinning mule, the spinning jenny, and the Arkwright water spinning frame, had been developed by the end of the 18th century, but the mechanized loom was yet to come.

CHAPTER 10

The Seventeenth Century

1600–1700

Historical Background

In 17th century Europe, the major powers were France, England, and Spain. Italy remained divided into small political units dominated by other countries. Holland had become not only independent of Spain, but wealthy and prosperous. The German princes, technically within the Holy Roman Empire, were sovereign powers, independent, free to make war or peace. The head of the Austrian Hapsburgs still had the title, Holy Roman Emperor, an illusionary honor. In reality the Austrian Hapsburgs had only their hereditary lands in eastern Europe.

The Renaissance styles in the arts had given way in the late 16th century to the Mannerist style. Mannerist styles stressed realistic representation of religious themes painted so as to appeal to the emotions of the beholder. Mannerism served as a bridge between the Renaissance and the Baroque styles. During the 17th century, the Italians again led the artistic transition from Mannerism to the vigorous Baroque style. Like the Renaissance, the Baroque style spread across the Alps and into the rest of Europe.

FRANCE

In France, the figure of Louis XIV would dominate the Baroque period. After the assassination of Henry IV in 1610, his young son became King Louis XIII. During a reign lasting until 1643, Louis XIII entrusted the government of France to Cardinal Richelieu who sought to centralize authority in the monarchy and to raise France to a dominant position in Europe. After Richelieu's death in 1642, Cardinal Mazarin carried on his work into the reign of Louis XIV, who succeeded his father on the throne in 1643 at the age of five years. At his death in 1715, after a reign of seventy-two years, Louis XIV's court had established a standard of grandeur to which other European monarchs would aspire but never equal.

During his youth, some great nobles engaged in an open rebellion, called the *Fronde* (a Parisian child's game), in an effort to ruin Cardinal Mazarin and to undermine absolute government. This episode, which endangered his life, left a strong impression on young Louis. As an adult, he resolved to forestall rebellions by the nobility and to bring them to court where they could not endanger the security of France.

Because the *Fronde* had also made Louis·wary of the city mobs, he moved his court away from Paris. At great expense, he had an enormous palace constructed outside Paris at Versailles where his father had a hunting lodge. The Palace of Versailles became the symbol of the glory and the majesty of Louis XIV's reign, serving as Louis's stage where he played the role of an absolute monarch, the epitome of a divine right king surrounded by fawning nobles.

For a member of the nobility to be forced to live on his ancestral estates in the provinces, instead of close to the court, meant that he was out of favor with the king, deprived of pensions and sinecures which could only be bestowed on those at court. By this tactic, Louis kept his nobles busy at court where he could keep an eye on them.

To be at Versailles a nobleman had to either live at the palace in the royal apartments or in squalid lodgings. To maintain appearances at court, a nobleman needed an expensive, varied wardrobe and funds to spend on life at court. Furthermore, nobles competed to participate in a complicated court ritual that included helping the king get up in the morning and prepare for bed at night. As a result, Louis XIV kept the nobles so busy waiting on him and spending money that they had neither the time nor the funds to plot against him.

In his search for glory, Louis tried to dominate Europe through a series of wars. However, the European powers reacted to his aggressions by forming alliances to thwart his ambitions. In the end, Louis's efforts at dominating Europe resulted only in exhausting the nation and impoverishing the people. Despite his sins and errors, Louis XIV set the style for absolute monarch, a style that was copied throughout Europe.

ENGLAND

While the French king grew more powerful, across the Channel the English monarchy was in difficulty. After the death of Elizabeth I, her cousin James VI of Scotland was crowned James I of Great Britain. The son of the ill-fated Mary Queen of Scots, James talked about divine right monarchy but backed away from real confrontation with Parliament over the question. During his reign, a radical Protestant religious faction within the Church of England, called the Puritans, continued to grow. Appearing in England during the reign of Elizabeth I, the Puritans, imbued with John Calvin's teachings, wanted to "purify" the Church of England of the remnants of Roman Catholic ritual and practice. Some Puritans, unhappy with James's religious policies, fled to Holland and from there in 1620 they sailed in the *Mayflower* to the New World, but other Puritans chose to remain in England.

James I's son, Charles I (1625–1649), a king who took very seriously the theory of divine right, could not escape a showdown with Parliament over money and religion. The royal income could keep up neither with inflation nor with the growing royal expenses. Moreover, Charles antagonized Puritans and other Englishmen by trying to compel religious conformity to the practices of the Church of England and by levying taxes without consent of Parliament. Civil war broke out in 1642, and by 1646 the king was a prisoner. In 1649 Charles I was beheaded, the monarchy abolished and a republic, the Commonwealth, proclaimed.

Oliver Cromwell, commander of the New Model Army which had defeated the royal forces, led the Commonwealth and later the Protectorate, a form of military dictatorship, until his death in 1659. Because no Puritan leader could fill Cromwell's place, and with civil war threatening, there was no alternative but to restore the monarchy and to invite the eldest son of Charles I to return in 1660 and rule as Charles II. He had taken refuge in France at the court of Louis XIV.

The new monarch, Charles II, brought to the throne a taste for French styles and a bevy of royal mistresses. A witty, shrewd politician, Charles schemed, plotted and bribed to gain absolute power. With victory almost assured, he died suddenly in 1685 leaving no legitimate children. His brother James II succeeded to the throne.

A Roman Catholic, but an incompetent politician, James II pursued policies which frightened all political factions. The birth of a son who would be raised in the Roman Catholic faith, led leaders of English political parties to invite William of Orange to come over from Holland and help end the reign of James II. Deserted by his supporters at the news that William had landed with a Dutch army, James was allowed to escape to France in 1688.

William and his wife, Mary, the Protesant daughter of James II, accepted the throne offered them by Parliament. During their reign, 1689–1702, Parliament, through the Bill of Rights, limited the power of the monarch and protected the rights of individuals. Through the Toleration Act, Parliament granted freedom of worship to Protestant dissenters but not to Roman Catholics, nevertheless, religious persecution ended for English men and women.

SOCIAL LIFE

The French court at Versailles was the hub of upper class activity. Courtiers lodged either in the Palace, where housing accommodations were neither spacious nor luxurious except for the quarters of the royal family; in their own houses nearby; or in Paris. Those of sufficient rank attended the king at his *levee* or when he arose in the morning. The king lived most of his life in public, including dressing in the morning. He donned his breeches, then was handed his shirt by the highest ranking person present. Washing consisted of rubbing his face with cotton soaked in diluted, scented alcohol—washing in water was considered dangerous. (Baths were rarely taken.) The rest of his day was just as ritualized, and the activities of each and every person were carefully prescribed by court ettiquette. Rules even governed the length of the trains of dresses ladies could wear. The Queen's train was eleven ells long (one ell equaled about 28 inches), a daughter of the King, nine; his grand-daughter, seven; a Princess of the Blood (i.e., related but not a direct descendant of the King), five; and a duchess, three.[1]

Clothing was one of the major items of expense for courtiers. One writer of the period, St. Simon, speaks of spending 800 louis d'or for clothes for himself and his wife for the wedding of the Duke of Burgundy. One louis d'or is equal to about $5.00, so that St. Simon must have spent around $4,000 for costumes for this one occasion! Obviously not all clothing was so luxurious, nor should it be assumed that this is the cost of one or two items of clothing. The festivities of an elaborate wedding would have required many different changes of clothing.

In England during the reign of Charles I, the court was less important than it was to become under his son, Charles II. In the first half of the 17th Century, England was still largely rural, and many of the aristocracy lived on their country estates. Those members of parliment who lived in the country went to London for Parliamentary sessions, but returned home when Parliament had ended. Others lived in houses in London or in towns. After the end of the Civil War and during the Commonwealth, life continued to center in the rural areas, but when Charles II was restored to the throne, social life of the upper classes began to center more at Court, and London society became more important as a leader of fashion.

1. J. Levron. *Daily Life at Versailles in the 17th and 18th Centuries.* New York: Macmillan Company, 1968, p. 108.

In Holland where a prosperous middle class had developed as a result of Dutch interests in trade, the numbers of items of clothing owned by some individuals is remarkable. For example, a dowry for the daughter of a wealthy Amsterdam family was reported to include 150 chemises and 50 scarves. One upper class widow of the first half of the century was said to have 32 different ruffs and the inventory of the wardrobe of the mayor of one town listed 40 pairs of drawers, 150 shirts, 150 collars, 154 pairs of ruffled cuffs, 60 hats, and 92 night caps, 20 dressing gowns which were worn during the day for informal attire, a dozen nightgowns, and 35 pairs of gloves.[2]

Among the early Puritan settlers of New England, one might expect to find a population with little interest in fashion, living under somewhat primitive conditions. Indeed, the earliest settlers in New England did live in temporary structures under difficult conditions, but these structures were gone by 1660, replaced by more permanent houses. Wills of the period show that some houses were well-equipped while others had more frugal belongings.

An invoice of English goods shipped to New England about 1690 includes many fashionable accessories and fabrics for making suits and dresses. Cargo listed included felt and castor (beaver) hats for men and boys, hair powder, looking glasses, periwigs, wool hose, lace, girdles (belts), caps, fringe, cornette and fontange wires (supports for fashionable head dresses), and a wide range of fabrics including "worsted fancies," "striped silk crapes," "silk fancies," "camblett" (camlet—a wool fabric) as well as more mundane fabrics such as kerseys in brown, gray, and drab; linsey-woolsey (a linen and wool fabric), and cottons in shades of white, red, blue, and yellow. One well-to-do woman was sent a feather fan with a silver handle and "two tortoise fans, 200 needles, five yards of calico, silver gimp, blank (white) sarindin, a cloak, a damson leather skin, and two women's ivory knives."[3]

Religious and secular leaders did not always approve of such "fancies." In some communities sumptuary laws were passed that included provisions that neither men nor women "should wear clothing with more than one slash on each sleeve and another on the back." Cutwork, embroidery, needlework caps, bands, and head rails (scarves)

2. P. Zumthor. *Daily Life in Rembrandt's Holland.* New York: Macmillan Company, 1963, p. 61.

3. G. F. Dow, "Domestic Life in New England in the Seventeenth Century." Lecture delivered at the opening of the American Wing of the Metropolitan Museum of Art.

were among the items prohibited, as were ruffs, beaver hats, and long-shoulder-length, curled hair. One minister disinherited his nephew because he wore his hair fashionably long. That these laws were more ignored than observed is likely. Captain George Corwin, a merchant of Salem, Massachusetts, included in his large wardrobe a cloth coat trimmed with silver lace, a velvet coat, and accessories such as golden topped gloves, embroidered and fringed gloves, a silver hat band, and a silver-headed cane.[4]

17th Century Costume

PURITAN COSTUME

Descriptions by later historians of the civil strife between the Puritans and Cavaliers (or Royalists) in England often imply that these two parties wore styles of garments which separated one group from the other. The reality is that the Puritans followed much the same styles as the rest of the population. Distinctions between these factions were chiefly those of degree. Puritans decried excesses of dress and the wearing of more stylish clothes than was appropriate to one's station, whereas Cavaliers and their ladies stressed lavishly decorated costumes in vivid colors.

Puritan dress is often described as "sad-colored." As generally understood, "sad colors" were drab dress emphasized less vivid colors, wealthy Puritans wore clothing of fine quality albeit more restrained in decoration than those of their Cavalier neighbors. Soldiers who followed the Puritan cause cut their hair shorter, and avoided the elaborate curls of the Cavaliers, thereby earning themselves the nickname of "roundheads."

Cavalier or royalist sympathizers tended to wear broad-brimmed, flat-crowned hats trimmed with plumes, while the Puritans favored high-crowned, narrower brimmed *capotains*, but neither faction followed this pattern slavishly. Puritan women and Cavalier women alike wore aprons for every-day, those of the Puritans being less ornate as a rule.

The Puritan settlers in New England brought with them the styles current in England at the time of their sailing, 1620. In spite of the time required for fashion information to travel across the Atlantic, the colonists in New England and in Virginia tried hard to keep up with current European fashions.

4. *Ibid.*

SPANISH COSTUME

Although Spain had been the major fashion leader of Western Europe during the latter half of the 16th century, by the beginning of the 17th century Spanish styles were beginning to lag behind those of other countries. The Spanish tended to be more conservative than other nations, and this conservatism had the effect of prolonging styles like the ruff and the Spanish farthingale (in Spanish, *verdugado*) even after they had been abandoned by the rest of Europe.

Even the Spanish *mantilla*, the veil worn to cover the hair which has come to be associated with traditional Spanish costume is a smaller version of the mantle worn by women during the Medieval period and carried over into later times. Custom was strong in Spain, and tradition regulated the length of this veil according to the status of the woman as either widow, married woman, or unmarried girl. In some regions, an unmarried girl was expected to cover her face when outside of the house. This practice may have been borrowed from the Moors who occupied Spain for such a long time during the Middle Ages.

But the most notable of the Spanish costume practices in the 17th century was the belated adoption of the wide, French farthingale. Obsolete in the rest of Europe after the second decade of the 17th century, wealthy Spanish women took up the style only around the mid-1600's. The Spanish called the style the *guardinfante*. (See Figure 10.1.) Not precisely like the late 16th-century farthingale, the bodice had a long, wide basque that extended down over the top of the wide skirt. The bodice shoulder line was usually horizontal and showed similarities to necklines of costumes then being worn in the rest of Europe. (See Figure 10.4.) Sleeves were full and slashed to show contrasting underlines and generally ended in a fitted cuff. With these dresses women wore high chopines with wooden or cork soles which helped to elongate the figure somewhat to compensate for the width of the *guardinfante*. Not all Spanish women wore these excessively wide skirts which were a feature of court dress. Other women often placed a pad around the waist which slightly widened skirts.

Spanish men, too, changed styles slowly. They retained the ruff and trunk hose somewhat longer than men in the rest of Europe, however men's styles were never so extreme in their regional differences as women's. By 1700 the Spanish re-entered the mainstream of European fashion.

GARMENTS FOR MEN

Men's costume in the first two decades of the century retained the major elements characteristic of costume of the latter part of the 1500's. In these two decades, major elements of costume were: the shirt, the doublet, the jacket or jerkin, and trunk hose or knee-length breeches called Venetians. Trunk hose became baggy and full, extending to the knees. By the close of the third decade, however a different style had emerged, the first of three fairly distinct phases in men's clothing styles.

Costume for Men—17th Century

1625–1650

Item / Description

shirt—Now less an undergarment and more an integral part of the whole costume. Cut very full, made of white linen and with a flat collar (*falling band*) which replaced the ruff. Sleeve cuffs and collars were often lace or decorated with cut-work embroidery.

doublet—worn over the shirt and tied (*laced*) to breeches. Evolving forms, all with the waistline set somewhat above the anatomical waistline, included:
  · a short tabbed extension below the waist (earliest form.)
  · a skirt-like extension reaching to the hip (later form.) (See Figures 10.2 and 10.3.) Some doublets had panes or slits through which the shirt or a colored lining was visible. (See Figure 10.2.)

breeches—began at the waist and extended to the knee; cut either full throughout or more closely and tapering gradually to the knee. The lower edges might be decorated with ribbons and lace. (See Figure 10.2 and 10.3.)

outdoor garments—*circular capes*—worn over one shoulder, often secured with a cord that passed under the wide collar. (See Figure 10.3.) Cloaks and capes often had wide collars. (In France, such capes were called *Balagny cloaks* after a popular military hero.)

cloaks—worn over both shoulders.

cassocks or *casaques*—coats cut with wide, full sleeves and wide throughout the body, ending at thigh-height or below. One type of cape was convertible into a coat.[5]

footwear—*boots*—extending to the knee where they met the breeches. (See Figure 10.2.)

shoes—until 1630's toes were rounded; afterward, toes more square with rosettes and ribbon decorations over a high square tongue. (See Figure 10.3.)

hose—knee-length and worn under shoes or boots.

hair and head dress—*hair*—long and curling; beards trimmed to a point; large, curling moustaches. French and English men of fashion grew one lock of hair (a "love lock") longer than the rest. (See Figure 10.2.)

hats—large-brimmed with full feather plumes. (See Figures 10.2 and 10.3.)

1650–1680

Item / Description

shirts—collars or bands may be part of the shirt or a separate piece; these enlarged at the front to form a bib-like, often lace-trimmed construction; after 1665 a long linen tie was an alternative to the collar. Changes in the doublet caused shirts to become more visible and more important.

doublet—shortened, ending several inches above the waist. Straight and unfitted through the body, sleeves ended at the elbow; some sleeveless forms. (See Figure 10.4.)

breeches—variations:
· short, straight, ending at the knee.
· full and drawn in to tie at the knee.
· *petticoat breeches* or *rhinegraves*—either a skirt-like construction or a divided skirt, rather like a modern culotte. (See Figure 10.4.)

5. See N. Waugh, *The Cut of Men's Clothes.* New York: Theater Arts Books, 1964, p. 16.

10.2 Painting of *Henri, Duc de Guise* by Van Dyck. The Duke wears a doublet over a white shirt which can be seen at the front of his doublet and through the slashes in its sleeves. His collar, a falling band, and cuffs are decorated with lace and embroidery. His breeches extend below the knee and are decorated with lace where they meet his high boots. One lock of his hair is grown longer than the rest, tied with a ribbon and called a "love lock." He carries a wide-brimmed, plumed hat and a cloak over his arm. (*Photograph courtesy of the National Gallery of Art, gift of Cornelius Vanderbilt Whitney, 1947.*)

canons—full, wide ruffles attached at the bottom of breeches. (See Figure 10.4)

outdoor garments—cloaks or capes; coats—cut full, some versions to the knee which obscured the costume beneath.

footwear—shoes with elaborate rosette, ribbon, and buckle trimmings. Preferred to boots for fashionable dress. *Boots*—for riding and in bad weather.

10.3 *The Ball* by Abraham Bosse depicts fashionable men and women of the third and fourth decades of the 17th century. Note the coat worn over the shoulder in the manner of a cape by the gentleman in the right foreground. (*Photograph courtesy of the Metropolitan Museum of Art, Rogers Fund, 1922.*)

The term *galoshes* appears in contemporary records, but the form is uncertain. The Cunningtons suggest they may have been made of leather with wooden soles and fastening with buckles.[6] Descriptions make them sound very much like pattens.

hair and head dress—*hair*—Some men shaved their heads and wore long, curling wigs. Others dressed their own hair in long, curling styles. *hats*—wide-brimmed, low-crowned, feather-trimmed hats. (This style associated with "Cavaliers" or supporters of the British royal family.) High-crowned, small-brimmed *capotains*. (This style associated with supporters of the Puritan faction, opposed to the King, in England.) Men wore hats indoors and out and in church.

6. C. W. Cunnington and P. Cunnington, *Handbook of English Costume in the 17th Century.* Boston: Plays, Inc., 1972, p. 59, 60

1680–1710

Item / Description

shirts—Little changed from forms earlier in the century.

cravats—Long, narrow, scarf-like pieces separate from the shirt that were worn instead of collars. (See Figure 10.5.)

NOTE: Of one "dandy" with an excessively long cravat it was said that "his cravat reached down to his middle and had stuff enough in it to make a sail for a barge."[7]

coats—Knee-length coats replaced doublets as outer garments. Called *surtouts* or *justacorps* by the French and *cassocks* by the English, such

7. R. Edwards and L. Ramsey, Editors. *The Connoisseur's Complete Period Guides.* New York: Bonanza Books, 1968, p. 448.

10.4 In the painting of 1665, *A Game of Skittles* by Dutch artist Pieter de Hooch, the men wear petticoat breeches with waist-length jackets over white shirts. The man at center right of the foreground has a pair of *canons* at his knees. (*Photograph courtesy of the Cincinnati Art Museum, gift of Mary Hanna.*)

10.5 Costume made for the wedding of Sir Thomas Isham in 1681. Men's outer coats had lengthened to the extent that they hid the knee breeches beneath. (*Photograph courtesy of the Victoria and Albert Museum.*)

garments had fitted straight sleeves with turned-back cuffs, and buttoned down the front. They completely covered the breeches and waistcoat. (See Figure 10.5.)

waistcoats—Cut along the same lines as the outer coat, but slightly shorter and less full. Before 1700 most were sleeved; later some were made without sleeves.

breeches—cut with less fullness than in earlier periods; ended at the knee.

hair and head dress—*wigs*—grew larger, the hair built-up somewhat on the top of the head. Some wigs were dusted with powder to make them white, but most were worn in natural colors. *hats*—somewhat superfluous given the large scale of the wigs. More often carried under the arm than worn. Flat hats with brims turned or "cocked" up at one or more points were often seen, especially one with the brim turned up at three points to form a triangle. Nineteenth century writers called this a *tricorne* however that term does not appear in the 17th or 18th centuries.

footwear—similar to that earlier in the century. Knee-length stockings worn with knee-breeches.

Costume for Women—17th Century

The wheel farthingale retained its hold on fashion in the first years of the 17th century. Gradually, however, the farthingale flattened in front and the whole line of the costume grew softer and more square, necklines low and rounded. In Spain and Holland the stomacher of the dress elongated into a rigidly boned, U-shape and the sides of the gown remained wide and full. Sleeves were multi-layered with fitted sleeves under hanging sleeves, and the ruff became even more enormous. (See Figure 10.6.)

Although the farthingale lingered on at the Spanish court, it went out of style elsewhere in Europe and the transition to a new style was complete by about the end of the third decade.

1630–1660

Item / Description

chemise—white, linen undergarment.

gowns—Generally made with bodices and skirts seamed together at the waist which was slightly elevated. Gowns opened at center front. The outer layer was worn over an underbodice, a boned, stiffened garment like a corset that had a long, U-shaped section called a *stomacher* at the front and this filled in the upper part of the gown.

skirts—A separate garment worn under the gown, visible at the front when the gown was open or seen when the outer skirt was carried looped-up over the arm. Even when skirts of outer gowns were closed in front, a second layer or under skirt was worn. The French called the outer layer the *modeste* and the under layer the *secret*. (See Figure 10.7.)

jackets—Worn in combination with skirts instead of gowns. These bodices had short tabs (*basques*) extending below the waist. Jackets worn at home were often quilted, looser in fit than fashionable dress and without elaborate sleeve constructions. (See Figure 10.8.)

sleeves—Often very full on gowns and fashionable jackets. They were puffed out, frequently paned. Contemporary writers refer to stylish sleeves, paned and tied into a series of puffs as *virago sleeves.*

necklines—Tended to be low, some V-shaped, some square, some horizontal in shaping.

10.6 *Paola Adorno,* an Italian Marquise, painted by Van Dyck, wears costume characteristic of Spain and the Low Countries in the first several decades of the 1600's. (*Photograph courtesy of the Frick Collection.*)

collars—Stiff ruffs had been replaced by *falling ruffs,* gathered collars that sloped from neck to shoulder or wide collars tied under the chin with strings. Also seen were large neckerchiefs. Horizontal necklines were often edged with a wide, flat collar that in present-day terms would be called a bertha.

outdoor garments—Usually capes, cut full and with flat, turned-down collars. Some were fur-lined.

hair and head dress—*hair*—divided behind the ears and the back hair drawn into a roll or chignon at the back of the head while the front hair was arranged in curled locks around the face.
hats—worn indoors and out, but women also went bareheaded. Styles included:
· wide-brimmed, "cavalier-style" hats
· capotains, frequently worn over a white, close-

10.7 Lady of the mid-17th century has pulled up her outer skirt (*modest*) to reveal her underskirt (*secret*) (*New York City Public Library Picture Collection.*)

fitting small cap or coif.
· squares of fabric sewn or pinned to form a cap or tied under the chin.
· hoods for out-of-doors.

footwear—Shoes similar in shape to those described for men. For bad weather: clogs with toe-caps, instep straps, no heels, and wooden soles that protected the shoes and raised them out of the wet streets.

1660–1680

Item / Description

gowns—Changed somewhat in shaping and silhouette.

bodices—lengthened and narrowed, becoming long-waisted and more slender with an extended V-shaped point at the front. (See Figure 10.9.)
necklines—tended to be low, wide, and horizontal or oval in shape and frequently were edged by a wide lace collar or band of linen called a *whisk*. (See Figure 10.10.)
sleeves—set low on the shoulder, opening into a full puff that ended below the elbow.

10.8 *Queen Henrietta Maria of England with her dwarf,* by Van Dyck. The tabs of the jacket in the style of 1625–1660 can be seen where they extend below the waistline. (*Photograph courtesy of the National Gallery of Art, Washington, D.C., Samuel H. Kress Collection.*)

skirts—either fell straight to the floor and were closed all round or were split at the front and pulled back into puffs or looped up, over the hips. Decorations for gowns often consisted of a row of ruffles down the front or lines of jeweled decoration or braid placed on top of seam construction lines. (See Figure 10.10.) Heavy satin fabrics seem to have been fashionable for formal dresses. Pastel colors predominate in paintings, but actual fabrics of the period are also brightly-colored.

10.9 *The Intruder*, by Gabriel Metsu. The lady at the center of the picture is partially undressed. Her braid-decorated outer skirt is draped across the chair in the foreground, as is her characteristically Dutch velvet, fur-trimmed outer jacket. On her head is a linen nightcap. She has just taken off her back-less shoes, which are on the floor. The woman seated by the window wears a jacket similar to the one on the chair. (*Photograph courtesy of the National Gallery of Art, Andrew Mellon Collection, 1937.*)

undergarments—consisted of chemises, under-petticoats (not to be confused with visible, decorative, outer petticoats or skirts), and drawers which though worn for some time on the continent were not worn in England at this period. Chemises usually showed slightly at the neckline and the edge of sleeves.

1680–1700

Item / Description

undergarments—underwent no major changes.

gowns—*Evolved* gradually from those prevalent between 1660 and 1680, with these features:
   necklines—revealed less bosom and became more square.

10.10 Dutch woman from after 1660. Her open overskirt displays the decorative underskirt beneath. The panel of ribbons at the front is a typical feature of many women's costumes of this period. (Portrait of a Lady Standing *by Gerard ter Borch. Photograph courtesy of the Cleveland Museum of Art, the Elizabeth Severance Prentiss Collection.*)

NOTE: This may have been as a result of the influence of Madame de Maintenon, conservative widow whom King Louis XIV of France is believed to have married secretly.

> *corsets*—visible at the front of the bodice, heavily decorated, and ending in a pronounced V at the waist. Separate stomachers could be tied or pined to the front of the corset to vary the appearance of a dress.
>
> *underskirts*—seen through the split overskirt, and ornamented with embroidery, ruffles, pleated edgings, and other trimmings.
>
> *overskirts*—generally split at the front and looped up in complex drapery with a long, back train. Skirts were often so heavy that they required additional support from whalebone, metal, or basket-work supports. (See Figure 10.11.)

mantua or manteau—a new cut for women's dresses. Instead of cutting the bodice and skirt as separate pieces that were sewn together, bodice and skirt were cut in one length from shoulder to hem. Cut to fall full in back and front, the garment was worn over a corset and an underskirt. For casual wear (the style is thought to have originated to provide a less confining costume for women) it was loose, but for more formal wear it was pleated to fit the body at front and back and belted. Front skirt edges were sometimes pulled to the back and fastened to form a draped effect.[8] (See Figure 10.12.)

outdoor garments—Capes in shorter or longer lengths still predominated. Coats, cut like men's cassocks, were worn for riding or walking. Long, broad scarves were worn around the shoulders, as were *tippets* or short, waist-length capes.

hair and head dress—Built up high, on top of the head, with long curling locks at the back and sides. On top of the hair a device made of a series of ruffles held in place with wire supports and known as the *fontange* in France and the *commode* in England and the American colonies. Over a period of about thirty years the style evolved from a small bow tieing up the hair in front to an elaborate, tall structure of three or four lace tiers in front and a cascade of ruffles and bows in the back.

NOTE: The fontange is said to have been named after one of the mistresses of Louis XIV who sup-

8. N. Waugh. *The Cut of Women's Clothes*. New York: Theatre Arts Books, 1968, p. 66.

10.11 Lady of the Court of Versailles (around 1680) wears dress with draped overskirt. (*New York City Public Library Picture Collection.*)

posedly emerged from the woods during a royal hunt in a somewhat disheveled state, thought to have been the result of an amorous encounter with the King. Using her lace garter to tie up her hair, she is said to have begun this fashion.

footwear—Shoes became more pointed at the front, heels were higher and narrower. Brocades and decorated leathers were used for fashionable shoes.

> *pantofles*—heelless slippers or mules though worn throughout the century became especially fashionable toward the end of the period. (See Figure 10.9.) Stockings were knitted both by machine and by hand from wool or silk and some had knitted or embroidered decorations.

10.12 Mantua-style dress, c. 1690–95, worn with the head dress called the *fontange*. *(Photograph courtesy of the Metropolitan Museum of Art, Rogers Fund, 1933.)*

Costume of Men and Women— 17th Century

Item / Description

accessories—*gloves*—worn by men and women and sometimes scented with perfume.
  handkerchiefs and purses—carried by men and women. Purses might be made of beaded leather or embroidered.
  fans—for women, made of feathers or of the folding types.

muffs—made of silk velvet or **satin**, fur, or fur-trimmed fabrics were carried by ladies.
  face masks—worn by ladies who wanted to protect their faces against the weather or to engage in flirtations without being recognized.
  aprons—the practical cotton or linen varieties worn to protect the garment beneath as women went about their household tasks; decorative ones made of silk or lace and lavishly embroidered worn as an attractive accessory to fashionable dress.

jewelry—Men wore neck chains, pendants, lockets, rings, and in the first part of the century, earrings. Women wore necklaces, bracelets, earrings, rings, and around the waist on chains mirrors and pomander balls, small balls of perfume placed in decorated, perforated boxes that might be shaped like an apple. (The French word *pomme* from which the word pomander derives means apple.)

cosmetics and grooming—used by both men and women and included perfume—applied to the person and to articles of clothing. Paint and powder: lead combs were used to darken the eyebrows, lips and fingernails were colored red by some women. (Artificial eyebrows made of mouse skins are mentioned by contemporary satirists.) Other grooming practices:
  · patches, small fabric shapes glued to the face to cover an imperfection or skin blemish.
  · night masks worn by ladies to protect, soften the skin and remove wrinkles.
  · from 1660–1700 some women used "plumpers," small balls of wax placed in the cheeks to give the face a fashionably rounded shape.

COSTUME FOR CHILDREN

Whereas many costume historians identify the first changes in clothing for children that reflect changes in attitudes toward them as taking place in the late 1700's, Aries in a social history of the family and childhood argues that the first important changes in costume for children come as early as the beginning of the 16th century. The changes he identifies were well-established and had become common practice during the 17th century at least for upper class children.[9]

The practice for many centuries had been to dress children, once they were released from their swaddling clothes, in the same styles as the adults of

9. Aries. *Centuries of Childhood, A Social History of Family Life.* New York: Alfred A. Knopf, 1962, p. 52ff.

10.13 Except for the ribbons of childhood on the dresses of two of the children whose backs are turned, these boys and girls are dressed in clothing like those of the adults of the period after the mid-17th century. (*Painting entitled* Dance of the Boys and Girls, *by Mathieu Le Nain. Photograph courtesy of the Cleveland Museum of Art, gift of Mrs. Salmon P. Halle in memory of Salmon Portland Halle.*)

their region and class. Starting in the 16th century, this changed for small boys, but not for girls. The nursery-age boy was first dressed not in the clothing of his elders but in the same dress as his sisters, who were, in turn, dressed like small women. Later he was dressed in a long robe which buttoned or fastened down the front. As a result, the sequence of costumes worn by boys was first swaddling clothes, and then a skirt, robe, and apron. About age three or four the boy donned the long robe, and at six or seven he was first dressed in adult male styles. Louis XIII received his first doublet and breeches at age seven. (See Figure 10.13.)

In England the occasion on which a young boy was presented with his first pair of breeches was called his "breeching" and was an occasion for celebration by all of the family and its friends.

Aries points out that the distinctive item of costume for small boys was the robe, which was not worn by adults or by girls. Here, he says, was a clear example of a costume exclusively for a child, and it had its origins in costume of the past. During

10.14 Front and back views of a dress for a boy or girl from after 1690 that has "ribbons of childhood" behind the sleeves. (*Photograph courtesy of the Smithsonian Institution.*)

the High Middle Ages men wore long robes. When these robes went out of general use, replaced by the shorter jackets for men, they continued to be used by priests, certain professions and in upper class families by children. This was not a universal practice in Western Europe. Children in Renaissance Italy seem not to have followed it, but French, German and English children did.

Other vestiges of earlier styles were also preserved in children's dress. The infants' cap worn by children is almost identical with the medieval coif. Attached to the shoulders of the robes for boys and dresses for girls was a broad ribbon of fabric that hung down the back. Many writers identify these ribbons as "leading strings," small strings used to help hold the child upright when he or she learned to walk and retained for another two years or so to help control the child's movements. Aries disagrees, pointing out that in many portraits of the time both leading strings *and* these ribbons are depicted. Leading strings were narrow, rope-like in construction, as compared to the flat ribbons of childhood. Instead, he argues convincingly, they

are probably a stylized or atrophied form of the hanging sleeves that were part of the medieval costume. (See Figure 10.14.)

Of the origins of these archaic styles for children Aries says it was obviously out of the question to invent a costume out of nothing for them, yet it was felt necessary to separate them in a visible manner by means of their dress. They were accordingly given a costume of which the tradition had been maintained in certain classes, but which adults no longer wore. The adoption of a special costume for children which became generalized throughout the upper classes from the end of the 16th century, corresponded with the beginnings of the formation of the idea of childhood as a separate stage of life.[13]

Infants were swaddled, tightly wrapped in bands of linen that inhibited movement. The major occasion in the baby's first year of life was the christening. Christening robes and accessories differed little from those of later centuries. Charles I of England's christening clothes have been preserved and they

13. Aries, *op. cit.,* p. 57.

consisted of undershirts open at the front and closed by small crossed tabs, binders for the stomach, bibs, a small cap, and a long, embroidered christening gown.

During the 17th century one other form of dress for young boys can be observed in a few portraits. It is almost a compromise between the dress of adult and child. Boys of age five to seven sometimes wore the waistcoat of the first half of the century with a long, full, gathered skirt.

Summary

The clothing of the 17th century continued the trend of earlier centuries toward a greater internationalism in style. The courts of Europe, and particularly that of France, provided a stage for the display of luxurious fashions and innovations. Such styles were all the more easily spread both at home and abroad because of the ready availability of printed descriptions and drawings of persons in fashionable dress.

At the same time, regional differences in dress persisted. Clothing worn at court of Spain, which clung to the styles of the late 16th century for more than fifty years is the most obvious example of regional dress, but styles that were preferred by and associated with the Italians, the Dutch, the French, and the English can also be identified.

For the costume historian the 17th century provides a far more complete picture of dress than in earlier periods. The many portraits painted and drawings made, not only of the well-to-do but also of every day life among the lower classes, are supplemented by an increase in printed materials that touch on current fashion and greater numbers of actual garments remaining in museums, particularly in England.

Selected Readings

BOOKS CONTAINING ILLUSTRATIONS OF COSTUME OF THE PERIOD FROM ORIGINAL SOURCES

Bechtel, E. *Jacques Callot.* New York: George Braziller, 1955.

Blum, A. *Costume of the Western World: Early Bourbon.* London: George Harrap and Company Ltd., 1951.

Brown, C. *Dutch Painting.* New York: E. P. Dutton, 1976.

Brown, D. *The World of Velazquez, 1599–1660.* New York: Time-Life Books, 1969.

Cumming, V. *A Visual History of Costume: the 17th Century.* New York: Drama Books, 1985.

Fletcher, J. *Rubens.* New York: Phaidon Publishers, N.D.

Gerard Ter Borch, 1617–1681. Munster: Landesmuseum. N.D.

Reade, B. *Costume of the Western World: The Dominance of Spain.* London: George Harrap and Company Ltd., 1951.

Thienen, F. V. *Costume of the Western World: The Great Age of Holland.* London: George Harrap and Company Ltd., 1951.

PERIODICAL ARTICLES

De Marly, D. "Indecent Exposure." *Connoisseur,* Vol. 206, (827), Jan. 1981, p. 1.

Marshall, R. K. Seventeenth Century Babies." *Costume Society of Scotland Bulletin,* No. 13, Spring 1974, p. 2.

Marshall, R. K. "Three Scottish Brides—1670–87." *Costume,* No. 8, 1974, p. 41.

Murray, A. "From Breeches to Sherryvallies." *Dress,* Vol. 2, 1976, p. 17.

Nevinson, J. L. "Van Dyke Dress." *Connoisseur,* November 1964, p. 166.

Strong, R. "Charles I's Clothes for the Years 1633–1635." *Costume,* Vol. 14, 1980, p. 73.

Swan, S. B. "The Pocket Lucy Locket Lost." *Early American Life,* Vol. 10 (2), April 1979, p. 40.

DAILY LIFE

Ashley, M. *Life in Stuart England.* New York: G. P. Putnam's Sons, 1964.

Coate, M. *Social Life in Stuart England.* London: Methuen and Company, Ltd.

Defourneaux, M. *Daily Life in Spain in the Golden Age.* New York: Praeger Publishers, 1966.

Erlanger, P. *The Age of Courts and Kings. Manners and Morals, 1558–1715.* New York: Harper and Row Publishers, 1967.

Godfrey, E. *Home Life Under the Stuarts.* New York: Frederick Stokes Company, N.D.

Goubert, P. *Louis XIV and Twenty Million Frenchmen.* New York: Pantheon, 1970.

Levron, J. *Daily Life at Versailles in the 17th and 18th Centuries.* New York: Macmillan Company, 1968.

Scott, G. T. *Life in a Noble Household, 1641–1700.* New York: Alfred A. Knopf, 1937.

Zumthor, P. *Daily Life in Rembrandt's Holland.* New York: Macmillan Company, 1963.

Color
in
Costume

~

Costume
in
Color

he pages which follow present a chronological survey of historic costume in color. The concept stressed in this section is *color*. In many periods one can identify colors that tend to predominate. Where this is possible, the following pages present illustrations of costume that show the kinds of colors prevalent in various periods.

Color may also have a symbolic function. The modern, Western association of white with weddings and black with mourning are examples of color symbolism. Custom may also play a role. "Tennis whites" were for many years required if one were to be permitted to play at the more exclusive tennis clubs. "Black tie" still connotes a customary costume for formal affairs. Pastel colors are often viewed as "more appropriate" for infants and small children than dark or vivid colors.

And, of course, color adds immeasureably to our enjoyment in viewing costume in exhibit or in pictures. It is an essential component in the aesthetic aspects of all types of dress.

One must, however, note some of the problems in considering color in historic costume. In the periods preceding the 18th century, actual items of costume are relatively rare. Sources of information come, mainly, from the arts and the writings of the various periods. From written descriptions one can get only a general idea of color. Artists' representations may also present difficulties. In some periods, for example the Mesopotamian and Assyrian, the representations available that depict costume are usually made in an uncolored stone or pottery. Similar problems exist in regard to Greek costumes. The pictures on vases are rendered without color and those statues that were once colored have, in the hundreds of years since their creation, been bleached away. A few wall paintings have survived that demonstrate that Greek costume was, indeed, brightly colored.

In the Middle Ages and the Renaissance we obtain much of our information from the paintings and sculpture that remains. An assumption is made that the artists of the period were depicting costume colors in an accurate way, but it is possible that artistic conventions may have led to the over-representation of some colors and the under-representation of others. We cannot be absolutely certain that the colors we see in the paintings of the period are exactly the same as those seen by the citizens of 16th century Florence as he or she strolled through the piazza on a summer afternoon.

From the 18th century onwards, more actual items of costume remain. Yet even in viewing items of historic costume one can experience difficulties. Before the mid-19th century, fabrics were dyed with natural materials. Dyestuffs were derived from animal, vegetable, or mineral sources. The durability or fastness of some of these colors was limited, and in the years since they were dyed color changes may have taken place. Exposure to light is particularly destructive of color. By examining hidden areas of costumes (such as seams, facings, and the like) one can often see that the original color was much brighter and more intense than it would appear from a superficial look at the external portion of the costume.

This use of natural materials for dyeing also placed limits on the range of colors used in clothing. The introduction of aniline dyes, the first synthetic dyes, in the mid-19th century contributed to the use of more intense (some would even say, garish) colors sometimes seen in the latter part of that century, as manufacturers took advantage of this new technology.

In spite of these cautions, however, a good deal can be learned about the uses of color in costume and the following pages present an overview of color use in Western dress.

1 Egyptian works of art depict individuals clad in white, solid, and multicolored fabrics. It is not clear whether multi-colored effects were created by weaving, appliqué, or beading. (*Photograph courtesy of the Metropolitan Museum of Art, Rogers Fund, 1933.*)

2 Only rarely does Greek art show colors of costumes. Here a woman wearing a gold-colored Ionic *chiton* has a lavender *chalymidon* over her shoulder. (*Photograph courtesy of the Metropolitan Museum of Art, Classical Purchase and Rogers Funds, 1979.*)

4 The Byzantine Empress Theodora wears a *paludamentum* of purple, a color associated with royalty, while her female retainers are dressed in colorful brocades probably woven from silk produced by the Byzantine silk industry. (6th century A.D.) (Corte de Teodora. *Ravenna S. Vitale. Photograph courtesy of Scala/Art Resource, New York.*)

3 Roman frescoes depict women in *stolas* of varying colors, over which they wore *pallas* of contrasting hues. The young girl in this picture may be the daughter or maidservant of the woman playing the cithara. She wears only a *stola*. (*Photograph courtesy of the Metropolitan Museum of Art, Rogers Fund, 1903.*)

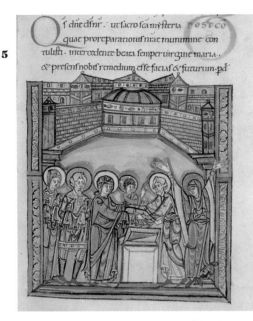

5 Byzantine influences appeared in European dress of the upper classes during the early Middle Ages. Bands of embroidery on the tunic of the second figure on the left show Byzantine influence, while other figures wear *undertunics*, *outer tunics* and *mantles* of various solid colors. (11th century) (*Photograph courtesy of The Pierpont Morgan Library,* © *1988, M641 f.18.*)

6 The elaborately patterned long *tunic* of the king (at center) and the elaborately patterned fabrics of the *tunics* and *mantles* of the bishops who supervise his coronation contrast with the solid color, short *tunics* of the men of lower status who stand on either side. (12th century) (*Photograph courtesy of The Pierpont Morgan Library,* © *1987, M736 f.8v.*)

7 The Virgin, often shown wearing blue—a color associated in the Medieval Period with purity— is flanked by the donors of this art work who are dressed in costumes that show their family colors. (First half of the 14th century) (*Photograph courtesy of The Pierpont Morgan Library,* © *1987, M700 f.3v.*)

8 The traditional black, hooded capes of medieval mourners contrast with the clerical robes and the colorful, though ragged, tunics and hose of the gravediggers. (c. 1460) (*Photograph courtesy of the British Library.*)

9
10
11

Love of color, says Umberto Eco, is evident not only in medieval art, but also in everyday life, clothing, ornament, and weapons. (see Umberto Eco. *Art and Beauty in the Middle Ages.* New Haven: Yale University Press, 1986, Chapter IV.) Paintings of the 15th century not only show color variations, but subtle fashion variations, as well. In **Figure 9** (*Photograph courtesy of the Metropolitan Museum of Art, Robert Lehman Collection, 1975.*) a bride and groom of about 1449 consult a goldsmith. Contrast her elaborately-patterned gown with its wide sleeve and her double-horned headdress with the tall, pointed *hennins*, predominantly solid-colored fabrics, and narrow sleeves of the ladies of the late 1400's in **Figure 10.** (*Photograph courtesy of Beinicke Rare Book and Manuscript Library, Yale University.*) Note how high the sleeve caps of men's garments of the late 1500's have grown in **Figure 11** when compared to those of the goldsmith in Figure 9. (*Photograph courtesy of The Pierpont Morgan Library, © 1987, M457 f.8.*)

Color in Costume/Costume in Color **169**

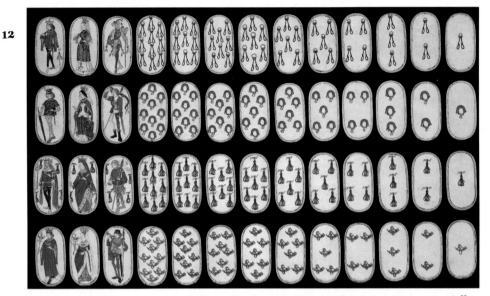

12 Playing cards from 1475 show fashionable dress for men and women. Note especially the parti-colored costume of the jesters. No longer part of fashionable dress, particoloring persisted in some specialized usages. (*Photograph courtesy of the Metropolitan Museum of Art, The Cloisters Collection, 1983*).

13 Master dyers of Florence transformed the silks and wools woven in the city into a rainbow of colors ranging from violet to *sanguine* (blood red) to *burnet* (near black) and Renaissance artists capture these varied colors in their paintings. (*Photograph courtesy of the Metropolitan Museum of Art, Rogers and Gwynne Andrews Funds, 1935.*)

14 Stiffly-rigid styles often in black or white with elaborate embroidery and lace were characteristic of the Spanish styles that influenced all of Europe in the 16th century. (c. 1584) (Infanta Isbella Clara Eugenia with Magdalena Ruiz *by Felipe de Liano. Photograph courtesy of the Prado Museum.*)

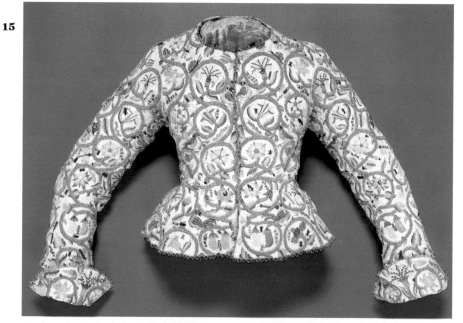

15 Embroidery in multi-colored yarns decorates this jacket for a girl of the late 16th or early 17th century. (*Photograph courtesy of the Metropolitan Museum of Art, Rogers Fund, 1923.*)

16 Robert Rich, Second Earl of Warwick, (Figure 16) wears the every day dress of a wealthy English aristocrat of about 1632–35. By contrast the Dutch gentleman in petticoat breeches of the mid-
17 1600's (Figure 17) wears black, a predominant color in the Netherlands. His female companion is more colorfully dressed. (*Photographs courtesy of the Metropolitan Museum of Art; Figure 16: The Jules Bache Collection, 1949, Figure 17: Gift of Henry G. Marquand, 1980.*)

18

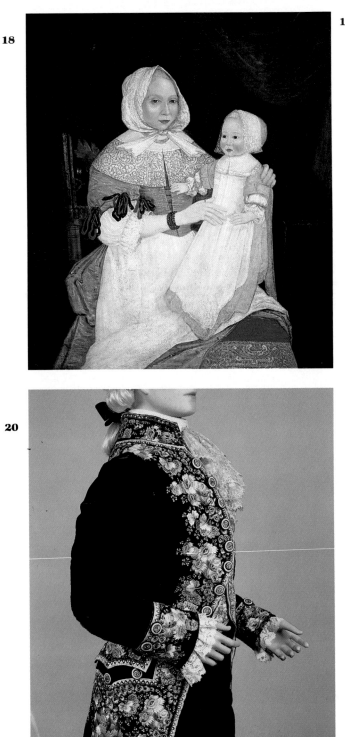

18 These Massachusetts settlers dressed for their portraits in light and bright colors, contrary to the stereotype of the drab and dark-colored dress of the Puritans. (*Mrs. Elizabeth Freake and Baby Mary, by an unidentified artist, c. 1674. Photograph courtesy of the Worcester Art Museum, Worcester, Massachusetts, gift of Mr. and Mrs. Albert W. Rice.*)

19

19 Styles of about 1700 are shown on a "dressed" fashion print, one which has had actual fabrics glued in place. (Cavalier and the Lady Drinking Chocolate. *Photograph courtesy of The Pierpont Morgan Library,* © 1987.)

20

20 Men's outer coats and waistcoats of the 18th century were heavily embroidered with silk in vivid colors. (c. 1770) (*Photograph courtesy of the Philadelphia Museum of Art, gift of Charles F. Saake.*)

21 "The redcoats are coming!" This cry of Americans during the Revolutionary War referred to the bright red coats worn by British soldiers such as the famous General Burgoyne. (General John Burgoyne *by Sir Joshua Reynolds, 1723–1792. Copyright © The Frick Collection, New York.*)

22 Although white wedding dresses had not yet become customary in the 18th century this bride wore cream satin and gold. (1729) (Wedding of Stephen Beckingham and Mary Cox *by William Hogarth. Photograph courtesy of the Metropolitan Museum of Art, Marquand Fund, 1936.*)

23 Silk brocades with floral patterns in pastel and light colors were among the more widely-used fabrics for women's dresses in the 18th century. (England, 1775–85) (*Photograph courtesy of the Cincinnati Art Museum, John J. Emery Endowment.*)

24 The simple white dress with puffed sleeves of the Empire Period was frequently worn together with a long, narrow shawl woven with a multi-colored paisley design like the one draped over the arm of this woman. (*Comtesse Daru by Jacques-Louis David, 1748–1825. Copyright © The Frick Collection, New York.*)

25

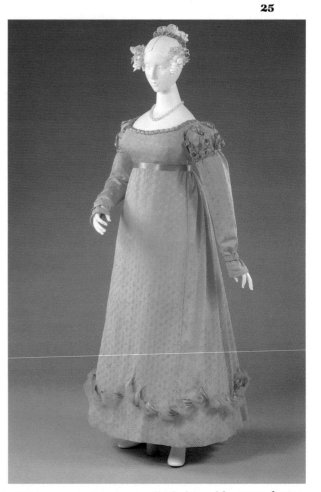

25 Pink was noted as especially fashionable around 1820, and can be seen in this crepe dress which shows the evolution toward the more elaborately decorated skirts of the early Romantic Period. (England, 1818–22) (*Photograph courtesy of the Cincinnati Art Museum, gift of Webb and Stacy Hill, by exchange.*)

26 Men's dress in the 19th century lost much of its color. Of all of the items of men's wear, waistcoats were most likely to provide touches of brightness. (*1834, Italian fashion plate.*)

27 Both the *pelisse* and the dress are made in colors that fashion commentators of the period called "amber," "apricot," or "citron." The white, embroidered *pelerine* is a typical feature of dresses of the period, and its shape is echoed in the collar of the *pelerine*. (*Dress, England, 1830–33, museum purchase, gift of Mr. and Mrs. J. G. Schmidlapp, by exchange; coat, United States, 1828–36, gift of Mrs. Chase H. Davis; photograph courtesy of the Cincinnati Art Museum.*)

29 During the Crinoline Period plaid fabrics were extensively used not only for women's dresses, but also for children's clothing and for men's waistcoats. (c. 1854) (*Photograph courtesy of the Metropolitan Museum of Art, Costume Institute, Gift of Mrs. Edwin R. Metcalf, 1969.*)

28 By the late Romantic Period, white had become the customary color for brides.

30 While the silhouette of Crinoline Period styles was achieved through the use of the hoop, some of the more vivid colors in fabrics and trimmings were often due to the growing use of coal tar dyes, first synthesized in 1856. (United States, 1856–58) (*Photograph courtesy of the Cincinnati Art Museum, gift of Mrs. Jesse Whitley.*)

31 Traditional mourning customs of the Victorian era were closely followed. Black fabrics, trimmed in black crepe were worn for specified periods, and the amount of black as well as the duration of its wearing varied according to the relationship of the wearer to the deceased. (c. 1875) (*Photograph by Taishi Hirokawa, courtesy of Kyoto Costume Institute.*)

31

32 The sailor dress, in white, tan, or navy with colored trim was the Victorian equivalent of sportswear, and its exact configuration varied with the current styles. These examples show the leg-o-mutton sleeve of the 1890's. (See also Figure 38.) (*Photograph courtesy of Fairchild Visuals, from* All American: A Sportswear Tradition.)

33 White and pastel colors and a great deal of lace were among the hallmarks of fashion in the Edwardian Period. (France, 1903–06) (*Photograph courtesy of the Cincinnati Art Museum, gift of the estate of Elizabeth W. H. Chatfield.*)

34 Paul Poiret, designer of exotic and dramatic clothes for women may have been influenced by the Ballet Russe which appeared in Paris in 1909 when he designed this garment in 1911. (*Photograph courtesy of the Metropolitan Museum of Art, Purchase, Irene Lewisohn Trust Gift, 1983.*)

35 The pleated gowns of Fortuny were usually made in bright solid colors, while his patterned fabrics were in rich, often dark shades influenced by Renaissance and Oriental designs. (1915–35) (*Left: tea dress, museum purchase, gift of Mrs. James Morgan Hutton, by exchange, with evening jacket, gift of Mr. and Mrs. Charles Fleischmann in memory of Julius Fleischmann. Right: tea dress, museum purchase, gift of family and friends in honor of the birthday of Margery B. Behr, with evening coat, gift of Patricia Cunningham in memory of Mrs. Alfred Lewis Flesh. Photograph courtesy of the Cincinnati Art Museum.*)

36 Men's wear was rarely lightened with color in the 20th century. Dark pin-striped suits in dark blue were worn for business before World War I. For leisure and sports, however, more colorful shirts could be worn. (*Illustrated by J. C. Leyendecker, 1912. Courtesy of The Arrow Company.* © 1988 Cluett, Peabody & Co., Inc.)

37 Men were not allowed on the courts of tennis clubs if they were wearing any color other than white until the 1970's. (*Photograph courtesy of Fairchild Visuals, from* All American: A Sportswear Tradition.)

38 The duster in tan showed the effects of the dirt kicked up by open automobiles less than if it had been made in darker or lighter shades. (c. 1905) (*Photograph courtesy of Fairchild Visuals, from* All American: A Sportswear Tradition.)

39

39 The "flapper" and the "sheik"—as drawn by John Held Jr. became the personification of "flaming youth" and 1920's styles: he in his colorful argyle pullover and she with her stockings rolled and her lips and cheeks rouged. (*Photograph courtesy of Jones, Brakeley & Rockwell, Inc.*)

40

40 Evening dresses in the 1920's were short, and often made from heavily beaded fabrics with hints of Art Deco style in the geometric patterning. (*Photograph courtesy of the Philadelphia Museum of Art, gift of Mrs. Basil R. Beltran.*)

41

SAFARI
SILKS OF A NEW ADVENTURE

To Africa . . . the new playground . . . The chic world goes for sun-bathing in Tunis, sport-flying over the Mountains of the Moon, journeying "On Safari," that jungle-hunt for fantastic game. And Africa, country of amazing contrast, savage and sophisticate . . . this is the theme of Safari . . . silks patterned in the keener color, the bolder rhythm of a new adventure.

▲ ▲ ▲

The Zebra design, "Punda" appears in this Schiaparelli pajama by Saks-Fifth Avenue. Safari prints for resort and town will also be shown in dresses, ensembles and silks by the yard.

BELDING HEMINWAY COMPANY
Madison Avenue at 34th Street • New York

41 Colorful lounging pajamas and beach pajamas were one of several ways in which women were able to wear the trousers that had heretofore been worn exclusively by men. (c. 1929) (*Photograph courtesy of Belding Heminway Company, Inc.*)

42 Multi-colored prints, often large in scale, were widely used in the 1930's. (c. 1934) (*Illustration by Eric. Courtesy* Vogue. *Copyright © 1934 (renewed 1962) by The Condé Nast Publications Inc.*)

44 When World War II caused silk supplies to dry up, many women preferred to paint their legs with leg makeup rather than wear ill-fitting rayon stockings. (*Photograph courtesy of Elizabeth Arden Inc.*)

43 Schiaparelli was most closely associated with the color called "shocking pink," but other designers such as the American Norman Norell also used this color for dramatic effect as seen here in one of his designs. (1941) (*Illustration by Eric. Courtesy* Vogue. *Copyright © 1941 (renewed 1969) by The Condé Nast Publications Inc.*)

45

45 Hawaiian shirts made a strong impact on the men's wear market in the late 1940's. (*Reprinted from* The Hawaiian Shirt *by H. Thomas Steele, Abbeville Press, Inc., 1984. Photograph courtesy of H. Thomas Steele.*)

47 As skirts grew shorter, women combined brightly-colored panty-hose with mini-skirts. (1969) (*Photograph courtesy of Fairchild Visuals, from* Fashion Silhouettes of the 20th Century.)

47

46

48

46 The lavish ball gowns which were one of the trademarks of designer Charles James typify the post-New Look, figure-hugging styles of the 1950's. Although he used color effectively, some of his most dramatic gowns were done in black and white. (1956) (*Photograph courtesy of the Cincinnati Art Museum, museum purchase: gift of Mr. and Mrs. J. G. Schmidlapp, by exchange.*)

48 The vivid colors characteristic of the mid-60's are seen in this short "cocktail" dress. (1965) (*Photograph courtesy of the Goldstein Gallery, University of Minnesota.*)

49

49 Not only dresses, but also underwear, utilized bright prints in the late 60's. (*Illustration by Phillip Castle from* Vogue *1968 © The Condé Nast Publications Ltd.*)

50 Surreal, cubist, and op art, all influenced fashion in the 60's.

50

51 By the late 60's, men were able to choose from more colorful items. From right to left the men in the photo are: John Weitz (fashion designer), Peter Jaeger (stockbroker), Martin Stahely (marketing manager), Count Ferdinando Sarmi (fashion designer), Barry Gary (radio commentator), all clad in a group of early John Weitz apparel. (*Photograph courtesy of John Weitz, Inc.*)

51

CHAPTER 11

The Eighteenth Century

1700–1800

Historical Background

Upon the death of Louis XIV in 1715, his great-grandson, Louis XV, became king of France at the age of five. During the period of the Regency, when the King was too young to reign alone, a gradual change in the Baroque art styles that had predominated in the previous century had taken place. The new style lines were less massive, still curved but the curves were more slender and delicate, and an emphasis was placed on asymmetrical balance. This new style, Rococo, reached its height during the reign of Louis XV.

The king, at whose court these styles flourished, lacked the intelligence and the common sense needed for the task of governing France. Lazy, egotistical, bored with affairs of state, he sought entertainment through hunting as often as possible. His other great passion was women. Perhaps the most famous of his mistresses and paramours was Madame de Pompadour who encouraged authors and helped artists while serving as the king's political advisor.

During much of Louis's reign, France engaged in costly wars which brought little but defeat and debts. Louis's half-hearted efforts never succeeded in solving the nation's mounting fiscal crisis. His lavish court contrasted sharply with the lives of the ordinary citizens. Louis XV died in 1774, more hated and despised than any French king for many generations.

Despite the lamentable condition of the finances of France, the nation dominated the culture of western Europe. France still set the style in fashion, literature, decorative arts, and in philosophical theories. French had become the international language of Europe, preferred by royalty and aristocracy.

The grandson of Louis XV succeeded him on the throne. Louis XVI was a well-meaning, pious king, able to work well with his hands but unfit for the heavy task which confronted him. His wife was of little help to him for he had married an attractive young Austrian princess, Marie Antoinette. In her first years as queen, she was immature, frivolous and with an intense dislike for the customs and etiquette of the French court which was not surprising since she was only fourteen when she married Louis. Her unpopularity with both the older nobles and the people did little to support the monarchy.

At the same time, writers called *philosophes*, convinced that by using reason and science a better world could be created, used the press to unleash a wave of criticism aimed at the abuses in French society and government. The success of the American Revolution, which France helped finance, encouraged Frenchmen who wanted to reform government and society. Their opportunity came in 1789 when the bankruptcy of the French government forced the calling of the Estates General which declared itself a National Assembly, abolished feudalism and began to write a constitution. France was undergoing a revolution. After defeats in war, the revolution was taken over by radicals who ended the monarchy, and eventually executed the king and queen in 1793. The Old Regime was abolished.

With the mid-century changes in philosophy, there had been related changes in styles of art. The Rococo styles were replaced by a neo-classical revival. Excavations in Italy, in 1719 and 1748, uncovered the ruins of two Roman cities, Pompei and Herculaneum, destroyed by the eruption of Mt. Vesuvius in 79 A.D. near Naples. The discovery of these remains fueled a revived interest in classical antiquity. Although the influences neo-classical styles would exercise on women's dress did not arise until near the close of the century, neo-classical styles in art and architecture were evident from mid-century onward.

For the first half of the century the influence of the French court styles were also felt elsewhere in continental Europe. In Prussia, Frederick the Great (1740–1786) patterned his court on the French court, building Rococo and Neo-classical palaces. Empress Maria Theresa of Austria, whose daughter Marie Antoinette became queen of France, maintained loose links with France. Spain, too, was closely tied to France because the great grandson of Louis XIV, Philip V, became Spain's first Bourbon king in 1700. He and his successors would attempt modest reforms. In Italy, first Spain and then Austria dominated the peninsula; only the Venetian Republic remained independent, and at the end of the century, even Venice lost its autonomy when it was handed over to Austria by Napoleon.

In England, the Georgian era had begun. Except for a short period at the beginning of the century when Queen Anne, daughter of James II, reigned, the Hanoverian kings, George I, II and George III, who were of German extraction, ruled England. Late in the century, English ideas would exert strong influence on France, particularly in field of reforming the government and civil rights.

SOCIAL LIFE IN THE 18TH CENTURY— FRANCE

During the minority of Louis XV, Versailles was abandoned and the center of the French administration was moved to nearby Paris. When Louis came of age, he returned to Versailles and for most of the rest of the 18th century the palace was again the center of royal life. Madame Pompadour, an official mistress of King Louis XV, was a major influence on styles in costume and the arts during his reign. Her patronage assured artists and artisans of success, and in return they named styles in such diverse areas as fans, hairdos, dresses, dishes, sofas, beds, chairs, ribbons, and the rose pattern of her favorite porcelain after her.[1]

The court became somewhat less important during the reign of Louis XVI, in large part because Queen Marie Antoinette, an Austrian, found the French court etiquette stifling. No wonder, when the ceremony required of her on arising not only that one person hand her the chemise and a different person her petticoat and dress, but also if a person of higher rank entered the room, the task had to be turned over to her. The Queen changed this procedure after the cold winter day on which the following incident (described by her attendant) took place:

> . . . the Queen, quite undressed, was about to slip on her chemise. I was holding it unfolded. The Lady-in-waiting entered, hastened to remove her gloves and took the chemise. Someone scratched at the door, which was opened; it was the Duchesse de Chartres. She had removed her gloves and came to take the chemise, but the lady-in-waiting handed it, not to her, but to me. I gave it to the Duchesse. Someone else scratched at the door: it was the Comptesse de Provence; the Duchesse de Chartres passed her the chemise. The Queen had folded her arms over her bosom and looked cold. Madame saw her strained attitude, just dropped her handkerchief, kept her gloves and while passing the chemise over the Queen's head, ruffled her hair.[2]

The Queen's dispensing with this and some other traditional court etiquette added to the strains between the royal family and the older, more conservative nobility. Furthermore, the Queen was extravagant at a time when the economy of France was in difficulty. She spent a great deal on jewelry, and on an average she ordered 150 dresses a year and spent the equivalent of about $40,000 on clothes. In one year when she wished to wear a dress that matched her ash blonde hair she sent a lock of

1. W. Durant and A. Durant. *The Age of Voltaire.* New York: Simon and Schuster, 1965, p. 282.
2. J. Levron. *Daily Life at Versailles in the 17th and 18th Centuries.* New York: Macmillan Company, 1968, p. 194.

hair to Lyòns, a city in the south of France where the silk industry was located, in order to be sure the fabric was dyed precisely the right color.[3]

For a period she abandoned the palace at Versailles for life at the Petite Trianon, a small chateau on the grounds of the palace built to simulate a country farm house where she and the rest of her court favorites played at being "country folk." There they started a fashion for peasant-style dresses and hats. Although the importance of the Queen's life style as a cause for the French Revolution is often over-stressed, it is true that her lack of popularity with both the old nobility and the people were factors in the decline of support for the monarchy.

FASHIONABLE LIFE—ENGLAND

The organization of society in England was less centered on the court than that of France. Even though the center of fashionable life was London, small towns and country estates also had their own social class structure and took an interest in fashionable dress. A brief review of the apprenticeships to which a young man of the provinces could apply himself shows the diversity of occupations related to clothing and fashion: clothiers, collar-makers, cordwainers (shoemakers), glovers, lacemakers, linen drapers, mantua-makers (dressmakers), peruke (wig) makers, tailors, weavers, wool combers, wool winders, and woolen drapers.[4]

Fashionable clothing was divided into categories according to the time of day the costume was worn or the sort of occasion for which it was appropriate. A man divided his garments among "undress" or lounging clothes; "dress," slightly more formal outfits for daytime or evening wear; and "full dress" or the most formal evening dress. His "nightgown" was not a sleeping garment in the modern sense, but a dressing gown or informal robe worn indoors. He also had a "powdering jacket" which he wore to keep the powder off his clothing while having his wig powdered.

The clothing a woman wore around the house was her "undress," "half dress," or "morning dress." Her "habit" was either a riding costume or a tailor-made costume. Her "coat" was not for out-of-doors, but was her petticoat. The garment we call a "coat" today, she would have called a "great coat." She never called a dress a "frock," because that term was applied to a type of man's coat (a "frock coat") or to children's dresses. And although by the end of the century she was wearing what the 19th Century fashion magazines dubbed a "bustle," she called it a "false rump."

The man of means who did not have to work for a living got up late, breakfasted and received his friends at home (wearing his "night gown") in the morning. In the afternoon he went out to a popular spot or to the shops, and then on to dinner; after dinner, to a play or coffee house. During the summer season he might go to a spa, a fashionable resort, to take the curative waters for real or imagined ailments. A man who paid a great deal of attention to his dress was called a "beau," a "coxcomb," or a "fop."

Fashionable ladies spent their mornings in bed where they reclined while receiving guests. Several hours were required for the late-rising lady to dress. In the afternoon she visited friends, or drank tea. Dinner was taken about 4 P.M., and her evenings were spent in card-playing and dancing.

Not only the wealthy aristocrats, but also the middle class, which was a growing segment of English society, kept up with fashion. The middle class as well as the upper classes traveled to spas for vacations. In addition to the spas there were many other places where the middle class lady or gentleman could observe the most recent styles. Many of the forms of entertainment, especially the outdoor amusement parks and the theatre, provided opportunities for the mingling of the social classes. Nor was it uncommon for the rich daughters of merchants to marry into upper class families.

CLOTHES AND THE POOR IN ENGLAND

Among the poor, simply keeping dressed was a problem. In the country women could obtain wool, spin, and weave or knit garments but in town clothing had to be purchased and for those on a small income prices were very high. W. H. Hutton in his autobiography described how it took him two years to save enough money to purchase a good suit of clothes. Unfortunately the suit was stolen, and it took him another five years to save for a replacement. Thefts of clothing were common. Some thieves were even so enterprising as to cut holes in the backs of carriages through which they grasped a passenger's wig and whisked it away.[5]

The poor purchased clothing from second-hand clothes dealers. These dealers obtained their stocks from the servants of good families to whom cast-off clothing was routinely given, or from thieves.

3. *Ibid.*

4. D. Marshall. *English People in the 18th Century.* London, Longmans, 1969, p. 84.

5. *Ibid.*

In some towns breeches clubs were formed where each member contributed a small amount to a common fund. When the fund was large enough, a name was drawn and that person received a pair of breeches. The club continued to function until every member had obtained a pair.

THE AMERICAN COLONIES

The cities of Philadelphia, Baltimore, New York and Boston in America were very like their British counterparts, and people living in these towns and nearby areas followed European fashions. Some clothes were imported, others were modeled after the styles shown on fashion plates or fashion "babies," small dolls from Paris which were dressed in detailed copies of current styles.

Working class dress was designed for convenience. A common costume for working class women consisted of a chemise and over this a petticoat skirt and a short garment that was like a jacket or overblouse.[6] To these "short gowns" were added a serviceable apron and a kerchief at the neck, together with some kind of a cap covering the hair. (See Figure 11.1.)

Farmers and artisans wore loose smocks over breeches. Made of coarse linen for summer and wool in winter, these garments were pulled over the head and tied at the neck with strings. Laborers often placed a leather apron over the smock. On the frontier men adopted a costume derived, in part, from Indian styles. They, too, wore a loose smock or a shirt made of fringed deerskin, or, sometimes, of coarse homespun decorated with fringes. For traveling through wooded regions, Indian-style deerskin leggings were worn. Close-fitting caps of coonskin, fox, bear, or squirrel often had a long, hanging tail sewn to the back.

English and American Quakers dressed somewhat differently from the rest of the population. Quaker men wore plain hats and no wigs. Women wore simply-cut gowns and, at first, peaked, steeple-shaped hats, later replaced by unadorned bonnets. By the end of the century Quakers were tending to give up their distinctive dress.

18th Century Costume

COSTUME FOR MEN

The major elements of men's costume consisted of underdrawers, a shirt, waistcoat, an outer coat,

6. For a fuller discussion of the nature of these costumes see C. Kidwell, "Short Gowns," *Dress*, Vol. 4, 1978, p. 30 ff.

knee-length breeches, hose, and shoes. Hats and wigs were added on appropriate occasions, along with other accessories and outdoor wear. Although these elements remained constant throughout the century, the styles of the first and second halves of the centuries do show some differences.

Item / Description

underwear—underdrawers, shirts, collars, and cravats were classified as "underwear." (See Figure 11.2.)

   shirts—similar cut to those of preceding centuries and having a ruffled frill at the front of the neck and the sleeves.

   collars and *cravats*—first half of century: gathered to a neckband and neckcloths or cravats wound around the neck and knotted under the chin, concealing the collar. Second half of century: neckbands lengthened evolving into a collar that was sewn to the shirt. For both: white cotton or linen fabric.

NOTE: One style of wearing the cravat pulled through the buttonhole and twisted loosely, the *Steinkirk*, was named after a battle in which soldiers were supposed to have twisted their cravats loosely around the neck. Evidence, however, indicates that the style originated several years *before* the battle for which it was supposed to have been named.

   underdrawers—closed at the waist with drawstrings or buttons. Made of white cotton or wool, and ending at the knee.

NOTE: After 1770 those men who considered their calves not fashionably shaped might wear "artificial calves," padding strapped to hose or strapped to the leg. (See Figure 13.12.)

MEN'S STYLES UP TO MID-CENTURY

coats—by 1700 extra fullness was added to straighter cut characteristic of 1680's. Ending about the knee, coats buttoned: to the hem until 1720, and to the waist after 1720. (See Figure 11.3.) Buckram stiffening was used to hold out full skirts of coats; side seams were usually left open from below the waist to accommodate swords.

   pockets—had flaps, with scalloped edges; were generally positioned at hip level.

   sleeves—until 30's tended to end in large full attached cuffs either closed all around or open at the back. Cuffs that reached to the elbow were called "boot" cuffs. Alternative styles had

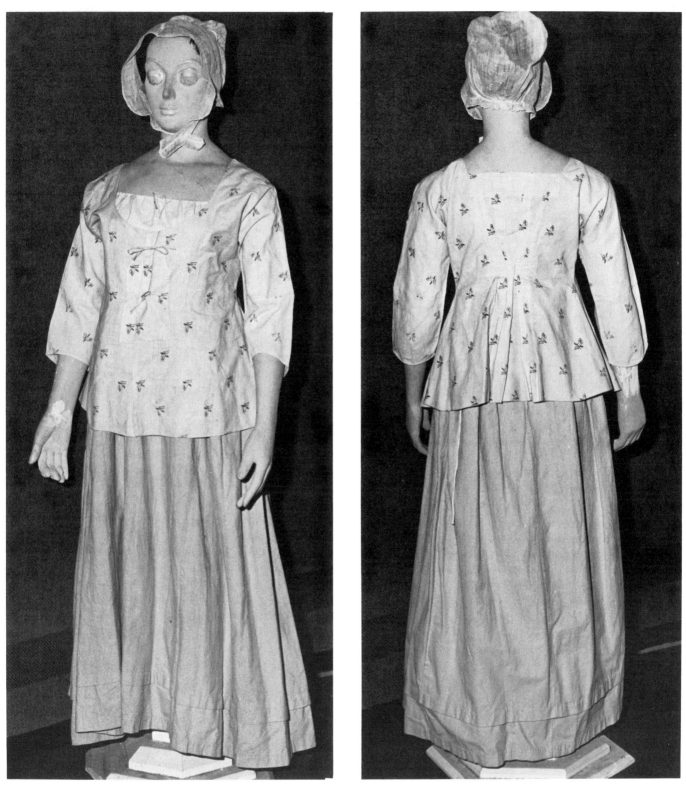

11.1 Petticoat and short gown, front and back views. Late 18th century. (*Photograph courtesy of the Germantown Museum, photographer: Philip Mossburg III.*)

11.2 Undergarments of the 18th century from England. Made of flannel for warmth, they include (left) underdrawers, (center) a shirt, and (right) an undervest. (*Photograph courtesy of the Metropolitan Museum of Art.*)

no cuffs and were slit at the back to expose the sleeve ruffle.

waistcoats—followed the lines of outercoats, ending close to the knee; were made with and without sleeves. Usually matched the outer coat in color and fabric.

NOTE: waistcoats without sleeves were worn at home without an outer coat as casual wear.

breeches—cut moderately full, with seat cut very full and gathered to a waistband that rode, loosely fitted, below the waist. Ending at knee; often just barely visible when coat was closed. Closed at front with buttons or after 1730 with a "fall," a square, central flap which buttoned to the waistline.

frock coats—after 1730 considered suitable for country wear. Cut was looser, shorter than dress coats, with flat, turned-down collars. After 1770, were accepted for more formal wear, also. Predominant fabrics were serge, plush, sturdy woven cloth; not embroidered. (See Figure 11.6.)

NOTE: The frock coat was an instance of adoption of working class costume by the upper classes.

CHANGES AFTER THE MID-CENTURY

Item / Description

coats—fullness decreased, side pleats eliminated, the front of coat curved toward the side. By 1760 a narrow stand-up collar appeared. Silhouette narrowed, as did sleeves which were longer and generally cuffed. (See Figure 11.4.)

waistcoats—sleeveless, shorter, both single and double-breasted. Since coats were worn open, the fabric became a center of attention and more brocades, or elaborately-embroidered silks were used.

breeches—fit more closely, fall or flap closing predominated. (See Figure 11.5.)

fabrics—for suits and coats: daytime or less formal evenings—plain woven wool, plush, velvet, silk including satin trimmed with lace, braid or fur; full dress—cloth of gold, silver, brocades, flowered velvet, or embroidered materials. For breeches: sturdy woven cloth, plush, or serge for casual wear; silk satin or velvet for evening; leather, especially buckskin for riding.

11.3 (*Far left*) Ditto suit, first half of the 18th century. Of mauve silk with a design of white flowers with green stems, this suit shows the sleeve cuff construction and long waistcoat characteristic of the first half of the century. (*Photograph courtesy of the Metropolitan Museum of Art.*)

11.4 (*Center*) Moss green velvet embroidered coat, embroidered waistcoat, and satin breeches worn between 1774 and 1793. This costume reflects the shorter waistcoat styles and standing collar characteristic of the second half of the century. (*Photograph courtesy of the Metropolitan Museum of Art, gift of Henry Dazian, 1933.*)

11.5 (*Far right*) Men's knee breeches, c. 1780–90. The front closing is of the fall or flap type. (*Photograph courtesy of the Smithsonian Institution.*)

11.6 (*Left*) Three gentlemen in a country scene are dressed in informal frock coats. The figure at the right holds a three-cornered hat in his hand and wears what appear to be knee-length spatterdashes or gaiters over his shoes. (Painting of the *Honorable Henry Fane with his guardians, Inigo Jones and Charles Blair*, painted by Joshua Reynolds.) (*Photograph courtesy of the Metropolitan Museum of Art, gift of Junius S. Morgan, 1887.*)

NOTE: coats did not necessarily match breeches or waistcoats. When all were made of the same fabric, the suit was called a "ditto" suit. Cunnington notes that this term is first encountered after 1750, (See Figure 11.3.) although such suits were seen earlier.

neckwear—Changes seen after 1730: cravats tended to be replaced by "stocks," a linen square folded to form a high neckband, stiffened with buckram, and fastened behind the neck. Often a length of black ribbon tied in a bow at the front was worn over the stock.

OTHER TYPES OF GARMENTS IN THE 18TH CENTURY

Item / Description

casual dress worn at home—variously known as a nightgown, morning gown, dressing gown, Indian gown, or banyan, this comfortable loosely-fitted garment was worn throughout the century. Cunningham in a detailed study suggests these variations:
- loose, full kimono style—more often seen in the early part of the century. (See Figure 11.20.)
- more form-fitting style, similar to a man's coat, with set-in sleeves. (See Figure 11.7.)

Each of these basic styles could have additional variations.[7] Fabrics included cotton calicos; silk damasks, brocades, velvets, taffetas, or satins; and wool worsteds and calamancos.

NOTE: Writings of the period indicate these garments were worn out-of-doors as well as at home; many men had their portraits painted in these gowns.

  caps—were worn at home instead of wigs. Two depicted styles were: cap with round crown and flat, turned-up brim that fit close against the crown (See Figure 11.7.); or shapeless crown and rolled brim, somewhat turban-like.

outdoor dress—until mid-century, capes or cloaks cut full and gathered at the neck under a flat collar. After mid-century, full wide-skirted great-coats (*surtouts*), ending below the knee. Sleeves generally cuffed, some coats had as many as three broad, falling, cape-like collars, each shorter than the one below.

footwear—*stockings*—long, above the knee.
  shoes—until 1720, square-toed, high square

heels, and large square tongues. Later shapes were rounder, heels not so high. Decorative buckles were placed at the base of the tongue. Red heels for court dress and for fashionable men were favored before 1750 and after 1770.
  boots—various sizes and shapes, worn for riding, traveling, hunting, and by the military.
  slippers and dress shoes—had low heels, flat soles.

hair and head dress—*hair styles*—most men who could afford them wore wigs. Styles varied, major changes were: until 1730's, long, "full-bottomed" wigs like those of the 1600's, although fullness gradually shifted to the back. Brushing the hair straight back from the forehead and into a slightly elevated roll (*toupee* or *foretop*) began in the 30's. (See Figure 11.9.) Hair was dressed higher after 1750 and wider in the '80's, paralleling women's hair styles. Other popular styles included wigs with queues (a lock or pigtail at the back), and club wigs or *catogans*) with queues doubled up on themselves and tied at the middle to form a loop of hair. Colors varied, but powdered wigs were preferred for formal dress. Wigs were made of human hair, horse hair, and goats' hair.
  hats—less important as wigs grew more important. Important styles were: three-cornered hats, flat hats carried under the arm rather than being worn (*chapeau bras.*) Two-cornered hats appeared about 1780 (See Figure 11.8), and top hats, called "round hats," were used for riding in the 1770's.

accessories—and *jewelry* included such varied items as muffs, walking sticks, watches, decorated snuff boxes for carrying powdered tobacco which was inhaled, rings, and some brooches and jeweled shoe buckles.

cosmetics and grooming—men used powder and perfume. Men tended to be clean-shaven.

COSTUME FOR WOMEN

The shape of women's costume during the 18th century was provided through a variety of supporting garments worn beneath the outermost clothes. The silhouette of a long slender bodice and a skirt with back fullness discussed in Chapter 10 continued until about 1720. Wide hoops (in French, *paniers*), used first in England about 1720 and slightly later in France, came into widespread use by the end of the second decade and remained a part of every day costume until about 1770–1780. Between

7. See P. Cunningham, "Eighteenth Century Nightgowns: the Gentleman's Robe in Art and Fashion." *Dress*, Vol. 10, 1984, p. 2 ff.

11.7 Seated man wears a striped satin banyan with matching waistcoat. His manservant combines a ruffled shirt and embroidered waistcoat with purple and black figured silk breeches. He holds a nightcap of embroidered silk in his hand. (*Photograph courtesy of the Costume Institute of the Metropolitan Museum of Art.*)

11.8 Two-cornered hat of the 18th century. (*Photograph courtesy of the Metropolitan Museum of Art, bequest of Marie P. James, 1911.*)

1720 and 1780, the shape of the hoop varied thereby causing changes in the silhouette of the garments it supported. Although hoops were adopted by all classes, not every woman wore hoops. Even after the hoop went out of style, it was preserved in the required formal dress worn at the English court. Between 1770 and 1780 the hoop was supplanted by hip pads and bustles as support garments.

Item / Description

undergarments—*hoops*—construction was similar to the construction of the farthingale of the 16th century.

At first: cone shaped; made of circles of whalebone sewn into petticoats of sturdy fabric, each hoop increasing in size as it moved nearer the floor.

In the 1720's: shape became rounded like a dome.

In the 1730's: favored shape was narrower from front to back and wider from side to side.

In the 1740's: extremes of width were reached, some hoops reached a width of two to three-quarters yards; these wide styles remained until the 1760's.

NOTES: The French called these hoops *paniers*, which means basket and some hoops did produce the effect of perching a basket on either hip, however the term derived from the fact that both baskets and paniers might be made of wicker.

Extreme width made it necessary for ladies to enter rooms sideways. Small railings were built around the edges of table tops and other furniture to prevent the sweeping of teacups and *object d'art* from the tables to the floor. Some paniers were hinged so that they could be folded up under the arms when necessary for mobility.

Caricatures and contemporary literary sources are full of gibes at ladies for wearing such an "outrageous" style. Male commentators in English journals offer these observations:

The Spectator of 1711: ". . . the hoop petticoat is made use of to keep us [i.e., the male sex] at a distance." *The Weekly Journal*, in 1717 appealed to women to "find one tolerable convenience in these machines."

The Salisbury Journal noted that the swaying hoops revealed ankles and legs, scolding ladies whom they accused of making their petticoats short so "that a hoop eight yards wide may indecently show how your garters are ty'd."

Although initially hoops were made of whalebone, and whalebone hoops sewn into a petticoat

continued in use throughout the period, both metal and whalebone frames without a petticoat attached and separate paniers, of wicker, one for each hip were also in use.

chemise—worn under hoops. Knee-length; cut full, with wide neckline edged with lace. This lace often showed at the neckline of the outer dress. Sleeves were full, to the elbow, but not visible.

drawers—not yet universally worn.

underpetticoat—placed over the chemise but under the hoop. A fairly straight garment, made of cambric, dimity, flannel, or calico and in winter often quilted for warmth. ·

stays—corsets, made of coarse fabric unless they were intended to be a visible part of the costume when they were covered at least in front by dress fabric. Both front and back were boned. Most laced up the back, although some laced at front and back and for stout and pregnant women, side lacings were sometimes

11.9 Satirical drawing of 1777 pokes fun at the tight lacing of corsets and the hair styles of that period. (*Photograph courtesy of the Smithsonian Institution.*)

added. (See Figure 11.9.) Some had fronts constructed to allow the insertion of a decorative, V-shaped stomacher.

jumps—loose, unboned bodices worn at home to provide relief from tight corseting.

NOTE: Some dress bodices were so heavily boned as to make stays superfluous and in this case they were not worn.

COSTUME FOR WOMEN

1715–1730

Item / Description

gowns—Either open or closed at center front, and either loose or fitted. The most commonly worn included:

• *robe battante, robe volante, innocente, or sacque*—a gown that was unbelted, loose from shoulder to floor. Made with pleats at the back and at the shoulder in front, sacques were worn over a dome-shaped hoop and might have either a closed front or be worn open over a corset and petticoat. (See Figure 11.10.)

NOTE: After the death of Louis XIV and until Louis XV reached adulthood, rigid court etiquette relaxed somewhat. The loose-fitting gown is sometimes cited as evidence of this lack of formality.

• *pet-en-lair* was a short, hip-length version. *mantua-style* gowns, cut in one piece from shoulder to hem, fitted to the body in front and back were more popular in England than in France. Many were open in front and the petticoat visible. Petticoats were often decorated with quilting.

hair and head dress—*hairstyles*—fairly simple as compared to the fontange styles which went out of use about 1710. Hair was waved loosely around the face, and twisted into a small roll or bun worn at the top of the head, toward the back, or alternatively arranged around the face in ringlets or waves. Women, like men, might powder their hair for formal occasions. *hats*—worn indoors and out. *For indoors:* pinners, circular caps with single or double frills around the edge, worn flat on the head; *mob caps*, with high, puffed-out crowns located toward the back of the head and wide, flat borders that encircled the face. Lace trimming much used; long lace or fabric streamers (*lappets*) often suspended from the edge or to tie under the chin. White indoor caps might also be worn out-of-doors, under other hats. *For outdoors:* hoods, small straw or silk hats with narrow brims and trimmed with narrow ribbon bands.

1730–1760

Item / Description

gowns—Replacing the loose sacque were either the *robe a la Francaise*, with a full, pleated cut at the back and a fitted front (See Figure 11.11.), or the *robe a l'Anglaise*, with a close fit in the front and at the back. (See Figure 11.12.)

NOTES: The robe *a la Francaise* was more popular in France, *a l'Anglaise* with the English, though both styles were worn in both countries and in America.

The term "Watteau back" came to be attached to the loose-fitting, pleated back styles in the 19th century when similar styles were revived. The term was not used in the 18th century. Watteau was an 18th century painter who often depicted women wearing sacques.

Generally, gowns had open bodices and skirts which allowed the display of decorative stays and petticoats. Some stays were decorated by embroidery, others were covered with ribbons (*eschelles*) or masses of artificial flowers or lace. Necklines were usually low and square or oval in shape. Petticoats of formal gowns were usually made from the same fabric as the gowns, thereby giving them the appearance of being a single garment. Sleeves generally ended below the elbow, finishing in one or more ruffles (*engageants*.)

two-piece garments—The short sacque or *pet en lair*. A jacket (in French, *casaquin*) fitted through the bodice and flaring out below the waist almost to the knee. Sleeves were tight, with a small, turned-back cuff. Separate tops were worn over petticoats or skirts.

hair and head dress—*hair*—styles began to change by 1750 when hair was combed back from the face, smooth and high on top in *toupee* fashion, then arranged in a bun at the top of the head or a plait at the back. *Also seen:* close, tight curls called *tete de mouton* (sheep's head, in translation.)

hats—indoor caps remained much the same, though a few variations were added. *For outdoors:* large flat straw hats with low crowns and wide brims, called *bergere* or shepherdess hats, and tied under or over the brim; three-

11.10 Both the lady in the foreground of the painting and her maid who gives "The Alarm" in the background wear loose sacque garments, also known as *robes battante, volante,* or *innocente. (Photograph of painting* The Alarm *by Troy, 1823, courtesy of the Victoria and Albert Museum.)*

11.11 *Robe a la Francaise* of the mid-18th century. Made of yellow flowered silk, the wide skirts of the dress are supported by a frame called *paniers*. (*Photograph courtesy of the Metropolitan Museum of Art, bequest of Mrs. Maria P. James, 1911.*)

cornered hats, jockey caps of black velvet with a peak at the front which were worn for riding.

1760–1790

Item / Description

gowns—After 1770, the robe *a la Francaise* modified, as paniers were replaced by hip pads. Excess fabric was pulled through pocket slits in such a way that the bunched fabric hung through the pocket to form a drapery. By 1780 this robe was no longer fashionable. The robe *a l'Anglaise*, with slight modifications in waistline placement and a fuller bodice, persisted into the 80's. (See Figure 11.13.) Skirt fullness swung from sides to back in the late 1770's, and a "false rump" pad tied at the back of the waist supported the fullness.

NOTE: contemporary references indicate "false rumps" were filled with cork or other light cushioning materials. The *London Magazine* of 1777 issued this warning to prospective bridegrooms:

> Let her gown be tuck'd up to the hips on each side
> Shoes too high for to walk or to jump;
> And to deck the sweet creature complete for a bride
> Let the cork-cutter cut her a rump.
>
> Thus finish'd in taste, while on Chloe you gaze
> You may take the dear charmer for life;
> But never undress her—for out of her stays,
> You'll find you have lost half your wife.

In the late 70's and 80's some skirts shortened, revealing the leg above the ankle. (See Figure 11.15.) A brief listing of the many gown styles in use would include:
  · the *polonaise*—from about 1770–85. An overdress and petticoat in which the overskirt was puffed and looped by means of tapes and rings sewn into the skirt. A hoop or bustle supported the skirt. (See Figure 11.14.)

11.12 From left to right: dress *a l'Anglaise* in floral striped, ribbed silk with a lace *fichu*; man's court suit, c. 1770; ball gown, *a la Francaise*, with overskirt open at the front to show matching underskirt; and formal dress, *a la Francaise*, of blue satin. (*Photograph courtesy of the Metropolitan Museum of Art.*)

11.13 *Robe a l'Anglaise* of 1775–1795 is fitted close to the waist at front and back. A scarf or *buffon* fills in the low-cut neckline. (*Photograph courtesy of the Smithsonian Institution.*)

NOTE: In subsequent periods the term polonaise is used very broadly to refer to any over-skirt that is puffed or draped over an underlayer.

· closed or "round" gowns, i.e., gowns closed all the way down the front.
· dresses resembling buttoned great coats with wide lapels or revers at the neck.
· *chemise a la reine*, a white muslin gown which resembled the chemise undergarment of the period, but having a waistline and a soft, fully-gathered skirt. This garment, made of muslin

imported from India, was a forerunner of styles from the beginning of the 19th century. (See Figure 11.15.)

two-piece garments—A long, fitted jacket (the *caracao* bodice) similar in style to the aforementioned *casaquin* in its cut. (See Figure 11.16.) A jacket based on men's riding dress, worn with a skirt and a man's hat.

hair and head dress—*hair-styles*—grew to extreme sizes.
   1760's—dressed higher, frizzed around the face, later arranged in sausage curls flat against the head, running from ear to ear.

11.14 Brocade overdress from 1775–1789 has skirt with puffed draperies that are often referred to as a *polonaise*. (*Photograph courtesy of the Smithsonian Institution.*)

11.15 *Antoine-Laurent Lavoisier and his wife*, 1788, painted by Jacques-Louis David. Madame Lavoisier wears a muslin dress of the *chemise de la reine* style. Her hair is dressed *a la herisson* or "hedgehog" fashion. (*Photograph courtesy of the Metropolitan Museum of Art, purchase, Mr. and Mrs. Charles Wrightsman Gift, 1977.*)

1770's—maximum size was reached: a towering structure supplemented by feathers, jewels, ribbons, and seemingly almost anything a lady could perch on top of her head. (See Figure 11.9.)

NOTE: In 1768 the *London Magazine* was talking about hair styles raised "a foot high and towerwise."

1780's—height diminished, but fullness was retained in the "hedgehog" fashion, with hair curled, full and wide around the face and long locks hanging at the back. (See Figures 11.15 and 11.17.)

hats—small day caps were little used when hair styles grew to exaggerated sizes. *Outdoors:* hoods, large enough to cover the hair, including *calashes* or *caleches*, made of a series of semi-hoops sewn into the hood at intervals. These hoops supported the hood without crushing the hair, and folded flat when not in use.

Other hats—perched on top of the tall head dress, until the flatter hedgehog style over which enormous hat structures with great quantities of lace, ribbons, feathers, and flowers were set flat on the head or at an angle.

18TH CENTURY OUTDOOR GARMENTS FOR WOMEN

Item / Description

cloaks—cut full, to fit over wide skirts. Lengths varied, some being full-length and others ending at the waist or hip. Some hooded. Fabrics included velvet and wool and fur-trims for cold weather; silk or other lightweight fabrics for warm weather. (See Figure 11.18.)

overcoats—cut like a man's greatcoat, though more closely fitted. Used in the last two decades after the style for hoops had passed.

other wraps—large scarves, shawls, wraps with or without sleeves that covered the upper part of the body. Smaller shawls, and short capes covering the shoulders and upper arms. Narrow fur or feather pieces like a modern-day stole but called "tippets" and worn around the shoulders.

11.17 Hairstyle of the third quarter of the 18th century. (*Photograph courtesy of the Cleveland Museum of Art, John L. Severance Fund.*)

11.16 Day dress, c. 1778. Gown of yellow-gold satin with a *caraco* bodice, in the pseudo-shepherdess style popular at the court of Louis XVI. This dress is said to be from the wardrobe of Queen Marie Antoinette. The child's dress of the 18th century is probably of an earlier date, and is made of green and gold flowered silk. (*Photograph courtesy of the Metropolitan Museum of Art.*)

footwear—shoes—had pointed toes, high heels, tongues, and side pieces called latchets that fastened over the instep.

backless slippers (mules).

Late 1880's—Chinese slippers with small, low heels and turned-up toes, held on the foot by a drawstring in a casing around the top of the shoe.

NOTE: Oriental influences are evident in all the decorative arts of the 18th Century, although in clothing they are most evident in men's dressing gowns and in fabric decoration.

clogs or *pattens*, overshoes that protect against wet and muddy surfaces, made of matching or other fabrics; had sturdy leather soles, built-up arches, and latchets that tied across the instep to hold the clog in place. (See Figure 11.19.) Country people wore wooden clogs or metal pattens to raise the shoe out of the mud.

stockings—extended to the knee, were held in place with garters. Fabrics used included cotton, wool, or silk knits.

accessories—gloves—usually extended to the elbow. Mittens were gloves that were open at the base of the thumb and fingers.

muffs—small until the 70's, after which they enlarged. Mostly made of feathers, fabric, or fur (which often had matching tippets.)

pockets—not yet sewn into dresses, but were small bags sewn onto a ribbon and tied around the waist. They were reached through a slit in the skirt. After 1760, some women carried a small bag, as well.

other accessories—folding fans, various sizes and shapes, parasols, black masks covering full or half face and mounted on sticks and held up before the face. These masks were often worn to balls.

jewelry—necklaces: rows of pearls, chains, lockets, pendants, and crosses, often with matching earrings. Gold watches worn around the neck, jeweled hair pins, hair ornaments, jeweled buckles for shoes.

cosmetics and grooming—Lips, cheeks, and fingernails could be colored red with rouge. Eyebrows were shaped with scissors or by plucking, and blackening with combs of soft lead. Patches and plumpers (noted in the 17th century) continued in use. Perfumes used. Creams, smeared on bands of cloth and wrapped around the head were worn at night to remove wrinkles. In place of soap,

11.18 Cloak from the 18th century. (*Photograph courtesy of the Smithsonian Institution.*)

women used "wash balls"—a combination of rice powder, flour, starch, white lead, and oris root. The lead was probably injurious to the skin.

COSTUME FOR ACTIVE SPORTS FOR MEN AND WOMEN

riding costume—Men had no special riding or hunting costume, but wore frock coats, breeches (preferably of buckskin) and high boots. Toward the end of the century top hats developed for riding.

11.19 Women's shoes of the early 18th century. The shoe at the bottom is worn with a matching clog. (*Photograph courtesy of the Victoria and Albert Museum.*)

Women wore a costume adapted from every day styles worn by men, consisting of a shirt, waistcoat, outer coat, and skirt. Coat and waistcoat reached almost to the knees until after mid-century, when they shortened and became fuller and more flared. By the end of the century a variation modeled on men's greatcoats appeared. Women wore three-cornered hats, black velvet jockey caps, and high-crowned, narrow-brimmed hats for riding.

bathing—both men and women were bathing in the sea in England by the 18th century, and written evidence together with engravings indicate that nude bathing was done in segregated areas. At most resorts, however, special costume was worn. Jackets and petticoats of brown linen or long, loose sacks of flannel are cited by Cunnington and Mansfield.[8] Sea bathing was not popular

8. P. Cunnington and A. Mansfield. *English Costume for Sports and Outdoor Recreation.* New York: Barnes and Noble, 1969, p. 261.

in America until after 1800, but bathing at spas and springs was considered beneficial to health. A blue and white checked bathing gown exists which is said to have belonged to Martha Washington. It's cut is similar to that of a chemise, although the sleeves are narrower and the neck higher. Lead disks are wrapped in linen and attached to the gown near the hem, which probably served to keep the gown in place when the bather entered the water.[9]

other sports—such as tennis, skating, and in England golf and cricket as well, were played by men and, more rarely, women, but no special costume had developed for these games.

COSTUME FOR CHILDREN

First Half of the Century

· *Babies*—in swaddling clothes.
· *After infancy to age six or seven*—both boys and girls wore skirts.
· *After six or seven*—both boys and girls wore adult styles, although the ribbons of childhood were still appearing on young and even adolescent girls' dresses until about 1770. (See Figure 11.20.)

NOTE: Some children were sent away to boarding schools, and some ran away from school. Descriptions of runaway children provide some descriptions of how children were dressed. One boy aged 11 or 12 was wearing "sad color kersey coat trim'd with flat new gilded brass buttons, a whitish callamanca waist coat with round silver buttons, silver edging to his hat, rolled white worsted stock. Sad color sagathy stuff britches with silver plate buttons."[10]

Sad color was any dull color. Kersey was a closely-woven twill cloth, callamanca was a glazed fabric with raised stripes of the same color, and sagathy was a lightweight serge.

Second Half of the Century—Styles specially for children, different from either previous or current adult dress, came into being. Jean-Jacques Rousseau, a French philosopher, is often given credit for inspiring this change. His writings do stress the importance of modifying current clothing practices in the direction of greater freedom for children, but Macquoid points out that changes

9. See C. B. Kidwell. *Women's Bathing and Swimming Costume in the United States.* Washington, D.C.: Smithsonian Institution Press, 1968, p. 14.

10. J. Ashton. *Social Life in the Reign of Queen Anne.* New York: Charles Scribner's Sons, 1929, p. 50.

11.20 Informal family group at home. The child wears a dress in the style *a l'Anglaise.* The mother in a combing jacket has not yet had her hair arranged. The father in a banyan with a matching waistcoat is already wearing his powdered wig. (*Group portrait by Drouais. Photograph courtesy of the National Gallery of Art, Samuel H. Kress Collection, 1964.*)

11.21 Children, late 18th century. Girls are dressed in white muslin dresses; the boy wears a skeleton suit. (*Photograph of painting by John Hoppner, courtesy of the Metropolitan Museum of Art, bequest of Thomas W. Lamont, 1948.*)

in English styles for children had already begun to take place before the publication in 1760 of *Emile*. Macquoid notes that portraits of little girls in sacques after 1720 are very rare, in spite of the fact that they were popular for wear among adult women, and that boys were dressed in straighter, less full coats than their elders.[11]

Moore suggests that paintings by the artist Joshua Reynolds may have helped to spread styles from England to the continent, because he liked to paint children in unadorned costume or in costumes from his own stock of clothes which were not necessarily part of actual street dress.[12]

The importation of muslin from India may also have had an impact on children's dress. This sheer white fabric was at first very expensive and artists enjoyed painting wealthy children dressed in the soft folds of the fabric.

But even if the less restrictive styles for children were not a result of Rousseau's philosophy

of child rearing, his recommendations must have lent this trend considerable support. In the light of previous practices his recommendations are quite revolutionary. Summarized briefly, the guidelines he laid down for children's dress included:

(1) for infants, "No caps, no bandages, no swaddling clothes." Instead he recommended loose and flowing flannel wrappers that were neither too heavy to check the child's movements nor too warm to prevent his feeling the air.

(2) for older children, nothing to cramp or hinder the movement of the limbs of the growing child. No tight, closely-fitting clothes, no belts.

(3) keeping children in frocks (skirts) as long as possible.

(4) dressing children in bright colors. He says, "Children like the bright colors best, and they suit them better too."

(5) "the plainest and most comfortable clothes, those which leave him most liberty."[13]

Although clothing for children did not reach the ideal recommended by Rousseau, it did im-

11. P. Macquoid. *Four Hundred Years of Children's Costume*. London: the Medici Society, Ltd., 1925, p. 100.

12. D. L. Moore. *The Child in Fashion*. London: B. T. Batsford Ltd., 1953, p. 12.

13. J. J. Rousseau. *Emile*. London: J. M. Dent and Sons, 1933, pp. 27, 91, 92.

prove significantly during the second half of the century. One of Rousseau's strongest statements was about the detrimental effects of swaddling infants. Whether due to his influence or not, the practice was, at least in England and the United States, pretty well given up by the end of the century.

For toddlers up to age six or seven: dresses or robes.

For boys over six or seven, after 1780: long straight trousers, a white shirt with a wide collar that finished in a ruffled edge. Over the shirt a jacket which was either a shorter, simplified version of those of adults or cut to the waist and double-breasted. This costume was called a "skeleton suit." (See Figure 11.21.)

NOTE: Just how boys came to wear trousers is not clear. In the adult world trousers were worn in the 17th and 18th centuries by Italian comic actors, and by city laborers in the 18th century. English sailors seem to have been the first Englishmen to wear long trousers. Moore suggests that it may have been by way of copying the sailor's costume for young boys that they first were used.[14]

For girls—simple straight dresses, often of white muslin. Dresses tended to have slightly elevated waistlines. (See Figure 11.21.) Out of doors, girls wore long or short cloaks. Small, white linen mob caps were worn indoors and out. Some small girls appear in portraits in large, decorative hats, similar to those of adult women.

After age 11 or 12—boys and girls assumed adult dress.

Summary

Costume history before the 19th century generally focuses on the clothing of the well-to-do. Pictorial evidence as well as the clothing that is preserved in museums leads to this upper class bias. As can be seen from Figures 11.1 and 11.9, clothing of less affluent people and servants was relatively simple and practical, with some general reflection of the lines of fashionable dress. These differences in style also served to reinforce the class distinctions that permeated society. The fairly decorative dress of servants of the nobility (see Figure 11.7) was a statement of a sort of reflected glory, as if the status of

the master would be diminished if his servant were inadequately attired.

Thorsten Veblen's theory of the leisure classes can easily be applied to the styles of the 18th century. His view was that clothing can be a means of establishing conspicuous consumption and conspicuous leisure. The costliness and lavishness of 18th century clothing illustrates the principle of conspicuous consumption, and the inconvenience of the tall headdresses and wide paniers, conspicuous leisure in that the wearer could not possibly be accused of doing any productive work!

It is rarely possible to point to clear, unambigious parallels between costume and current events, but it is tempting to see the variability of styles, the extremes of size and shape, and the lavishness of decoration as evidence of a frantic attempt on the part of the French nobility to escape the political realities that will shortly lead to the bloody French Revolution.

If such analogies were so clear-cut, however, then one would expect to see quite different styles in America following 1776, and yet women of the American democracy also powdered their hair and donned paniers. One can note that American styles were less extreme and lagged a little behind those of the European courts.

From an overview of the 1700's, one can draw some general conclusions. The effects of increasing international trade on costume were demonstrated not only in the styles of some shoes and in men's robes or dressing gowns, but also in the use of Indian muslins and woven brocades and damasks from the Orient.

Attitudes toward children, shaped by the writings of Rousseau, seem to have been changing at about the same time that clothing for children changed. Greater freedom in both childrearing methods and in clothing for children show interesting parallels.

Protests against the values of contemporary society were expressed through clothing as well. Quaker men avoided wearing fashionable wigs; and both men and women of the Quaker faith wore subdued colors without elaborate embellishments.

Clearly a major role of clothing was the establishment of socio-economic status. Although advances in the technology for manufacturing cloth were beginning to have an impact on the availability of fine fabrics, the enormous amount of hand labor required to make both men's and women's clothing shows not only the wealth of the owner, but also the ready availability of low-paid men and women who spent hours in sewing and embroidering these garments.

14. Moore, *op. cit.*, p. 12.

At the end of the Century the French Revolution in 1795 marks the end of the *Ancien Regime,* a way of life in which the aristocracy was separated from the rest of the population. Styles in clothing changed radically at the time of the Revolution. These changes will be discussed in the next chapter. If the styles of the 18th century are contrasted with those of the beginning of the 19th century, one can see clear visual evidence of radical political change, a rare instance of revolution rather than evolution in styles.

Selected Readings

BOOKS CONTAINING ILLUSTRATIONS OF COSTUME OF THE PERIOD FROM ORIGINAL SOURCES

Blum, S. *Eighteenth Century French Fashion Plates.* New York: Dover Press, 1982.

Cobban, A. *The 18th Century.* McGraw-Hill Book Company, 1969.

Gaunt, W. *The Great Century of British Painting: Hogarth to Turner.* New York: Phaidon, 1971.

Halls, Z. *Men's Costume: 1580–1750.* London: Her Majesty's Stationary Office, 1970.

Halls, Z. *Men's Costume: 1750–1800.* London: Her Majesty's Stationary Office, 1973.

Little, N. F. *Paintings by New England Provincial Artists: 1775–1800.* Boston: Museum of Fine Arts, 1976.

Maeder, E. *An Elegant Art.* New York: Harry N. Abrams, 1983.

Shesgreen, S. (Ed.) *Engravings by Hogarth.* New York: Dover Press, 1973.

Schonberger, A. and H. Soehner. *The Rococo Age.* New York: McGraw-Hill Book Company, Inc., 1960.

PERIODICAL ARTICLES

Brobeck, S. "Images of the Family: Portrait Paintings as Indices of Family Culture, Structure, and Behavior. 1730–1860." *Journal of Psychohistory,* Vol. 5 (1), Summer, 1977, p. 81.

Davis, R. R. Jr. "Diplomatic Plumage: American Court Dress in the Early National Period." *American Quarterly.* September 1968, p. 164.

Cunningham, P. "Eighteenth Century Nightgowns: The Gentleman's Robe in Art and Fashion." *Dress.* Vol. 10, 1984, p. 2.

Kidwell, C. "Short Gowns." *Dress,* 1978, p. 30.

Ribeiro, A. "The Macaronis." *History Today.* Vol. 28 (7), July, 1978, p. 463.

Rowe, A. P. "American Quilted Petticoats." *Irene Emery Roundtable in Museum Textiles, 1975 Proceedings.* Washington, D.C.: The Textile Museum, 1975, p. 161.

Smith, D. J. "Army Clothing Contractors and the Textile Industries of the 18th Century." *Textile History.* Vol. 14 (2), Autumn 1983, p. 153.

Trautman, P. "An 18th Century American Tailor: Myth and Reality as Seen Through One Tailor's Surviving Records." *Clothing and Textiles Research Journal,* Vol. 3, No. 2, Spring 1985, p. 25.

DAILY LIFE

Andrieux, M. *Daily Life in Papal Rome.* New York: Macmillan Company, 1969.

Andrieux, M. *Daily Life in Venice at the Time of Casanova.* New York: Praeger Publishers, 1972.

Brander, M. *The Georgian Gentleman.* Farnborough, Hants, England: Westmead, 1973.

Douville, R. and J. Casanova. *Daily Life in Early Canada.* New York: Macmillan Company, 1968.

Fairchilds, C. *Domestic Enemies: Servants and Their Masters In Old Regime France.* Baltimore: Johns Hopkins University Press, 1984.

George, M. D. *London Life in the Eighteenth Century.* Hamondsworth, England: Penguin Books, 1966.

Jaret, J. *England in the Age of Hogarth.* New Haven, Conn.: Yale University Press, 1986.

Levron, J. *Daily Life at Versailles in the 17th and 18th Centuries.* New York: Macmillan Company, 1968.

Marshall, D. *English People in the 18th Century.* London: Longmans, 1969.

Vussard, M. *Daily Life in Eighteenth Century Italy.* London: Allen and Unwin, 1962.

A Woman's Life at the Court of the Sun King. Letters of Liselotte von der Pfalz. Baltimore: Johns Hopkins University Press, 1984.

Wright, L. B. *Everyday Life in Colonial America.* New York: G. P. Putnam's Sons, 1965.

PART V

The Nineteenth Century

1800–1900

Political events in Europe and the United States provided an almost kaleidoscopic backdrop against which the fashions of the 19th century should be viewed. In France, the Revolution of 1789 and the republic shortly gave way to the first Empire, founded by Napoleon Bonaparte. He re-established a court and made Paris the center of power and fashion. After his overthrow, the Bourbon monarchy was restored under Louis XVIII in 1814. For the remainder of the century France experienced a variety of governments: kings (Charles X, 1824–30, and Louis Philippe, 1830–48); another republic, the Second, with Louis Bonaparte as President, who then became Napoleon III, establishing the Second Empire. After 1870 France had the Third Republic lasting through the remainder of the century.

In Great Britain, the unlucky King George III, who became mentally unstable, had to allow his ministers and his son, the Prince Regent to govern for him. The Prince gathered around him a fashionable circle of men and women who set the styles for the upper classes. On the death of his father in 1820, the Prince became George IV. His scandalous personal life helped make him an unpopular king. After his death in 1830, William IV succeeded him, and he in turn was followed by a niece, Victoria,

who came to the throne in 1837 at the age of eighteen and ruled Great Britain and the Empire until her death in 1901. Through her personality she helped to restore the popularity of the monarchy. So strong was her influence that her name has often been used to describe the greater part of the 19th century—"the Victorian Age."

In mid-century, the forces of nationalism altered the map of Europe. For centuries, Italy had been a geographical expression, a land controlled by stronger powers. Under Napoleon, Italy was treated as a vassal state, but enjoyed many beneficial reforms, only to have them disappear after Napoleon's fall when Austria became dominant. This experience impelled some Italians to think about establishing an independent Italy, freed of reactionary forces. Revolutionary movements to establish a republic failed. However, in an alliance with Napoleon III of France, Piedmont, the only genuinely independent Italian state, defeated Austria, and established an independent Italy in the north in 1859. A military expedition under Giuseppi Garibaldi conquered southern Italy. By 1861, the unification of Italy was completed except for Venice and Rome, and Victor Emmanuel became the first king of Italy.

In central Europe, Austria dominated the German

states, until defeated by Prussia in 1866 in a short war. In 1870 after defeating France, Prussia united the German states in the German Empire.

In the United States the 19th century was the era of westward expansion as new territories were added. In 1800 sixteen states composed the United States, all east of the Mississippi River. After a bloody Civil War over slavery, 1860–1865, a united country of 45 states stretched from the Atlantic Ocean to the Pacific Ocean. At the same time, the expanding nation which offered so many opportunities for a new life attracted millions of immigrants who came primarily from Europe.

Industrialization

The Industrial Revolution which had begun in the preceding centuries, accelerated during the 19th century. The Industrial Revolution brought a fundamental change to industry, resulting in increased production of goods at lower prices, and ultimately a higher standard of living. But in the process it reshaped the pattern of life of men and women. The transition from an economy that had been primarily agricultural with household industries to an economy dominated by great factories was harsh and often cruel.

The Industrial Revolution produced the factory system which involved the migration of people from rural areas to towns and cities that were unprepared to receive them. At the same time, industrial changes produced squalor and misery for many workers who were required to work long hours under unsafe conditions for low pay. Because of the factory system, workers gravitated to towns where crowding and poor housing conditions gave rise to large slum areas. The crowding, poor sanitation, overwork, and poor nutrition contributed to the spread of disease.

The laborers in factories who were most abused were the women, children, and the unskilled. Even those who worked at home were subjected to exploitation. An anonymous author described a swindle perpetrated on sewing girls in New York in the 1850's. These girls were given pantaloons to sew, but only after depositing a security payment. When the garments were finished, she brought them back, expecting to be paid. The man behind the counter examined the bundle, and declared that she had ruined them, and refused to pay her. When the frightened girl asked for the return of her deposit, she was told that she had ruined seven or eight dollars worth of merchandise, and was not entitled to the return of the deposit. The "ruined" garments were subsequently pressed, sorted, and packed up for sale.[1]

For the industrial capitalists, however, industrialization brought wealth and luxury. The early Victorian period in England also saw the Middle Class achieve greater numbers and a more important place in society.

19th Century Morality and Values

The reign of the Prince Regent, later King George IV, in the first three decades of the century was "memorable for the dissolute habits" of the monarch. "Regency life was characterized by expensive flamboyance of costume and endless sessions with one's tailor, barber, and valet preparatory to attending glittering salons, gambling halls, prize fights, modish brothels, and, in extreme cases, early morning duels."[2]

Such behavior, however, was replaced during the remainder of the century by a code of conduct which was determined by "rigid notions about the right ordering of society and individual behavior."[3] As these standards were set by the increasingly influential middle classes, the term "middle-class morality" is often applied to a code of behavior which stressed obedience, male authority, religious piety, thrift, hard work, and sexual morality.

Any references that might have an even vaguely sexual connotation were improper. Classics such as Shakespeare's plays were published with "off-color" sections removed. In the United States for a visit, British Captain Marryat reported an incident during a visit to upper New York State in the 1840's. While walking with a lady over some rough terrain, the lady slipped and obviously hurt her leg. When he inquired as to whether she had injured her "leg," she was visibly offended and upset. When he asked what he should have said, "her reply was, that the word *limb* was used; 'Nay,' continued she, 'I am not so particular as some people are, for I know

1. *Glimpses of New York City* quoted in W. S. Tryon, *A Mirror for Americans: Life and Manners in the United States 1790–1870*. Volume 1. *Life in the East*. Chicago: University of Chicago Press, 1952, p. 222 ff.

2. R. D. Altick. *Victorian People and Ideas*. New York: W. W. Norton and Company, Inc., 1973, p. 9.

3. W. J. Reader. *Life in Victorian England*. New York: G. P. Putnam's Sons. 1964, p. 6.

those who always say limb of a table or of a pianoforte.' "[4]

Just because the Victorian middle class espoused a strict morality does not mean that all 19th century persons practiced these virtues. Prostitution was not uncommon among working class women who were often driven to the streets by poverty. Their patrons were from all classes of society. Nevertheless, respectable women were expected to marry and to bear children as a "duty." Sexual pleasure, especially for women, was held to be sinful.

Dress Reform

The role of respectable women for most of 19th century society was limited by tradition to that of wife and mother. Even so, at the mid-century feminists had begun to agitate for a more important place in society. Being denied the right to vote was a symbol of oppression of women in the eyes of the suffragists. Another symbol of the oppression of women to some feminists was fashion, particularly those fashions that tended to confine and hamper women.

Several specific efforts at dress reform were mounted. The first of these was advanced by the suffragists, between 1851 and 1854. Although the costume was called "Bloomer costume" after Amelia

Bloomer one of the women who wore this full-skirted, short dress that was placed over full trousers, other feminists such as Susan B. Anthony, Lucy Stone, and Elizabeth Cady Stanton also adopted the style. The Bloomer costume, however, provoked ridicule, and was given up.

Later attempts at dress reform included the Aesthetic Dress of the 1870's and 80's—a reform based on an artistic ideal rather than on a political philosophy, and the "Rational dress" of the 1880's which represented an attempt to provide women with more healthful clothing that did away with tight corseting and lacing.

The End of an Age

Queen Victoria died in 1901. The Victorian Era had actually ended before her death, if one defines that era by the attitudes discussed heretofore. By the end of the century the sense of an absolute code of correct behavior, the self-confidence and self-righteousness that had characterized Victorian attitudes had passed. The era that followed, shortened though it was by the First World War, ". . . was electric with an exultant and slightly self-conscious sense of liberation—liberation, that is, from the stuffiness, the obscurantism, the false verities, the repressions and taboos now attributed, fairly or not, to the Victorian mind."[5]

4. Quoted in A. Nevins. *American Social History as Reported By British Travelers*. New York: Augustus M. Kelley, Publishers. 1969, pp 245–246.

5. Altick, *op. cit.*, p. 301.

CHAPTER 12

The Directoire Period and the Empire Period

1790–1820

The *Directoire* and the Empire periods encompass the years from 1790, just after the beginning of the French Revolution, until 1820. The dates assigned to the *Directoire* (c. 1790 to 1800) include major events of the French Revolution and the establishment of the Directory, a government by a five man executive. The Empire period coincides generally with the period during which Napoleon Bonaparte was the head of state in France. Indeed, the name of the period is derived from the title of his era, the Napoleonic Empire.

Historical Background

FRANCE

The Revolution and the Directory—Social, political, and economic grievances, high unemployment and high prices, along with a bankrupt government combined to produce conditions ripe for revolution in France in 1789. Peasants, who bore the heaviest load of unjust taxation, did not lead the revolution, that role belonged to the urban bourgeoisie who resented the nobility's privileges and monopoly of

high offices in government, church, and the armed forces.

Unable to solve the national financial crisis, Louis XVI summoned the Estates General, representatives of the three estates of the realm, to meet in 1789. It had not met in over a century and a half. Soon after its opening session, the Estates General proclaimed itself a National Assembly and began to reform France by abolishing feudalism, adopting the Declaration of the Rights of Man and by drafting the first written constitution in French history. After war broke out in 1792 and began to go badly for France, Parisian rioters, frightened by the defeats on the battlefield, overthrew the monarchy. The first French republic was established; the king was tried and executed in 1793. Doctrinaire radicals, the Jacobins, resorted to a "Reign of Terror," 1793–1794, in an effort to save the nation from defeat. Although they saved France, the Jacobins were overthrown in 1794 and a new government established, a *Directoire* (in English, Directory), an executive of five men. The Directory ruled France for the next five years.

During the Revolution fashions for women did not change radically from those of the pre-revolutionary period. Citizens were expected to declare their revolutionary ardor by displaying the revolutionary colors—red, white, and blue—so these colors were fashionable and appeared often in dresses. Red-white-and blue flowers or ribbons were seen on costumes or hats.

For a time, men's costumes took on a number of symbolic meanings. For many generations trousers had been worn only by men of the laboring classes, and so the revolutionaries adopted the dress of the lower classes. In the earliest stages of the revolution these men were called, derisively, "sans culottes," meaning "without kneebreeches." The nickname persisted, and when it became clear that the revolution was succeeding, the term lost its negative connotation. Soon men who wanted to be sure their loyalty to the revolution was not questioned dressed in the peasant fashion, in the *carmagnole*. The carmagnole was made up of a short woolen or cloth jacket of a dark color. It was hip length with fullness at the back, cut rather like a smock. Trousers were made of the same material, or of red, white and blue striped drill. A red waistcoat was worn, and wooden shoes called clogs or sabots. A soft woolen peasant's cap of red color which followed the line of the classical Phrygian bonnet became a symbol of the revolution.

When the Terror ended and the Directory was established, the passions aroused during the revolution began to cool. At this point in France styles for women changed radically. A new style, elements of which are thought to have appeared first in England, became fashionable. Based on Ancient Greek forms and cut with little or no sleeve, a low, round neckline, and a high waist, the dress fell straight to the floor. Soft clinging fabrics such as muslin or linen were employed. Many were sheer and under these dresses some women wore little underwear aside from the chemise and no corseting. Others who were quite bold wore pink tights to give the illusion of flesh.

Men abandoned the carmagnole, returning to costumes similar in their basic aspects to those from before the revolution: a fitted coat, a waistcoat, and knee breeches. Extremists in fashion were assigned nicknames. The *merveilleuse* (the marvelous ones) were women who affected the most extreme of the directoire styles, with long flowing trains, the sheerest of fabrics, necklines cut in some extreme cases to the waistline, and huge, exaggerated jockey-like caps. The men, known as *incroyables* or "incredibles" wore waistcoats of loose fit at the shoulders, excessively tight breeches, and cravats or neckties and collars that covered so much of their chins that one wonders if they could be heard or understood when they spoke. Both the men and women affected a shaggy, unkempt hairdress. (See Figure 12.1.)

The Empire—The French Revolution had opened careers to young men of talent. A young Corsican, Napoleon Bonaparte, a second lieutenant in artillery in 1789, a brigadier general by 1795, saved the Directory from a mob with a "whiff of grapeshot." Promoted to major general, his victories over the Austrians in Italy, 1796–1797, and his victories in Egypt against the British and the Turks, 1798–1799, made him the hero of Paris. However, the Directory governed ineffectively, the war again went badly. Because they feared another Terror, conspirators joined with Napoleon in staging a coup in 1799, overthrowing the Directory. It was replaced by an executive of three consuls, but Napoleon as First Consul had dictatorial power. By 1804, after consolidating his power, he was crowned, "Emperor of the French." In the next ten years, Napoleon instituted legal and educational reforms, reorganized the government, making it more efficient, competent and honest. Napoleon extended his hegemony over all of Europe, defeating all but Great Britain. In 1812, finding it necessary to attack Russia, his armies marched to Moscow but the Tsar refused to surrender. With winter coming on, Napoleon had to retreat. Harrassed by Russians, the defeat became a rout. It was the beginning of the end for Napoleon. In 1814 he abdicated and went to the Island of Elba.

After the establishment of the Empire, the basic style lines that had been worn by both men and women during the Directoire continued, but the extremes of nudity and the styles of the merveilleuse and incroyable disappeared. In part this may have been because Napoleon was somewhat conservative in his attitudes, and considered the more extreme styles as immoral. The newly established court also provided a stage for the display of fashions, and more elaborate fabrics and styles began to appear as the Emperor attempted to recreate the elegance of the old regime.

Napoleon tried to encourage French industry by stimulating the demand for French goods, and he restricted the importation of fabrics from abroad particularly muslin and printed cottons from India. Shawls were a popular fashion item imported from India. Napoleon ended their importation and ordered that they be copied in France. However his first wife, Josephine, continued to have her own shawls imported without his knowledge. She must have helped to stimulate the French industry almost single-handedly, as an inventory of her wardrobe

12.1 Styles of the early Empire Period. Women's dresses are cut low, from fabrics that cling and reveal the body. Their hair styles show strong Greek and Roman influences. The man on the left wears an exaggeratedly high collar and cravat; his coat cut full and somewhat loose over the shoulder. Such styles were associated with fashion extremists, the *incroyables* and *merveilleuse* of about 1800. (*Courtesy of the Metropolitan Museum of Art, Harris Brisbane Dick Fund, 1938.*)

in 1809 included 666 winter dresses, 230 summer dresses, and 60 cashmere shawls.

ENGLAND

In England, King George III reigned throughout this period. A pious, virtuous man who enjoyed the simple life, he wrote articles on farming, under the byline, "Farmer George." This unlucky gentleman, who had to preside over the loss of the American colonies in 1776, had periods of intermitant insanity. By 1810 his condition had become permanent; he could no longer rule. The Prince of Wales had to be named as Regent to act for his father. During the Regency Period, 1811–1820, the English court and fashionable society were organized around the Prince Regent, who had an eye for the ladies and for whom the pursuit of pleasure was possibly his

most active pasttime. His cleverness and gracious manners, gave him the title, "the first gentleman of Europe." As a result, the court became the center of fashion in England.

For the greater part of the period, the English remained at war with France, resolved to block Napoleon's ambition to become supreme in Europe. The defeat of the French fleet at Trafalgar in 1805 ended any danger of French invasion of the British Isles. Final peace came only with the defeat of Napoleon at Waterloo in 1815.

For a time, at the beginning of the Empire period, English and French women's dress styles diverged. While the French were narrowing the silhouette as it fell from the elevated Empire waist, the English placed a padded roll under the waistline to create a fuller, rounded line to the skirt. It is thought that these differences developed because England and

12.2 White embroidered cotton dress of the round gown type which exhibits the fullness at the elevated waistline that characterized English styles of 1800. (*Photograph courtesy of the Smithsonian Institution.*)

France were at war, and trade and dissemination of ideas were restricted. After about a year or two, the English line narrowed and became like that of the French. (See Figure 12.2.)

UNITED STATES

Styles in the United States paralleled those of Europe. Imported fashion engravings provided information about current fashions from Paris and London.

THE ARTS OF THE PERIOD

The revival of interest in the arts of classical antiquity that had begun in the second half of the 18th century continued during the Empire period. This interest accelerated as a result of the military campaigns of Napoleon in Italy, where Roman ruins abounded, and because of the political emphasis on the revival of the republican ideals of ancient Greece and Rome. Many French artists painted huge canvasses depicting events in ancient history. Architecture emphasized classic styles. When Napoleon took his armies to Egypt, he included on his staff artists who sketched the ruins of Egyptian civilization, and a number of Egyptian influences began to find their way into furniture and design.

The renewal of interest in the arts and philosophy of the ancient world paralleled the revival of many classical elements in the new costume style for women that was based on an interpretation of the styles worn by women of Greece of the Golden Age. Taken largely from statuary and from Greek vase painting, the dress styles were predominantly white in color. Over the years since their creation the color of Greek and Roman statues had been bleached away leaving them completely white. This led to the assumption that classical costume had been white.

At the same time the new style provided a sharp contrast to the silhouette of the *ancien regime*, or the pre-revolutionary period. It marked an extreme and distinct break with the earlier period. Fashion is generally evolutionary rather than revolutionary, but the costumes of the Empire Period mark one of those rare instances in which a revolutionary change in fashion takes place. This change in fashions parallels an equally revolutionary change in the political structure of the country in which the styles developed. It is not far-fetched to say that the revolutionary change in women's dress styles was a visible symbol of the revolution in political thought that caused both the American and French revolutions.

Empire Costume

COSTUME FOR WOMEN

Item / Description

undergarments—During the Directoire Period (c. 1895–1900) very fashionable women ceased wearing corsets and wore, at most, a lightweight chemise as underclothing. For most women, however, these undergarments were used:

corsets (more commonly known as "stays.")— cut in a straight line and so as to push the breasts up and out. Use of false bosoms is noted, these were made of wax or cotton.

NOTE: One disgruntled lover lamented:
"My Delia's heart I find so hard, I would she were forgotton
For how can hearts be adamant when all the breast is—cotton."[1]

chemise—made of cotton or linen and worn closest to the body.
petticoat—placed over the chemise by some women. Poor women and African slaves in the Americas often wore petticoats in combination with short gowns (see page 186) as street clothing. While the skirts of dresses remained narrow, undergarments were cut fairly straight, but as skirts widened toward the end of the Empire Period, both the chemise and petticoat gained in breadth.
drawers—new to England and the American colonies, continental European women seem to have worn cotton or linen drawers much earlier. From this time on they became a basic part of women's underclothing. Unlike modern underpants, they were usually open through the crotch area, an important convenience when women needed to relieve themselves.
pantalettes—Long, straight, white drawers trimmed with rows of lace or tucks at the hem became fashionable for a short time around 1809. While the fashion did not long continue for adult women, young girls wore them throughout this and subsequent periods.
padded rolls—bustle-like, these constructions were placed under dresses at the back of the waistline during the closing years of the period. The result was to give a peculiar forward slant to the body which was known as the "Grecian bend."

dresses—silhouette—Tubular, with a waistline placement just under the bosom. Skirts reached to the floor. To achieve the straight line and incorporate the gathered fullness, supple and light-weight fabrics had to be used. A small concentration of gathered fabric at the back of the skirt was a vestige of the back-fullness characteristic of the last part of the 1700's. Trained and untrained dresses were made until about 1812 when skirts shortened.
fabrics—Lightweight cotton and linen muslins

1. *The Oracle*, an English periodical of 1800.

12.3 Printed cotton round gown of 1800. (*Photograph courtesy of the Smithsonian Institution.*)

and soft silks. In the Directoire period plain white, undecorated "Grecian-style" gowns were fashionable, but with the coming of the Empire pastel shades or white with a variety of delicate embroideries were more often used.

dresses—Several different constructions were utilized. These included:
· dresses open at the front to display an elaborate, decorated "petticoat" which was not an undergarment but a visible underskirt. This type of dress was often worn as evening wear.
· *round gowns*—daytime or evening dresses that did not open at the front to show a petticoat. (See Figures 12.2 and 12.3.)

• *tunic dresses*—an underdress with a loose shorter (ranging from hip to ankle) tunic or outerdress on top. (See Figure 12.7.)

• *apron or high stomacher dress*—a complex construction in which the bodice was sewn to the skirt at the back only. Side front seams were left open to several inches below the waist; a band or string was located at the front of the waist of the skirt. The lady slipped the garment over her head, put her arms into the sleeves, then tied the waist string around the back like an apron. The bodice often had a pair of underflaps that pinned across the chest, supporting the bust. Front closing of the outer bodice was made either by wrapping it across the bosom like a shawl or lacing it up the front over a short undershirt (a *habit* shirt), or by buttoning it down the front.

On these dresses, the following necklines:
• low-cut, round, or square.
• higher necklines, often finishing in a small ruff or ruffle or with a drawstring that tied around the neck.

Major sleeve types were:
• short, puffed or fitted—the most common type.
• sheer oversleeves placed over the aforemen-

12.4 From left to right: Empire dress of embroidered muslin with a spencer of figured silk; small child in embroidered muslin dress and wearing pantalettes; ribbed silk dress, c. 1807–12; muslin dress (1804–1814) with multicolored bead embroidery and embroidered muslin scarf. (*Photograph courtesy of the Costume Institute of the Metropolitan Museum of Art.*)

tioned short sleeves.
· long sleeves, either fitted or full.
· full, long sleeves tied into sections of short puffs.
· a single puff at the shoulder, with the rest of the sleeve fitted to the arm.

outdoor garments—shawls or stoles in varying sizes and shapes. (See Figure 12.4.)

NOTE: In Winter these provided relatively little protection. A flu epidemic during the Directoire Period gained the nickname "muslin fever" after the practice of wearing lightweight muslin dresses with so little covering over them.

spencer—a short jacket (worn by both men and women) that ended at the waistline which in the case of women's styles was just under the bosom. Made with sleeves and sleeveless, the color usually contrasted with the rest of the costume. Spencers were worn indoors as well as out. (See Figure 12.4.)

pelisse—similar to a modern coat, generally full-length and following the typical Empire silhouette. For winter, especially when made of silk or cotton, pelisses had warm linings. (See Figure 12.5.)

cloaks or capes—Cut full or three-quarter

12.5 On the left a silk walking dress (c. 1805–1810) in chestnut brown faille and green-gold satin worn with a leghorn hat tied "gypsy" fashion and at the right a red, silk taffeta *pelisse* (c. 1816–1818). The *pelisse* is padded throughout for warmth; the hat is a poke bonnet. (*Photograph courtesy of the Metropolitan Museum of Art.*)

length. The terms mantle and cloak were used interchangeably.

hair and head dress—*hair*—styles were often based on Greek prototypes: combing the hair back from the face to gather it in ringlets or coils at the back of the head, while the hair around the face was arranged in soft curls. Other styles included a short, curly style with the name *a la victime* or *a la Titus*.

NOTE: The former term was a reference to the short haircuts given to victims about to be guillotined during the French Revolution; the latter to short hair depicted on statues of Roman men.

hats—a variety of styles which included:
• jockey caps, especially for riding. (Riding was one of the few sports in which women could participate.)
• turbans—especially fashionable after Napoleon's invasion of Egypt.
• small fabric hats similar to military helmets of classic antiquity.
• bonnets—having crowns of fabric or straw and wide brims.
• toques—high, brimless hats.
• "gypsy hats"—with a low crown and a moderately wide brim, worn with ribbon tied over the outside of the brim and under the chin.
• small muslin or lace caps worn indoors by mature women.

Hats were worn not only out-of-doors but also for evening events such as the theatre or balls.

footwear—*shoes*—usually made of leather, of velvet or satin and often in colors matching dresses or pelisses. Shoes had no heels, were flat. Major types were:
• slippers, some with cris-cross lacings which ran up the leg to below the knee.
• short boots, reaching to the calf. Boots closed at the sides with laces or buttons or at the back with laces.
• pattens—with small platforms of wood or steel that fastened over shoes for bad weather.

accessories—*gloves*—with short-sleeved dresses, long gloves, ending on the upper arm or above the elbow. Made of leather, silk, or net.
reticules or *indispensibles*—small handbags, often with a drawstring at the top.

NOTE: In earlier periods when skirts had been full, pockets placed under the skirt were used for carrying small personal objects. The narrow silhouette of the Empire period made such pockets impractical, so the reticule replaced the pocket. Some found the device amusing and took to calling it a "ridicule."

muffs—large in size, often of fur, swansdown, or fabric.
parasols—some pagoda-shaped, moderate to small in size.
fans and decorative *handkerchiefs* were also carried.

jewelry—Included necklaces, earrings, rings, small watches that pinned to the dress, and brooches, some of which served the function of closing the dress. Bracelets were worn high on the arm in imitation of those on Greek and Roman statues and vases.

COSTUME FOR MEN

Item / Description

undergarments—*drawers*—similar to those shown in Figure 11.2, and usually made of linen or cotton.

shirts—cotton or linen fabrics were used to make full-cut shirts with high, standing collars that reached to the cheek. The front of the shirt was generally pleated or ruffled.

neckwear—*cravats*—large squares of fabric folded and wrapped several times around the neck and tied in front.
stocks—stiffened neckbands that buckled or tied behind the neck.

suits—consisting of a coat; a waistcoat, worn beneath the coat; and either breeches or trousers. Clothing for "dress" (formal occasions) and "undress" (less formal occasions) usually differed only in color or quality of fabric, buttons, and accessories.
colors and fabrics—Rarely were the three parts of the suit the same color. Generally they contrasted. Colors were light or dark, bright or subdued. Wool was used in a variety of weights and qualities; for formal occasions and especially at the French or English courts, lavishly decorated velvets and silk fabrics were suitable.
coats—Coat fronts generally ended at the waist, either curving gradually back from the waist into two tails that ended slightly above the knee; or with a cut-in, a rounded or square space at the front where no skirt was attached and with the tails beginning where the cut-in ended. (See Figures 12.6 and 12.7.)

12.6 View of man's coat of 1804 from the back shows the cut of the tail coat. As accessories the gentleman wears a top hat and riding boots. (*Fashion plate, 1804.*)

12.7 Gentleman of 1802 in tail coat, knee breeches, and two-cornered hat is dressed for a ball. His waistcoat is visible between the end of his coat and the beginning of his breeches. His companion wears a dress with a short overskirt or tunic. (*Fashion plate, 1802.*)

Coat collars generally had a notch where the collar joined the lapel. Some coats had velvet facings applied. Closings were both single and double-breasted. Pockets were located in the pleats of the coat tails, or at the waist. Some coats had false pocket flaps.

waistcoats—Sleeveless, only the front was visible when a coat was worn therefore the back was made of plain cotton or linen fabric or of the waistcoat lining fabric. Collars generally stood upright; some were cut so that the upper and lower edges formed a step-like structure, i.e., were "stepped." About two inches of waistcoat were visible at the bottom of the coat when it was closed and only a small edge of the waistcoat was visible at the open neck of the coat. (See Figure 12.7.)

breeches or trousers—*breeches*—pants ending at the knee. Until about 1807 breeches were worn extensively.

trousers—extended to the ankle.

pantaloons—at this period were generally defined as fitting the leg more closely than trousers which were made in close-fitting, moderately full, and very full styles. These latter trousers were based on the dress of Russian soldiers and in the fashion press were referred to as *Cossacks*. Tight pantaloons or trousers had an instep strap to keep them from riding up the leg.

NOTE: Trousers had been introduced for fashionable wear during the French Revolution, but were discarded again by fashion leaders immediately following the Revolution. After 1807 they returned as acceptable fashions.

dressing gown or banyan—Usually ankle-length, cut with a full, flared skirt. Fabrics used included decorative damasks or brocades of wool, cotton, or silk. Some had matching waistcoats.

NOTE: According to Coleman, "in the eighteenth and early nineteenth centuries this outfit was not confined to 'at home' wear as its descendant the robe or dressing gown, is today. It was accepted for street and office wear."[2]

outdoor garments—Overcoats or great coats for cold weather; very full, either single or double-breasted, coats had collars and lapels and were either knee or full length. Some had one or more capes at the shoulder. Cloaks no longer fashionable, but were sometimes worn for travel.

Spencers were worn by men as well as women, but for men they took the place of the coat with a suit.

hair and head dress—*hair*—generally worn short; faces clean-shaven although side whiskers were somewhat long.

hats—*Top hats* the predominant form, with either taller or shorter crowns and medium-sized brims. Brims rolled up slightly at the sides, dipping in front and back. (Figure 12.6.) The *bicorne* was a two-pointed hat worn with the points from front to back or from side-to-side. When worn for evening and carried flattened, under the arm, it was called a *chapeau bras* (French for "hat for the arm.") (Figure 12.7.) Hats were made from silk, wool felt, or beaver (felted beaver fur mixed with wool.)

footwear—*shoes*—made with low, round heels and rounded toes. Early in the period shoes closed with decorative buckles, but were gradually supplanted by a tie closing at the front.

boots—named for military heroes or well-known army units (Examples: Napoleons, Wellingtons, Cossacks, and Hessians.) True military boots were high in front, covering the knees, and scooped down behind the knee in back so that the knee could be bent easily. *Other boot styles:* turned-down tops with contrasting linings; shorter boots to be worn over close-fitting trousers.

accessories—*gloves*—short, made of cotton or leather. Hand-carried accessories included canes

2. E. A. Coleman. *Of Men Only.* New York: Brooklyn Museum, 1975, p. 6.

and quizzing glasses, i.e. magnifying glasses mounted on a handle and worn around the neck.

NOTE: Some authors claim that the fad for quizzing glasses led some dandies to have their optic nerves loosened surgically in order to justify the acquisition of a glass, but this is most likely an example of the exaggerated claims often made for the impact of fad or fashion.

jewelry—For men, limited to rings and decorative watch fobs and occasionally decorative brooches worn on the linen of the shirt or neckcloth.

cosmetics—Some very fashion-conscious men used rouge to heighten their color, bleached their hands to whiten them, and used substantial quantities of eau de cologne.

COSTUME FOR CHILDREN

boys—Aged infant to about four or five—skirts similar to those of little girls, although generally slightly shorter. By age four or five, trousers were usually worn under skirts.

After age six or seven—*skeleton suits:* a loose shirt with wide, frilled collar and ankle-length trousers that began high; the trousers generally buttoned to the shirt. After age 11 or 12, boys were dressed much the same as men.

footwear—slippers or soft boots.
hair dress—long or short.
outer wear—overcoats.

girls—*dresses*—cut along same lines as those of adult women, but shorter for both little girls and young adolescents. Under dresses girls wore *pantalettes.*

footwear—slippers or soft boots, made of leather or fabric.

head dress—hair styles natural for small girls; adolescents adopted fashionable adult styles, particular Grecian styles. Bonnets were among the most popular hat styles.

outer wear—shawls and pelisses.

Summary

Clothing for men and women during the Directoire/ Empire period provides a marked contrast with the styles of the preceding century. For men, the acceptance of trousers in place of knee breeches represented the triumph of a style that had once been associated with working class men. Moreover, the accepted styles for men for the rest of the 19th century and on into the 20th century that will be described in the coming chapters will continue to reflect the more somber color range and plainer fabrics that first became acceptable for upper class men in these first two decades.

By comparison with men's costume, women's dress utilized more decorative fabrics, a greater variety of colors, and many different style details. This will continue in subsequent periods. The elevated "Empire" waistline that was established in the 1790's persisted throughout the first two decades, but by the close of this costume period, subtle changes were occurring in the silhouette of clothing. As the skirts of dresses shortened and widened perceptibly (the waistline located at the anatomical waist was not achieved in ladies' dress until almost 1840) the evolution from the Empire styles into those of the Romantic period had clearly begun.

Selected Readings

BOOKS CONTAINING ILLUSTRATIONS OF COSTUME OF THE PERIOD FROM ORIGINAL SOURCES

Ackermann's Repository of the Arts, reprinted by Dover Publications, New York, 1979.

Coleman, E. *Changing Fashions: 1800–1970.* Brooklyn, N.Y. The Brooklyn Museum, 1972.

Gibbs-Smith, C. H. *The Fashionable Lady in the 19th Century.* London: Her Majesty's Stationary Office, 1960.

Of Men Only, A Review of Men's and Boy's Fashions, 1750–1975. Brooklyn, N.Y.: Brooklyn Museum, 1975.

White, W. J. *Working Class Costume from Sketches of Characters, 1818.* London: Costume Society and Victoria and Albert Museum, 1971.

PERIODICAL ARTICLES

Anninger, A. "Costume of the Convention: Art as Agent of Social Change in Revolutionary France." *Harvard Library Journal*, Vol. 30 (2), April 1982, p. 179.

Bradfield, N. "Studies of an 1814 Pelisse and Bonnet." *Costume*, 1973, p. 60.

Deslandres, Y. "Josephine and La Mode." *Apollo*, Vol. CVI, No. 185, July 1977, p. 44.

Harris, J. "The Red Cap of Liberty: A Study of Dress Worn by French Revolutionary Partisans, 1789–94." *Eighteenth Century Studies*, Vol. 14, No. 3, Spring 1981, p. 283.

DAILY LIFE

Ashton, J. *Social England Under the Regency.* London: Chatte and Winders, 1899.

Langdon, W. C. *Everyday Things in American Life, 1776–1876.* New York: Charles Scribner's Sons, 1941.

Laver, J. *The Age of Illusion: Manners and Morals 1750–1848.* New York: David McKay Company, Inc., 1972.

Low, D. A. *That Sunny Dome: A Portrait of Regency Britain.* Totowa, NJ: Rowman, 1977.

Margetson, S. *Leisure and Pleasure in the 19th Century.* New York: Coward McCann, Inc., 1969.

Peterson, H. L. *Americans at Home: From the Colonists to the Late Victorians.* New York: Charles Scribner's Sons, 1971.

Robiquet, J. *Daily Life in France Under Napoleon.* New York: Macmillan Company, 1963.

Wharton, A. H. *Social Life in the Early Republic.* New York: Benjamin Blom, 1969.

CHAPTER 13

The Romantic Period

1820–1850

The name assigned to the period in costume from about 1820–1850 in this text is the Romantic Period. The term "Romantic" has been applied to much of the literature, music, and graphic arts of this same era. Romantic art and literature emphasized emotion, sentiment, and feeling. Romanticism represented a reaction against the formal classical styles of the 17th and 18th centuries. Romantics rejected the classical insistence on rules governing creative work. Romantics were concerned more with content and less with form; they preferred to break rules. Romantic writers assumed that "empirical science and philosophy were inadequate as a means of answering all the most important questions concerning human life."[1] Romantic artists appealed to the emotions.

Romanticism was a form of rebellion against restrictions on artistic expression. The artist or the writer should express his innermost feelings in any form he chose. Romanticism had a new set of values—the innermost emotions should be fully expressed. Art should please the senses. Imagination was more important than reason.

Romantics ignored social conventions, including

1. R. W. Harris. *Romanticism and the Social Order*. New York: Barnes and Noble, 1969, p. 19.

marriage. They resorted to tears, violent emotions, loving and hating fiercely. A true romantic heroine fainted easily because of inner spiritual turmoil. Romantic life style included beards, long hair, and unusual clothing. English poets such as Lord Byron, Shelley, and Keats were non-conformist in their life styles, as well as in their poetry.

Romantics preferred other times and places, and one of their favorite times was the Middle Ages. Romanticism invented the historical novel. Writers, such as Walter Scott, wrote popular historical novels filled with the legends and history of Scotland and medieval England. In France, Alexander Dumas the Elder wrote swashbuckling historical novels, including *The Three Musketeers* and *The Count of Monte Cristo*. Subjects of romantic paintings were often events from the past, as well as Oriental and Mediterranean scenes of violent action. Some Romantic artists painted moonlit ruins, ghosts, mysterious forms. The romantic love of the unusual and fantastic found expression in tales such as Mary Godwin Shelley's *Frankenstein*.

These trends in the arts were reflected in costume. After 1820 elements that can be related to Romanticism in the arts began to appear, especially in women's dress. Many costumes showed conscious attempts to revive certain elements of historical dress, such as neck ruffs, the ferroniere (a chain with a jewel worn at the center of the forehead), or sleeve styles from earlier costume periods. Costume balls at which men and women appeared dressed as figures from the past were in vogue. The leading Romantic poet, Lord Byron, inspired some styles or names of styles in men's dress. Fashionable colors were given names such as "dust of ruins" or "Egyptian earth."

After the Revolution of 1848–49, Romanticism declined. Although some artists and writers continued to work in the Romantic vein, the period of major influence of the Romantics was over.

Historical Background

The Romantic Movement was played out against the following political background. In England, the Prince Regent finally became King George IV in 1820, but the scandals surrounding his marital life made him unpopular. During his reign, the first professional police force was created with headquarters at Scotland Yard, and Roman Catholics were permitted to sit in Parliament. William IV, an eccentric old sailor, with little political sense, succeeded his brother on the throne in 1830. In his reign, Parliament enacted the famous Reform Bill, redistributing the seats in the House of Commons and extending the franchise. When William died without an heir in 1837, his eighteen year old niece, Victoria, became queen. Victoria ruled until 1901, and gave her name to an age. She restored the prestige of the monarchy, recapturing the respect and admiration of the English people.

In France after the fall of Napoleon, the Bourbon monarchy was restored. Louis XVIII, brother of the executed Louis XVI, became king and granted the nation a written constitution. The restoration of the Bourbons contributed (along with the historicism of the Romantic writers) to the revival of styles from earlier monarchial periods and to an interest in costume balls.

In 1824, Louis's brother succeeded him as Charles X. A king lacking in common sense, his attempt to restore royal absolutism led to revolution in July 1830. The revolution was led by an alliance of journalists, republicans, unemployed working men, and students who had been enthusiastic supporters of the rebellious spirit of Romanticism. They expressed their rebellion not only through political actions but also in their style of dress. They wore clothes deliberately different from fashionable men, working clothes; they discarded stiff collars and neckcloths.

After three days of fighting, Charles X abdicated in favor of his grandson, but the Parisians wanted no more of the Bourbon dynasty. Leaders of the *bourgeoisie* (middle class), fearing another republic, succeeded in having the crown offered to Louis Philippe, the Duke of Orleans, the head of the younger branch of the Bourbon family, whose father had been an aristocratic supporter of the French Revolution. He now became the King of the French. But his reign was filled with social and economic unrest because he proved too conservative. His unwillingness to make reforms in the electoral system led to the outbreak of revolution in 1848. France established a second republic and the voters elected Louis Napoleon as president but in 1852 the Second Republic became the Second Empire. Meanwhile, the revolution in France led to a tidal wave of revolution which swept over Austria, the German states and Italy.

In the United States during the same period the westward expansion had begun. Texas was annexed in 1845, and after a war with Mexico, New Mexico and California were ceded to the United States. Then the Oregon territory was acquired, giving the United States government control over virtually all of the territory now part of the United States.

The United States had also in the Monroe Doctrine of 1823 given notice to the European powers that the American continent was no longer open to colonization. But at the same time that Americans were becoming politically independent of Europe, American people continued to follow the pattern of styles set abroad.

WOMEN'S ROLES AND CLOTHING STYLES

Romantic poets often emphasized the maiden who died for love or the one whose hard-heartedness caused despair in her lover. According to one analysis of women's attitudes in the 19th century, it was distinctly unstylish to appear to be in good health. Circles under the eyes were cultivated and rice powder was liberally applied to produce a pale look. The middle class woman was expected, furthermore, to be a "perfect lady."[2]

With industrialization and the growing movement of business out of the home and into an external workplace, women's roles were increasingly confined to the home. Affluent women were severely

2. C. W. Cunnington. *Feminine Attitudes in the 19th Century.* London: Heinemann, 1935.

limited in their activities. The home was the center of entertainment, and well-to-do women served as hostesses for their husbands. For this role they required a substantial wardrobe of fashionable clothes. They supervised the servants, who did all of the household tasks. Women dressed in the most stylish gowns of the 1830's and 40's when sleeves were set low on the shoulder would not have been able to raise their arms above their heads, and were virtually incapable of performing any physical labor. Accomplishments such as sewing, embroidering, modeling in wax, sketching, painting on glass or china, or decorating other functional objects were encouraged, but most had seamstresses who would come to the home to make the more complicated garments.

Women from working class families, from rural areas, and pioneers, however, did toil at a wide variety of tasks. Their garments were less hampering, more practical in form, and made from less expensive fabrics. Even so, their dresses followed the basic style lines and silhouette of the period. (See Figure 13.8.) The fashionable bonnet of the Romantic Period was transformed by farm and pioneer women into a sunbonnet, a practical covering to protect the face and head from the hot sun.

SOURCES OF FASHION INFORMATION

A major source of fashion information was women's magazines which carried a number of features about current styles. Introduced in Europe in the late 18th century, these periodicals included hand-colored prints showing the latest styles, together with a printed description. The major American fashion magazines of the 19th century, *Godey's Lady's Book* and *Peterson's Magazine* began publication in 1830 and 1842 respectively. From the 1830's up to the present time fashion magazines have served as an excellent primary source of information about what was considered to be the newest fashion.

Fashion magazines clearly demonstrated the influence of Paris styles on women's fashions. Descriptions of plates in both English and American magazines usually emphasized that these were the "latest Paris fashions." Descriptions were heavily larded with French phrases and French names for garments or fabrics.

The 1840's also marked the beginning of photographic portraiture. Louis Daguerre of France perfected his photographic process and it immediately became fashionable for individuals to sit for their "daguerreotypes." These pictures not only provide

13.1 Dress of 1824 shows transition from Empire to early Romantic period styles. Waistline has been moved to a somewhat lower level than during the Empire, the skirt is more bell-shaped, and sleeves are growing a little larger. (*New York City Public Library Picture Collection.*)

a record of styles actually being worn but also allow comparison of the idealized fashion plates and artists' painted portraits with real clothing. From 1849 on, when the process became established in the United States, there is a wealth of photographic material documenting costumes.

Yet another source of information can be found in historic costume collections. Items from the period between 1820 and 1850 are more plentiful than those from earlier periods, although the largest number of items tend to be wedding dresses, ball gowns, and other "special" clothing. Everyday dresses, men's, and children's costumes are rarely represented in quantity in collections.

Romantic Period Costume

COSTUME FOR WOMEN—1820–1836

The period between 1820 and 1825 was a period of transition between the Empire styles and the newer Romantic mode. A change in the location of the waistline took place gradually. By 1825 the waistline had moved downward from just under the bust to several inches above the anatomical location of the waist. (See Figure 13.1) By 1825 along with the changes in waistline placement, women's dresses had developed large sleeves which continued to grow larger and gored skirts which were widening and becoming gradually shorter. (See Figure 13.2.)

types of dresses— Dresses were frequently identified in fashion magazines according to the times of day or the activities for which they were intended. As a result fashion plates generally carried captions such as "morning dresses," "day dresses," "walking" or "promenade dresses," "carriage dresses," "dinner dresses," or "evening" or "ball dresses." Morning dresses were generally the most informal, often being made of lingerie-type fabrics such as white cotton or fine linen with lace or ruffled trimmings. Day dresses, promenade or walking dresses, and carriage dresses are often indistinguishable one from the other, especially in summer.

Item / Description

undergarments—*drawers*—more and more worn by women of all social classes. No substantive changes in their construction.
   chemises—still about knee-length, wide, and usually with short sleeves. (See Figure 13.3.)
   stays—as dress silhouettes placed greater emphasis on a small waist, stays shortened and laced tightly to pull in the waist.
   petticoats—Multiple layers worn to support the ever-wider skirts of dresses.
   bustles—in the form of small, down or cotton-filled pads tied on around the waist and located at the back. (See Figure 13.3.)

dresses for daytime—Without trains and fastening at the front or at the back.
   necklines—usually high, to the throat and finishing off with a small collar or ruff; or V-shaped; or draped with cross-over folds arranged in various ways. Open necklines were generally filled in with white linen or cotton "chemisettes."

13.2 Plum-colored silk dress with *gigot* or leg-o-mutton sleeves, 1830. (*Photograph courtesy of the Smithsonian Institution.*)

20's and 30's—many bodices had wide, V-shaped revers extending from shoulder to waist in front and back. Wide, matching or white-work cape-like collars also popular.
   sleeves—exceptionally diverse. Fashion periodicals gave many different names to the styles they showed. The following are the major varieties identified by the Cunningtons:[3]
   · Puffed at shoulder then attached to a long sleeve, which was fitted to the wrist or, alternatively, a small puff covered by a sheer oversleeve. Decorative epaulettes (*mancherons*) sometimes placed at the shoulder. *Marie* sleeve: full to the wrist, but tied in at intervals with ribbons or bands. (See Figure 13.4.)

3. C. W. Cunnington and P. Cunnington. *Handbook of English Costume in the 19th Century.* London: Faber and Faber, 1970. p. 385 ff.

Patent French Improver

ah! that's just the thing!

13.3 Caricature of 1831 shows the down-filled hip pad called a bustle that was worn under full-skirted dresses. Other underclothing depicted includes a corset cover with short, full, puffed sleeves, several layers of petticoats, and a pocket suspended from the waist into which the lady is tucking a handkerchief. These pockets were reached through openings in the skirt seams. (*Photograph courtesy of the Smithsonian Institution.*)

· *Demi-gigot:* full from shoulder to elbow, then fitted from elbow to wrist, often with an extension over the wrist. (See Figure 13.5.)
· *Gigot*—also called *leg-of-mutton* sleeves: full at the shoulder, gradually decreasing in size to the wrist where they ended in a fitted cuff. (See Figure 13.2.)
· *Imbecile* or *idiot* sleeves: extremely full from shoulder to wrist where they gathered into a fitted cuff. (See Figure 13.11.)

NOTE: The name "imbecile" derived from the fact that its construction was similar to that of sleeves used on garments for confining mad persons— a sort of "strait jacket" of the period.

waistlines—generally straight until about 1833 when some V-shaped points were used at the front. Buckled belts or sashes often are seen at the waist.

skirts—long, ending at the top of the foot until c. 1828 when they shortened. From the end of the 20's until about 1836, skirts were ankle-length or slightly shorter, then in 1836 they lengthened again, stopping at the instep.

shaping—from about 1821 to 1828, skirts were fitted through the hips with gores, gradually flaring out to ever-greater fullness at the hem. About 1828, skirts were fuller through the hips and this fullness was gathered or pleated into the waist. Fabrics used included muslins, printed cottons, challis, merino, batiste.

pelisse-robe—the name given to a dress for daytime that was adapted from the pelisse worn out-of-doors. A sort of coat-dress, it closed down the front with buttons, ribbon ties, or, sometimes, hidden hooks and eyes.

dresses for evening—These differed from daytime dresses in details, but not in basic silhouette. Necklines were lower, sleeves were shorter, skirts were shorter. In the 20's necklines tended to be square, round, or eliptical; in the late 20's and 30's, off-the-shoulder. (See Figure 13.5.) *Fabrics:* silk satins or softer gauzes and organdy held out by full petticoats.

neckwear and dress accessories—In the daytime necklines were filled in with a number of fillers (also called "chemisettes" or "tuckers") that were separate from the dress and could be varied. *Pelerines*—wide, cape-like collars extending over the shoulders and down across the bosom were especially popular. (See Figure 13.4.)

The *fichu-pelerine* was a variant that added two wide panels or *lappets* that extended down the front of the dress and passed under the belt. (See Figure 13.6.) Other accessory items included the *santon*, a silk cravat worn over a ruff, and the *canezou*. This latter item illustrates the confusions in terminology. In some fashion plates the canezou appears as a small, sleeveless spencer worn over a bodice, and in others as a garment synonymous with the pelerine.

hair and head dress—*hair*—generally parted at the center. In the early 20's: tight curls around the forehead and temples, with the back arranged in a knot, bun, or (for evening) ringlets. After 1824: elaborate loops or plaits of false hair were added. About 1829 the style known as *a la Chi-*

13.4 Dress of gray silk with detachable *pelerine* and Marie sleeves. (*Photograph courtesy of the Metropolitan Museum of Art, gift of Mrs. Frank D. Millet, 1913.*)

13.5 Evening dress of the second half of the 1830's with *demi-gigot* sleeves. This dress shows some evidence of the change in silhouette that took place after 1836. (*Photograph courtesy of the Smithsonian Institution.*)

noise was created by pulling back and side hair into a knot at the top of the head while hair at forehead and temples was arranged in curls. (See Figure 13.7.) Day caps, white and lace- or ribbon-trimmed, worn indoors by adult women.

hats—usually large-brimmed with high, round crowns and large feather and lace decorations or bonnet styles (See Figures 13.6 and 13.11.), one of which, the *capote*, had a soft fabric crown and a stiff brim.

Hair ornaments included jewels, tortoise shell combs, ribbons, flowers, and feathers. For evening hair ornaments were favored over hats, although berets and turbans were also worn.

1836–1850

Item / Description

dresses—*silhouette*—About 1836 a major change began: the buoyant, full form gradually became more subdued. A change in sleeve construction has been described as being like a baloon that started to deflate. While fullness in the sleeves did not entirely disappear, it moved lower on the arm until about 1840 when sleeves became narrower and more closely fitted. At the same time, skirts lengthened. The result was a subtle change in the feeling of the costume from one of lightness to one of a heavier, almost drooping quality. (See Figure 13.8.)

13.6 *Fichu-pelerine.* (Petite Courrier des Dames. *April 15, 1834. Picture Collection, New York City Public Library.)*

13.7 Madame Raoul-Rochette in a drawing of the 1830's by Ingres wears her hair in the style known as *a la Chinoise.* *(Photograph courtesy of the Cleveland Museum of Art, purchased from the J. H. Wade Fund.)*

bodice—predominantly one-piece; some two-piece jacket and skirt styles. These included:
· front-buttoning jacket bodices with short *basques* (extensions of the bodice below the waist.)
· *gilet corsage*—made in imitation of a man's waistcoat.

NOTE: France being the fashion capital, French terms appear frequently in descriptions of fashions on fashion plates or in women's magazines. *Gilet* is French for waistcoat and *corsage* means bodice.

Bodices generally ended at the waist which, increasingly, came to a point at the front and closed with hooks, buttons, or laces down the front or back.

sleeves—Set low, off the shoulder after 1838. The Cunningtons identify these sleeve constructions:
· *bishop* sleeve—at this period made with a row of vertical pleats at the shoulder which released into a soft, full sleeve gathered to a fitted cuff

at the wrist. (Unfashionable after the early '40's.)
· sleeve *en bouffant* or *en sabot*—alternated places of tightness with puffed out expansions. A variation of this construction, the *Victoria*, had a puff at the elbow.
· tight sleeves with these variations: decorative frills above the elbow, short oversleeves, or epaulettes at the shoulder.
· a new style, seen early in the 1840's, fitted at the shoulder and widening about half way between the elbow and wrist into a funnel or bell shape.

White lace- or embroidery trimmed cotton or linen undersleeves were sewn into the wide open end of the sleeve and could be removed for laundering.

skirts—Full, that fullness gathered into the waist. Innovations in skirt constructions dating from about 1840 included:
· edging skirt hems with braid to prevent wear.
· sewing pockets into skirts. (Prior to this time, pockets were made separately from dresses and tied around the waist, reached through slits

13.8 On the left is a daytime dress of the 1840's made of *barege*, a fabric made from a blending of silk and wool fiber. Contrast this garment with the one on the right, an everyday dress made of cotton fabric and worn with embroidered apron belonging to a woman of more modest means. (*Photograph courtesy of the Smithsonian Institution.*)

in the skirts. Trimmings included ruchings (pleated or gathered strips of fabric), flounces, scallops, and cordings. Many fashion plates show skirts with flounces, either one or two or row on row, for the entire length of the skirt.

NOTE: The styles depicted on fashion plates are not necessarily representative of the styles worn by ordinary women. For example, although fash-

ion magazines of the 1840's show skirt decorations arranged in a vertical panel at the front or horizontally around the skirt, most extant examples of costumes in collections lack such trims.

evening dresses—(See Figure 13.9.) Comparable to daytime dresses in silhouette; major differences were in:

· neck lines—off the shoulder either straight

13.9 Evening dress of 1837 made of gold brocade. The sleeve shows a good example of the shifting of fullness to a lower position on the arm which took place in the latter half of the 1830's. (*Photograph courtesy of the Smithsonian Institution.*)

13.10 Striped silk quilted *pelisse*, c. 1830. (*Photograph courtesy of the Metropolitan Museum of Art, gift of Mrs. Frank D. Millet, 1913.*)

across or with a dip at the center (*en coeur*). Many had *berthas* (wide, deep collars following the neckline.)
· trimmings—greater quantities; more use of lace, ribbon and flower trims.
· fabrics—silks, moiré, velvet, and organdy especially.
· skirt construction—some with overskirts opened at the front or closed and puffed up.

hair and head dress—*hair*—(See Figures 13.8 and 13.9.) parted in the middle, pulled smoothly to the temples where it was arranged in hanging sausage-shaped curls or in plaits or with a loop of hair encircling the ears. At the back, hair was pulled into a bun or chignon.
hats—Adult women continued to wear small white cotton or linen caps indoors. Some had long, hanging lappets.

• *bonnets*—the predominant hat shape, and both utilitarian and decorative types were worn. Sunbonnets—to keep the sun from the faces of women who worked outdoors. These were made of quilted cotton or linen with a bavolet or ruffle at the back of the neck to keep the sun off the neck. Fashionable bonnets—often worn with bonnet veils attached to the base of the crown and worn either hanging over the brim or thrown back over the crown. Fashionable bonnet styles included drawn bonnets, made from concentric circles of metal, whalebone or cane and covered in silk; capotes (with soft crowns and rigid brims), and small bonnets that framed the face.

For evening, hair decorations were preferred over hats.

OTHER ELEMENTS OF COSTUME FOR WOMEN, 1820–1850

Item / Description

outdoor garments—*pelisse*—Followed the general lines of dress and sleeve styles until the mid-1830's (See Figure 13.10.) when it was replaced by a variety of *shawls and mantles*—worn for day and evening out of doors. Until about 1836

13.11 *Pelerine-Mantlet.* (Petite Courrier des Dames. *June, 1834. Picture Collection, New York City Public Library.*)

13.12 Caricature of 1822 depicts the artificial assistance required by some men to achieve a fashionable silhouette: pads at the shoulder, chest, hip, and calf and a tight corset. (Monsieur Belle Taille. *Photograph courtesy of the Smithsonian Institution.*)

full-length mantles were worn; later they shortened. Evening styles were made in more luxurious, decorative fabrics such as velvet or satin and trimmed with braid.

Fashion terminology for mantles proliferates. Some of the more commonly seen terms include:

mantlet or *shawl-mantle*—a short garment rather like a hybrid between a shawl and a short mantle with points hanging down at either side of the front.

pelerine-mantlet—with a deep cape, coming well over the elbows and having long, broad front lappets worn over, not under, a belt. (See Figure 13.11.)

burnous—a large mantle of about three-quarter length with a hood, the name and style deriving from a similar arab garment.

paletot—about knee-length and having three capes and slits for the arms.

pardessus—a term applied to any of a number of garments for outdoor wear that had a defined waistline and sleeves and were from one-half to three-quarters in length.

footwear—*stockings*—generally knitted of cotton or silk or worsted wool. For evening in the 30's and 40's, black silk stockings were fashionable. *shoes*—mostly slipper-type. Toes became more square after the late 1820's. (See Figure 13.3.) Very small heels are applied in the late 40's.
· *For evening:* black satin slippers seem to predominate until about 1840 when ribbon sandals and white satin evening boots appeared.
· *For cold weather:* leather shoes or boots with cloth gaiters (a covering for the upper part of the shoe and the ankle) in colors matching the shoe. Rubber galoshes or overshoes were introduced in the late 1840's.

accessories—*Gloves:* worn daytime and evenings. Daytime gloves, short and of cotton, silk, or kid; evening gloves long to the elbow until the second half of the 1830's when they shortened. Gloves, cut to cover the palm and back of the hand but not the fingers were called mittens or mitts. Hand-carried accessories included reticules, handbags, purses, fans, muffs, and parasols. When hats were very large (20's and 30's) parasols were often carried unopened. Parasols of the 40's were small and included carriage parasols that had folding handles.

jewelry—In the 20's and 30's: gold chains with lockets, scent bottles, or crosses attached; chatelaines (ornamental chains worn at the waist from which were suspended useful items such as scissors, thimbles, button hooks, penknives), brooches, bracelets, armlets, and drop earrings. In the 30's a narrow tress of hair or piece of velvet ribbon was used to suspend a cross or heart of pearls around the neck (called a *Jeanette.*) In the 40's less jewelry was worn. Watches were suspended around the neck or placed in a pocket made in the skirt waistband.

cosmetics and grooming—Rice powder was used to achieve a pale and wan appearance, but obvious rouge or other kinds of face paint were not considered "proper."

COSTUME FOR MEN—1820–1840

Item / Description

undergarments—no major changes from earlier periods. Some men used corsets and padding to achieve a fashionable silhouette. (See Figure 13.12.)

shirts and neckwear—*shirts*—cut with deep collars, long enough to fold over a cravat or neck-cloth wrapped around the neck. Daytime shirts had tucked insets at the front; evening shirts had frilled insets. Sleeves were cuffed, closing with buttons or studs.
stocks—wide, shaped neckpieces fastening at the back were often black.
cravats—square, were folded diagonally into long strips and tied around the neck, finishing in a bow or knot.

suits—*coats*—Variations of the frock coat included "military" frock coats (worn by civilians but with military influences evident) which had a rolled or standing collar and no lapel. Riding dress frock coats had exceptionally large collars and lapels. (See Figures 13.13 and 13.14.)
waistcoats—worn under the outer or suit coat. At least one, sometimes more, waistcoats were worn and these were arranged so as to show off only at the edge of the suit coat.

13.13 Left to right: Boy in tunic suit, blouse which has large, *demi-gigot* sleeves, and is worn over contrasting trousers. Man in frock coat, top hat, and trousers. Man dressed for riding in a riding coat, knee-breeches, and boots. (*From Petit Courrier des Dames, March 1834, New York City Public Library Picture Collection.*)

13.14 Left to right: Boy's coat is made of plaid cotton, his hat of silk. The gentleman wears a green wool tailcoat, linen trousers with a fall front closing, and a top hat of straw. The girl is dressed in a dark green silk *pelisse* and a white dimity cap. (2nd quarter of the 19th century.) (*Courtesy of the Metropolitan Museum of Art, The Costume Institute.*)

• *Basic cut:* sleeveless with either straight, standing collars or small, rolled collars without a notch between the collar and lapel. The roll of the collar extended as far as the second or third waistcoat button.

• Both single and double breasted waistcoats were worn (although in the 20's single-breasted styles predominated for daytime wear.)

• Evening waistcoats were black (often velvet) (See Figure 13.15.) or white or among the ultra-fashionable English "Dandies" of the 20's in colors contrasting with dark, evening dress suits.

trousers or *pantaloons*—(See Figures 13.13 and 13.15.) these terms used interchangeably. Generally close-fitting, with an ankle strap or slit that laced to fit the ankle.

NOTE: In the 20's it was fashionable to use a different color, or at the least a different shade of the same color, for each part of the costume.

1840–1850

The following changes can be seen in men's costume:

Item / Description

suits—*coats*—The tail coat became strictly a dress coat; consisting of coat, waistcoat, and trousers. Although older men continued to wear knee-breeches for daytime and all men wore them for court dress and formal occasions and for riding, trousers or pantaloons were more consistently worn as part of the suit. Coat styles were usually either of the tail coat or frock coat types.

• *tailcoats*—single or double-breasted, the double-breasted coat with large lapels; single-breasted styles with smaller lapels. Collars were cut high behind the neck, with the rolled collar joined to a lapel to form either a V-shaped or M-shaped notch.

13.15 Man at left wears an opera cloak over his evening clothes and carries a *chapeau bras.* Man at right wears a frock coat and carries a top hat. (*1834, Italian fashion plate.*)

NOTE: Until 1832 coat sleeves were cut full through the armscye, and gathered into the armhole opening making a full puff at the joining. Later this gathering disappeared, and sleeves fit into the armhole more smoothly. The most fashionable of men's coats had padded shoulders and chest areas, the width helping to emphasize a narrow, sometimes corseted, waist. This heavy padding disappeared after about 1837.

> • *frock coats*—A more casual garment than tail coats, frock coats fitted the torso, had collar, lapel, and sleeve construction, chest and shoulder padding as described above, but at the waist had a skirt flared out all around ending at about knee level. (After c. 1830, the skirts shortened somewhat.) After 1830 frock coats were more generally worn during the day, while tail coats were more often used for evening dress. Frock coats were worn for "undress" or casual wear. Coats became longer-waisted, skirts narrower and shorter, and sleeves fitted into armholes without gathers.
> New coat styles:
> • *riding coat or newmarket*—differed from the tail coat in that the coat sloped gradually to the back from well above the waist, rather than

having a squared, open area at the front.
· jacket—single-breasted, with or without a seam at the waist. Jackets had side pleats, no back vent. The front closing was fairly straight, curved back slightly below the waist to stand open. Collars and lapels were small, pockets placed low, with or without flaps.
· *Waistcoat changes*—these lengthened, developed a point at the front (called a *Hussar front* or *beak.*) Lapels narrowed, were less curved. By the end of the 40's, however, lapels grew wider again and were sometimes worn turned over the edge of coat collars and lapels. Wedding waistcoats were white or cream-colored; evening waistcoats were made of silk satin, velvet, and cashmere.
trousers—By 1840 breeches were limited to sportswear and ceremonial fulldress. Fly front closures were gaining popularity.

dressing gowns—Worn at home, especially in the mornings, and made of vivid colors. The cut did not change markedly from styles of the Empire Period.

OTHER ELEMENTS OF COSTUME FOR MEN, 1820–1850

Item / Description

outdoor garments—much the same as in the Empire Period. After the 20's the Spencer went out of fashion.

> greatcoats—a general term for overcoats. (See Figure 13.16.) Single or double-breasted, often to the ankle. Collars had a deep roll; coats were made with and without lapels.
> box coats—were large, loose greatcoats with one or more capes at the shoulder. (In the 1840's this coat was likely to be called a *curricle* coat.)
> *paletot*—a term first used in the 1830's, but the styles to which the term was applied vary over time. At this period it appears to have been a short greatcoat, either single or double-breasted, with a small flat collar and lapels. Sometimes it had a waist seam, sometimes not.
> *chesterfield*—a term used first in the 40's and then applied to a coat with either a single or double-breasted closing, although the double-breasted closing has since been more closely associated with this term. The coat had no waistline seam, a short vent in the back, no side pleats, and often had a velvet collar.

13.16 Overcoat of the 1830's. Note fullness in sleeve cap and close fit through the body, characteristics that disappear in the 1840's. (*Photograph courtesy of the Smithsonian Institution.*)

NOTE: The chesterfield was named after the Sixth Earl of Chesterfield who was influential in English social life in the 1830's and '40's.

mackintosh—a waterproof coat made of rubber and cut like a short, loose overcoat. Invented at this time, mackintosh was named after its inventor. Waterproof cloaks and paletots are also mentioned.

NOTE: These early mackintoshes were not met with universal approval. The Cunningtons quote complaints that ". . . the mackintosh is now becoming a troublesome thing in town from the difficulty of their being admitted to an omnibus on account of the offensive stench which they emit."[4]

cloaks—especially used for evening dress. (See Figure 13.15.) Cut with gores and fitting smoothly at the neck and shoulder, capes had both large flat collars and semi-standing collars. Some had multiple capes at the shoulders. Late in the period evening cloaks became more elaborate, many with large sleeves with slits in front that allowed the sleeve to hang behind the arm like a Medieval hanging sleeve. Lengths varied. In the late 30's and the 40's a short, round, full so-called *Spanish cape* lined in silk of a contrasting collar was worn for evening.

hats and head dress—*hair*—worn short to moderate in length; in loose curls or loosely waved; cut short at the back. Beards, beginning with a small fringe of whiskers, returned to fashion around 1825, and gradually grew to larger proportions.

hats—the top hat the predominant form for day and evening. Different names were applied to styles, based on subtle differences in shape. The crown was a cylinder of varying height and shape, ranging from those that looked like inverted pots to tubes with a slight outward curve at the top. Brims were small, sometimes turned up at the side. A collapsible top hat for evening was fitted with a spring so that the hat could be folded flat and carried under the arm. *Derby* hats (in the United States) or *bowlers* (in England) began to be worn. These hats had stiff, round, bowl-shaped crowns with narrow brims. Caps were favored for sports.

footwear—*stockings*—generally knitted from worsted, cotton, or silk. Elastic garters were invented in the 1840's.

shoes—with square toes, low heels. Shoes lacing up the front through three or four eyelets come into use in the 1830's. Formal footwear was open over the instep and tied shut with a ribbon bow.

spatterdashers or *spats*—(i.e., gaiters) were made of sturdy cloth and added to shoes for bad weather or for hunting. Those worn for

4. *Ibid.* p. 142.

sports ended below the knee; those for every day were ankle length.

boots—important for riding.

NOTE: The first rubber soles for shoes were made about 1832. By the 40's rubber overshoes, galoshes, and elastic-sided shoes were available.

bedroom slippers—worn at home. Women's magazines frequently included patterns for making needlepoint slippers as a gift for gentlemen.

accessories—*gloves*—made of leather (especially doeskin and kid), of worsted wool, or of cotton for daytime; of silk or kid for evening.

pocket handkerchiefs—Men who took snuff (a tobacco that was inhaled) particularly required these as inhaling snuff causes sneezing. Canes and umbrellas were carried.

jewelry—was limited to cravat pins, brooches worn on shirt fronts, watches, jeweled shirt buttons and studs, and decorative gold watch chains and watches.

COSTUME FOR CHILDREN

Children of the late 18th century through the Empire Period escaped, to some extent, from wearing uncomfortable, burdensome clothing. This was thanks to the relative simplicity of adult women's clothing and the tendency to dress children in less constricting styles intended for them rather than in adult styles. During the Romantic Period the clothes for children reverted, to some extent, to less comfortable clothes based on adult fashions.

boys—in skirts until age five or six when boys donned trousers.

Suits—*skeleton suit*—until about 1830, a carryover from the Empire Period (See Figure 13.17.)

· *Eton suit*—short, single-breasted jacket, ending at the waist. The front was cut square, the lapels wide. With it, a turned down collar and a necktie; a vest or waistcoat; and trousers.

NOTE: This style derived from the school boy clothing worn at Eton School in England. This style with minor variations remained a basic style for young boys for the rest of the century.

· *tunic suit*—consisting of a jacket, fitted to the waist where it attached to a full, gathered or pleated skirt that ended at the knee. It buttoned down the front, often had a wide belt. Usually worn with trousers, some versions for small boys aged three to six combined the tunic jacket

13.17 Left to right: Boy's tunic suit and matching trousers, c. 1838; woman's dress of moiré silk with *gigot* sleeves and a double *pelerine* of white, embroidered mull, c. 1836; boy's wool suit, c. 1830. Note that the children's sleeve constructions are similar to styles popular for adult women. (*Photograph courtesy of the Metropolitan Museum of Art, Costume Institute.*)

with frilled, white drawers. (See Figures 13.13 and 13.17.)

jackets—in combination with *trousers*, the jackets cut like those of adult men, however boys did not wear frock or dress coats.

girls—*dresses*—like those of women, but shorter and with low necklines and short sleeves.

pantalettes—white, lace-trimmed drawers, or leglets, a sort of half-pantalette that tied around the leg, worn under dresses.

head covering—inevitably some kind of hat, bonnet, or starched lingerie cap.

boys and girls—*footwear*—Ankle-high boots for boys and girls; slippers more seen on girls than on boys. White cotton stockings for both.

NOTE: Both boys' and girls' costumes in fashion plates of the period are curiously like fashion plates of adult styles. When narrow waists for both men and women were emphasized in the drawings, the children were likewise given abnormally small waists. During the time that women's sleeves ballooned out to enormous proportions, not only little girls but also little boys were depicted in the awkward, large sleeves. (See Figure 13.13.)

Summary

The Romantic Period was one of evolution in fashion. For women this evolution can be seen in the gradual shift of the waistline from the Empire placement to a lower position, slightly above the natural, anatomical waist, and finally by the close of the period to the natural position. Sleeves, too, evolved year-by-year, first enlarging gradually until they reached maximum dimensions, then collapsing with the fullness moving gradually down the arm. Hemlines shortened gradually, then lengthened just as gradually.

In men's styles there were echoes of the changes in women's styles and an evolutionary development. The sleeves of men's coats grew larger, then smaller again. The skirts of frock coats widened, then narrowed.

By the end of the period a new fashionable look had been established that was a marked contrast to that seen in the early years of the 20's. Women had become "genteel instead of jolly"[5] . . . "the bounce was gone, replaced by a sensitive fragility."[6]

Selected Readings

BOOKS CONTAINING ILLUSTRATIONS OF COSTUME OF THE PERIOD FROM ORIGINAL SOURCES

Fashion Magazines: *Godey's Lady's Book Peterson's Magazine*

Boehn, M. *Modes and Manners of the 19th Century*. New York: E. P. Dutton and Company, 1909, Volume 2.

Coleman, E. A. *Changing Fashions: 1800–1970*. Brooklyn, N.Y.: Brooklyn Museum, 1972.

5. C. W. Cunnington. Feminine Attitudes in the 19th Century.
6. G. Squire. *Dress and Society*, p. 159.

Gibbs-Smith, C. H. *The Fashionable Lady in the 19th Century*. London: Her Majesty's Stationery Office, 1960.

Holland, V. B. *Hand Coloured Fashion Plates, 1770–1899*. London: B. T. Batsford, 1955.

Ormond, R. *Early Victorian Portraits*. London: Her Majesty's Stationery Office, 1973.

Tarrant, N. *The Rise and Fall of the Sleeve, 1825–1840*. Edinburgh: Royal Scottish Museum, 1983.

PERIODICAL ARTICLES

Back, A. M. "Clothes in Fact and Fiction, 1825–1865." *Costume*, No. 17, 1983, p. 89.

Coleman, E. J. "Boston's Atheneum for Fashions." *Dress*, Vol. 5, 1979, p. 25.

Finkel, A. "*Le Bal Costume*: History and Spectacle in the Court of Queen Victoria." *Dress*, Vol. 10, 1984, p. 64.

Tandberg, G. G. "Field Hand Clothing in Louisiana and Mississippi during the Ante-bellum Period." *Dress*, Vol. 5, 1980, p. 90.

Tandberg, G. G. and S. G. Durand. Dress-up Clothes for Field Slaves of Ante-bellum Louisiana and Mississippi." *Costume*, No. 15, 1981, p. 40.

DAILY LIFE

Burton, E. *Pageant of Early Victorian England, 1837–1861*. New York: Charles Scribner's Sons, 1978.

Chancellor, E. B. *Life in Regency and Early Victorian Times*. London: B. T. Batsford, Ltd., 1927.

Eisler, B. *The Lowell Offerings: Writings by New England Mill Women (1840–1845.)* New York: J. B. Lippincott Company, 1977.

Lacour-Gayet, R. *Everyday Life in the United States Before the Civil War*. New York: Frederick Ungar Publishing Company, 1969.

Langdon, W. C. *Everyday Things in American Life, 1776–1876*. New York: Charles Scribner's Sons, 1941.

Laver, J. *The Age of Illusion*. New York: David McKay Company, Inc., 1972.

Page, T. N. *Social Life in Old Virginia Before the War*. New York: Charles Scribner's Sons, 1897.

Uzanne, L. O. *The Frenchwoman of the Century: Fashions, Manners, Usages*. New York: George Routledge and Sons, 1887.

Wright, L. B. *Everyday Life in the New Nation: 1787–1860*. New York: G. P. Putnam's Sons, 1972.

CHAPTER 14

The Crinoline Period

1850–1869

The "Cage Crinoline," the major fashion innovation for women in the 1850's, provided the name for this period. The increasing width of women's skirts had led to the use of more and more stiffened petticoats. When the hoopskirts of the 18th century were revived to hold out these voluminous skirts, the editor of *Peterson's Magazine* hailed its revival.

> There can be no doubt, that, so long as wide and expanded skirts are to be worn, it is altogether healthier to puff them out with a light hoop than with half-a-dozen starched cambric petticoats as has been the practice until lately. Physicians are now agreed that a fertile source of bad health with females is the enormous weight of skirts previously worn. The hoop avoids that evil entirely. It also, if properly adjusted, gives a lighter and more graceful appearance to the skirt.[1]

Worth and the Paris Couture

Who invented the hoopskirt—or rather who chose to revive it, for it had been used in much the same

1. *Peterson's*, September 1856, p. 204.

form in the early 1700's and 1500's—is not clear. Many sources have given the credit to Charles Frederick Worth, but there is no evidence that he actually originated the style. Charles Worth was an Englishman who can claim to be the founder of the French couture. With a hundred seventeen francs and unable to speak a word of French, he came to Paris to work in the fabric houses. While an employee of the Maison Gagelin, he began to have his attractive French wife wear dresses he had designed. Soon customers began to request that similar designs be made for them. After leaving Gagelin in 1858, he set up his own establishment. However, he was aware that to be successful he must gain the patronage of influential women, and so he presented his designs to the Princess Pauline Metternich, wife of the Austrian ambassador, and an important figure at the court of Emperor Louis Napoleon III and the arbiter of Paris fashion. The success of the gowns Worth made for the Princess helped him to win the favor of the Empress Eugenie, and soon all of fashionable Paris waited in the anterooms of his salon.

Worth dressed the most respectable as well as the most notorious women of the world. His clients ranged from Queen Victoria to Cora Pearl, a well-known courtesan. His designs were sold wholesale

235

for adaptation by foreign dressmakers and stores. A unique aspect of Worth's talent was his engineering because he designed clothes so that each part would fit interchangeably with another. For example, each sleeve could fit any number of different bodices and conversely each bodice any number of sleeve styles. Bodices could fit any number of skirts.

Until the 1880's Worth worked as a couturier. After his retirement his sons continued the business, organizing the couture, which had expanded since their father opened his salon, into the *Chambre Syndicale*, an organization of couturiers that still regulates the French *haute couture*. In the 1920's and 1930's the House of Worth declined in importance, and closed after World War II although a perfume bearing the name of Worth is still sold.

Historical Background

In this era the accepted ideal of womanhood was the virtuous wife and mother. The British found the perfect example of their ideal in their young queen, Victoria. In 1840 she married a German Prince, Albert, and for her people became the model of sedate, respectable motherhood. She brought to the throne a sense of a loving family, something especially lacking among recent British monarchs.

In mid-century, Britain enjoyed prosperity marked by increasing imports and exports, expanding production of iron and steel, and industrial growth. Other nations not only envied her industry but tried to emulate her success. Nothing so symbolized the well being of Britain more than the Great Exhibition of 1851 presented in an especially designed great glass building in Hyde Park. There over 7,000 British exhibitors demonstrated their products as evidence of Victorian progress.

FRANCE

Worth helped Paris once again become the fashion center of Europe. The city had passed through bloody days: revolutions in 1830 and again in 1848 with fighting in the streets. A Second Republic, proclaimed after King Louis Philippe had abdicated in 1848, enjoyed a short life. The nephew of Emperor Napoleon I, President Louis Napoleon, staged a coup d'etat and in 1852 after a carefully staged plebiscite approved an empire, assumed the title, Napoleon III.

During the Second Empire, France regained the leadership of Europe; again Paris became a world capital. In the glamorous city, the Tuileries Palace became the center of social life where the beautiful Empress Eugenie presided over a glittering court. To the Palace flocked kings, princes, princesses, statesmen and their ladies, bejeweled and dressed in the best of Paris fashion. Once again, masked balls became the rage, offering ladies the opportunities to display their gowns.

Although his glittering court was the most brilliant and colorful since the old monarchy, Louis Napoleon was himself a man of conservative and simple tastes. In the morning he dressed in a dark blue coat, a waistcoat, and grey trousers. The ribbons of the Legion of Honor and a military medal were the only symbols of authority that he wore. For the evening he wore the typical evening dress of the period for concerts and official dinners: a tail coat with black knee breeches and silk stockings, and for really gala events he dressed in a general's uniform, with the tunic covered with orders and crosses.

His wife, a Spanish countess and much younger than he, Eugenie de Montijo, was considered quite beautiful. Although she dressed lavishly for state occasions, Eugenie really had little interest in clothes. Actually she was reluctant to adopt new fashions even after they had become popular. At home she wore a plain black dress. Eugenie followed fashion; she was not a fashion setter.

Nevertheless the arrangements for the storage of her wardrobe were formidable. Her dressing room was located directly beneath a group of rooms in which wardrobes with sliding panels were located. Here her clothing was arranged in perfect order. Four dressmaker forms with the exact measurements of the Empress served a twofold purpose. They made it unnecessary for Eugenie to try on her clothes too often when they were being made. When her costume for the day had been selected, the figure was dressed, and the form—complete with all parts of the costume—was lowered by elevator through an opening in the ceiling of her dressing room.

To be invited to the court or to one of the royal residences required a considerable wardrobe. A visiting American socialite described her wardrobe for a week at one of the royal residences.

> I was obliged to have about twenty dresses, eight day costumes (counting my traveling suit), the green cloth dresses for the hunt, which I was told was absolutely necessary, seven ball dresses, five gowns for tea . . .[2]

2. L. Hegermann-Lindencrone. *In the Courts of Memory.* New York, 1912. p. 60.

But the glamorous Second Empire had to end. Although Napoleon III did much for the economic life of the Empire, including the rebuilding of Paris, his foreign adventures led to his downfall. In the 1860's his fortunes began to decline. After Prussia defeated France in 1870, the Emperor abdicated and fled to Britain where he spent the remainder of his life in exile with Eugenie and their son. The Second Empire vanished to be replaced by the more somber Third Republic. Paris, however, never conceded its position as the fashion center of Europe.

UNITED STATES

In the United States the Crinoline period coincided with the Civil War. Then the American population was about 23 million, and a little more than half of these people lived west of the Alleghenies. Twelve percent of the population was foreign born. In 1850 there were 141 cities of more than 8,000 population, containing sixteen percent of the population.

By this time, thanks to the industrial revolution, the annual output of mills and factories had surpassed the value of agricultural products, and manufacturing was concentrated in the northeastern states. Already the nation was bound together by a network of turnpikes, rivers, canals, and railroads. By 1870 East and West were connected by transcontinental railroads.

Although education remained predominantly private, the foundations of public school education had been laid. In 1862 Congress passed the Morill Act establishing the land grant system of higher education. The new colleges were intended to emphasize a more practical education in agriculture and industry.

The women's rights movements had begun and would get increased impetus through an alliance of this movement with the anti-slavery and temperance (anti-alcohol) movements. Women still lived under many legal and social restrictions. They had no legal control over property; they lacked the vote; and as late as 1850, some states allowed a husband to beat his wife with a "reasonable instrument."

Religion had a strong influence in pre-Civil War America; some forms of religious expression were allied with an interest in Utopian societies. Some of these groups even developed their own form of dress. The costume worn by women of the Oneida colony in New York State, composed of a bodice, loose trousers, and a skirt ending slightly above the knees, may have influenced the "Bloomer costume." Bloomer costumes were similar in style, and were worn by some feminists of the 1840's.

The Civil War and Costume—National divisions over slavery came to a head in the War between the North and South. Although the war had little direct influence on the continuity of western fashion, which in any event was being set abroad, women living in the beleaguered South were forced to rely on their ingenuity to keep up with fashion.

Because the Union fleet was blockading southern ports, the importation of foreign and domestic goods ceased. Moreover, the major manufacturers of textiles were located in the North so that even domestically produced goods were unavailable. In addition, fashion magazines were printed in Northern cities such as Philadelphia and Boston.

For one southern woman, the first year of the war presented little difficulty because "most of us had on hand a large supply of clothing." But southern women continued the practice of giving away clothing they had tired of only to regret it later, wondering how they "could ever been so foolish as to give away anything so little worn." They were grateful for the popularity of skirts and blouses which could be made from scarves, aprons, or shawls, and for tight sleeves which could be cut down from the wide ones so popular in preceding years.

Women had to patch their clothes and piece them with scraps cut from wornout clothes.

> Black silk was a favorite material for piecing out our old clothes, because it suited everything . . . An old black silk skirt with nine flounces was a treasure in our family for nearly two years, and when that store was exhausted, we fell back upon the cover of a wornout silk umbrella.[3]

Inflation also took its toll. Milliners paid $150 for an old velvet bonnet which they then renovated and sold for $500. In the final year of the war, $1,000 was not considered an unreasonable price for a hat.

The Sewing Machine—The first patents on the sewing machine were taken out in the 1840's. Public response to the new device was not overwhelming because the cost was relatively high, at least $100. In 1857, James Gibbs, a Virginia farmhand, devised a simpler, less expensive type of sewing machine which he marketed for about $50.

But it was Isaac Singer, mechanic, unemployed actor, and inventor who developed one of the most successful sewing machines. Singer's sewing ma-

3. Elzey Hay, "Dress Under Difficulties; or Passages from the Blockade Experience of Rebel Women," *Godey's Lady's Book*, July, 1866, p. 36ff.

chines became one of the first domestic appliances manufactured on a production line basis using interchangeable parts. Consequently, the Singer sewing machines could be produced in quantities sufficient enough to reduce the price substantially.

Singer also pioneered in innovative sales methods. He displayed his sewing machines in elaborate showrooms where pretty young ladies not only demonstrated the sewing machines but also taught purchasers how to operate them. Singer sold his machines to seamstresses on the installment plan: five dollars down and the remainder, with interest, in monthly installments. To interest respectable ladies in purchasing sewing machines, Singer sold his machines at half price to church connected sewing societies in the hope that each member would soon want to own her own sewing machine. The Singer Company also allowed fifty dollars on an old sewing machine when purchasing a new one.

But it was the Civil War that demonstrated the usefulness of the sewing machine. The war generated an immediate and enormous demand for the ready-to-wear uniforms: the Northern Army wore out over a million and a half uniforms a year. Such quantities could only be supplied by using sewing machines.

During the war, the Northern Army collected statistics on the form and build of American males. These statistics were useful to manufacturers of civilian clothing in developing the ready-to-wear clothing industry after the Civil War. Then the sewing machine became a vital force in the development of this industry. Without the sewing machine, it would have been impossible to produce sufficient quantities of clothing to meet the needs of the growing American population.

Seamstresses soon saw the benefits of the sewing machine in increased speed, particularly those who were hired by clothing manufacturers to do piece work in their homes. The first major savings in time were in simple items, men's shirts, aprons, calico dresses, which had been the first items to be mass produced.

Soon sewing machines were used in the productions of men's and boy's suits and overcoats. In the 1860's, a first rate overcoat which required six days of steady sewing by hand could be finished with the help of the sewing machine in three days.

The sewing machine also contributed to the popularity of fashions such as ready-made women's cloaks and the hoop-skirt insomuch as these garments could be manufactured cheaply and in quantity by using sewing machines instead of hand-sewing. Attachments for sewing machines made possible the easy addition of braiding, tucking and pleating to fabrics, and the use of these trimmings increased accordingly.

Early Attempts at Dress Reform—The "Bloomer" Costume—The increasing numbers of petticoats required to support the skirts of the late 1840's were certainly uncomfortable and hindered easy movement. A group of American feminists combined their interest in women's rights with a desire to reform a costume that they saw as confining and impractical. "Women are in bondage; their clothes are a great hindrance to their engaging in any business which will make them pecuniarily independent," said Lucy Stone, a leader of the movement. Mrs. Stone, Susan B. Anthony, Elizabeth Cady Stanton, and Amelia Bloomer were among the women who adopted a special costume. (See Figure 14.1) Mrs. Bloomer endorsed the costume and promoted its

14.1 Amelia Bloomer wearing the so-called "Bloomer Costume." The drawing is based on a daguerrotype of Mrs. Bloomer. (*New York City Public Library Picture Collection.*)

use, but did not originate the style. Nevertheless, it was named after her. The Bloomer costume consisted of a pair of full trousers gathered in at the ankle, over which a dress with a knee-length skirt was placed. Attempts were made to promote its use in England, where cartoonists had great fun caricaturing the style.

Few women outside the feminist movement took up bloomers, which provoked a great deal of ridicule, leading some feminists to conclude that emphasizing the costume was counter-productive. When the hoop skirt became fashionable, Mrs. Bloomer found the cage crinoline a "comfortable and practical garment," and she and others willingly discarded the Bloomer costume. The cut of the trousers, however, retained the name "bloomers," and as some women's undergarments had a similar cut, they were nicknamed "bloomers." Today the term is often applied to any full pants gathered in at the bottom.

Crinoline Period Costume

Many costume collections have substantial numbers of garments dating from this period of time. Furthermore, the practice of photography was so wide spread that it was the rare family that had not immortalized its members in photos. Women's magazines regularly printed hand-colored fashion plates and their descriptions. As a result, there is a wealth of detailed information about fashions from this period available to the fashion historian.

The basic silhouette of women's costume (and also, therefore of children up to age five or six and girls older than six) fits closely through the bodice to the waist, then the skirt immediately widens into a full round or dome-shape. Armhole seams are placed below the natural shoulder on the upper part of the arm. (See Figures 14.3 c and e.)

Fabrics used are fairly crisp, with enough body to enhance the fullness of the skirt, even though it is supported by a hoop. Among the silks used for better dresses, one sees a great many taffetas, particularly plaid and striped patterns and "shot" or irridescent fabrics created by weaving one color in the lengthwise yarns and another in the crosswise yarns. Every day clothing, little of which remains, underwear and much children's clothing were made of washable cotton or linen. Wool fabrics appear in every day and dressier clothing for women and suits for men. Outerwear for men, women, and children is usually wool. One also sees an attractive silk and wool blended fabric, relatively sheer, crisp and lightweight, called *barege*.

While knowledge of silhouette and costume detail are useful in dating historic costume, clues as to dates can sometimes be found within the costume itself. For example, men's waistcoats or trousers in this period and later may have buckles which are used to adjust their fit. Some of these buckles will contain a patent number and even the date of the patent. Other closures such as hooks and eyes, snaps and some buttons are marked with patent numbers and the dates of patents can be easily ascertained.

COSTUME FOR WOMEN, 1850–1870

Item / Description

undergarments—Consisted of chemise and drawers, worn under a corset and a hoop, and a petticoat placed on top of the hoop. Undergarments were made of cotton or linen.

 chemise—knee-length, short and full; without much decoration.

 drawers—about knee length, trimmed at edges with tucking, lace or embroidery. Crotch left open and unseamed. In winter some women wore colored, flannel drawers for warmth.

 corset—boned and closing with laces or hook fasteners. While skirts were full at the waist, corsets were short, not too tight over the hips.

 hoop (*cage crinoline*)—Either a series of whalebone or steel (only after 1857) hoops sewn onto tapes or into a fabric skirt. Shapes varied with changes in the fashionable silhouette: 1850's-round; 1860's flatter in front and fuller at the back. (See Figure 14.2.)

 petticoats—Single petticoat decorated with lace, embroidery, tucking was placed over the hoop. Additional layers, flannel, or quilted petticoats could be worn in winter.

 camisole—waistlength, shaped to the figure, with short sleeves and buttoned down the front.

daytime dresses—(See Figure 14.3.) One-piece or increasingly, two piece with separate bodices and skirts.

NOTE: Some two-piece garments were made with both a day time and an evening bodice that could be worn with the same skirt.

 princess dress—One-piece, cut with bodice and skirt in one (no waist seam) and shaped

14.2 Cartoonists found the hoop an irresistible target. The drawing to the left shows a harried husband of 1858 being asked by his wife's maid if he can find room for her hoop in his suitcase. In the drawing below, the hazards of public transportation for hoop-wearing ladies are noted. (*New York City Public Library Picture Collection.*)

to fit at the waist through the cut of gored sections.

bodices—General shape often achieved through curved seams in back; darts in front. Armhole is dropped below the natural shoulder line. Necklines are high, without attached collars and usually finished in bias piping. Silk or wool garment bodices usually lined with cotton fabric; occasionally some boning. Separate washable collars (and cuffs) worn. *Separate bodices for daytime*—Generally either ending at waist and fastening up the back or front with buttons or hooks and eyes, or cut to look like a jacket with basques flaring out below the waist.

NOTE: Basques are extensions of bodice below the waist. Before 1860 they are generally cut in one with the bodice; later often are separate pieces sewn to bodice at the waist. Some extended about six inches below the waist and even all around; others were short in front, long in back.

sleeves—Many open at the end, worn with removable lace or muslin undersleeves (In French: engageantes.) Most common types* were:
· bell-shaped, narrow at shoulder and gradually widening to end between elbow and wrist
· "pagoda" shaped, narrow at the shoulder and expanding abruptly to a wide mouth at the end: sometimes shorter in front, longer in back
· double-ruffle
· closed sleeves (especially in 60's) of various types such as: pleated into armhole with released fullness gathered into wristband; close

* Fashion magazines give styles a wide variety of fashion names.

fit to wrist with epaulettes at armhole; series of puffs from shoulder to wrist.
· like a man's coat sleeve, with inner seam under the arm and outer seam down the back of the arm; no gathers at shoulder and relatively fitted for length of the arm.

blouses—Separate blouses worn with skirts. The red "garibaldi blouse" was especially popular in the 1860's. (See Figure 14.4.)

NOTE: Garibaldi blouse was inspired by the red shirts worn by Italian soldiers who fought under General Giuseppe Garibaldi to unify Italy.

skirts—widened throughout 50's and into the 60's (some 12 to 15 feet in circumference), with these shape changes: early 50's dome-shaped; 60's more pyramid-shaped with fullness toward back; by late 60's less fullness at waist, gored instead of gathered and waistline located somewhat above natural anatomical placement. Skirt styles included plain, undecorated skirts; two or more flounces sewn onto an under skirt; layered skirts, each layer cut shorter than the last to form a flounce; rows of narrow frills; and double skirts with outer skirt layers puffed or looped up. Skirts are usually lined, either altogether, half way, or with a band of lining around the underside of the hem to keep the skirt from being soiled.

a

b

c

d

e

f

14.3 *Carte de visite* type photographs from the Crinoline Period. The first two figures, a and b upper left, wear open sleeves with *engageants*. The woman on the left wears her hair in a chenille snood, the one on the right has on a small lingerie cap. The girl (c) at upper right has sleeves of the jacket type which are decorated at the top with epaulettes. The outlines of the hoops underneath their skirts can be seen clearly in the photographs of the woman and child at lower left (d and e). The woman on the right (f) wears her hair in sausage curls or ringlets around her face. On her head is a small cap with hanging ribbon lappets. All of the figures part their hair in the center. All except the little girl wear detachable white collars. (*Photographs from the author's collection.*)

14.4 Fashion plate depicts girl, on left, wearing a red Garibaldi blouse with a black taffeta skirt. Her hair is enclosed in a red, net snood, possibly of chenille, and her small, flat hat with feathers at the side is tipped forward. Her companion is wearing an evening dress with horizontal bands of pleated fabric at the neckline and short, puffed sleeves. The bodice dips to a deep V at the waist. The underskirt, visible beneath the puffed up overskirt, is made with horizontal tiers of small pleats. In one hand the lady carries a folding fan, in the other a small bouquet. Both were popular accessories for evening dress. (*New York City Public Library Picture Collection.*)

NOTE: Braid placed at hem edge helped to reinforce and keep hem edge from fraying as it touched the ground.

dress accessories—To vary appearance or to protect garments:
- washable aprons (elaborately embroidered silk aprons were worn for decoration, not practicality)
- separate collars and undersleeves, white and washable and trimmed in lace and/or embroidered
- fichus, shown as being worn criss-crossed and tied in back.

- canezou, a fashion term applied to a variety of accessories including fichus, muslin jackets worn over bodices and chemisette neck fillers. (The term canezou seems to go out of use after this period.)

evening dress—Differences from day time mostly seen in cut of neck, sleeves, types of fabrics used, and elaborateness of decoration. Frequently two-piece; some princess style.

necklines—Mostly "off the shoulder" either straight across or with a dip at the center (*en coeur*), and often with a wide bertha trim (a folded band of fabric hanging suspended around the neckline).

sleeves—short, straight, and often obscured by the bertha. (See Figure 14.5.) In late 60's, some sleeveless dresses had shoulder straps or ribbons tied over the shoulders.

skirts—frequently double, with decorative effects achieved by looping or puffing up the outer layer; trimmed with artificial flowers, ribbons, rosettes, or lace. (See Figure 14.4.)

outdoor garments—generally divided among:
- sleeved, unfitted coats of varying lengths (See Figure 14.6.)
- sleeved, fitted coats of varying lengths
- loose capes, cloaks, and shawls, without sleeves (See Figure 14.6.)

NOTE: Tendency of fashion magazines to assign names to each of a number of different styles tends to confuse terminology.

Among the names encountered for these garments:[4]

pardessus—sleeved outdoor garment.

paletot—sleeved outdoor garment that fitted the figure.

pelisse-mantle—double-breasted, sleeved, unfitted coat with wide, flat collar and wide, reversed cuffs.

mantle—three-quarter-length coat, fitted to waist in front, full at the back, with either long loose sleeves or full, shawl-like sleeves cut as part of the mantle.

shawl-mantle—loose cloak, reaching almost to the skirt hem.

talma-mantle—full cloak with tassled hood or flat collar.

rotonde—shorter version of the talma-mantle.

burnous—a hooded cape.

4. Definitions based on Cunnington, *Handbook of English Costume in the 19th Century*. London: Faber and Faber, p. 453 ff

14.5 Evening dress of about 1860 with wide bertha collar. The lady wears a pair of black lace mitts, her hair is arranged in long ringlets. Her companion wears what appears to be a dark frock coat, dark vest and light trousers. The photograph may be a wedding portrait. (*Photograph from a glass plate negative courtesy of the Huntington Historical Society, Huntington, New York.*)

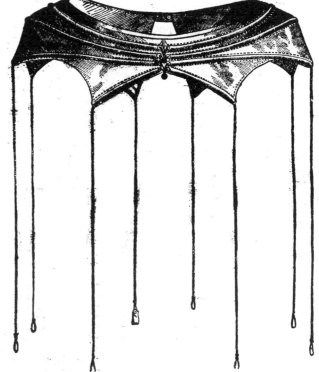

zouave—short, collarless jacket, trimmed with braid. Often worn over a Garibaldi shirt. (See Figure 14.7.)

NOTE: Zouave jacket derived from the costume of Algerian troops that fought as part of the French army. During the American Civil War, a regiment called the Zouaves fought for the North and adopted, in part, the costume of the French Zouaves.

hair and head dress—*hair*—generally parted in the center and drawn over the ears smoothly or in waves, pulled into a bun or plaits at back of the head. Pads, placed under the hair at the side, helped to give a wider appearance. For evening, curls arranged at the back of the

14.6 (*Above*) Outdoor garments from 1863, on the right a full, plaid mantle trimmed with cording and tassels, worn over a dress with a skirt having a band of matching plaid around the hem. The figure on the left wears a coat of the *pardessus* type, closed with frogs. The skirt under the jacket is raised from the ground by means of a *porte jupe* or dress elevator. The drawing below depicts a dress elevator, which was placed under the skirt and fastened to the hem of the skirt with loops that enclose buttons. A tab at the front of the elevator is pulled to raise the device in much the same way that one would raise a modern-day Venetian blind.

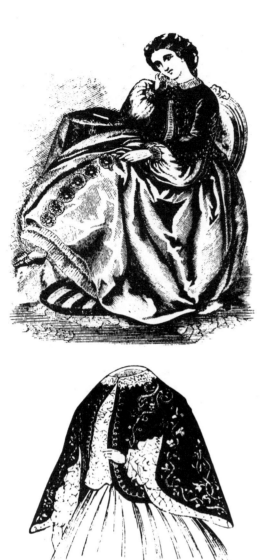

14.7 Two versions of the popular *zouave* jacket. The description accompanying the drawing recommends that the jacket be made of black velvet or cashmere and that it be worn over a white silk or muslin vest. The applied decoration is of braid.

neck. In the 1860's, quantity of hair massed at the back enlarged. False hair supplemented natural hair as required. In daytime, hair was usually confined in a net. (See Figures 14.3 to 14.7.)

head coverings—small, muslin "day caps" with long lappets or ribbons were still worn by some older and married ladies. Hair nets, of colored silk or chenille. Bonnets continued to be worn, but in the 60's, small hats were more fashionable, and included hats with low, flat crowns and wide, flexible brims; bergere straw hats similar to those of the 18th century; sailor hats;

and "pork pie" hats with low, round crowns and small brims turned up at one side. *For evening*—beaded hair nets, lace kerchiefs, hair ornaments made of flowers or fruit, and jeweled hair ornaments.

footwear—*stockings*—Made of cotton or silk, with white the preferred color, but also colored and plaid stockings.

daytime shoes—square toes, low heels, rosette trimming over the toes in some styles.

evening shoes—made of white kid or satin; in the 60's often colored to match the gown.

boots—cut to above the ankle and closed with lacing, buttons, or with elastic sides.

accessories—*gloves*—short and fitted for daytime, except for "sporty" gauntlets with wide cuffs. White gloves, short in the 50's, long and elbow-length in the 60's worn with evening dress. Fingerless mitts, often of lace, for day or evening.

hand-carried accessories—included handkerchiefs, folding fans of moderate size, and small muffs. Parasols were small, dome-shaped, often of silk and lined inside. Carriage parasols had folding handles.

jewelry—bracelets, earrings, brooches, necklaces. Fashionable materials included coral, cameos, cabochon stones (i.e., cut in convex form but without facets), colored glass and jet.

cosmetics—Use of "paint" considered in bad taste among "ladies of quality" but fashion magazines did offer regular advice about home-made cosmetic remedies.

NOTE: Examples of recommended cosmetics: "a tablespoon of gin thrown into lukewarm water will remove redness in the face produced by exertion."[5] "Water to thicken hair and prevent its falling out: distil (sic) and cool as slowly as possible two pounds of honey, a handful of rosemary, and twelve handfuls of the curlings or tendrils of grapevines, infused in a gallon of new milk."[6]

COSTUME FOR MEN—1850–1870

Item / Description

undergarments—Next to the skin, long or short cotton or linen underdrawers and an undervest of cotton or linen in the warm months and, sometimes, wool in the winter.

5. *Godey's*, July 1854, p. 91
6. *Ibid*, November 1864, p. 439

shirts—no major changes from earlier styles. Points of the collar extended to the jaw. Exposed only slightly at the neck, shirts lost decorative tucking or ruffles in the daytime. Evening shirts had embroidered or ruffled fronts. Most shirts were white; some colored shirts for country or sports wear.

ties and cravats—wrapped around the collar.

suits—*coat*—variations included:
- *dress coats* (formerly called tailcoats)—cut with a short, square "cut-in" in front and tails at the back. Worn for formal occasions both day and evening in the 50's, but by the 60's strictly for evening. Evening coats were black, some with velvet-faced lapels. Worn open, coats did not button shut leaving the waistcoat visible. (See Figure 14.8.)
- *frock coat*—construction the same as in the previous decade: fitted through the torso, the skirt not overly full. In the 1860's the waistline dropped somewhat and the waistline was less well defined. These coats lengthened after 1855, were longer for the rest of the period. (See Figures 14.9, 14.11 and 14.12.)

- *morning coats* (riding coats or Newmarket coats) curved back gradually from the waist, the curve becoming less pronounced in the 60's.
- *sack jacket*—(called lounging jackets in England)—loose, comfortable jackets with no waistline. They had straight fronts, center vents in back, sleeves without cuffs, and small collars with short lapels. (See Figure 14.10.)
- *reefers* or *pea jackets* were loose, double-breasted jackets with side vents and small collars. These were also worn as overcoats.
- *waistcoats* for daytime—ended above the natural waist. Both single and doublebreasted styles. The latter had wider lapels. For evening waistcoats were single-breasted and longer. (See Figure 14.11.)

trousers—no instep straps after 1850, but fitting close to the leg. Also seen were pegged-top styles, wider at the top and narrowing gradually to the ankle. After 1860, legs widened somewhat. For daytime, some striped and checked fabrics. Colored strips of fabric covered side seams of some styles. Suspenders (In En-

14.8 Men and boys dressed for a formal occasion. (Gentleman's Magazine. *January 1854.*)

14.9 Left to right: Hunting garb, a *paletot*, and a frock coat, vest, and trousers. (Modes de Paris, *c. 1850.*)

14.10 Man wearing sack jacket, a loosely-fitted coat, introduced in the late 1840's for casual wear. (*Fashion plate, c. 1850.*)

14.11 Gentleman of about 1860 wears a plaid waistcoat which is double-breasted and has a wide lapel. His collar stands upright, the points reaching to his jaw. Around the collar he has wrapped a cravat which is tied in a knot, the ends hanging. (*Photograph courtesy of the Huntington Historical Society, Huntington, New York.*)

gland, "braces") held trousers in place; alternatively some were constructed with a tab and buckle at the back of the waistband and did not require suspenders.

NOTE: An embroidered or needlepoint pair of suspenders was considered an appropriate gift from a lady to a gentleman.

New, after 1850, was a sportswear garment called *knickerbockers*. Knickerbockers were cut with loose legs and belted into a band that buckled just below the knee. The term was later shortened to "knickers."

NOTE: Knickerbockers seem to have evolved from the fitted knee breeches worn for riding, shooting, and hunting.

outdoor garments—the trend toward looser, more comfortable clothing was evident in overcoats, some being fitted with a defined waist; others loose, with no clear waistline definition; or combined coat-capes with loose fit and cape-like or full sleeves and/or an over-cape. (The term *paletot* continued to be used to refer to the general category of overcoats.) (See Figure 14.9.)
Named styles included:
  · The *chesterfield*, either single or double-breasted.
  · The *frock overcoat*, cut along the same lines as the frock coat.
  · *Inverness cape*, a large, loose overcoat with full sleeves and a cape ending at wrist length.
  · *Raglan cape*, actually a full overcoat with an innovative sleeve construction. Instead of setting the sleeve into a round armscye, it was

joined in a diagonal seam running from under the arm to the neckline.

· Wide variety of *capes* or *cloaks* with sleeves, and a man's version similar to the lady's talma mantle was worn for evening. Waterproof coats, such as the *mackintosh*, continued in use.

Men also wore large shawls over suits for out-of-doors.

dressing gowns—made in decorative fabrics, worn with nightcaps in the privacy of one's home. Also smoking jackets, loose jackets cut like a sack jacket and made in velvet, cashmere, or other decorative fabrics and worn with small, tasseled caps.

hair and head dress—*hair*—fairly short, curly or waved; long, full side whiskers were stylish. Moustaches in the 50's; by the 60's being clean shaven was no longer fashionable.

hats—the *top hat* was the predominant style. Other styles: the *wide awake*, with a low crown and wide brim and made of felt or straw; *caps* for casual wear and in the country; *derbies* (bowlers), *straw hats* with flat crowns and narrow brims.

footwear—included laced shoes, half or short boots with elastic-sides or buttoned or lace closings; and long boots. Short or long gaiters or spatter-dashers (spats) were added to shoes for sports-wear.

accessories—canes, umbrellas with decorative handles, and gloves.

jewelry—largely confined to watches and watch chains, tie pins, rings, and a variety of ornamental buttons and studs.

14.12 Boy and girl on the left wear similarly-cut *zouave* jackets; the girl with a gathered skirt, the boy with a pair of trousers. Their leather boots reach to the ankle. On the right side, a small boy still dressed in skirts wears a white shirt, checked skirt with belt and band of trim in velvet, lace-trimmed drawers, knee-length stockings, and ankle-high boots. The man standing beside him wears a frock coat and light-colored trousers.

14.13 Left to right: Child's dress in wool with *soutache* braid trim, c. 1869; mother's dress, c. 1860; infant's christening gown, c. 1860; and girl's dress, c. 1869. (*Photograph courtesy of the Metropolitan Museum of Art, Costume Institute.*)

COSTUME FOR CHILDREN—1850–70

Item / Description

NOTE: Before the age of five or six, boys and girls were dressed alike, wearing skirts. (See Figures 14.12 and 14.13.)

dresses—shorter versions of the styles worn by adult women. Skirts lengthened as girls grew— at four, dresses ended just below the knee (for boys and girls); by age sixteen, skirts for girls lengthened to two inches above the ankle. Hoops were worn by older girls to hold out skirts. Pantalettes continued in use until the end of the period when they were no longer worn. (See Figure 14.13.)

footwear—mainly ankle-high boots or slippers (See Figures 14.12 and 14.13.), striped or plain colored stockings.

hair and head dress—Boys generally had short hair; girls' hair was often dressed in tight ringlets around the face. Hats for boys were smaller versions of men's hats, or caps. Girls' hats also resemble those of adult women.

Boy's styles, after age 5 or 6:

trousers or short pants—cut similarly to adult men's (See Figure 14.8.)

knickerbockers—cut full to the knee where they

14.14 Children in this picture wear clothing of the late 1860's with narrower, gored skirts. Younger girls wear shorter skirts while the older girl in the center wears a skirt reaching to the ground. The boy in the center wears a modified form of the tunic suit, with a sailor hat. The boy and girl at left, rear, wear jackets of the unfitted cut that was popular at the time and pill box hats. (*New York Public Library Picture Collection.*)

gathered in to a band and buttoned or buckled closed.

knickerbocker suits—added a short, collarless jacket to these pants, and for older boys, a vest as well.

sailor suits—made up of trousers or knickers, a blouse with a flat, square collar and a V-shaped neck opening.

NOTE: The sailor blouse style was known as a "middy," the word derived from "midshipman."

Eton suits, tunic suits, and jackets plus trousers—similar to those of preceding period. (See Figures 14.8 and 14.14.)

sports—for the beach, knitted wool jersey suits.

outdoor garments—mostly smaller versions of adult men's coats, including inverness, chesterfield, and ulster styles.

Summary

During the Crinoline Period fashion changes in women's clothing were concentrated more in variations in detail than in major silhouette alterations. To be sure, the shape of the hoop-supported skirts did evolve from a dome-like shape to one more pyramidal. The period might be considered a product of the Industrial Revolution and technology. Surely it would have been difficult for so many women of all social classes to adopt the hoop so quickly without the factories to produce the steel from which the hoops were made and the sewing machines that permitted their assembly at relatively low prices and in great quantities.

And while women were being confined inside the steel structure of the hoop, men were gaining greater comfort and freedom in their clothing. The sack suit, which in its cut and shape can be said to be the closest 19th century ancestor of the men's sport jacket of today, was a comfortable, unconfining jacket that men accepted readily and have made a staple in their wardrobes ever since.

Selected Readings

BOOKS AND OTHER MATERIALS CONTAINING ILLUSTRATIONS OF CONTEMPORARY STYLES FROM ORIGINAL SOURCES

American Fashion Magazines: *Godey's Lady's Book Graham's Magazine, Peterson's Magazine*

Blum, S. *Fashions and Costumes from Godey's Lady's Book* New York: Dover Press, 1985.

Gernsheim, A. *Fashion and Reality.* London: Faber and Faber, 1963.

Ginsburg, M. *Victorian Dress in Photographs.* New York: Holmes and Meier Publishers, Inc., 1983.

The House of Worth: The Gilded Age in New York. New York: Museum of the City of New York, 1982.

Kunciov, R. (Editor). *Mr. Godey's Ladies.* New York: Bonanza Books, 1971.

Of Men Only. Brooklyn, N.Y.: Brooklyn Museum, 1975.

Reader, W. J. *Victorian England.* New York: G. P. Putnam's Sons, 1973.

Richardson, J. *La Vie Parisienne, 1852–1870.* New York: Viking Press, 1971.

Rosenblum, R. *Jean-Auguste-Dominique Ingres.* New York: Harry N. Abrams, Inc., N.D.

Tozier, J. and S. Levitt. *Fabric of Society: A Century of People and Their Clothes.* (1770–1870). Carno, Powys, Wales: Laura Ashley, 1983.

PERIODICAL ARTICLES

Adler, S. "A Diary and a Dress." *Dress,* Vol. 5, 1980, p. 83.

Beck, J. F., P. Haviland, and T. Harding. "Sewing Techniques in Women's Outerwear 1800–1869." *Clothing and Textiles Research Journal,* Vol. 4, No. 2, Spring 1986, p. 20.

Foote, S. "Bloomers." *Dress.* Vol. 5, 1980, p. 1.

Gunn, V. "The Establishment of a Chronology of Local Photographers as a Resource for the Study of 19th Century Costume in Ohio." *Proceedings of the Association of College Professors of Textiles and Clothing,* 1978, p. 98.

Hay, E. "Dress under Difficulties; or Passages from the Blockade Experiences of Rebel Women." *Godey's Lady's Book,* July 1866, p. 36.

Hollander, A. "When Worth Was King." *Connoisseur,* Vol. 212, December 1982, p. 114.

Richmond, R. "When Hoops did Tilt and Falsehood was in Flower. Women's Fashions of the 1860's." *American History Illustrated.* Vol. 6 (1), April 1971, p. 23.

DAILY LIFE

Barton, N. *The Victorian Scene.* London: George Weidenfeld and Nicolson, 1968.

Burton, E. *The Pageant of Early Victorian England.* New York: Charles Scribner's Sons, 1972.

Evans, H. and M. Evans. *The Victorians.* New York: Arco Publishing Company, Inc., 1973.

Hibbert, C. *The Horizon Book of Daily Life in Victorian England.* New York: American Heritage Publishing Company, 1975.

Langdon, W. C. *Everyday Things in American Life, 1776–1876.* New York: Charles Scribner's Sons, 1941.

Lacour-Gayet, R. *Everyday Life in the United States Before the Civil War- 1830–1860.* New York: Frederick Ungar Publishing Company, 1969.

Margetson, S. *Leisure and Pleasure in the 19th Century.* New York: Coward-McCann Inc., 1969.

Peterson, H. L. *Americans at Home. From the Colonists to the Late Victorians.* New York: Charles Scribner's Sons, 1971.

Reader, W. P. *Life in Victorian England.* New York: G. P. Putnam's Sons, 1964.

Richardson, J. *La Vie Parisienne.* New York: Viking Press, 1971.

CHAPTER 15

The Bustle Period and the Nineties

1870–1900

Two separate costume periods are included in this chapter. The first, the Bustle Period, derives its name from the bustle, a device which provided the shaping for a silhouette with marked back fullness. The concentration of fullness at the back of the costume that had evolved gradually during the late 1860's at first required a modification of the hoop and eventually led to the construction of devices which either alone or in combination with the hoop supported the fullness which came to be concentrated more and more at the back.

In the 90's this silhouette altered. The name most often given to the last decade of the 19th century in the United States is "the Gay Nineties." In France, the period is frequently called "La Belle Epoque." Both names convey a sense of fun, good humor, and indeed, the western world seemed to be emerging from the serious moralistic tone of the Victorian era.

Historical Background

1870–1890

By the time that the bustle became a popular fashion, Queen Victoria had been ruler of Great Britain for just over thirty years, and would remain Britain's ruler for another thirty more. During the earlier years of Victoria's reign, the British people had come to share a common ideal with particular emphasis on the importance of morality and high standards of conduct. The British Empire had grown to include lands across the world. In 1870 when the Bustle Period began, industrial England was in the midst of a great economic boom. In the following twenty years there was a gradual extension of voting rights, and passage of legislation to clean up the slums and to improve sanitary conditions. These years were unmarked by major internal or international upheavals for England.

In France, the period began with the shock of the Franco-Prussian war when French armies were defeated and Napoleon III surrendered to the victorious Prussian armies. Peace did not come to France until after a revolution, which ended the Second Empire and replaced it with the Third Republic. In the spring of 1871 the people of Paris endured a bloody civil war, the Commune, a struggle of Paris radicals against conservative France.

In the United States the Civil War had ended, the country was united from East to West by the railroads, and the settlers were moving westward in ever-increasing numbers. Industrialization, urbanization, and immigration were continuing apace, and with them the corresponding problems of labor strife, poverty, and exploitation of laborers. But Americans remained optimistic and the long peace and economic expansion that followed the Civil War provided opportunity for many native and immigrant Americans to improve their economic status.

1890–1900

The decade of the 1890's in the United States saw the continuation of trends cited in the preceding decades. The frontier was closing, urban centers were expanding, as the country moved toward the new century.

In Europe, too, the social conventions of the Victorian era continued, but there were signs of changes in attitude. In England the Prince of Wales, heir to the throne, was enormously popular, while the Queen was considered somewhat old-fashioned. The Prince, a ladies' man, lived a life style of which his mother disapproved. One of his favorite spots for escaping from parental constraints was Paris, then considered the pleasure capital of Europe. In popular dance halls like the Moulin Rouge, risque dances and songs were performed; the Folies Bergere had opened; and a new form of entertainment called the strip tease became popular. Houses of prostitution flourished. They ranged from the lavish, beautifully furnished houses visited by the Prince of Wales to rooms in the most degraded quarters of the city.

For those who came to Paris for more sedate pleasures there were the fashion houses of Worth and Paquin, as well as outdoor cafes, the theatre, and strolling on tree-lined boulevards.

SOCIAL LIFE

It is difficult for urban dwellers today to realize that the first apartment house in New York City was built in 1870. It was a five-story walk-up, patterned after the apartment buildings of Paris. With increased pressure for housing that developed as urban centers grew, it was not long until this first luxurious building had inspired a host of imitations, including the notorious, crowded tenements which housed the poor.

But whether they lived in sprawling suburban Victorian houses, on farms, or in city apartments, the Americans of 1870 were family-oriented, and father was the head of the household. Even so, increasing numbers of women were entering the work

force. In 1890 there were 3,704,000 women employed in a variety of jobs outside the home. By 1900 that figure had reached 5,319,000. The census of 1890 shows that women were concentrated in occupations such as teaching, domestic and personal services (i.e., as nurses, laundresses, servants, and waitresses), bookkeeping and accounting, selling, and dressmaking. Many were employed in agriculture; more than 226,000 were farm-owners or overseers, and 447,000 were listed as hired help on farms. There were even 60 female blacksmiths and more than 4,800 physicians and surgeons. Seven out of every ten colleges had become co-educational by 1900.

The tendency for women to go out of the home to work was probably responsible for the development of less cumbersome clothing for women, which was particularly evident in the 1890's. Fashion magazines do not always accurately reflect this trend, whereas photographs of women at work show clearly that they wore their skirts shorter than those shown in magazines and with relatively little decoration. Many of the items in historic costume collections reinforce the notion of excessive decoration and elaborate construction because most women did not save their "every day" clothing. Everyday clothing is more readily seen in mail order catalogs and candid photographs of the period.

SPORTS FOR WOMEN

Defining sport as recreational activity that requires more or less vigorous bodily exertion, one can say that women did not enter into real participation in active sports until well into the 19th century. True, women had ridden horses for recreation as well as for transportation for a number of centuries. They also ice skated and played croquet, but it was after 1870 that women increasingly participated in tennis, golf, roller skating, hiking, and even mountain climbing. Women also "bathed" in lakes or the sea, but few did any real swimming. Bathing and riding required special costumes. Other sports needed only slight modifications of daytime costume, except for shortening skirts a little, tennis or croquet players and skaters or golfers tended to follow the fashions of the period. When cycling became the rage, however, a special costume was devised.

Bicycles first appeared in the early 19th century but had not really caught the public fancy. The English bicycle with a front wheel five feet high and a rear wheel of 8 inches intrigued a few manufacturers when it was shown in the Philadelphia

Centennial exhibition of 1876. By 1885 more than 50,000 Americans had taken up cycling and by 1896 the number swelled to an estimated 10 million.

The first lady cyclists pedaled decorously in their long skirts, even while wearing bustles, but in the 90's a bifurcated garment, a sort of full knicker, was devised as a practical costume for the sport. While relatively few women actually adopted knickers (called "rationals" in England), the style did mark the first use of bifurcated garments for women that had achieved some modest success. Once these knickers had been accepted for one sport they were also adopted for other activities such as mountain climbing. It was not until the late 1920's, however, that large numbers of women began to wear anything approximating men's trousers.

READY-TO-WEAR CLOTHING

Ready-to-wear clothing for men had been available for some time. By 1879 most men bought at least part of their clothing in stores. Corsets, crinolines, bonnets, and cloaks were about the only ready-made items that most ladies bought through the 1860's. The average housewife counted sewing among her many skills and for the more affluent a dressmaker was easily employed. The entry of more women into the work force after 1870 made for changes in clothing production and consumption, as did the development of department stores. The first women's garments to become available in stores were underclothes and "wrappers;" soon after dresses, suits, and walking costumes were being advertised. A vogue for shirtwaists and skirts in the 90's gave a tremendous impetus to manufacturing and by 1910 "every article of female clothing could be purchased ready-made."[1]

A number of technological developments had made the move to mass production possible. The invention of the sewing machine was a major factor. In 1863 Ebeneezer Butterick, a tailor, had patented a special type of tissue paper pattern which he sold successfully. The unique feature of these patterns was that they were made in different sizes. Prior to this time seamstresses had to enlarge small patterns printed in fashion magazines and adjust them to the correct size. The sized paper dress pattern helped to standardize sizes, a necessity for ready-to-wear clothing.

Cutting out each garment by hand was a time-consuming process. Unless some way could be

found to speed up this step, no great quantity of garments could be made efficiently. The first device for cutting large numbers of pattern pieces at the same time was a long knife which was worked up and down through slots in the table. This device could cut eighteen thicknesses of cloth at one time. A cutting machine powered by steam was introduced about 1872, but the device was stationary and the fabric had to be brought to it, making it awkward and cumbersome to use. After 1890, use of electricity for manufacturing allowed the development of smaller, more efficient cutting machines. The first of these cut twenty-four thicknesses; later models could do up to one hundred.

The efficiency of the garment industry was also based on the piece-work concept in which each operator completed only one step in the manufacturing process. The division of labor, characteristic of less expensive clothing, among a number of different workers made it possible even for a novice to acquire sufficient skill to handle a single component.

Sociological factors also contributed to the development of the garment industry. The absorption of ever more women into the work force on a full-time basis decreased the amount of time they had available for dressmaking for themselves and their families and at the same time created more of a demand for clothing to wear to work. The industry developed over a period of time when great waves of immigrants, many of whom possessed excellent tailoring and dressmaking skills, were entering the United States and seeking work. Even the American ideal of a society in which "all men are created equal" helped to foster acceptance of ready-made clothing that, as Kidwell put it, "served to obliterate ethnic origins and blur social distinctions." Nothing comparable evolved in Western Europe where not only was the immigrant labor force lacking, but where the more clearly-defined social class structure did not lend itself so readily to the acceptance of a mass-produced supply of clothing suitable for all but the wealthiest. Even in the United States the rich continued to purchase their clothing in Paris or from custom dressmakers and tailors.

THE VISUAL ARTS AND COSTUME

The entire Victorian Period in the arts was markedly eclectic, featuring many styles that derived from earlier historical periods. In architecture Gothic and Renaissance styles were among the more important examples of this tendency. Most of the important styles in furniture or interior design were also based on earlier furniture or architectural styles and in-

1. C. B. Kidwell and M. C. Christman. *Suiting Everyone.* Washington, D.C.: The Smithsonian Institution Free Press, 1974, p. 137.

cluded not only Gothic and Renaissance revivals, but also revivals of Rococo, Louis 16th, and neo-Greek forms.

Revivals of historic styles were also evident in women's dress, particularly in the years between 1870 and 1890. Some dresses had hanging sleeves similar to those of the Middle Ages or the Renaissance, others had "Medici" collars, derived from the 16th and early 17th century, and many skirts were cut with polonaises inspired by the costumes of the 18th century. Shoes were made with "Louis" heels, modeled after those worn at the court of Louis 14th, and garments were given fashion names such as the "Marie Antoinette fichu" or the "Anne Boleyn paletot."

A reaction against the traditional and conservative nature of art was stirring, however. Artists such as Courbet and Manet had begun to challenge the traditional painting styles as early as the 1860's. They were followed in the 70's and 80's by the Impressionists who received a hostile reaction not only from the traditional salon painters and critics, but also from the public. When in 1874 their work was refused admission to the official French salon, a show of art works approved by the established art world, they set up a separate show called the *Salon des Independents*, which became an annual event. By the 1890's the Impressionists had gained a substantial following among the public and had become the acknowledged leaders of the art world. The direct influence of Impressionist art on costume of the period for either men and women was, however, minimal.

AESTHETIC DRESS

In the 1880's and 90's a dress reform movement directly related to attempts to reform the arts in England did have some impact on clothing styles. The dress reforms of the Bloomer movement proposed by the American women's rights proponents had been based chiefly on the premise of a need for more comfortable and convenient clothing for women. "Aesthetic dress," of the latter part of the 19th century, had different philosophical origins.

Its origins lay in the Pre-Raphaelite Movement, a group of painters who opposed the direction of English art of the 1840's. They took their themes from Medieval and Renaissance stories. Not only did they make costumes for their models to wear, but the women of the group also adopted these dresses for themselves. The costumes while not wholly authentic, were based on drawings from books on costume history published in the 19th

century. From the 50's through the 70's, Pre-raphaelite dress was limited to this group of artists and a few others. By the 1880's and 90's, the costume had begun to catch on with those who espoused the Aesthetic Movement in the arts, a popularized form of Pre-Raphaelite philosophy that attracted painters, designers, craftsman, poets, and writers.

One of the major proponents of Aestheticism was the poet and playwright Oscar Wilde. Wilde in his lectures on Aestheticism sometimes wore his own version of Aesthetic costume: a velvet suit with knee breeches and a loosely fitting jacket, worn with flowing tie and a soft, wide collar.

Women's Aesthetic costume generally had no stays. Sleeves were of the puffed, leg-of-mutton style. Dresses were made of Liberty-printed cotton fabrics or oriental silks and worn without petticoats. The wearer had a languid, drooping appearance that contrasted with the stiffly-constructed lines of fashionable, bustle-supported dresses. The satirists of the period had great fun mocking the Aesthetes with their emphasis on "art for art's sake." Most of the illustrations of Aesthetic dress come from the cartoons of George DuMaurier whose work appeared regularly in the British humor magazine, *Punch*. The operetta *Patience*, written by Gilbert and Sullivan, also poked fun at the Aesthetes. Indeed, its leading character was modeled on Oscar Wilde.

ART NOUVEAU

In the period between 1890 and 1910 yet another art movement had some influence on costume for women. Art Nouveau was an attempt by artists and artisans to develop a style with no roots in earlier artistic forms. Its proponents saw it as a revolt against the eclectic nature of art and design of the Victorian Period.

Art Nouveau designs emphasized sinuous, curved lines, contorted and stylized forms from nature, and a constant sense of movement. The silhouette of some women's dresses, especially in the first decade of the 20th century, echoed these lines. The stylized natural forms appeared in some dress fabrics and embroidered patterns in Art Nouveau motifs were often applied to garments. (See Figure 15.14.) Jewelry, the metal clasps of handbags, hat pins, and parasol and umbrella handles often show Art Nouveau influences.

In a sense the Art Nouveau movement formed a bridge between the artistic styles of the 19th century and those of the 20th century. Although Art Nouveau artists did not succeed in making a sharp break with traditional styles, this artistic philosophy which stressed the need for art to be divorced from the past led eventually to the true revolution in art that arrived with modern, abstract art after World War I.

Bustle Period Costume

COSTUME FOR WOMEN: 1870–1890

Back fullness was a feature of women's dress for most of the period between 1870 and 1890. To support this fullness a number of different structures called bustles were devised. The shaping of the back fullness, however, was not consistently the same for the entire period, and three somewhat different subdivisions can be identified within the overall period:

- c. 1870–1878—a full bustle created by manipulation of the drapery at the back of the skirt.
- c. 1878–1883—the sheath or cuirass-bodice.
- c. 1884–1890—large, rigid, shelf-like bustles.

Each of these somewhat different skirt shapes were supported by bustles and a number of other undergarments.

Item / Description

undergarments—*chemise*—of cotton or linen, generally short-sleeved and round-necked, extending to the knee. Decoration increased, with trimmings at the neck and sleeve and, often, tucking at either side of the front opening.

drawers—little change from those of earlier periods.

combination—a garment combining the chemise and drawers into one. Some models were knitted, others woven. In winter wool was preferred. Widespread acceptance of combinations after 1870 was probably related to a desire for less bulky underclothing to wear beneath dresses that fit quite closely. (See Figure 15.1.)

NOTE: At least one example of a combination was depicted in *Godey's Lady's Book* as early as 1858. It was described thus: "This garment combining the chemise and drawers has very many advantages. We recommend it to ladies traveling, to those giving out their wash, and to ladies boarding. It is also decidedly cooler for summer."

corset—long, curved, and supported with strips of whalebone, steel or cane; shaped to achieve a full, curved bustline, narrow waist, and smooth, round hip curve.

15.1 Knitted combination underwear, 1897. (*New York City Public Library Picture Collection.*)

bustle—Initially the bustle was supported by the cage crinoline of the preceding period worn with an added bustle, or the crinoline was shaped with greater fullness at the back. Other bustle-support constructions developed, ranging from padded, cushion-like devices to half hoops of steel. (See Figure 15.2.)

During the period when the narrow, cuirass bodice dress was fashionable fullness dropped to below the hips, and the trailing skirts were supported by a semi-circular frame.

petticoats—fullness increases and decreases as skirt widths change.

dresses—Throughout the period two-piece dresses with bodice and skirt matching predominated. The *Princess dress*, cut in one piece from shoulder to hem, without a waistline seam, was an exception. To achieve a fit that followed body contours through the torso, princess dresses were cut with many vertical seams and vertical darts (long, shaped tucks.) Although seen less frequently, skirts and blouses were also worn.

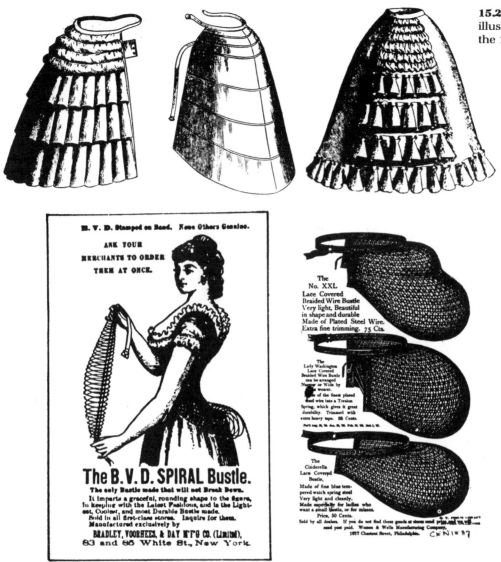

15.2 A variety of bustle styles illustrated in fashion magazines of the 1870's and 1880's.

daytime dresses, 1870–1878 (See Figure 15.3.)

bodices—generally of the jacket type with either:

· shorter basques (i.e. extensions of the bodice below the waist) at front and/or back.

· longer basques—forming a sort of over-skirt at the back of the costume.

necklines—High and closed or square or V-shaped. Open necklines were generally filled in with a decorative chemisette or lace frill. Even when the front of the bodice was cut low, the back neckline was high.

sleeves—close-fitting, ending about three-quarters of the way down the arm or at the wrist, or *coat sleeves*, fitted sleeves ending in a deep cuff. Sleeves were now set into the armhole higher, without a dropped shoulder.

skirts—Unless worn with a blouse rather than a bodice, skirts generally matched bodice in color and fabric. Overskirts often were draped to produce an apron-like effect at the front; back fullness was achieved by cutting both skirts and long basques with plenty of fabric and then looping or draping the fabric in various ways.

blouses—generally overblouses, cut loosely and belted at the waistline. Norfolk jackets (a men's coat style) were worn by women with skirts.

princess style—overdresses were sometimes combined with a separate underskirt. When the outer fabric was looped up or draped over the hip the style was known as a Princess polonaise.

evening dresses, 1870–1878—(See Figure 15.4.) Followed same lines as daytime dresses, chief differences were in use of more decorative fabrics,

15.3 Daytime dress of 1874. Pleated and fringed trimmings were applied to the sleeves, to the bodice and its elongated basques, and to the skirt. (*Photograph courtesy of the Smithsonian Institution.*)

15.4 Evening dress of 1873; this pink silk gown had elbow-length sleeves. (*Photograph courtesy of the Smithsonian Institution.*)

greater ornamentation, and cut of sleeves and necklines.

> *necklines*—Square, V-shaped, or round and low; many off the shoulder sleeves, sleeveless, short sleeve, or elbow-length sleeves finishing in ruffles.
>
> *bodices*—Many women had two bodices made for each skirt; one for daytime, one for evening wear.

daytime dresses, 1878–1883—(See Figure 15.5.)

> *silhouette*—modified, with gradual year-by-year diminishing of bustle dimensions, the change beginning as early as 1875 with the *cuirass bodice*, a long jacket ending in a point at the front and fitting smoothly over the hips. It required less back fullness. Gradually bustle fullness decreased.

> *skirts*—fitted smoothly over the hips, long heavily trained skirts had thin decoration concentrated low, at the back of the skirt. Skirts were held close to the knee in front by ties, restricting women's movements to small, mincing steps.
>
> *necklines*—Cut of necklines and sleeves, and trimmings used showed no radical changes. Decoration of many costumes, however became more asymmetrical.

daytime and evening dresses, 1883–1890.—(See Figure 15.6.)

> *silhouette*—Bustles returned, but they differed from earlier styles in that the back fullness had more the appearance of a constructed, shelf-like projection rather than the softer, draped construction of the 1870–1878 styles.
>
> *skirts*—rarely trained, usually ending several

15.5 Styles from the second phase of the bustle period. Princess style dresses, front and back views, on adults show focus of decoration at hem, particularly at the back. The child's dress, though shorter, is cut along similar lines. (*Print from* Demorest's Monthly Magazines, *April 1878.*)

15.6 Bustle dress of the third phase—c. 1882—worn in New York City. (*Photograph courtesy of the Metropolitan Museum of Art, Costume Institute.*)

inches above the floor.

bodices—jacket-style, short basques; polonaise bodices, and belted over blouses were all worn.

sleeves—generally close fitting, ending above the wrist. As early as 1883 some sleeves developed a small puff at the sleeve cap. In 1889 this puff, (called the kick-up) grew, becoming more pronounced, a forerunner of the extremely full sleeves which characterized the 90's.

necklines—high, fitted, boned collars were seen in almost all daytime dresses of the 1880's either as part of a blouse worn under a jacket, part of the jacket, or a part of the dress.

evening dresses—followed same silhouette as daytime dresses, but had increased trimming, some were trained. Ball gown sleeves were short, covering just the shoulders. By the close of the 80's, some evening dresses had broad or narrow shoulder straps in place of sleeves. Conservative ladies wore elbow-length sleeves.

OTHER ELEMENTS OF COSTUME FOR WOMEN: 1870–1890

Item / Description

negligee costumes—In the early 1870's, as new form of dress called a *tea gown* was introduced. Intended to provide some relief from the tight lacing; it was worn without a corset, loosely fitted, and softer in line than daytime or evening dresses. Ladies wore tea gowns for at home with other women friends.

Other negligee items that were worn before the day's toilette was complete or before retiring included wrappers, dressing saques, combing mantles, and breakfast jackets. (See Figure 15.7.)

sportswear—Although women were beginning to take more interest in active sports, the costumes worn for tennis, golf, yachting, or walking were made with bustles and elaborate draperies. The only concession to the activity of these pastimes was that they were cut slightly shorter than other dresses.

NOTE: On the origin of the term "jersey" as applied to knit fabrics, Lillie Langtry was an internationally famous stage personality who was born on the British Island of Jersey, hence her nickname "the Jersey Lily." She adopted a wool knit fabric as a tennis costume, and as a result the fabric became known as "jersey."

Bathing costumes (ie., bloomers or trousers with an overskirt and bodice,) remained the same, though the trousers shortened to the knee. Stockings covering the lower part of the leg, bathing shoes, slippers and a cap completed the outfit. Sleeves decreased in size, and in 1885 some bathing costumes were sleeveless. Even with these

15.7 (*Above*) A "Breakfast robe" from the 1870's. (*New York City Public Library Picture Collection.*)

15.8 (*Below*) Group of women and children by the sea from *Der Bazar*, a German publication, of 1874. The three figures in the center are dressed in bathing costume. (*New York City Public Library Picture Collection.*)

15.9 Ladies of 1889 dressed for winter. The lady at far left wears her dress just slightly shorter than the others for ice skating. (*New York City Public Library Picture Collection.*)

15.10 Outdoor garments for adult women and young girls. The garment at the far right is a dolman mantle. (*Italian fashion magazine, November, 1874.*)

modifications ladies could do little real swimming and their activity in the water was generally limited to a little splashing about in the shallower areas. (See Figure 15.8.)

outdoor garments—*jackets* were close-fitted at the back, loose or fitted in front, generally extending below the waist. Some were knee-length. They accommodated the bustle configuration of the particular year. Sleeves generally were coat-style with turned-back cuffs.

Paletot, sacque, and pelisse are terms applied to variety of coat-like garments, most of which were three-quarter length or to the floor.

Other coat styles included the *ulster,* or a long, belted coat often made with a removable shoulder cape or hood; chesterfield-style coats with velvet collars; and the dolman, a semi-fitted garment of hip to floor length—that was shaped like a coat but had a wide-bottomed sleeve that was part of the body of the garment (a sort of coat-cape). Cloaks and capes were cut in varying length, fitted to the shoulder and some fitted in the back and loose in the front. (See Figures 15.9 and 15.10.)

hair and head dress—*hair*—parted at the center, waved around the face and pulled to back of the head. Bangs or curled fringe covered the forehead. In early 70's, long hair was arranged in large braids, a chignon, or long curls cascading down back of the head. False hair was used lavishly. As the costume silhouette grew more slender, hair was worn closer to the head and arranged in a confined bun or curls at the nape of the neck. High boned collars worn so widely after 1884, led to dressing the hair high on the top of the head in a bun or curls.

hats—By the end of the 1880's only elderly women still wore caps indoors. Hats and bonnets exceedingly elaborate, with ribbons, feathers, lace, flowers, and flounces as trimming. When large curl masses or chignons were concentrated at the back of the head, hats were worn either tilted up, perched on the front of the head, or set back, resting on the chignon. When hair styles simplified, hats and bonnets were built up higher, crowns enlarged, brimless toques were in style. For sportswear, a straw sailor hat with low, flat crown and wide stiff brim was a popular fashion.

footwear—*stockings*—matched the color of the dress and/or shoes. Embroidered and striped patterns were popular. For evening in the 70's, white silk stockings with colored "clocks" (a

small design) were preferred, whereas black became more popular in the 80's.

shoes—made with pointed toes and medium high heels. Daytime shoes often matched dresses; evening slippers were of white kid or satin, often with flower or ribbon ornaments at the toe.

boots—less fashionable than shoes, were usually cut to the lower calf, closed with laces and shaped similarly to shoes. Rubber-soled shoes with canvas or buckskin tops were worn for sports such as tennis and boating; boots for hiking and skating.

accessories—*gloves*—lengths varied with sleeve lengths, longer gloves being worn with shorter sleeves, and evening dress requiring elbow or longer lengths. Popular styles for evening included folding fans of gauze with painted decorations or large ostrich plumes mounted on tortoise shell or ivory sticks. Muffs, usually small except for some large, fur ones.

parasols—large in size, with ornate handles, long points and trimmed with lace and ribbons.

boas—long, narrow, tubular scarves of feathers or fur.

jewelry—Utilized for evening more than for day, included bracelets, earrings (usually small balls or hoops), necklaces, jeweled hair ornaments. With daytime dresses women sometimes wore brooches.

makeup and grooming—Rouge and "paint" were unacceptable in polite, middle class society, but face creams, beauty soaps, rice powder and light scent were used.

COSTUME FOR WOMEN—THE NINETIES

Item / Description

undergarments—drawers and a chemise or the "combination" which united drawers and the chemise in one garment. Corsets placed on top of these. Some corsets in this period changed in shape, shortening to end below the bust, and thereby removing the support that had previously been provided. A specific garment to support the bust called the *bust bodice* was therefore introduced around 1890 and it can be seen as a forerunner of the brassiere. Other corsets followed the older styles and did not require a bust bodice. Bust improvers designed to fill out a deficient figure were commonly worn. Some were made of "flexible celluloid," others of fabric and stuffed with pads of cotton. Corset covers now known as *camisoles*. One or two petticoats. Most underwear was trimmed with quantities of lace, tucking, embroidery or other decoration.

dresses—*silhouette*—Although vestiges of the bustle remained in pleats or gathers concentrated at the back of the skirt, the silhouette of the 1890's could be described as hour-glass shaped. By mid-decade for both day and evening, sleeve styles were large and wide at the top, the waist was as small as the corset could make it, and the skirt flared out into a bell-like shape. (See Figures 15.11 and 15.12.)

bodices—two-piece dresses were constructed with lined and boned bodices, which usually ended at the waist and had round or slightly pointed waistlines. A few had short basques, extending below the waist. Shoulder constructions included yokes or revers with width at the shoulder produced by ruffles or frills. (See Figures 15.13 and 15.14.)

sleeves—The expansion that had begun in late 80's with enlargement of sleeve cap continued. Sleeves were still larger by 1893 and by 1895 had become enormous. These included: the leg-of-mutton sleeve with a full puff to the elbow, then a fitted sleeve from elbow to wrist or a wide top that narrowed gradually to the wrist—sleeves of softer fabric, full for the length of the arm, ending in a cuff. After 1897 sleeve size generally decreased and reminders of the larger sleeve styles could be seen in small puffs or epaulettes at the shoulder, the rest of the sleeve being fitted.

skirts—*gored*—fitting smoothly over the hips with some back pleating or fullness, the gores flaring out to a wide bell shape. Skirts were fully lined; some had bands of linen or buckram around the hem for stiffness.

NOTE: Fashion magazines and costume historians speak of skirts to the floor; however, candid photographs of women working show that for practical purposes, skirts of three or four inches from the floor were more often worn. Dresses for sportswear were also shorter.

shirtwaists—or *"waists"* were made in styles ranging from blouses with leg-o-mutton sleeves tailored to look like a man's shirt to styles covered with lace, embroidery and frills. (See Figure 15.13.)

15.11 Couple of the '90's dress for the photographer, she in leg-o-mutton sleeved bodice and bell-shaped skirt; he in a sack jacket, waistcoat and matching trousers. His "handle-bar" moustache was a popular fashion in this decade. (*Photograph courtesy of the Huntington Historical Society, Huntington, New York.*)

NOTE: Shirtwaists were among the first products of the growing American ready-to-wear industry.

tailor-made costumes—(See Figure 15.14.) matching jackets and skirts worn with a blouse, were the predominant fashion for wear outside the home. Styles ranged from severely tailored costumes modeled after men's suits to elaborately decorated models with ruffles and lace trimmings. Even the most severely tailored, however, had the enlarged sleeves of the period.

15.12 Back view of dress of the 1890's shows the pleating that was frequently concentrated at the back of the skirt. (*Photograph courtesy of the Smithsonian Institution.*)

These garments were made by tailors rather than dressmakers, hence the name.

evening dresses—with low V, square or round necklines until 1893, after which off-the-shoulder lines predominated. Sleeves were full, ending above or at the elbow usually large and balloon-shaped. When daytime sleeves grew smaller (c. 1897), evening dress sleeves also diminished to short, small puffs. Skirts were frequently trained. (See Figure 15.15.)

15.13 Young woman of the 1890's wears a decorative lace-trimmed shirtwaist blouse and skirt of brocade. (*Photograph courtesy of the Huntington Historical Society, Huntington, New York.*)

outdoor garments—mostly capes, many with high puffs at the shoulder to accommodate the large sleeves of dresses. Styles included: full capes of velvet or plush trimmed with fur or jet beading. Collars were high and standing or the neck finished in a ruffle. Coats hip-length had large sleeves, ranged in length from short fitted or full jackets to others three-quarters or floor length. chesterfield-style coats remained popular.

sportswear—Knickers (called "rationals" in England) worn with a fitted jacket were proposed as cycling costume in fashion magazines. (See Figure 15.16.) Some of these knickers were constructed with considerable fullness so that when

15.14 (*Above*) Tailor-made costume depicted in an advertisement of 1896 has large "leg-o-mutton" sleeves. The bell-shaped skirt would have been made with some fullness at the back, generally in the form of pleats or gathers.

a lady dismounted from her bicycle they gave the appearance of a full skirt. Other cycling costumes included divided skirts or a skirt worn over knickers. Many women simply cycled in their shirtwaists and skirts or tailor-made and maintained a dignified, if somewhat strained, upright position. Bathing costumes of the era were not only no more practical for swimming than those of the Bustle Period, but were perhaps even more cumbersome since they contained more fabric as they followed the lines of the dresses including large, puffed sleeves of elbow length, narrow waistlines and full, bell-shaped shirts ending at about knee length, all this was worn over bloomers of the same length and with dark stockings that come to the knee. A few bathing costumes were cut with knickerbockers instead of skirts, but even these were very full.

hair and head dress—*hair*—curled fringe at the front and the back twisted and arranged in a coil or curl at the top. The "Gibson Girl" favored an arrangement with deep, soft waves around

15.15 (*Below*) Ball gowns of the '90's. Left, dress c. 1898, made by Worth of Paris has an *Art Nouveau* scroll motif. Right, American evening dress of 1894–95 made in yellow moiré faille. (*Photograph courtesy of the Metropolitan Museum of Art, Costume Institute.*)

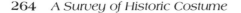

15.16 French advertisement of the 1890's depicts lady cyclist in a costume with wide bloomers, a fitted jacket, and leg-o-mutton sleeves. (*Photograph courtesy of Photo Arts Company.*)

the face. Hair was built up at the front in a "pompadour," the ears were uncovered.

hats—now worn only out-of-doors, were small to medium in size, some had no brim. Trimming tended upward, with lace, feathers, ribbons as the favored trims. For sportswear or work women wore men's styles including the fedora and the straw boater. Face veils were popular. For evening, hair decorations such as feathers, combs, and jeweled ornaments were worn.

footwear—stockings for daytime were made of cotton; for evening of black or colored silk. Shoes generally had slightly rounded toes, medium high heels. Boots either laced or buttoned to close.

accessories—Gloves were worn short during the day; long in the evening. Handcarried accessories changed little from those of the Bustle Period; boas remained popular.

jewelry—Art Nouveau design influence was strong in many items of jewelry. Watches that pinned to the dress were a fashionable accessory item.

cosmetics—Although only face powder and face creams were acceptable cosmetic items, a little tinting was sometimes added to these materials.

COSTUME FOR MEN: 1870–1900

Item / Description

evening coats—tail coats, tails about knee-length and slightly narrower at the bottom than at the top. In the 80's the cut of the dress tail coat altered somewhat, and a continuous, rolled collar faced in satin or some other silk fabric replaced the notched collar.

    tuxedo—in the 1880's a dress version of the sack suit jacket was introduced. It was called a *tuxedo*, (after its origin in Tuxedo, New York) in the United States, a dinner jacket in England. (See Figure 15.17.)

    shirts—white, generally plain, with two studs at the front, some pleated dress shirt fronts were worn after 1889. Collars fit closely and narrow bow tie was worn.

    waistcoats—matched the rest of the suit, were usually double-breasted.

    trousers—fairly narrow, matching the coat in color, and generally had a band of braid covering the outer, side seam.

daytime coats—Frock coats remained fashionable until the late 1890's when they had been supplanted for formal daytime wear by *morning coats*. Morning coats curved back from well above the waist, thereby displaying the lower part of the waistcoat. Lounge coats or sack coats continued to gain in popularity. (See Figures 15.17 and 15.18.) These had no waist seam; were cut straight or slightly curved in front, were either single or double-breasted. Reefers, similar in cut, were always square and the front double-breasted, with slightly larger lapels and collar than the sack jacket. After 1890 reefers went out of use as suit jackets, and were chiefly worn as overcoats. The Norfolk jacket was a belted sports jacket, cut without a collar or lapels.

    trousers—at this period were straight and fairly narrow, with daytime trousers cut slightly

15.17 A double-breasted sack jacket with contrasting trousers for the yachtsman; a tuxedo for dress; and a light-colored, double-breasted suit with a sack jacket and worn with a straw "boater" hat all were appropriate for summer wear in 1896. (Sartorial Arts Journal, *July, 1896.*)

wider than those for evening. Knickerbockers were worn for golf, hiking, tennis and shooting, together with knee-length stockings and sturdy shoes or high boots or gaiters.

outdoor garments—Lengths varied, shorter in the 70's, longer in the 80's and still longer in the 90's. Major styles, Chesterfield or top frock coat styles; (See Figure 15.19.) the inverness cape, as garment with full cape covering the shoulders and arms, or a cape in front that fitted into the armscye in the back so that from the front the cape was visible but from the back the coat looked like a conventional overcoat with full sleeves; and the ulster, a long, almost ankle-length coat with a full or half belt and, sometimes a detachable hood or cape.

hair and head dress—*hair*—short with a side or, less often, center part. Moustaches were popular, worn with side whiskers or a beard, although the trend was toward clean-shaven faces with moustaches.

hats—(See Figures 15.17 to 15.18.) mostly a continuation of those of earlier periods, including:

15.18 Young man of about 1880 wears a business suit and carries a derby hat. His sideburns extend into short side whiskers. (*Photograph courtesy of the Huntington Historical Society, Huntington, New York.*)

· top hats, the favored dress hat and folding top hats **for the** opera or theater. Evening top hats **were black**, silk plush, while gray, fawn and white were all used in the daytime.
· Bowlers or derbies, fedoras (low, soft hats, with the crown creased front to back), homburgs (a variant of the fedora made popular by the Prince of Wales), and a variety of caps worn for sports.
· Straw boaters, made of shellacked straw, for sports.
· The deerstalker cap, made famous through the illustrations of Conan Doyle's Sherlock Holmes stories.

15.19 At left and right the front and back views of a Chesterfield coat; at center the frock style overcoat. Hats worn include a derby (left), a top hat (center), and a homburg (right). (Sartorial Arts Journal, *January, 1896.*)

15.20 A mother, her small son, still dressed in skirts, and young daughter from about 1885. The boy's draped skirt and long buttoned bodice show a resemblance to the style of his mother's dress. (*Photograph courtesy of the Huntington Historical Society, Huntington, New York.*)

footwear—Patent leather shoes were used with both day and evening dress. They laced up the front. Elastic-side shoes, sturdy high shoes for work or hunting, oxfords, and gymnastic shoes of canvas or calf with rubber soles were all popular styles worn.

accessories—for men included such items as gloves and walking sticks. In general, jewelry was not considered masculine for men to wear, and was mostly limited to tie pins, watches, shirt studs and cuff links.

CHILDREN'S COSTUME—1870–1900

The basic approach to dressing children remained constant throughout the 19th century; infants and young children of both sexes were dressed alike. (See Figure 15.20.) After age five or so, boys no longer wore skirts but changed to trousers or knickers.

boys—knickers—1870's—became more fitted, resembling knee-breeches of 18th century. 1880's—like short trousers ending at the knee.

(See Figure 15.21.)
suits—
· Eton suit, like those of Crinoline Period.
· Sailor suit.
· Tunic suit, but with a narrower skirt and slightly lower waistline than earlier styles.
jackets—
· Reefers, cut like those of adult men.
· Blazer—made of striped or plain colored flannel, loosely fitted, with patch pockets and generally worn for sports.
· Norfolk jackets, especially with knickers.
shirts—had stiff, high collars.
outerwear—like those of adult men.

girls—dresses—like those of adult women in silhouette, but shorter in length.
· Large bustle constructions early in Bustle Period.
· About 1880 when adult cuirass style was worn, girls had dresses cut straight from shoulder

15.21 Boy dressed in knee-length knickers, c. 1880.

15.22 Adult and child from late 1890's. The little girl's dress falls from a wide, ruffled plaid yoke. (*Photograph courtesy of the Huntington Historical Society, Huntington, New York.*)

to hem with a belt located just a few inches above the hem line, at the knee.
· When bustles enlarged again, young girls wore bustles.
· 1890's—large leg-of-mutton sleeves also appeared in girls' dresses.
· Other style features: Russian blouses, Scotch plaid costumes, smocked dresses, and sailor dresses. (See Figure 15.22.)

boys and girls—Influences from Aesthetic Dress:
· *Kate Greenaway styles*—based on illustrations of children's books that showed little girls in dresses derived from Empire styles became popular with the Aesthetes and were imitated in girls' dresses for the 80's and 90's.

NOTE: Kate Greenaway styles have been revived periodically ever since for children and have influenced women's styles as well.

· *Little Lord Fauntleroy suits*—consisted of velvet tunic, ending slightly below the waist, tight knickerbockers, a wide sash, and a wide, white lace collar. Based on clothing worn by the hero of the children's book of the same name. (See Figure 15.23.)

NOTE: The similarity of this costume to that worn by Oscar Wilde was not coincidental. According to Cunnington, the author of *Little Lord Fauntleroy* was influenced by the comments of Wilde on his trip to the United States in 1882 when he declared that the Cavalier dress on which he based his "aesthetic" costume was the most artistic male dress ever known.[2] With this costume some boys wore long, curling locks. Many children's books of the time characterized the wear-

2. C. W. Cunnington and C. Beard. *A Dictionary of English Costume 900–1900.* London: Adam and Charles Black, 1972, p. 127.

15.23 Boy dressed in "Little Lord Fauntleroy suit." Although the suit is made from wool rather than velvet, the wide lace collar and cuffs, knickers, bow at the neck, and the long hair are typical of this style.

ers of Fauntleroy costume as "mama's boys" or "sissies," while boys forced to wear the costume are depicted as hating every moment and longing for the day when the barber would relieve them of these obnoxious curls. The truth is that relatively few boys actually wore little Lord Fauntleroy suits.

head dress—Boys wore their hair slightly longer until out of skirts, then hair was cut short like adult men's. Girls—hair was long, natural waves encouraged. Large bows might be worn in the hair. Boys wore caps; boys and girls wore sailor hats; both wore styles modeled on adults' hats.

Summary

Styles for women in the years between 1870 and 1900 went through a more rapid series of changes than did styles of any preceding period of comparable length. None of the distinct phases of costume can be said to have lasted even ten years. These changes were gradual, progressing year-by-year as the silhouette changed from one emphasizing the draped bustle, narrowing to the slim, cuirass bodice with both decorative detailing and trainings at the back, and returning to back fullness again in the rigid structure of yet another sort of bustle. When the bustle finally subsided, it was superceded by the hour-glass silhouette of the 90's.

Men's costume, contrariwise, showed little change in silhouette. The items of a man's wardrobe remained constant and varied little from year-to-year except in details such as the length of coats, or the width of trousers or lapels.

The budding women's American ready-to-wear industry, born in the last decades of the 19th century as a result of socioeconomic changes and technological advances in the United States, was beginning to be a factor in women's fashion, as it made possible the mass production and distribution of fashionable items such as the shirtwaist.

The more rapid movement of fashion changes for women, the more static nature of styles for men, and the transformation of certain segments of the ready-to-wear industry into a "fashion industry" foreshadowed important trends that would continue in the 20th century.

Selected Readings

BOOKS AND OTHER MATERIALS CONTAINING ILLUSTRATIONS OF COSTUME OF THE PERIOD FROM ORIGINAL SOURCES

Fashion Magazines, including: *The Delineator*
　　Godey's Lady's Book
　　Harper's Bazaar
　　Peterson's Magazine
Blum, S. *Victorian Fashions and Costumes From Harper's Bazaar: 1867–1898.* New York: Dover Publications, 1974.
Foster, V. *A Visual History of Costume: the 19th Century.* New York: Drama Books, 1985.
Gersheim, A. *Fashion and Reality.* London: Faber and Faber, 1963.

The House of Worth. Brooklyn, N.Y.: Brooklyn Museum, 1962.

Waller, G. *Saratoga: Saga of an Impious Era.* Englewood Cliffs, N. J.: Prentice Hall, 1966.

PERIODICAL ARTICLES

Bradfield, N. "Cycling in the 1890's." *Costume,* 1972, p. 43.

Haack, E. J. and J. A. Farrell. "Adult Costume in Iowa Towns, 1870–1880." *Home Economics Research Journal,* Vol. 9 (2), December 1980, p. 130.

Ormond, L. "Female Costume in the Aesthetic Movement of the 1880's and 1890's." *Costume,* 1968, p. 33.

Paoletti, J. "Clothes Make the Boy, 1860–1910." *Dress,* Vol. 9, 1983, p. 16.

Paoletti, J. "The Role of Choice in the Democratization of Fashion: A Case Study, 1875–1885." *Dress,* Vol. 5, 1980, p. 47.

Prellwitz, M. and M. D. Metcalf. "Documentation of 19th Century American Costume." *Dress,* Vol. 5, 1980, p. 24.

Schonfield, Z. "The Expectant Victorian (Late 19th Century Maternity Clothes." *Costume,* 1972, p. 36.

Walsh, M. "The Democratization of Fashion: the Emergence of the Women's Dress Pattern Industry." *The Journal of American History,* Vol. 66, 1979, p. 299.

DAILY LIFE

*Andrist, R. K. *American Century: One Hundred Years of Changing Life Styles in America.* New York: American Heritage Press, 1972.

Crow, D. *The Victorian Woman.* New York: Stein and Day Publishers, 1972.

*Fisher, J. *The World of the Forsytes.* New York: Universe Books, 1976.

Horn, P. *The Rise and Fall of the Victorian Servant.* New York: St. Martin's Press, 1975.

*Jenson, O., J. Kerr, and M. Belsky. *American Album.* New York: American Heritage Publishing Company, 1968.

Letheve, J. *Daily Life of French Artists in the 19th Century.* New York: Praeger, 1972.

The Nineties. New York: American Heritage Publishing Company, Inc., 1967.

This Fabulous Century. 1870–1900. New York: Time-Life Books.

* Also contains illustrations of costumes from contemporary sources.

PART VI

The Twentieth Century

1900–1970

The beginning of a new century is for many almost a magical period. It seems to mark some kind of a turning point, a new era and is marked by special celebrations, special expositions, pronouncements by public officials, and a rash of predictions of what the world will be like by the turn of the next century. This was certainly true of the beginning of the 20th century, and yet had people been able to look into the future to see the events of the next seventy years, it is likely that they would have chosen 1914 rather than 1900 as the beginning of a new era.

For it was in 1914 that the First World War began and it was after 1914 that nothing ever seemed the same again. For Americans, particularly, it marked the beginning of an expanded role in international politics and economics from which the country, try as it might, could never pull back.

In the 20's with prosperity for most Americans—the single largest exception to the general prosperity were the farmers—the country entered a period of reaction to the war that brought with it a revolution on the part of the young against traditional mores and values. Technology expanded, the buying power of individuals increased, and life for most people, though more frenetic, was marked by a higher standard of material comfort than ever before.

When the stock market crash came in 1929 and ushered in the Depression of the 1930's, all this changed. Not only the farmers but large numbers of middle class Americans experienced varying degrees of poverty. The Depression was not confined to the United States; its impact was worldwide. And with the rise to power in Germany of Adolf Hitler and in Italy of Benito Mussolini in the 30's, the stage was slowly being set for another international conflagration. It came in 1939 when Germany invaded Poland. The United States managed to stay out of the war until December 7, 1941 when the Japanese bombed Pearl Harbor.

The end of the war in 1945 was marked by yet another 20th century milestone, the development of atomic power. The United States emerged from the war as a "super power" and so did Russia. The older European powers that had exercised Western World leadership for so many centuries were devastated by the war and never regained their former positions of leadership.

The post-war period was marked politically by the "Cold War" between Russia and the United States and economically by a period of prosperity.

In the United States the returned veterans flooded the colleges, married or took up married life again, produced a bumper crop of babies and moved to the suburbs in large numbers. The Korean War from 1950–1953 disturbed the return to peacetime life for some Americans.

In 1957 the Russians announced that they had launched the first earth-orbiting satellite and thus began what has been called "The Space Age." The Americans made intense efforts to catch up. When John Kennedy was elected President in 1960 he vowed that Americans would reach the moon by 1970, and indeed the first manned moon landing was successfully accomplished July 20, 1969.

The 1960's in the United States could be referred to as the decade of protest and demonstrations.

The Civil Rights Movement pressed its demands for racial equality through passive resistance and mass demonstrations in the early 60's and when students of the late 60's first began to oppose the ever enlarging war in Vietnam, they borrowed these same tactics.

The end of the period covered by this survey of costume is 1969–70, a period when the Vietnamese involvement was still intense and Watergate was yet to come. Visible differences between 1900 and 1970 were many, but changes in attitudes and values were even more dramatic, as dramatic as the contrast between the corseted Gibson Girl of the turn of the century in her long, softly flowing skirts and soft pompadour and the blue-jeaned, bra-less college girl on a picket line of 1970.

CHAPTER 16

The Edwardian Period and World War I

1900–1920

Historical Background

THE UNITED STATES

The years preceding World War I in America have been called, by different writers, "the good years," "the confident years," the age of "optimism," "the innocent years," and even "the cocksure era." These appelations reflect a sense of well being that seemed to pervade the country.

The total population of the United States in 1900 was something over 76 million, forty percent of whom lived in urban areas. Only 41 million of these Americans were native born, and almost a half a million new immigrants entered the country each year. There were 45 states, New York the largest in population and Nevada the smallest.

The country was coming to depend more and more on a host of useful devices. The telephone, the typewriter, the self-binding harvester, and sewing machines were commonplace. Electricity was installed in many of the homes of America. And 8,000 automobiles were registered in the U.S. by 1900.

At the drug store soda fountain, ice cream sodas were ten cents, and orangeade was a nickel. Beef was ten cents a pound, and spring chicken seven cents a pound. Ladies could buy a tailor-made suit at the department store for ten dollars and a pair of shoes for $1.50. At the same time the average wage was twelve dollars a week or twenty-two cents an hour. Five percent of the population were unemployed, almost eleven percent were illiterate.

The Wright brothers made the first successful flight in 1903. In the same year a twelve-minute movie, *The Great Train Robbery*, was released, and a new industry was on its way.

GREAT BRITAIN AND FRANCE AT THE TURN OF THE CENTURY

The accession of Edward VII to the throne of the British Empire in 1901 after the almost seventy-year reign of his mother Queen Victoria raised in some of the British hopes for a fresh approach in politics. Britain was involved in the Boer War in South Africa when Edward became King, and the war dragged on until 1902.

Edward was a genial and worldly man with a wide range of interests. While Prince of Wales he had displayed an especially keen interest in women and such an active social life that his life style earned the disapproval of the Queen. One of the most popular cartoons of the era showed a rotund Prince of

Wales standing in the corner while the Queen scolded him.

Edward's name is generally applied to the first decade of the century: the Edwardian Period. He brought to the English throne an emphasis on social life and fashion that had been absent during the long years of Victoria's widowhood.

In France in the period from 1900 to just before World War I, a political system emerged that permitted a high degree of individual freedom. A remarkable number of creative artists and scientists who were active at the time can be cited. Important writers of the period included Zola, de Maupassant, Anatole France, Verlaine and Mallarmé. Monet, Manet, Renoir, Degas, Cezanne, and Gauguin were among the important painters of the era, and in music the composers Massenet, Saint-Saëns, Bizet, Debussy, and Ravel were active. In science the names of Pierre and Marie Curie and Louis Pasteur stand out.

WORLD WAR I

Events that led to the beginning of World War I developed rapidly and unexpectedly. The major European powers confronted each other in two heavily armed alliance systems. Germany feared encirclement by hostile powers. However, because of Germany's rise to power, other nations feared German domination of Europe. Indeed, some German leaders dreamed of such a goal.

The assassination of the Archduke Franz Ferdinand, heir apparent to the Austro-Hungarian throne, provided the spark for war. The Austro-Hungarian government, convinced of Serbian responsibility for the assassination, used the assassination as an excuse to declare war on Serbia. After Russia refused to stop mobilizing in defence of Serbia, Germany declared war on Russia and two days later on France, Russia's ally. Germany took these actions because the war plan required attacking first France and then Russia. To attack France, German armies marched through Belgium, whose neutrality had been guaranteed by the European powers. Consequently, Britain entered the war as an ally of France and Russia in defence of Belgium.

To Americans the war was far away. The average man and woman on the street, though likely to sympathize with the French and British and aghast at "the rape of Belgium," thought the United States was well out of it. But as the war dragged on, American sentiment changed and on April 2, 1917, President Woodrow Wilson called for a declaration of war against Germany.

When the fighting stopped on November 11, 1918, over 10 million soldiers had been killed and over 20 million wounded. Three great empires had collapsed. Western civilization had been forever changed.

The Effect of the War on Fashions—The War influenced styles of the period in Europe and America from 1914 to 1918 in a number of ways. The most obvious of these was in a move by women into more comfortable, practical clothes that were required for their more active participation in the variety of jobs that they had taken over from men. The prevailing costume during World War I had a relatively short skirt, several inches above the ankles. The skirt was fairly wide around the hem, a distinct change from the hobble skirt that had been the rage about 1912, and the fit through the body was comfortable. Military influences were evident in the cut of some jackets and coats which followed the lines of officers' tunics.

The war also affected colors and fabrics. Wool was in short supply, as it was diverted to the manufacture of uniforms for fighting men. And the chemicals used for certain dyestuffs restricted somewhat the use of dark colors.

After the war some of the clothing worn by soldiers passed into use by the general public. Sweaters were issued to soldiers, and the men who had become used to wearing these comfortable garments adopted them for general sportswear. For warmth the army issued a sleeveless vest-like garment to wear under the uniform. After the war these were sold as army surplus. The success the surplus stores had in selling these garments led manufacturers to add sleeves and make jackets over the same general pattern, and the buttoned, and later zippered, jacket for outdoor wear was born. Another postwar style that originated during the war was the trench coat. This water repellent coat of closely-woven cotton twill that was belted at the waist became a standard item of rainwear for men and after several decades was also adopted by women.

Influences on Fashion

THE FRENCH COUTURE AND PAUL POIRET

The turn of the century was marked, as such events often are, by a major exposition in Paris, the *Exposition Universelle*. In one of the exhibit halls members of the Parisian haute couture, the leading fashion houses of the era, presented exhibits showing their designs. Those who exhibited provide a roll call of the most important design houses of the time: Doucet, Paquin, Rouff, Cheruit, Callot Soeurs, Redfern, and Worth.

The original Worth, Charles, had died, and had been succeeded by his two sons Gaston and Jean Philippe. In the early part of the century Gaston engaged a young designer named Paul Poiret. Gaston saw in Poiret's work the kind of change he felt was needed for styles, but Jean Philippe and Gaston disagreed and Poiret left the house of Worth and in a few years opened his own establishment.

In any given fashion period there are sometimes designers whose influence is so great or whose work so captures the spirit of the age that they seem to serve as a focal point for style in that time. Poiret was such a figure. He was not only an outstanding designer, but also a colorful character whose personal idiosyncrasies help to perpetuate his legend.

Between 1903 and the First World War Poiret reigned supreme in the Paris couture. His customers submitted to his every wish, and he altered their way of dressing. The first radical step that he took was to do away with corsets. But while making gowns that were loose and free through the body, he put women into skirts with hems so narrow that they could hardly move. He is quoted as saying "I freed the bosom, shackled the legs, but gave liberty to the body."[1]

One of Poiret's major talents was for the use of vivid colors. Many writers have credited the color and oriental-influenced styles he devised to the popularity of the Russian Ballet and the costumes designed for the ballet by Leon Bakst. The Russian Ballet took Paris by storm in 1909, but Poiret disclaimed the influence of Bakst, saying that he had already begun to use vivid colors and a new style with strong oriental overtones before the arrival of the ballet. No matter which version of the development of these styles is accurate, the two complemented each other and helped to reinforce the popular lines and colors of the time.

In 1912 Poiret designed costumes for a show called *Le Minaret*. He put the women into hobble skirts over which he placed wide tunics. The tunic and hobble skirt became the rage. One of his designers was an artist named Erte' who, in turn, became a prominent fashion artist and designer for the stage as well as for women's clothing.

In addition to the styles he created, Poiret was

1. R. Lynam. *Couture*. Garden City, N.Y.: Doubleday Company, Inc., 1972, p. 63.

an innovator in other ways. He traveled abroad with a group of fashion models on which he showed his designs. He was also the first of the couturiers to begin marketing perfume, which he named after his daughter.

During and after the First World War the theatrical, colorful styles so characteristic of Poiret's work became outmoded. He never adjusted to the newer lines and look, and although his business continued into the twenties, he grew less and less successful. Eventually he dropped from public sight, and died in 1943. Some say that he died in poverty, others claim that he lived quietly but comfortably.

THE CHANGING ROLE OF AMERICAN WOMEN

Although increasingly larger numbers of women were entering the work force (over five million in 1900), most men and women considered that woman's place was in the home. Concessions to the more active life that women were leading were evident in styles, as skirts grew somewhat shorter and the shirtwaist blouse and skirt were widely adopted. Business was employing increasing numbers of women, especially as "typewriters."

But even the married lady who saw her role as wife and mother was getting out of the house more. Women's clubs increased in membership to more than one million by 1910. These groups focused on self-improvement or good works such as helping the poor.

The woman's suffrage movement stepped-up its campaigning for women's rights, but President Grover Cleveland spoke for many men and women as well when he declared "The relative positions to be assumed by man and woman in the working out of our civilization were assigned long ago by a higher intelligence than ours."

By the second decade of the century women were becoming even more adventurous. They drove cars, went out to work in increasing numbers (7.5 million in 1910 and a million more were added to the work force by 1920) and engaged in a variety of active sports from swimming to bobsledding. The clothes required for these active, competitive sports helped to modify the prevailing styles.

As women became more emancipated, support for the vote for women grew. After 1910 a series of public marches and rallies were held, and each one was larger than the last. The war caused a decrease in the activism of the suffragists and, at the same time, dramatized the place of women in American society, as women moved in to fill jobs that the soldiers had left behind. Women worked in factories, delivered ice, and directed traffic. Women became auto mechanics and operated elevators. On June 4, 1919, after the war had ended, Congress passed the 19th Amendment which guaranteed that the right to vote could not be restricted on account of sex.

AUTOMOBILES

The role of the automobile in American society is so thoroughly established that it is difficult to imagine what life must have been like before it came upon the scene. In 1900 the auto was a rich man's toy. Automobiles or "bubbles" as they were sometimes called cost upwards of $3,000 at a time when the average weekly wage was twelve dollars.

At first they were used for sport. Auto racing became a social event and in 1905 when the second Vanderbilt Cup Race was held, Manhattan society turned out in force. The newspapers reported the event as they would have reported a hunting party with descriptions of the crowds and their clothing. They reported that Mrs. Belmont wore tweed, a fairly sensible choice, while another dowager "dripped pearls" and yet another wore a large Gainsborough picture hat.[2]

Drivers of automobiles had no problems about what to wear. Automobiling costume was quickly established as a long cotton or linen duster, a cap with a visor (worn backwards at high speeds to prevent its being blown off) and goggles. Ladies wore face veils, green was preferred, and their coats sometimes had a more stylish cut, but like those of men they covered the costume beneath completely. Cars were open and roads unpaved, so the term "duster" was an appropriate one.

In 1908 Henry Ford made the first Model T which sold for $850. The car was no longer the rich man's toy. By the end of the next decade more than four million Model T Fords had been purchased by Americans and the age of the automobile had arrived.

AMERICAN HIGH SOCIETY

Although the average woman in small town America had no direct contact with the wealthy and socially prominent, she could easily be kept abreast of their doings through the press, particularly through the many magazines that were sold across the nation. Around the turn of the century mass circulation

2. W. Lord. *The Good Years.* New York: Bantam Books. 1965, p. 108.

magazines in the United States were available at low prices and in great variety. Their cost was kept low by the increasingly large quantities of advertising they carried.

Fashion magazines and women's magazines which carried a good deal of fashion information frequently printed photographs and drawings of the wealthy and stories of their latest escapades. The balls and weddings of the socially prominent were minutely described in *Vogue*, and a drawing of the bride's wedding dress often accompanied the article. From these photographs, articles, and drawings, fashion-conscious women across the country could keep up with the latest fashions in "society." By selecting similar styles from the growing number of pattern catalogs and ready-to-wear items women of more limited means were able to obtain less expensive versions of the most popular styles.

Costume of the Edwardian Period and World War I

COSTUME FOR WOMEN—1900–1920

Between 1900 and 1920, women's fashions in Europe and America changed with remarkable rapidity. Examination of day time and evening styles from this period is, therefore, simplified by sub-dividing the detailed examination of women's dress into the following phases:

- 1900–1908—Edwardian styles or styles with emphasis on an S-shaped silhouette.
- 1909–1914—Empire revival and the hobble skirt
- 1914–1918—World War I
- 1918–1919—Post-War Styles

1900–1908

Item / Description

undergarments—No radical changes from those of the 90's. Frilly, decorative petticoats and drawers continued to be popular, many had ruffles around the bottom and were edged with lace. Eyelet insertion with ivory, pink, or blue ribbon threaded through was a popular trim for all kinds of underclothing.

dresses—*silhouette*—S-shaped curve. The major features of women's dresses included a high boned collar, a style that had been continually in use since the late 1800's; a full, pouched bodice; and a skirt that was flat in front and emphasized a rounded hipline in the back. (See Figure 16.1.) The skirt after hugging the hips flared out to a trumpet shape at the bottom. Dresses were generally one piece, with bodices and skirts sewn together at the waistline; some princess-line, one piece dresses as well.

fabrics—Except for tailor-mades and shirtwaist styles made in imitation of men's shirts, the emphasis on frilly and much-decorated clothing required soft fabrics. Decorations included tucking, pleating, lace insertion, bands of applied fabric, lace, and embroidery. (See Figure 16.2.)

bodices—often quite complicated in construction, with full-bosomed cut almost universal.

Most closed with hooks and eyes or hooks and bars.

necklines—high boned collars predominated, others were square cut, v-shaped (with or without collars), and sailor collars. Frilly jabots were often placed at the neck.

sleeves—generally long, either close-fitting or bishop style, i.e., full below the elbow with fabric puffed or pouched at the wrist; in the last half of the decade, shorter (often ¾ length) sleeves. Other styles included: sleeves wide at the end and finished with ruffles or attached under sleeves, and kimono-style sleeves.

skirts—shapes achieved by goring, with skirts close-fitted to the knee in front, then full and flared to the hem. Some had back pleats. Lengths varied: some ended several inches off the ground, others had trains.

16.1 S-shaped silhouette of the Edwardian Period is evident in the silhouette of this summer dress. (*Photograph courtesy of the Huntington Historical Society, Huntington, New York.*)

16.2 This high school graduate of 1904 wears lace-trimmed, ruffled white dress with high, boned collar. (*Photograph courtesy of Melissa Clark.*)

separate blouses and skirts—a wide range of skirt styles were featured in mail order catalogs and pictured were variations such as pleating, decorative stitching, applied braid trim, and ruffled hems. Blouses (shirtwaists) came in great variety and displayed features much like the bodices of daytime dresses. (See Figures 16.3, 16.4.)

other garments—*tailor-made*—a major item of clothing for women. Jackets varied in length from waist to below the hip. Shorter jackets were generally fitted; long jackets were sometimes loose and sacque-like. Many imitated the cut of men's jackets. (See Figure 16.5.)
   tea gowns—were soft, frilly dresses worn in the late afternoon.

evening dresses—followed the same silhouette as daytime dresses.
   necklines—were generally low and square, round, V-shaped. Some had lace or sheer fabric fichus at the neck.
   sleeves—ruffled decorative sleeves covering the upper part of the arm or sleeveless styles with shoulder straps.
   skirts—full, often trained, in soft fabrics.

outdoor garments—chiefly cloaks and capes with high-standing (Medici) collars and wide revers, especially for evening wear. Coats were fitted or unfitted and made in many different lengths. Some were fitted at the back, loose in the front.

hair and head dress—*hair*—full and loose around the face, pulled into a chignon or bun at the back of the neck. An important style, the pompadour, had hair built high in front and sides around the face. The first permanent wave was given in London in 1904.
   hats—large in scale, styles included brimless toques and large-brimmed "picture hats." Decoration was lavish with artificial flowers, lace, buckles, feathers, and bird wings.

NOTE: In 1905, a single page of the Sears Roebuck catalog showed 75 different styles of ostrich feather decorations.

   hair ornaments—for evening included feathers, jeweled combs, and small skull caps of pearls called "Juliet caps," after the heroine of Romeo and Juliet.

footwear—*stockings*—generally of dark or neutral cotton lisle for daytime or silk for formal wear. Some decorated with colored clocks or lace insertion.
   shoes—pointed toes, long slender lines, heels

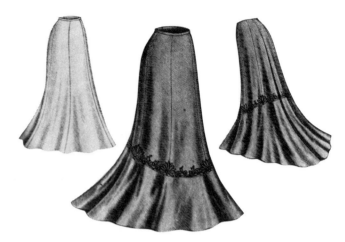

16.3 Gored skirts in three lengths. Left to right: "round length," "dip length," and "medium sweep length" from *The Designer, 1903.*

about 2–2½ inches high curved in the so called "Louis" style.
   boots—less fashionable than shoes, but when worn were high and buttoned or laced to close.

accessories—included large, flat muffs; decorative lace or silk parasols and trimmed with fringe or lace: serviceable oiled silk umbrellas; suede or leather daytime handbags or beaded evening bags; and long folding fabric fans or ostrich fans.
   belts—especially triangular-shaped, "Swiss" belts revived from the 1860's. Ruffles, boas, ribbons or cravats worn around the neck.

jewelry—in all qualities and prices and including: clasps, brooches, pendents, necklaces, chains, dog collars and long necklaces; pendent for single stone earrings. Jewelry was often made in the Art Nouveau style.

1909–1914

dresses—*silhouette*—By 1909 the S-shaped curve of the Edwardian period was being superceded by a straighter line. The full, pouched bodice decreased in size, and the location of the waistline moved upward. Skirts narrowed and grew shorter. Dresses were likely to be one-piece, although skirts, blouses, and tailor-mades had become a permanent part of women's wardrobes. The high boned collar gradually went out of fashion. This collar had been part of women's costumes for such a long time that the clergy were outraged that women would show their necks while health experts expressed fears for women's health and predicted

16.4 At a company picnic of about 1901, ladies wear cotton dresses or shirtwaists and skirts and men white shirts and bow ties. Almost all of the women have arranged their hair in a pompadour. (*Photograph courtesy of Almeda Brackbill Scheid.*)

an increase in pneumonia and tuberculosis. *costume detailing*—the Empire revival led to the use of a number of details in addition to the elevated waistline that were considered to have originated during the First Empire. (See Figure 16.6.) These included military collars, ruffled jabots, and wide revers or lapels. As is true with most costume revivals, these latter details were only very loosely based on men's costume of the early 1800's.

daytime dresses—*bodices*—retained some vestiges of its fullness of Edwardian period. Front-buttoned closing were used for many styles. *skirts*—From 1909–1911 a narrow, straight skirt predominated, (See Figure 16.6.) but by about 1912 a number of different skirt styles of more elaborate construction had become popular. (See Figure 16.7.) But whether the skirt was single or multiple layered, it maintained an exceptionally narrow circumference around the ankles. Women could barely take a full step in the most extreme of these skirts. They were called "hobble" skirts. Some were so tight that a slit had to be made at the bottom to enable women to walk.

Types included: peg-top skirts, with fullness concentrated at the hip then narrowing gradually to the ankles. Tunics were worn over underskirts. Tunics varied in shape from narrow tubes to wide, full-bottomed styles, and even multiple layers of tunic skirts.

NOTE: Paul Poiret designed a number of very exotic styles including the "minaret" tunic, a wide tunic, boned to hold out the skirt in a full circle and worn over the narrowest of hobble skirts. He also introduced the harem skirt, a full turkish style trouser which did not attract any significant following.

sleeves—generally tight-fitting, ending below the elbow or at the wrist, with cuffs of contrasting colors. Man-tailored shirtwaist blouses, complete with neckties and high tight collars were worn with separate skirts. Blouses lost the exceptional frilliness of the Edwardian period.

evening dresses—also emphasized the Empire revival. Most had tunics or layers of sheer fabric placed over heavier fabric. Trains were popular, sleeves were short, often kimono style and of

16.5 Two garments depicted in a pattern book of 1903. The pleated jacket on the right has the straight, loose cut seen on some styles of jackets from this period, while the dress on the left follows the S-shaped curved silhouette that is more typical of the Edwardian styles.

16.6 Empire style revival of 1911. (*French fashion magazine, L'Art de la Mode, 1911.*)

sheerer fabric than the body of the dress. Decorative touches included wide cloth belts or sashes, gold and silver embroidery and lace, beading, and fringe. (See Figure 16.8.)

tailored suits—jackets were cut to below the hips, with an overall line that was long and slender. (See Figure 16.9.) Narrow skirts were slit at the side or front.

outdoor garments—For daytime coats were long or three-quarter length, some closing at far left in a sort of wraparound style. Evening coats were looser, cut full across the back and often with cape-like sleeves. Some elaborately ruffled capes were also worn for evening.

hair and head dress—*hair*—less bouffant; waved softly around face and pulled into a soft roll at the back or toward the top of the head. *hats*—large, emphasizing height, many in the toque style or with turned-up brims. Face veils

were popular. Hats were decorated with artificial flowers, feathers, and ribbons. In keeping with the Directoire revival, tricorne hats were worn. (In actuality, tricornes were worn not in the Directoire or Empire periods, but earlier.)

footwear—no radical changes.

1914–1918

Item / Description

dresses—*silhouette*—During the wartime years the silhouette of women's clothes grew wider and skirts grew shorter. By 1915 skirts achieved fullness through pleating, gathering, or with gores. Hems raised to six inches from the ground in 1916 and as much as eight or more inches from the floor in 1917. Throughout the period the waistline was at normal placement or slightly above. (See Figure 16.10.)

16.7 Layered skirts that fit tightly around the ankles; the "hobble skirt." (*French fashion magazine*, L'Art de la Mode, *1913.*)

16.8 Evening dress, 1914, made of white satin and beaded net with lace and chiffon. The draped skirt and kimono sleeve are characteristic of evening styles of this date. (*Photograph courtesy of the Metropolitan Museum of Art, gift of Susan Dwight Bliss, 1937.*)

daytime dresses—one-piece dresses were still preferred. Coat dresses, either single or double-breasted and belted or sashed at the waist were a popular style. Necklines often V-shaped or squared, some had sailor collars.

    sleeves—generally straight and fitted.

    tailored suits—gained even greater popularity during the wartime years. Some had a distinctly military look, with jackets long and belted at or slightly above natural waistline. (See Figure 16.11.)

blouses—worn with skirts or suits. Typical features were: sleeves and yokes cut in one, leg-o-mutton sleeves, Medici or standing collars with open or round or square neck at the front.

sweaters—knitted sweaters that pulled on over the head ("pullovers") became popular after 1916. These had no discernable waist, were belted at the hip, and had long sleeves.

NOTE: Gabrielle Chanel, the designer, is often given credit for being the first person to interest women in knitted pullover sweaters.

evening dresses—followed daytime dress lines. Waistline placement tended to be slightly higher than the natural waistline. Skirts were full, with many having tiers of ruffles, floating panels of fabric, or layers of varying lengths. At the neck the decolletage might be filled in with flesh-colored or transparent fabric. Sleeves were short or

16.9 Suit styles of 1913 have elongated jackets. The coat (far right) is full at the back but narrow at the hem. (*French fashion magazine*, L'Art de la Mode, *1913.*)

16.10 Suit and two dresses of 1916 have shorter, fuller skirts that were part of the wartime styles. (*French fashion magazine*, L'Art de la Mode, *1916.*)

to the elbow. Sleeveless dresses had only narrow straps over the shoulder. Beading, gold, and silver embroidery remained fashionable trimmings. (See Figure 16.12.)

outdoor garments—coats grew wider to accommodate wider skirts. One popular style had a full back, others were full but loosely belted. Three-quarter coats were popular in 1916 and after. Military influence was evident in some coats.

hair and head dress—*hair*—worn closer to the face and shorter during the wartime period. More women tried permanent waves.
   hats—high rather than wide, smaller than before the war, with and without brims and often worn with face veils.

footwear—Stockings were dark for daytime, but pale for evening. Rayon stockings were introduced as an alternative to silk. Shoe styles did not change radically, but shoes were more visible as hemlines raised.

1918–1920

The post war period is really a transitional period from the wartime styles to the styles of the 1920's. By 1918 the war had had the effect of curtailing the supplies of fabrics, and the silhouette grew narrower again. In 1918 and 1919, there developed a narrower skirt with a less clearly defined waistline that was rather wide giving rise to the term "barrel-shaped." In 1919 after the end of the war, fashion designers turned back to narrower skirts, and hemlines gradually dipped to the ankle again. The silhouette remained loosely fitted through the waist. The chemise dress, a straight tube of the type that was to become so fashionable in the 20's is said to have been created first by the designer Jeanne Lanvin.

16.11 Women's suits of 1915 show military influence in the cut of the jackets and the style of the cap on the left. (*French fashion magazine*, L'Art de la Mode, *1915.*)

16.12 Sketch of an evening dress from the Worth collection of the World War I period. This dress was colored blue and silver. (*Costume Institute Library of the Metropolitan Museum of Art.*)

COSTUME FOR MEN—1900–1920

Item / Description

daytime dress—Over this period jacket styles varied in these ways: both single and double breasted suits were made, the popularity of each varying from year to year. In the early years of the century jackets and coats were cut long, buttoned high, had small lapels—a full cut through the torso gave men an almost barrel-chested appearance. (See Figure 16.13.) During the teens, jackets and coats gradually shortened. (See Figure 16.14.)

Except for summer when lighter weight flannel and linen fabrics were worn, suits were generally dark in color and dark blue wool serge was the most popular fabric.

Suit jacket styles included:
· *frock coats* were worn only by dignitaries on formal occasions or by elderly men.

· *morning coats* were still seen for formal occasions during the day. Before the war, morning coats were worn as suits with matching coat and trousers or with contrasting waistcoat and striped trousers. After the war, morning coats were worn only among the upper classes or political leaders as formal dress for weddings, diplomatic receptions, or inaugurations. Formal occasions required a top hat; for less formal events one might wear a derby or homburg.
· *lounge suits* or *sack suits* became the standard suit for men during the 20th century. Sack coats were worn for all occasions and even appeared for leisure time wear as "sports jackets." (The British preferred the term lounge coat. American tailors called these coats sack jackets.)

NOTE: Military influences crept into men's coats during the war, and silhouettes narrowed, shoulder lines became less padded and more natural.

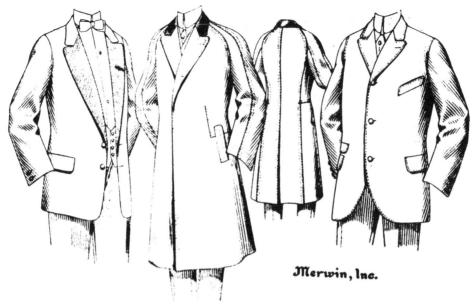

16.13 Left to right: evening dress of the tuxedo type, a chesterfield coat with velvet collar, and a business suit. (Sartorial Art Journal, *October 1911.*)

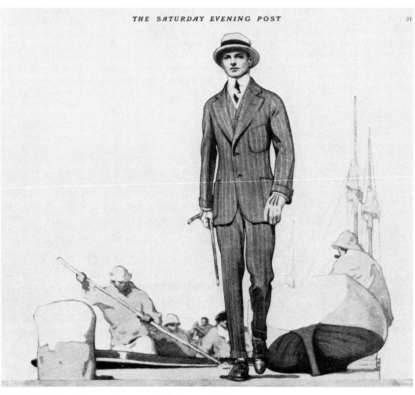

Hart Schaffner & Marx

Varsity Fifty Five *with patch pockets*

Young men like the variations we give to our Varsity Fifty Five model—patch pockets or plain; vest with roll-collar or no collar; one, two, or three button coats. So long as the main idea is right, the variations are a matter of preference.

16.14 Business suit, 1913. (*Photograph courtesy of Hart, Schaffner, and Marx.*)

16.15 Young man of the turn-of-the-century dressed probably to play baseball in a turtleneck sweater and padded knickers. (*Photograph courtesy of the Huntington Historical Society, Huntington, New York.*)

trousers—generally cut loosely around the hips, narrower toward the bottom. Some had turned up cuffs, others no cuffs, and were worn with and without sharply pressed creases. Applied waistbands were becoming more popular.

vests—just after the turn of the century were light or colored, but by the teens vests generally matched the suit with which they were worn.

shirts—when worn under coats and vests were visible only at the collar, above the vest, and at the end of the sleeves. Some shirts, particularly those for more formal dress, had stiffened fronts. Both white and colored shirts were worn, as well as patterns such as polka dots or stripes. In the first years of the century collars were high and stiff. The height gradually decreased and both soft and stiff collars were worn. Shirts worn by soldiers had softer collars, and after the war men continued to favor less rigidly-starched shirt collars.

NOTE: Collars were either part of the shirt or detachable, so that the same shirt could be worn for several days and by changing the collar and cuffs the wearer gave the appearance of a fresh shirt.

neckties—Those worn with shirts included bow ties (which could be purchased already-tied to clip into place, but these were considered unfashionable), "four-in-hand" ties, (today's standard necktie), and ascots, ties with wide ends that were worn with one end looped over the other and held in place with a tie pin.

sweaters—were generally worn by working-class men, with available styles including collarless cardigans that opened down the front, V-necked pullovers, and high-collared styles similar to the modern turtleneck. (See Figure 16.15.)

NOTE: Soldiers were issued sweaters as regulation army wear and after the war they remained popular, particularly for sports.

evening dress—*jackets*—either with matching trousers and a white waistcoat or dinner jackets (tuxedos, sack cut) with dark waistcoats and matching trousers were worn. Tail coats were double-breasted, but worn unbuttoned, and had rolled lapels or notched collars and lapels. Dinner jackets were generally single breasted. Evening jackets usually had lapels faced in silk. (See Figure 16.13.)

trousers—matched the jacket, had no cuffs, and a row or two of braid placed along the outer seams.

dress shirts—generally had stand-up collars and were worn with white bow ties. Shirts closed with studs. After about 1910, shirt fronts were pleated and had wing collars. After 1915, black ties for evening were gaining acceptance.

loungewear—for home consisted of dressing gowns, and smoking jackets, some of which had quilted lapels and were made in decorative fabrics.

sleepwear—Nightshirts were still worn by many men, but others wore pajamas.

underwear—was generally made of wool. Heavier knits were used for winter, lighter for summer. Union suits, with drawers and underwear in one were popular. In summer drawers had short legs; in winter, long.

outdoor garments—*overcoats*—cut to accommodate the wide cut of men's suits in the first decade, after which they became more fitted. Lengths varied, some being almost ankle length, others below the knee at midcalf, still other short "top coats" ended at the hip. (The top coat was worn by affluent men who could afford more than one overcoat.) Basic overcoat styles included:

- chesterfields and raglan sleeve coats, with versions for evening having velvet collars. (See Figure 16.13.)
- ulsters—made with whole or half belts and, detachable hoods or capes.
- inverness coats—with single or double capes.
- mackintoshes—the name given to almost any kind of rainwear.

NOTE: The process patented by Charles Mackintosh for placing a layer of rubber between two layers of cloth was still a popular means of applying a waterproof finish to fabric. Other waterproof finishes were made by oiling fabric to make "slickers," and during World War I Thomas Burberry created the "trench coat," a belted twill cotton gabardine of very close weave that had a chemical finish that made the coat water repellent.

In the second decade of the century military influences were evident. Collars took on a military shape, high and fitted, and coats became shorter. Trench coats became fashionable after the war. Fur coats were worn, especially after the war. Racoon was especially popular for motoring. Many fur collared and fur-lined coats.

jackets and casual coats—in the early years of the period, limited to working class men who wore heavy corduroy, leather, wool, and other utilitarian fabrics. Some jackets such as lumber jackets were associated with particular occupations. After the war interest in outdoor sports increased and jackets for recreation were adopted by the public at large. Growing use of casual outdoor garments may have been related to the post-war sale of surplus military sleeveless lined jackets. Veterans who remembered them as warm and comfortable quickly bought them, and manufacturers, seeing their popularity, made their own versions.

sportswear—Antecedents of the modern sports jacket, worn with unmatched trousers can be seen in the blazer, worn for tennis, yachting, or other sports and the Norfolk jacket, an English style of belted jacket for golf, bicycling, and hiking. Knickers, long stockings, sturdy shoes and a soft cap with a visor were often combined with these jackets. (See Figure 16.16.)

16.16 Golfing clothing, 1912. On the left, knickers and a norfolk jacket; on the right plaid suit with a half belt at the back. (*Sartorial Arts Journal, 1912.*)

riding—costumes differed from the traditional 19th century morning coat, breeches and boots. Instead, a jacket with a flared skirt was worn with jodphurs, a pair of trousers fitted closely around the lower leg and flaring out above the knee.

NOTE: Jodphurs originated in India where they were adopted by British colonials and subsequently spread throughout the West.

swimming—dress for men in England was made up of a pair of drawers, but in the United States was more likely to be either a knitted wool suit with fitted knee-length breeches and a shirt with short or no sleeves or a one-piece, short-legged, round-necked, sleeveless tank suit.

NOTE: Kidwell believes that bathing dress in the U.S. developed a more conservative character because men and women bathed together rather than, as was the custom in England until about 1900, separately.[3]

3. *Op. cit.*, p. 18

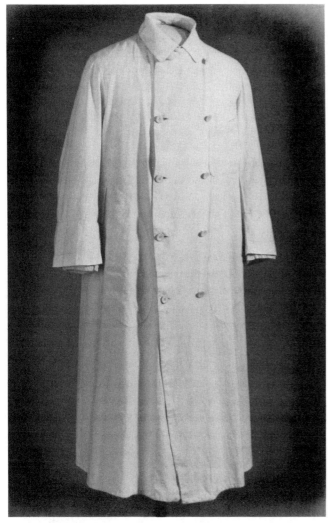

16.17 Linen duster or automobiling coat. (*Photograph courtesy of the Smithsonian Institution.*)

driving—some men wore sports coats and flannel trousers for driving, but long, linen dusters or leather motoring coats were more practical. To this were added goggles and peaked caps, worn with the peak at the back to avoid having them blown off. (See Figure 16.17.)

hair and head dress—*hair*—generally short. The war helped to diminish the popularity of beards and moustaches, as they were more difficult to keep clean in combat zones and interfered with gas masks.

hats—did not alter much from the latter part of the 19th century, and included top hats, now only for formal occasions; soft felt hats with names as homburg or trilby; derbies; and caps for leisure. Western-style Stetson® felt hats were worn in some parts of the United States; for summer men used panama straw hats and straw boaters and linen hats made in derby or fedora-like shapes.

footwear—*stockings*—were usually neutral colors, with a few stripes and multi-colored styles. Stockings had ribbed tops and were held up with elastic garters.

shoes—in the early part of the century, long, pointed toes; shoes laced or buttoned shut, and many were cut high, above the ankle. For dress, black patent leather slippers were popular. After 1910, oxfords (low, laced shoes) increased in use. Some had perforated designs on the toes, others were two-toned, some white buckskin for summer, but sturdy laced, high shoes were still favored by many for everyday. By the end of the decade, rounded more blunt toes were more popular.

accessories—gloves, handkerchiefs, scarves. Walking sticks were popular until automobiles came into widespread use.

jewelry—mostly limited to tiepins, shirt studs, rings, and cuff links. Wristwatches gained popularity as a result of their wartime use and because of the increased use of automobiles. (The inconvenience of pocket watches to soldiers and drivers proved the value of wrist watches.)

COSTUME FOR CHILDREN

Throughout history children's clothing shows clear similarities to that of adults. At times, particularly in the 20th century, the special needs of children for clothing that is reasonably practical have been recognized. In the first decade of the 20th century this recognition, while beginning, was not characteristic of all children's clothing. Moore calls the Edwardian period a time of transition in children's clothing as styles moved from impractical to more practical dress.[4]

girls—*dresses*—included white, light, or cream-colored lingerie dresses (one of the less practical styles) cut with waists low on the hip. For decoration on all dresses: embroidery, smocking, and lace. Other styles had more natural waistline placement, and full, bloused bodices similar to those of adult women.

· *For school:* navy blue serge popular; sailor dresses and hats remained popular. (See Figure 16.18.)

· *About 1910:* a favored style had a large, cape

4. Moore, *op. cit.*, p. 90.

16.18 Children dressed for cool weather around 1900. The girl at the left wears a coat with several shoulder capes, a style which appears frequently in mail order catalogs of Sears and Roebuck Company about 1900. Her hat is a wide-brimmed sailor style. The older boy at the center wears a turtlenecked sweater and a visored cap. The girl at the right has a short jacket. Her hat is a tam-o-shanter under which one can see her large hair ribbon. (*Photograph courtesy of the Huntington Historical Society, Huntington, New York.*)

16.19 Child from just after 1900 wears a checked pinafore over her lighter-colored frock. Even though the weather is warm enough for her to be outdoors without a coat, she wears heavy, dark stockings. (*Photograph courtesy of the Huntington Historical Society, Huntington, New York.*)

collar, low waist, sleeves full to the elbow then tight to the wrist.

· *Pinafores:* usually placed on top of other dresses to protect them. (See Figure 16.19.)

· *After 1910:* less white and more color in "best" dresses.

· *From 1914–1917:* belts dropped low, to the thighs.

· *Throughout the period:* skirts for young girls were about knee-length; longer but still a practical length for older girls.

· *Physical education uniforms:* gym tunics worn over blouses had sleeveless yokes, square necks, and belted full pleated bodices. This style remained popular in subsequent periods, as well.

boys—1900–1910—most small boys were still dressed in skirts until the age of four or five, the dresses followed the same lines as those for girls.

1910–1920—Little boys were more likely to be dressed in rompers, and when a little older, in knickers.

suit styles—sailor suits, Eton suits, Norfolk jackets, and sack suit jackets, all with or without belts. With jackets, shorts or knickers for younger boys; long trousers for older boys. (See Figure 16.18.)

outdoor wear—mackinaw coats in plaid or plain colors; Norfolk jackets; long cardigan sweaters, turtle neck sweaters.

boys and girls—Innovative styles included these from mail order catalogs of 1914: knitted tops and leggings for small boys and girls; sleeping garments with feet.

footwear—High laced shoes for both sexes. For dress wear girls wore flat slippers with strap(s) across the instep or a flat shoe with an ankle strap.

stockings—1900–1910—tended to be knee-length; during the war these shortened for girls. Boys wore knee-length socks with knickers.

Summary

The first two decades of the 20th century were characterized in women's clothing by rapid changes of fashion and in men's clothing by relative stability in styles. Influences such as increasing use of automobiles and the entry into the work force by more women, both before and during the War, probably helped to establish styles for women that were shorter, less confining, and more practical. Ever-increasing availability of ready-to-wear clothing of all kinds was another characteristic of these two decades.

World War I had an impact not only on the styles of the wartime period when military influences were evident in the cut and colors of both men's and women's clothing, but also on styles after the war. Garments such as trench coats, sweaters, and jackets that were part of military clothing issued were carried over into civilian use after the war to become permanent items of dress.

Selected Readings

BOOKS AND OTHER MATERIALS CONTAINING ILLUSTRATIONS OF COSTUME OF THE PERIOD FROM ORIGINAL SOURCES

Fashion Magazines such *Vogue* and *Harper's Bazaar*

Women's Magazines such as *The Delineator, Ladies Home Journal,* and *McCalls.*

Sears and Roebuck Mail Order Catalogs

Battersby, M. *Art Deco Fashion: French Designers: 1908–1925.* New York: St. Martin's Press, 1974.

Carter, E. *20th Century Fashion: A Scrapbook—1900 to Today.* London: Eyre Methuen, 1975.

Men's Wear: 75 Years of Fashion. New York: Fairchild Publications, 1965.

Schoeffler, O. E. (Ed.) *Esquire's Encyclopedia of 20th Century Men's Fashion.* McGraw-Hill Book Company, 1973.

Winter, G. *Golden Years, 1903–1913.* London: David and Charles, 1975.

The World in Vogue. New York: The Viking Press, 1963.

PERIODICAL ARTICLES

Behling, D. and L. Dickey. "Haute Couture: A 25 Year Perspective of Fashion influences: 1900–1925." *Home Economics Research Journal,* Vol. 8 (6), July 1980, p. 428.

Behling, D. "The Russian Influence on Fashion: 1909–1925." *Dress,* 1979, p. 1.

Doering, M. D. "American Red Cross Uniforms." *Dress,* Vol. 5, 1979, p. 33.

Feldkamp, P. "The Man Who Banned the Corset (Poiret)." *Horizon,* Vol. 14, Summer 1972, p. 30.

Helverson, S. "Advice to American Mothers on the Subject of Children's Dress: 1800–1920." *Dress,* Vol. 7, 1981, p. 30.

"Mario Fortuny: The Magician of Venice." *American Fabrics and Fashions,* Spring 1980, No. 119, p. 21.

DAILY LIFE

*Andrist, R. K. *American Century: One Hundred Years of Changing Life Styles in America.* New York: American Heritage Press, 1972.

**American Heritage History of the Confident Years.* New York: American Heritage Publishing Company, Inc. N.D.

*Churchill, A. *Remember When (1900–1940).* New York: Golden Press, Inc., 1947.

Kennedy, D. M. *Over There.* New York: Oxford University Press, 1980.

Lord, W. *The Good Years.* New York: Bantam Books, 1960.

**This Fabulous Century, Vol. 1, 1900–1910 and Vol. 2, 1910–1920.* New York: Time-Life Books, 1969.

* Also contains illustrations of costume from contemporary sources.

CHAPTER 17

The Twenties, Thirties and World War II

1920–1947

Historical Background—The United States

With the end of World War I, Europe and the United States hoped for "a return to normalcy." The American President, Woodrow Wilson, a strong proponent of the League of Nations, campaigned arduously for ratification of the Treaty of Versailles and membership in the League for the United States. These efforts cost him his health—he suffered a breakdown in 1919—and he was an invalid for the remainder of his seventeen months in office. In the end, the Senate defeated the Treaty and the United States never joined the League of Nations.

THE TWENTIES

Warren G. Harding was elected President of the United States in 1920. During his administration a separate peace resolution was approved and the "official business" of World War I finally was concluded.

In the early 20's, the United States settled down to a period of unequaled prosperity. From 1923 to 1927, business was booming. A survey of the consumer goods that sold most actively provides a key to the interests and life style that developed over

the period. Leading the sales charts were automobiles. Radios (commercial broadcasting to the public began in 1922), rayon, cigarettes, refrigerators, telephones, cosmetics, and electrical devices of all kinds were sold in huge quantities. The purchasing power of the dollar increased twofold for most Americans. There was a boom in higher education, self-improvement books sold briskly, and travel abroad increased. In 1928, 437,000 people left the United States by ship to visit some distant place.

This prosperity, however, had a dark side. While business was thriving and most people were increasingly affluent, the American farmer was experiencing hard times. The demand for agricultural products was fairly stable and the export market dropped off, creating surpluses. Cotton went into decline as rayon, a man-made fabric became more popular.

Another cloud on the horizon of the population was prohibition. The Eighteenth Amendment had been passed and the distilling, brewing, and sale of alcoholic beverages became illegal in 1920. In the long run the Amendment was ignored by many, but in the process of violating the law a new institution, the speak-easy, a clandestine drinking club for drinking, dining, and dancing, replaced the saloon. When prohibition was repealed in 1933 the speak-easy made a rapid transition into the nightclub.

Several other American institutions planted their roots firmly during the 20's. One was the chain store. These national or regional chains of stores served to bring the prices of consumer goods down and increase purchasing power. Installment buying took a firm hold, too.

With the spectacular success of Charles A. Lindbergh's transatlantic flight in 1927, flying took on a new importance. Passenger service was beginning by the end of the decade. A cross-continent flight combined with rail transportation (it was too dangerous to fly at night, so by night passengers took the train), took two days. And the first airmail service was initiated.

Changes in the Social Life of the Twenties—After World War I had ended, the social climate in Europe and in the United States changed. This change was especially pronounced in the United States. Not only had the war left people wondering whether their efforts had been justified, but other disturbing notions such as the sexual theories of Sigmund Freud and the changing roles of women resulted in a revolution in mores and values, especially among the young. Reactions varied. There were the romantic cynics like the novelist F. Scott Fitzgerald and his heroes and heroines. There were escapists who followed a ceaseless round of parties and pleasure. There were an increasing number of isolationists who saw America as having no important ties to Europe or the rest of the world. And, of course, there were the many average citizens who were increasingly bewildered by the many antics of the pleasure-seekers.

Writers of the period speak of a revolution in morality. This was evident in the behavior of the young, particularly young women. Until the first World War there were certain standards of behavior expected of "ladies." They were not supposed to smoke, to drink, to see young men unchaperoned, certainly they were expected to kiss only the boy they intended to marry. By the 20's all this had changed. The "flapper" as she was nicknamed seemed free from all of the restraints of the past. She smoked and drank, she necked in parked cars, she danced the Charleston until all hours of the night, and what's more she looked totally different as well. She was caracatured perfectly by John Held, Jr., whose drawings of flappers appeared often on the covers of *Life Magazine.*

1. M. Horn. *The Second Skin*. New York: Houghton-Mifflin Company, 1975, p. 107.

". . . the sensitivity of fashion to social problems provides a visible index of agitation and unrest. Drastic changes in clothing patterns are evidence of changes elsewhere."[1] Women's costume of the 20's provides the visible evidence of agitation and unrest of which Horn speaks. Never before in the history of costume in the civilized West had women worn skirts that revealed their legs. Except for a brief period after the French Revolution, women's hair had never been cut so short nor flesh-colored stockings been worn. Trousers as an outer garment had heretofore been strictly a man's garment. (The earlier attempts to introduce bifurcated garments for women had utilized "bloomers" which were cut differently than a man's trousers.) Rouge and lip color had not been used by "nice" girls. But during the 20's all of these things became commonplace. These were clear changes in acceptable dress for women that paralleled clear changes in the social roles of women.

THE DEPRESSION

Toward the end of the decade the bubble of the 20's prosperity burst. Business had been faltering after about 1927, but the stock market continued to rise to what astute financial observers felt were dangerous heights. On October 29, 1929 the stock market collapsed, the last of several drops which had each been followed by recovery, but this time the recovery never came and the United States and Europe sank into the period now known as "The Great Depression."

Unemployment was widespread. The American farmers who had never participated in the prosperity of the 20's were affected even more sharply during the Depression and those of the mid-West were further devastated by natural disasters that included floods and dust storms.

The Labor Movement which had made gains in the United States during World War I and shortly after had had no great successes in the 20's, but during the 30's unionization advanced. These advances were accompanied by violence and strikes, as industrialists did not capitulate to labor without resistance.

At the same time not everyone was poor. Many individuals and families retained their wealth. These were the group to which fashion magazines such as *Vogue* and *Bazaar* for women and *Esquire* for men turned for fashion news. They vacationed on the Riviera and in Palm Springs or at Newport, Rhode Island. They made headlines in the gossip columns and socialized with movie stars.

In Europe Fascism took root in both Germany

and Italy. Hitler came to power in Germany in 1933. In 1935, Italy invaded Ethopia and in 1936 Italy and Germany formed the Rome-Berlin Axis. In 1938 Germany annexed Austria and part of Czechoslovakia. World War II began on September 1, 1939 with the German invasion of Poland. The United States remained outside of the war but clearly sympathetic to the English and French until December 7, 1941 when Japan, which had been increasingly hostile to the United States during the 30's, attacked Pearl Harbor and as a result the United States entered the war. Wartime industrial production brought the United States out of the Depression. In the late 30's recovery had begun, but this recovery was not complete as the war began.

WORLD WAR II

Americans did not experience devastation of homes and communities during World War II, being outside of the zones of fighting. The war was brought home to them more directly by the drafting of young men and by military casualties. Scarce goods were rationed. These were largely foodstuffs and gasoline. Few clothing items were actually rationed except for shoes made of leather, which was in short supply. Guidelines called the "L-22 Regulations" were passed that restricted the quantity of cloth that could be used in clothing. Savings in fabric were made by eliminating trouser cuffs, extra pockets, vests with double-breasted suits and by regulating the width of skirt hems and the length of men's trousers and coat sleeves. The only garments exempt from restrictions were wedding dresses and burial gowns.

Many fabrics available before the war were in short supply. Nylon, invented in the late 30's had just begun to come onto the market when the war caused its diversion to military use. Wool was scarce. Silk supplies were disrupted because of the war in the Pacific.

Since most able-bodied men enlisted or were drafted into the armed services, women entered factories and took on jobs that were formerly held by men. In the factories women required specialized kinds of clothing, and coveralls, slacks, and turbans were generally adopted for jobs requiring active physical labor.

The war in Europe ended in May, 1945, but continued in the Pacific until August. With the cessation of hostilities the countries involved turned to rebuilding their devastated lands. The United States emerged from the fighting with its land unscathed and its economy intact, but millions of families had experienced the loss of one or more men in battle.

Some Influences on Fashions

THE MOVIES

Silent films had, by the 1920's, become a part of everyday life. In addition to providing a diversion, the movies brought visions of glamorous actors and actresses into every small town across America. Life depicted in films helped to re-enforce the hedonistic attitudes and helped to spread urban tastes, urban dress, and an urban way of living.

Film stars became fashion-setters. Rudolph Valentino was the idol of millions of American women, and men copied his pomaded, patent-leather look hair. In her first major film role the actress Joan Crawford personified the fast-living, shingled flapper of the 20's and women across the country aped her make-up, her hairstyle, and her clothes.

With the beginning of talking pictures in 1927 films became more popular than ever. In the early 30's reaction against some films which were thought to have too much nudity and sex, led to a strict code of propriety as to what could or could not be shown on the screen. Many films of the 30's did not at all reflect the bleak economic picture of the Depression. Women were lavishly gowned and houses magnificently furnished. Off screen the movie star was a fashion influence. Greta Garbo's broad-shouldered, natural beauty served to set one ideal of feminine beauty of the era. Other women bleached their hair blonde in imitation of Jean Harlow. Thousands of mothers curled their daughters' hair into ringlets like those of Shirley Temple, the famous child star.

During the war, movies stressed patriotic themes. Among the screen heros of the day were the "clean-cut American boy" like Van Johnson, and the rugged individualist like Spencer Tracy. Teen-aged girls wore page boy hair like June Allyson or draped a wave over one eye in the "peek-a-boo" style of Veronica Lake. Movie studio publicity offices printed "pin-up" pictures of actress Betty Grable in a backless bathing suit and high heels. Films were made in Technicolor®, and Americans flocked to the movies throughout the war.

ROYALTY AND CAFE SOCIETY

European royalty and ex-royalty as well as cafe society influenced fashion. During the 20's and 30's one man who was an important style-setter was the English Prince of Wales who later became King Edward VIII, and left his throne to marry American divorcee Wallis Simpson. During the 30's wealthy Americans and Europeans were photographed at fashionable resorts in the United States and abroad. Much of the sportswear that became popular for tennis, riding, and skiing was first worn by the rich— few others had the leisure and money to engage in these activities in the 30's. Some of the debutantes of the late 30's caught the imagination of the public, and gossip columns were full of news about coming out parties and cotillions and charity balls. Brenda Frazier, one of these "debs" helped to publicize a new style, the strapless evening gown.

SPORTS

Participants in both spectator sports and active sports gained in numbers. Attendance at sporting events in the 20's broke all previous records. Baseball, college football, boxing, tennis, and golf were widely followed. Women as leading sports figures were new phenomena. The interest in watching sports had the logical side effect of increasing participation in sports and the widespread prosperity made this participation easy for many. Sports stars appeared in films, so that they became known through these films to a national audience that would otherwise have seen them only in photographs.

As active sports for everyone became more widespread, sports clothing became more important. Special costume was required for some particular sports. The move to expanded outdoor recreation reinforced the need for practical, casual dress as a general category.

THE AUTOMOBILE

Once the automobile had become practical transportation rather than a sport, special costume for motoring disappeared. As women began to drive routinely, the need for shorter and less cumbersome skirts was evident. Although day time skirts did drop fairly low to just above the ankle in the early 30's, and again in the 50's, skirts have never reached all the way to the floor for everyday wear after 1910 and it is possible that the automobile has been, in part, responsible for this.

The automobile also may have been responsible for the abandonment of the parasol or sun shade, as women walked less and a parasol was impractical in an open car and unnecessary in a closed car. Cars encouraged the use of wrist watches which were easier to look at while driving than pocket watches, and probably made smaller hats preferable. Canes and walking sticks went out of style.

Cars allowed workers to live in suburban areas and commute to the city, and made new recre-ational opportunities possible by carrying individuals and families out of the city and into the countryside. Both of these aspects of car use contributed to the growing use of casual sports clothes.

THE FRENCH COUTURE

From 1920 until Paris was cut off from contact with England and America by the German occupation during World War II, the French couture maintained its position as the arbiter of style in clothing for women. Although the couture in general was influential, in each period certain designers stood out from the rest. Just as Poiret had occupied a special place among the designers of the late Edwardian Period and before World War I, so did the designs of Chanel typify the style of the 20's, Vionnet the early 30's, and Schiaparelli the later 30's.

Gabrielle "Coco" Chanel began to work as a designer before World War I. During the war she had a small shop at Deauville, a seaside resort, where she had great success in making casual knit jackets and pullover sweaters. She designed comfortable, practical clothes, buying sailor's jackets and men's pullovers which she combined with pleated skirts. Soon she was having these garments made specially for her own clients.

After the War she returned to Paris and set up a salon which became one of the most influential in Paris. She is credited with making the suntanned look and costume jewelry popular, but her real genius lay in designing simple, classic wool jersey styles.

In the late 20's Chanel went to Hollywood briefly to design for films. It had been the practice to dress the film stars in the most elaborate possible costumes, even when these were not appropriate for the time of day. Chanel insisted that the costumes be appropriate for the action of the drama, and was in this way responsible for a new authenticity in film clothes. She continued to be a leading designer in the 30's. She closed her shop during World War II and she did not re-open after the War. In 1954 she came out of retirement and she surprised the fashion world by re-entering the couture. She went on to have a highly successful second career as a leading couturiére.

Madeleine Vionnet began to work as an apprentice in a dressmaker's shop at the age of thirteen. She worked at the important fashion house of Callot Soeurs and later for Doucet. Her plain, unadorned but well-cut designs were not acceptable to this house where elaborate and lavish clothes were the mode, so she left in the years before World War I to set up her own shop, but was not especially successful until after the war in the early 20's, at which time the house of Vionnet became part of the haute couture.

Her distinctive talent was in the cutting of dresses. She originated the bias cut, a technique for cutting clothing to utilize the diagonal direction of the cloth which has greater stretch and drapes in such a way that the body lines and curves are accentuated. During the 30's when this cut was especially fashionable she was one of the most sought-after of the French designers. She has been compared to an architect or sculptor. Clearly she completely understood the medium of fabric and through cutting and draping created styles of such simplicity and elegance that they are still admired. She retired in 1939, and although she lived on until 1975, she never returned to the couture.

Elsa Schiaparelli, an Italian designer, worked in Paris in the 30's where she began by creating sweaters in bizarre designs. Hers was a flare for the theatrical. By the end of the 30's she was an exceedingly popular designer whose emphasis on color and unusual decorative effects was widely praised. She is credited with being the first couturiére to use zippers—she put them on pockets in 1930 and in dresses in 1934 and 1936. Her other innovations included the first evening dress with a matching jacket, and skirts to match sweaters. She worked with artists such as Salvador Dali who designed fabrics for her. She had a talent for gaining publicity for her work. In the mid-30's Schiaparelli labeled a vivid pink color that she used "shocking pink." When the war broke out she came to the United States where she continued to work during and after the war.

Chanel, Vionnet, and Schiaparelli were only three of the influential Paris-based designers of the 20's and 30's. Other important couturiers included Jeanne Lanvin, Jean Patou, Edward Molyneux, Lucien Lelong, Maggie Rouff, Robert Piguet, Madame Grés, Marcel Rochas, and Jacques Heim.

AMERICAN DESIGNERS

Although the French couture continued to work on a limited basis during the War, international press coverage could not be given to the designs created there. As a result a number of talented American designers were featured in the magazines like *Vogue* and *Harper's Bazaar* to an extent that might not have been possible had they been competing with the French Couture. Once established these designers continued to have substantial following,

although the operation of the fashion industry in America was quite different from the operation of the French Couture.

The French *haute couture* is represented by a trade association called the *Chambre Syndicale*. This group defines the *haute couture* as firms which create models that may be sold to private customers or to other segments of the fashion industry who also acquire the right to reproduce the designs. In the period between the wars the designs of the French haute couturiers were sold to private customers and to retail stores where they were copied and resold to customers of the store. Through this system the designs originated by the couturiers influenced international fashions.[2]

In the United States, by contrast, fashion designers generally worked for ready-to-wear manufacturers. Although many of the fine department stores in large cities maintained custom dressmaking or tailoring departments, and smaller towns and cities had a number of local dressmakers, most American women purchased their clothing ready-made in local stores.

The American fashion designer, therefore, usually worked for the dress manufacturer. He or she prepared a line of designs for a given season. Most dress firms produced clothing for four seasons: spring, summer, fall, and holiday. Some also had a resort line. These clothes were shown in New York to buyers for stores across the country, or in lower priced dresses samples were taken directly to the stores by salesmen. Orders were placed by buyers for items from the line. Those which did not receive an adequate number of orders were not put into production.

American designers for the most part worked in this system, and still do. Even the highest priced fashions are produced in this way. One exception to this rule was Mainbocher, an American-born designer who went to Paris in the 20's to work as a fashion editor. He opened his own couture house in Paris in 1929. When the war came, he left Paris and returned to New York where he continued to work as he had in Paris, following the practices of the French couture.

Among the American fashion designers of the period between 1920 and the end of World War II, certain figures stand out. Claire McCardell is one such figure. Sally Kirkland, writing about McCardell in *American Design*, says that "Many think Claire McCardell was the greatest fashion designer this

2. Latour, *op. cit.*, p. 58.

country has yet produced. Certainly she was the most innovative, independent, and indigenous of American designers.[3]

Claire McCardell was born in Frederick, Maryland, in 1905. She studied at the Parsons School of Design and in Paris. Her first individual collection was done for Townley Frocks in 1931 when the head designer with whom she worked was killed accidentally. She remained with this firm until 1938 when it closed. There she designed chiefly sportswear and casual clothes. She designed under her own name after 1940 and had her greatest success in the 40's and 50's. Her clothing was considered radical at first and was difficult to sell, but when women found her designs fit them well and were comfortable, they looked for more of the same.

Some of the important styles and design features that she is credited as originating or making popular include matching separates, a new idea at the time; dirndl skirts; the "monastic," a bias cut, full tent dress that when belted followed the body contours gracefully; hardware closings; spaghetti or shoestring ties; the diaper bathing suit; ballet slippers; and the poncho. She died in 1958.

Another prominent American designer, Adrian, gained his earliest recognition as a designer for films. Throughout the 20's and 30's he designed both for contemporary and period films, and the name Adrian became synonymous with high fashion and glamour. In 1941 he opened his own business. The firm of Adrian Ltd. continued in business throughout the 40's but had to be closed in 1952 when the designer had a severe heart attack. His recovery was long and slow. When he felt ready to return to active work it was to work on designs for the musical comedy *Camelot*; however, he died in 1959 before completing the work on the play.

Two other American designers who came to prominence during the wartime period should also be mentioned. These are Norman Norell and Pauline Trigere. Norell was a native of the United States, Pauline Trigere was French and came to America in 1937. Although both Norell and Trigere were more influential in the period to be discussed in the next chapter, they were active in the 40's as well. Both worked for Hattie Carnegie for a time. Then Norell joined a fine tailor, Anthony Traina, to form the firm of Traina-Norell and later, in 1960, went off on his own. Trigere formed her own business after

leaving Carnegie in 1942 and showed her first collection in that year, a group of twelve dresses.

After the end of World War II, the French couture resumed its operation, and its primacy as the center of international fashion design. American designers had, however, shown that they could create innovative and original styles, and had earned an important place in the world of fashion design. In recognition of the importance of American design in the post-war period, fashion magazines while prominently featuring Paris design continued to give extensive coverage to American designers, as well.

Costume

COSTUME FOR WOMEN—1920–1930

Item / Description

dresses—*Silhouette* was straight, without indentation at the waistline; a figure with a flat bosom and no hips was the ideal. When a dress had a belt, the belt was placed at the hipline. Dresses were almost inevitably one-piece. (See Figure 17.1.)

Skirt lengths were, at the beginning of the period, long and reached almost to the ankle, but gradually they moved upward. By 1925 they were about eight inches from the floor, by 1926–27, fourteen to sixteen inches and some even as short as eighteen inches from the ground. Once the skirts reached this elevation, they began to lengthen again. The first move toward longer lengths was observable in a tendency to cut skirt hems unevenly, with panels, flares, scalloped, or pointed segments of the skirt. By the end of the decade, skirt lengths had dropped.

daytime dresses—one-piece styles predominated; some coat dresses with cross-over, left to right, closings. (See Figure 17.2.)

necklines—usually ended at the base of the throat or lower, with round, V-shaped, bateau, or cowl styles. Round, high, and V-necklines often were finished with collars or bias ruffles.
sleeves—when dresses had sleeves, they were often long. Many dresses were sleeveless.
bodices—generally were plain and cut straight to the hip. Some had embroidered decorations or pleating.
skirts—tended to be more complex in cut than bodices, with use of bias cutting to produce

3. Sally Kirkland in *American Fashion*. New York: Quadrangle/New York Times Book Co., 1975, p. 211.

17.1 Styles of 1922 reflect the introduction of a new silhouette: narrow with a dropped waistline. In the post-war period hemlines had lengthened. (*French fashion magazine,* L'Art de la Mode, *1922.*)

interesting effects; pleats and gathers placed off center; scalloped hems; godet insets; and paneled effects to achieve "handkerchief" skirt styles.

blouses—usually elongated, low-hipped, and straight overblouse. Middy blouses were a popular style, sweaters followed similar lines. (See Figure 17.3.)

tailored suits—had matching jackets and skirts, with jackets ending at the hip or below. When belted, the belt was placed well below normal placement. Some opened at center front, closed on the left. Long lapels that rolled to a low closing were fashionable. (*Ensembles*—were matching dresses and coats or skirts, overblouses, and coats.)

evening dresses—were made in the same lengths as daytime dresses, and grew shorter as daytime dresses grew shorter. Generally sleeveless, with deep V or U shaped necklines, some bodices were

17.2 Daytime dress, 1924–1928. This two-piece dress of green silk crepe was made from a skirt and separate overblouse. The hat is a cloche. (*Photograph courtesy of the Smithsonian Institution.*)

supported over the shoulder by small straps.

skirts—often more complex in cut than for daytime dresses, and used such effects as floating panels, draped areas, layered skirts. As the decade progressed, the tendency to cut skirts un-

17.3 Styles of 1927, including jodphurs, which were worn by both men and women for riding, hats in the cloche style, and a suit of the type made famous by Chanel. (*French fashion magazine, L'Art de la Mode, 1927.*)

evenly also appeared in evening styles. Decorations included beading, which sometimes covered an entire dress. Fashionable fabrics included chiffon, soft satins and velvets, and for the robe de style garments, silk taffeta. Geometric Art Deco designs were frequently used as fabric patterns.

NOTE: In 1919 Jeanne Lanvin introduced a bouffant skirt, reminiscent of the crinoline period. An evening dress of this type with a dropped waistline and full skirt was a popular alternative to the tubular silhouette. It was called the *robe de style*. (See Figure 17.4.)

outdoor garments—the most characteristic coats closed over the left hip, often with one, large decorative button or several small ones. Some coats, known as "clutch" coats, had to be held shut as they had no fastening.

Young women (and young men) wore raccoon coats for motoring or to football games. Fur and fur-trimmed capes and wraps were popular among the more well-to-do. Sweaters, long and belted low, were popular for sportswear.

underwear—as depicted in mail order catalogs came in wide variety of styles. Items included brassieres, which replaced the "bust bodice" of earlier periods. Drawers or "knickers" became "panties" in the 20's. These were short, buttoned or elasticized at the waistline and often very decorative. Underclothing was generally intended to suppress the curves of women who did not naturally possess the fashionably flat figure.

An evolution of the combination was a garment alternately known as "camiknickers," "step-ins," or "teddies," a combination of the camisole and panties. A straight cut chemise or petticoat was renamed the "slip" and was a parallel to the garment called by that name today. Corsets were worn by larger women. These were boned or made with elastic panels, or both. Garters suspended from the corset held up the stockings; women who did not wear corsets wore garter belts to hold up their stockings.

sleepwear—consisted of either nightgowns or pajamas, both of which had long, straight lines.

footwear— *stockings*—The short skirts caused women to focus greater attention on hosiery. In the early years of the decade, dark stockings or white stockings continued in use, but as skirts grew shorter, tan or flesh colored stockings replaced them. More luxurious stockings were silk, but rayon was coming into widespread use for less expensive stockings.

NOTE: Cartoons of George Held Jr. depict the "flapper" of the period in stockings rolled below the knee, skirts above the knee and rouge on the knees.

shoes—Heels were two to two and a half inches in height, toes pointed or rounded. Commonly seen styles included pumps, with a strap across the instep or T-shaped straps which crossed the instep and down the center of the foot; oxfords, especially for sports; and dressy evening slippers of fabric or gold or silver leather. Russian-style wide-topped boots were worn. (One photo of the period shows how neatly a flask of bootleg whiskey fit into the top of this boot.) Young women affected the style of wearing their overshoes for bad weather or galoshes open and flapping.

NOTE: It is to this practice that some have attributed the origin of the term *flappers* although

17.4 Three evening dresses of the 1920's. The two in the left-hand picture follow the tubular silhouette and are decorated with beading. The dress on the right was designed by Jeanne Lanvin and has the wide skirt she created in the *robe de style.* (*Photograph (left) courtesy of the Smithsonian Institution. Photograph (right) courtesy of the Wadsworth Atheneum, Hartford.*)

a variety of derivations are claimed for the word. Another suggested origin is the large hair bows worn by young girls in the post-world war I period which flapped on the backs of their heads. Most dictionaries of word origins indicate the word derives from the flapping of the wings of young birds. The parallel is then made with the young, human "fledgling" of 15 or 16 who is "trying her wings." The term had been applied to young girls before the twenties, and the use of the word prob-

ably received reinforcement from the flapping of the galoshes of the young girls of the 20's. In the 20's it was applied quite specifically to fashionable and "modern" young women in their late teens and twenties.

Hair and head dress—*hair*—women's hair styles of the 1920's were one of the more revolutionary developments in fashion. Except for the Empire Period, in which short hair was fashionable, no other earlier costume periods can be cited in which women cut their hair short. Viewed at first as a radical style, by 1923 it had become accepted fashion and college girls across the country were singing (to the tune of Jingle Bells).

"Shingle bob, shingle bob, cut it all away . . ." To have ones hair *bobbed* was to have it cut. The *shingle* was an exceptionally short cut in which the back hair was cut and tapered like that of a man. Although the most fashionable cut was short with the hair tapering off to the nape of the neck, many variations were seen. Some women cut their hair short, with bangs at the front and the hair turned under at the ends on the sides and in the back. Others followed the extreme *Eton crop*, a style in which hair was exceptionally closely-cropped and dressed like that of the men.

NOTE: Frederick Lewis Allen pointed out the widespread nature of the style for short hair in the United States. "In the latter years of the 20's bobbed hair became almost universal among girls in their 20's, very common among women in their 30's and 40's, and by no means rare among women of sixty."[4]

Some women wore their bobbed hair straight, others with a *marcel wave*, a style made up of a series of deep waves all over the head. The old fashioned, open hairpin was replaced by the bobby pin, with its tight spring clip. By the end of the decade, however, women started to let their hair grow again and small curls began to appear at the back of the head. Of course some women never did cut their hair, but even those with longer hair usually wore it dressed straight or waved close to the face with a tight bun at the back of the neck. *hats*—with short hair, hats could be fitted close to the head. Just as the bob was the prevailing hair style, a small, close fitting hat called the *cloche* became the predominant hat form. (See Figure 17.2.) In general cloches had small or larger brims that turned down around the face. Some larger, summer hats with wide, downturned brims almost hid the face entirely. Berets were popular for sports. Headbands, popularly known as *headache bands*, some jeweled and others with tall feathers attached were popular for evening, as were turbans.

4. F. L. Allen. *Only Yesterday*. Perennial Press, New York: Harper and Row, 1964. p.87.

1930–1947

Item / Description

dresses—The beginnings of a change in silhouette came in the late 1920's when hemlines began to lengthen and belts moved gradually closer to the natural waistline. The silhouette of the 1930's emphasized the natural form of the woman's body. Bosom, waistline, and hips were clearly defined by the shape of clothing. (See Figure 17.5.)

One-piece dresses, skirts and blouses, and tailored suits remained the staples of women's wardrobes for daytime wear. Hemlines fell—they were about 12 inches from the ground in the first several years of the decade and by 1932 went as low as ten inches. Indeed, some fashion magazine pictures of high fashion garments show a hemline that comes almost to the ankle. By mid-decade, the skirt length started upward again—13 or 14 inches off the ground and by the end of the period skirt lengths had reached 16 or 17 inches from the floor.

The wartime period, with its restrictions, essentially "froze" styles of the late 30's and 1940–41. By the war period, skirts had become shorter, ending just below the knee, and had grown fuller. Shoulders had broadened, and shoulder pads were inserted into all garments to provide greater width. Bias cut was rarely used. (See Figure 17.6.)

daytime dresses—*necklines*—generally high. In the first half of the decade, cowl necklines, cape collars, and soft finishes such as bows and jabots predominated; later V-necklines and collared dresses were more important. Yoke constructions were common.

sleeves—tended to be long and full, gathered to a wristband; or short, many with a cape construction. Other sleeve styles included full, raglan sleeves; magyar or "bat wing" sleeves; and, at the end of the decade, short, puffed sleeves.

skirts—usually narrow but flaring until the end of the period when greater fullness appeared. Most were cut in several gores; some had bias cut pieces set onto a yoke that covered the hips; others were made with box pleats or shirred sections, and a few tunic constructions of layers were seen.

suits—remained a basic item of women's wardrobes. Made in firmer fabrics, their line was not so supple as that of most dresses. (See Figure 17.7.) Some styles were clearly modeled after

17.5 (*Left*) Summer dresses of 1934. Most are made with cape sleeves and have bias shaping in the skirts. (*Stella, 1934.*)

17.6 (*Bottom left and below*) Dresses and suits from the *Vogue Pattern Magazine* during the period of World War II both utilized large, square shoulder pads and had slim skirts. (*Reproduced courtesy of the Butterick Patterns Archives/ Library.*)

17.7 (*Top left*) Sketch by Gaston of a Vionnet suit from 1937. Shoulder pads were growing appreciably wider at this time. (*Costume Institute Library, Metropolitan Museum of Art.*)

17.8 (*Bottom left*) Backless evening gowns with halter tops and a fur-trimmed evening jacket of 1933. (Tres Parisien, *1933.*)

17.9 (*Above*) Dinner dress, the jacket of which is made with a flared peplum, designed by Mark Mooring around 1940. The turban-like hat was a popular accessory at the time. (*Courtesy of the Metropolitan Museum of Art.*)

men's suits. Except for some square, boxy jackets of the early 30's, suits curved in to fit closely at the waist. Styles were both single and double breasted, some were belted. Jacket lengths were shorter in the early 30's, longer toward the end; wide lapels in the early years, narrower, longer lapels later. Wartime suit styles included bolero suits with short curving jackets that ended above the waist and Eisenhower jackets, based on military jackets that were slightly bloused above the waist and gathered to a fitted belt at the waist.

blouses and sweaters—worn with separate skirts. Blouses showed no major differences from dress bodices. Pull-over wool sweaters were made in decorative patterns or plain colors, with short or long sleeves. Sometimes belts were worn over sweaters. Matching short-sleeved sweaters and long-sleeved cardigans were popular in the early 40's. In the mid-40's adolescents wore large, loose pullovers called "sloppy joes."

NOTE: Sweaters were especially popular during the war. Movie stars who were photographed in tightly fitting sweaters for "pin-up" pictures were called "sweater girls."

separate skirts—In the 30's generally cut with little fullness. Construction details included gores, pleats that released fullness low and below the hip, top-stitching, and panel insets. In the 40's, and during the war, skirts were fuller and shorter. About 1945, *dirndl skirts* (full, gathered skirts) became fashionable.

evening dresses—evening and daytime dress lengths were markedly different. Evening gowns always reached to the floor. Bias cut styles were utilized until the late 30's. Such dresses followed the body to the hips, where they flared out. Other common characteristics of evening dresses included bare-backed gowns cut low to the waist at the back, halter-type bodices, sleeveless and full, cape-like or puffed sleeved styles. (See Figure 17.8.) Toward the end of the 30's, less ornamentation, less detail in construction and more severe lines were more common. Blouses and skirts, and evening suits, with long skirts and matching jackets of plain, uncluttered lines under which soft, frilly and often backless or sleeveless blouses or bodices were worn. (See Figure 17.9.)

Strapless gowns appeared in Hollywood films of the late 30's. Brenda Frazier, a debutante of the period also helped to make these styles popular.

outdoor garments—In the early 30's many coats were cut with decorative detailing around the neck and shoulder lines. Large collars were often made of fur. (See Figure 17.10.) Some coats had leg-o-mutton sleeves. Closings tended to be at the left, often with only one button. Overall the line was slender until the latter part of the decade when more boxy, fuller coats, some in three-quarter length, some ending at the hip, and some in full length were popular. Forties styles included features such as large collars and revers, heavily padded shoulders, raglan and dolman sleeve constructions, and plain, straight box coats. Fur coats were popular and the increased affluence of Americans who worked in highly-paid, wartime industry brought these coats within the means of many more women. Military influence was evident in the war years. The military trench coat was often seen.

undergarments—Emphasized the curves of the figure. Brassieres of the 30's were cut to lift and emphasize the breasts. Corsets extended above the waist slightly. Rigidly boned corsets were still worn by large women, but smaller women wore corsets in which the shaping was achieved by elasticized fabric panels. Terminology changed; panties became "pantie briefs" and then "briefs" as they grew shorter in order to fit under active sportswear. Older women continued to wear fuller, looser "drawers" or "bloomers." Slips fitted the torso and were fuller in the cut of the skirt. Lower-priced underwear was made of cotton, rayon, or acetate; more expensive ones of silk.

sleepwear—continued to offer a choice between nightgowns and pajamas.

hair and head dress—*hair*—in the early years of the 30's, hair was relatively short, usually waved softly, and with short, turned-up curls around the nape of the neck. As the decade progressed, fashionable hair styles grew longer; toward the end of the decade the page-boy bob (straight hair turned under at the ends) and hair dressed on top of the head in curls or braids (the "upsweep") were more fashionable. During the war some women dressed the hair in a high pompadour at the front and sides of the face while arranging the hair in a long, U-shaped roll at the back; others wore a short, curly hairstyle called a "feather cut."
hats—In the early 30's these were small in scale, of many different shapes and usually tipped

at an angle, either to one side, front, or back. Additional styles included berets and sailor hats, and wider-brimmed styles in the latter 30's. When up-swept hair styles were worn, higher hats and small hats with face veils were fashionable.

NOTE: Milliners found inspiration in many sources, including the Middle Ages and some hats were shown with wimple-like scarves draped under the chin and attached to the hat at or above the ear.

Hats for evening became fashionable, especially turbans and decorative veils, artificial flowers, and ribbons. Snoods returned to fashion for the first time since the Civil War era, possibly as a result of the popularity of motion pictures such as *Gone with the Wind* and *Little Women.*

In the 40's hats tended to be small; styles included pillboxes and small bonnets. Many women went hatless, but to be considered well-dressed a lady *had* to wear a hat.

footwear—stockings—made in flesh tones of silk or rayon and seamed up the back. Cotton and wool stockings were for sportwear. Ankle socks were worn by young girls and for sports. In the 40's teen-aged girls wore these socks so constantly that adolescent girls came to be known as "bobby-soxers." Shortages of fabrics for stockings during the war led women to paint their legs with "leg makeup" to simulate the color of stockings. Some even went so far as to paint a dark line down the back of the leg in imitation of the seams.

NOTE: During the war, leather shoes were rationed. Each adult was entitled to two new pairs per year. Shoes made of cloth were exempt from restriction, and so cloth shoes with synthetic soles were readily available.

OTHER ELEMENTS OF COSTUME FOR WOMEN-1920–1947

sportswear—Throughout the period from 1920 to 1947 women were becoming more active participants in sports. As a result women adopted both specific costumes for individual sports such as tennis, swimming, and skiing and general, informal dress for spectator sports and outdoor activities. (See Figures 17.11 and 17.13.) By 1928 such clothing was referred to as *spectator sports styles,*

17.10 Fur-trimmed coat designed by Schiaparelli in 1937. (*Costume Institute Library, Metropolitan Museum of Art.*)

by fashion magazines. By the 30's, the clothing industry identified this new category of clothing as *sportswear.*

Except for basically unsuccessful attempts by dress reformers of the 1860's to introduce bloomers and the knickers worn by women for cycling, trousers for daytime wear had remained essentially a man's garment until the 1920's. Harem skirts, it is true, were introduced by Poiret in the preceding period, but these exotic bifurcated garments were hardly like men's trousers nor were they widely worn. In the late 20's, women began to appear in garments made like men's trousers for casual wear. The general term *slacks* was used to designate these garments. By the 30's the style was well-established, but slacks remained a sportswear item. During the war many women found slacks a useful garment for working in factories. Adolescent girls began to wear men's

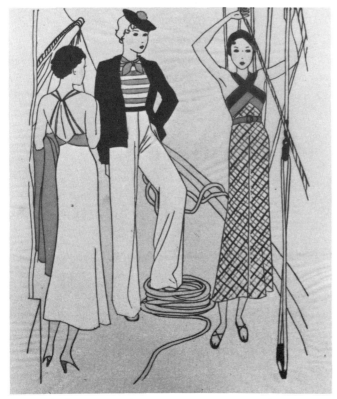

17.11 Slacks, acceptable by 1934 as sportswear for women, and halter-top sundresses. (Tres Parisian, *1934.*)

work jeans in blue denim for casual dress.

In the 20's and on into the early 30's, beach pajamas were worn. These were long, full, trousers with matching tops, either separate or seamed together, that were worn for leisure activities. Some even had large, matching hats.

active sportswear—*tennis*—white clothing was traditional. Tennis dresses grew shorter as did dress skirts in the 20's, and remained shorter even when daytime dresses lengthened again. The 30's bodices of tennis dresses were sleeveless and collarless; skirts were either short or divided culotte-style and shorts were also commonly worn for tennis.

golf—no special costume was required but tweed skirts with pullover sweaters worn over a blouse seemed to be favored.

swimming—costume altered radically. In the early 20's a fairly voluminous two-piece tunic and knickers was a carry-over from the teens, but gradually the knickers grew shorter, armholes grew deeper, necklines lower, and one-piece tank suits became popular for women. (See Figure 17.12.) Knee-length stockings were worn only in the first years of the 20's. By the

17.12 Bathing suit, 1925–27. Black wool knit bathing suit was made in one piece, the trunks being attached at the waist. This suit was made by the Gantner and Mattern Company and worn in California. (*Photograph courtesy of the Smithsonian Institution.*)

end of the 20's, the modern concept of costumes in which women could really "swim" rather than "bathe" had been established. (The first women to wear the more revealing tank suits were often arrested for "indecent exposure.") In the 30's bathing suits with halter tops or low-cut backs became popular, the lines similar to those seen in some evening gowns. Knitted wool, rayon, acetate, and cotton were utilized. In the early 30's *Lastex*, a fabric made from yarns with a rubber core covered by another fiber was used to make bathing suits that had stretch and were more form-fitting and wrinkle free than other fabrics.

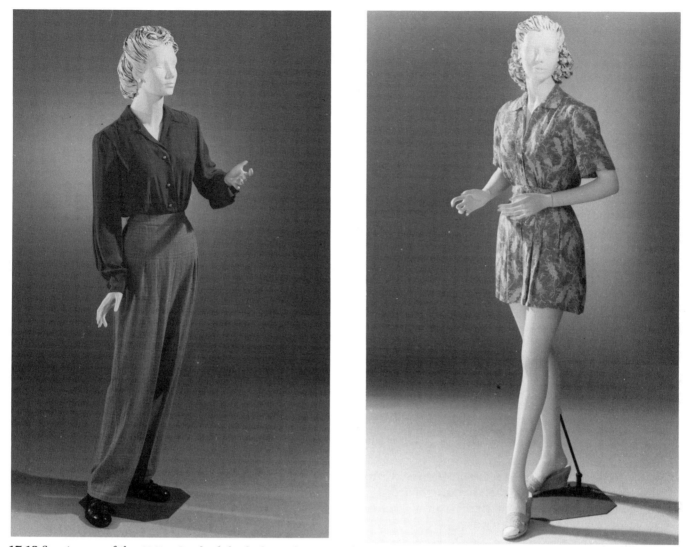

17.13 Sportswear of the 1940s. On the left, slacks and a crepe blouse, on the right, a one-piece playsuit. (*Photographs courtesy of the Smithsonian Institution.*)

Also in the 30's, two-piece bathing suits with either a brassiere-like or halter top and shorts made their first appearance. Women could choose from a variety of bathing suit styles including one-piece or two-piece styles with either shorts or skirt-like constructions.

skiing—clothes consisted of full trousers and a sweater or, especially in the 30's and after, matching jackets. Close-fitting ski clothing was not introduced until after World War II.

riding—called for jodphurs worn with high riding boots, shirts, and tweed jackets.

accessories—included umbrellas (parasols were hardly used) which were practical rather than fashionable, with long or short handles and in conservative colors; fans of ostrich feathers for evening during the 20's but not after; and a wide variety of handbags, which ranged in size from serviceable large leather bags to dainty, beaded evening bags barely big enough to hold a handkerchief and a lipstick. From a vast variety a few especially fashionable items stand out.

In the 20's: evening bags of brocade, embroidered silk, glass or metal beads, or wire mesh in gold and silver. Daytime leather bags often flat, envelope type with a small strap for holding.

In the 30's: bags on frames with straps and pouch-shaped.

In the 40's: shoulder strap bags.

gloves—worn for daytime, out-of-doors throughout the period. In the 30's long evening gloves were worn. During the war, cotton gloves replaced leather due to shortages. Gloves often matched either dresses or hats and/or handbags in color or fabric.

scarves—made of fabrics that contrasted with dresses were an important accessory in the mid-40's. Throughout the period fur scarves, stoles, and skins were worn around the neck; often the head and paws of the animal were retained for decoration.

jewelry—in the 20's, plentiful, especially long, dangling earrings which looked well against short haircuts and long necks. Many brooches, bracelets, and shorter necklaces were made with Art Deco designs, and long strands of pearls or beads were popular accessories.

In the 30's, jewelry was more subdued, and included short pearl necklaces and jeweled clips in pairs placed at the neckline or on collars. Although earrings were generally worn in the evening, many fashion magazines showed women modeling daytime dresses without earrings.

In the 40's, upswept hair styles contributed to greater interest in earrings, many of which were large in scale. Rhinestones were popular for evening; other jewelry included brooches for collars and lapels, short necklaces, and bracelets.

cosmetics and grooming—During the 1920's cosmetics (popularly called "make-up") became an accepted part of women's fashion. Prior to this time most women who used cosmetics did so in secret. In the 20's cosmetics became essential to achieving a fashionable look.

NOTE: This notation from *Only Yesterday* may serve to dramatize the magnitude of the change that took place. Back in 1917, according to Frances Fisher Dubuc, only two persons in the beauty culture business had paid an income tax; by 1927 there were 18,000 firms and individuals in this field listed as income tax payers.[5]

Fashionable ladies plucked their eyebrows into a narrow line, which was then emphasized with eyebrow pencil. Rouge and lipstick in bright shades; some flappers even went so far as to rouge their knees. (Lipstick in a round metal tube had been invented in 1915.) Powder completed an almost mask-like appearance that the most fashionable women attempted to achieve.

COSTUMES FOR MEN—1920–1947

No dramatic changes in men's costume took place from the 1920's through the end of World War II. For the well-to-do the English tailor retained his reputation as the best in the world. The English tailor was to men's clothing what the French couturier was to women's. Fashion influences from England were also given a boost by the popularity of the youthful Prince of Wales. The king, who after his abdication became the Duke of Windsor, was always very much interested in clothing, and his adoption of a style was sure to give it importance throughout the men's wear industry. Sack suits remained the basis of suits for almost every occasion. Vests, trousers, and jackets matched in color and fabric. Only wealthy and prominent individuals still wore morning coats and then only for very formal occasions. White suits for summer were worn by those who could afford variety in their wardrobes. F. Scott Fitzgerald's character Jay Gatsby was portrayed as wearing a white suit at his fabulous summer parties on Long Island, and the white linen or flannel suit became symbolic of an upper class life style.

business suits—1920's—jackets—had fairly natural shoulder lines, fairly wide lapels and pronounced waists. Single and double-breasted styles were worn and sleeves were short enough to show at least half an inch of cuff. (See Figure 17.14.)
  trousers—Widened through the legs during the 20's.

NOTE: The impetus for wider trouser legs is thought to have come from a fad that developed at Oxford College in England. Students at Oxford were forbidden by dress regulations from wearing knickers to classes. In order to be able to change quickly from the acceptable long trousers to knickers, the students took to wearing trousers with excessively wide legs that could be slipped on over the knickers. After classes, off came the *Oxford Bags.*[6] The style spread to other young people and Oxford bags with legs as wide as 32 inches in diameter were soon seen in America, too. Although most men never wore Oxford bags, trousers grew generally wider and remained fuller in cut.

---

5. F. L. Allen. *Only Yesterday.* New York: Perennial Library, Harper and Row, Publishers, 1964, p. 88.

6. O. C. Schoeffler and W. Gale. *Esquire's Encyclopedia of 20th Century Men's Fashion.* New York: McGraw-Hill Book Company, 1973. p. 12

Some Styles That Are Being Featured in New York Shops

The various styles presented here have been shown in past issues of this publication as worn by smartly dressed men at important sources of fashion. They have been predicted for some time as the coming developments in masculine attire, and are shown here as evidence of the fact that they have arrived on the retail market and are reported to be selling well.

Above—The two button, small notch lapel jacket of authentic style is promoted by Browning, King & Co.'s shop in East Forty-fifth street.

Above — Three models of custom-made shoes ready for wearing at Saks-Fifth Avenue. The lower sketch is of a straight tip brown, buckskin sports shoe.

At left. The tan polo coat is recommended by Tripler and other shops.

Above—Tripler leads the way in fashions by featuring the double-breasted dinner jacket in midnight blue with square end bow tie.

Left—The three-button, peaked lapel jacket, similar in style to coats turned out by leading London tailors, is advocated by Browning King & Co. in black and white sharkskin. The tab collar to match shirt in fine stripes and small patterned ties are to the fore at Saks Fifth Avenue.

17.14 Men's wear fashions from 1920's (*Illustration reproduced courtesy of* Men's Wear Review.)

shirts—White and colors, and had narrow collar styles, which included button-down collars (a new form), collars designed to be pinned together under the tie with a tie pin, those with a tab fastening points of the collar together under the tie, and the Barrymore collar (named after actor John Barrymore) with long points. *neckties*—styles continued to emphasize four-in-hands, bow ties, and ascots.

business suits—1930's—*jackets*—wider at the shoulders, more fitted at the hips. (See Figures 17.15 and 17.16.) In the latter part of the decade a style known as the "English drape suit" was introduced and became the predominant suit cut. Cut for greater comfort, it had more fabric in shoulders and chest and therefore fell softly with a slight drape or wrinkle through the chest and shoulders. After the Prince of Wales wore a plaid suit while on a visit to the United States, plaid suits became more popular, along with pin-stripes, and lighter summer suits. Summer fabrics included lightweight worsted wools, gabardine, and linen. Rayon, also called "artificial silk," was the first man-made fiber to gain widespread use. It was made into some men's suits, as well as other garments.

NOTE: Trousers first used zippers instead of buttons for fly front closing about 1930. Although the first zipper had been patented as early as 1893, two decades were required to perfect the machinery required to manufacture slide fasteners. In the 20's B. F. Goodrich registered the trade name *zipper*. These closings were first applied to men's rubber galoshes.

shirts—made in white, considered more formal, in colors and with stripes or checks. Collar styles included tab and button-down styles; California collars, seen on film actors such as Clark Gable, which had shorter, wider points than the Barrymore collar of the 20's; and Windsor or spread collars designed to be worn with the larger Windsor tie knot. Some collars also had short, rounded shapes.

business suits—1940's—Wartime restrictions modified the English drape cut somewhat. To conserve wool fabric, which was in short supply, restrictions were imposed on the quantity of fabric that could be used in suits. The American War Production Board decreed maximum lengths for jackets and trouser inseams in each size, ruled out the making of suits with two pairs of trousers, eliminated waistcoats with double-breasted suits,

17.15 Advertisement from the 1930's showing a variety of men's suit styles from Hart, Schaffner, and Marx men's wear company. (*Photograph courtesy of Hart, Schaffner, and Marx.*)

cuffs, pleats in trousers, and over-lapping waistbands.

NOTE: The *zoot suit* was thereby eliminated. This unusual fashion, one of the few that had originated at the lower end of the socio-economic ladder, had been adopted by teen-age boys in the early 40's. It became a mark of status among some of the young, and was associated with the popularity of "jitterbugging," an especially athletic type of dancing. The suit was an extreme form of the sack suit of this period, with excessively wide shoulders, long, wide lapels, and a longer jacket. The trousers were markedly pegged.

informal daytime clothing—1920–47—During this period a whole new category of clothing for men

This season . . . we're ready

to treat you *Rough*

We're referring, of course, to the new "rough fabrics"! For this spring—according to all indications, smartly dressed young men are going to show a distinct preference for softer, rougher materials—such as shetlands, cheviots, etc. And we have prepared for such a demand—with the result that you'll find here a complete selection of rich, rugged suitings that offer some of the best-looking patterns and colorings you've ever seen. Styled in either the two or three-button coat, these rougher materials tailor up into suits that show a definite trend away from the smoother-finished type of clothing that most men have been accustomed to in the past few years.

17.16 Man's double-breasted suit from the 1930's worn with a straw "boater" hat. (*Photograph courtesy of the Smithsonian Institution.*)

developed. It is generally classified as "sports-wear," but would perhaps be more accurately termed "leisure" or "casual" clothing, as it was worn not only for active sports but also for occasions requiring informal clothing to be worn during a man's leisure time.

sports jackets—were jackets without matching trousers, cut along the lines of business suit jackets and worn with contrasting fabric trousers. (See Figure 17.17.) These were made in more colors and fabrics than regular suit jackets and worn with vests in matching or contrasting colors, pullover sweaters, or shirts. Some were cut with half belts or belted all the way around. Norfolk jackets with a pleat in the back were adopted by golfers. The Prince of Wales made

tweed jackets popular.

knickers and shorts—During the 20's sports jackets were often combined with knickers or plus fours (a fuller version of knickers) and argyle socks. In the 30's trousers or shorts replaced knickers to some extent. Walking shorts, based on military costume of British Colonial soldiers had been adopted by the well-to-do for vacation wear. They were worn with knee-length stockings and often had matching shirts. Shirts for leisure as opposed to those for wearing with suits were a new development in men's wear. Some styles worn were:

· *1920's and 30's*—polo shirts—knitted shirts with attached collars and short, buttoned, neck vents, and, most often, short sleeves. This style

17.17 Men's styles of the 1930's. Counter clockwise from top right: bathing suit, sports shirt and trousers, double-breasted sports jacket worn with straw boater, white dinner jacket, knit polo shirt. (*Illustrations by L. Fellows from* Esquire, *January, 1936. Reproduced by courtesy of the magazine. Copyright © 1935 by Esquire Inc.*)

originated as costume for polo-players, but was adopted generally for informal wear in the 20's and after. (See Figure 17.17.)
· *1930's and after*—"dishrag" shirts of net fabric, first worn on the Riviera; basque shirts, striped, wide crew-necked shirts; and dark blue linen sport shirts patterned after one worn by the Prince of Wales.
· *African bush jackets*—short-sleeved tan cotton jackets with four large flapped pockets made to imitate styles worn by hunters and explorers in Africa.
· *Late 1930's*—Cowboy shirts in bright colors and fabrics with button-down pockets on the chest and pointed collars, and Western shirts in solid or plaid wool or gabardine with crescent shaped pockets in front.
· *About 1938*—Hawaiian printed shirts in vivid colors.

NOTE: In spite of the Depression, there were still wealthy individuals who wintered on the Riviera or in Palm Beach and summered in Newport or other fashionable resorts. These persons set styles that filtered down in less expensive versions to the general public.

· Sportswear trousers were made in a variety of colors and patterns with many plaid, checked, and striped designs.
· Sweaters, popular for golfing and other sports. Multi-colored sweater patterns were worn in imitation of a sweater worn by the Prince of Wales in the 20's; turtlenecks made an appearance in the 30's.

evening dress—tail coats were reserved for the most formal occasions.
  jackets—for evening generally were of the tuxedo type, made in black or "midnight" blue. (See Figure 17.14.) Tuxedos had either rolled collars faced in silk or notched collars. Lines of jackets followed the lines of daytime business suits. In the 20's, single-breasted styles were preferred; in the 30's double-breasted. From the late 20's on, some men substituted a cumberbund, a wide pleated fabric waistband, for the waistcoat. Waistcoats after the 30's often had a sort of halter-type construction and no back. In the 30's and after, white dinner jackets, especially for summer, were worn. (See Figure 17.17.) Wartime restrictions required all dinner jackets be single-breasted.
  trousers—for evening followed lines of daytime trousers but had no cuffs and added a line of braid following the outer seam line.

bow ties—dark ties with dinner jackets, white ties with tails.

NOTE: Except for more affluent men, most no longer owned evening clothes, but rented them for special events.

sleepwear—Pajamas had largely replaced night shirts. The cut varied: in the 20's the jacket was long, below the hip, often belted. Russian influence was evident in the late 20's and 30's in styles that had standing collars, and closed far to the left. Some buttoned down the front, others slipped over the head. Robes ranged from kimono-style silk to ornately patterned flannels that buttoned down the front and tied shut with a corded belt.

underwear—for the more conservative men, one-piece, knitted union suits were available with short or long sleeves or legs. Other underwear had no sleeves and ended at the knee or above. Boxer shorts were introduced in the 30's, and the style was inspired by the shorts worn by professional boxers. Other new styles of the 30's included "athletic shirts" of knitted cotton that were adapted from the top of tank swimsuits; and fitted, knit shorts. One of the trademark names for these knitted shorts, "Jockey shorts," has since become an almost generic designation for this style of men's underwear. During World War II servicemen wore knit undershirts with short sleeves, called "T-shirts." After the war civilian men continued to wear these undershirts and they eventually found their way into general sportswear, as well.

NOTE: In the 30's film "It Happened One Night" actor Clark Gable appeared bare-chested and without an undershirt. *Esquire's Encyclopedia of Men's Fashion* credits this film with beginning a fashion for going without undershirts that severely affected the underwear industry. Other motion picture influences cited were the "Wallace Beery" shirt, a ribbed-knit undershirt with a buttoned vent at the front of the neck, worn by the character actor of that name.[7]

Clothing for Active Sports—1920–1947—*tennis*—Knitted shirts worn with white flannel trousers were popular until the 30's when some men substituted white shorts for the trousers.

NOTE: White was mandatory as a color on tennis courts. Many clubs forbade play to those wearing colors.

7. Schoeffler and Gale, *op. cit.*, pp. 374–375.

17.18 Golfing outfit; jacket from 1930, knickers from 1928. (*Photograph courtesy of the Smithsonian Institution.*)

17.19 Ski outfit, the pants from 1940 and the jacket from 1937. The skis, goggles, gloves, boots, and ski poles all date from the same period. (*Photograph courtesy of the Smithsonian Institution.*)

golf—clothes consisted mainly of shirts, sweaters, or jackets combined with knickers in the 20's and slacks or shorts in the 30's and after. (See Figure 17.18.)

swimming—1920's: costumes included these alternatives: one-piece suits held on over the shoulders with shoulder straps, sleeveless knit pullover shirts with or without sleeves and worn with short trunks, the pullover worn either out, over the trunks or tucked into trunks belted at the waist. Upper sections of bathing suits often had deep armholes and straps across the armhole to maintain a snug fit.

1930's: tops decreased in size until eventually men stopped wearing any covering for the upper part of the body.

1940's: only bathing trunks were worn.

skiing—was taken up as a sport only after World War I. In the 20's skiers wore wool sweaters and plus fours; in the 30's wind-resistant jackets were adopted and worn with long trousers cut full and gathered into an elasticized cuff at the ankle. (See Figure 17.19.)

outdoor garments—Generally followed the predominant jacket silhouette. Coat styles included chesterfields, and raglan-sleeved coats, with either buttoned front closings or fly-front closing in which a fabric placket obscured the buttons.

1920's: Racoon coats were popular among the young college crowd and tweed and herringbone patterned fabrics were used for casual coats. Polo coats made of tan camels' hair were worn by a British polo team playing exhibition matches in the United States and the style swept the United States and continued on into the 30's. (See Figure 17.14.) The classic cut of this coat was double-breasted, with a six-buttoned closing, and a half belt at the back. Other camels' hair coats included single-breasted box coats, belted raglan sleeved coats and wrap around coats without buttons and tied with belts. Trench coats, slickers, and waterproof coats modeled after fishermen's foul-weather gear were worn as rain coats.

1930's: styles included continuation of many 20's types and added the English guards' coat, a dark blue coat with wide lapels and an inverted pleat in the back and a half belt. Zip-in linings to make cold weather coats convertible to use in warmer temperatures were introduced. Short jackets with knitted waistbands and cuffs, parka jackets with hoods (copied from Eskimo cold weather wear), lumber jackets or mackinaws (made of heavily-fulled wool), and leather jackets for the affluent were some of informal coat styles.

1940's: styles were influenced markedly by military garments, and included pea jackets, the double-breasted dark box jackets of American sailors, and Eisenhower or "battle jackets" which were short, bloused jackets ending in a belt at the waist.

hair and head dress—Throughout the period hair was short. In the 20's many men controlled their hair with glistening hair dressings and pomades in imitation of the film star Rudolph Valentino whose hair looked as if it were plastered to his head. Faces were generally clean-shaven, some men wore pencil-thin moustaches. In the 30's, hair was worn waved and parted on the side. Moustaches were more likely to be worn by older than by younger men; in the 40's moustaches went out of fashion.

NOTE: Some writers attribute the decrease in popularity of moustaches in the 40's to the fact that Adolf Hitler wore a moustache.

Hat styles altered very little. Major forms continued to be fedoras (becoming more popular), derbies (becoming less popular), homburgs, straw boaters and panama hats, and sports caps. During the 30's, the *pork pie-* a low-crowned, soft felt hat that could be rolled up was used for sportswear.

footwear—*Stockings* became more colorful as a result of the availability of machinery for making fancy-patterned hosiery. In the 30's, argyle, chevron, and diamond patterned socks became popular. Elastic-topped socks were introduced and did away with the need for garters.

High *shoes* went out of style in the 20's and oxfords became the predominant fashion. White and two-toned shoes were worn in summer. Moccasin style shoes were introduced in the 30's, adapted from shoes worn by Norwegian fishermen and nicknamed "weejuns." Other 30's styles included sandals, cloth shoes for summer, crepe-soled shoes, and higher shoes that ended at the ankle, closing either with laces (*chukka* boots) or a strap and buckle across the ankle (*monks' front*).

Wartime rationing made leather shoes and tennis shoes with rubber soles scarce. Composition soles were used to conserve leather. Galoshes or overshoes and rubbers changed little over the period. Galoshes closed at the front with snaps or zippers.

accessories—were relatively few for men, and chiefly consisted of gloves, handkerchiefs, scarves, umbrellas, canes, and jewelry such as watches, tie pins, shirt studs, cuff links, and rings.

COSTUME FOR CHILDREN

Item / Description

girls—*dresses*—Toddlers wore loose, smock-like dresses, often falling from a yoke at the neck; most had matching bloomers that could be seen beneath the short skirts. Smocking and embroidery were favored decorations.
  • *1920's*—young girls dresses, like those of adults, were unfitted.
  • *1930's*—waistlines of dresses returned to anatomical placement. Older girls' dresses often had fitted bodices with skirts attached and a sash tied in the back. Skirt fullness varied according to whether adult skirt styles were wider or narrower. Puffed sleeves were commonly seen.
  for school—skirts and blouses common in the 30's and 40's, some with straps or suspenders. (See Figure 17.20.)
  other garments—pullover and cardigan sweaters; slacks for sportswear for younger girls once pants had been accepted for women.

17.20 A selection of illustrations of children's clothing from a *Vogue Pattern Magazine* of 1933. *(Reproduced courtesy of the Butterick Pattern Archives/Library.)*

NOTE: The popularity of Shirley Temple, a child actress, influenced clothing styles for little girls in the 1930's.

outdoor wear—
· *1920's*—straight, narrow coats.
· *1930's*—princess line coats, often with fur trimmed collars.
· 1944 *Sears and Roebuck Catalog* shows a cross-section of coats for young girls including princess line, single-breasted chesterfields with velvet collars, "boy" coats cut straight with patch pockets, and wrap coats with tie belts. Leggings were available to match dress coats for cold weather.

boys—The custom of dressing small boys in skirts had ended. They wore romper suits or short pants, instead.

NOTE: Although boys' styles showed some minor differences from decade to decade, a boy could expect to spend the first few years of his life in short pants (in warm weather), then graduate to knickers, and finally into long trousers.

jackets—for dress occasions included:
· *1920's*—long and belted, or Norfolk jackets.
· *1930's & 1940's*—less likely to be belted, shorter, cut like those of adult men. Some had matching vests. (See Figure 17.21.)
shirts—1930's—polo shirts common for everyday dress. Cotton knit pullovers with napped undersurfaces appeared in the early 30's and by the 1940's this garment was being called a "sweatshirt."
special play clothes—Pre-school boys contin-

17.21 Boys' clothing styles of 1934. Young boys generally wore short pants; slightly older boys wore knickers. (Stella, 1934.)

ued to wear sailor suits, but other items appeared.

17.22 Page from Sears catalog, 1935. Interests of small boys of this period are reflected in the cowboy, Indian, aviator, and Buck Rogers space suits that could be purchased. (*Illustration reproduced courtesy of Sears, Roebuck and Company.*)

· *1920's*—"Tom Mix" outfits were advertised. (Tom Mix was a popular cowboy film star.) On the same page of the Sears Catalog were advertised Indian suits, policemen suits, and other cowboy outfits.

· *1930's*—cowboy and Indian suits remained popular and baseball players' suits and flyers' uniforms were added. (See Figure 17.22.)

· In the *1940's*, during the war, military uniforms for boys were advertised.

outdoor wear—Dress coats followed the lines of men's dress coats in each decade.

· *1920's*—mackinaws remained popular and a "lumber jack" jacket with knitted waistband ending just below the waist.

· *1930's*—"Fingertip" length, boxy jackets added, and in the late 30's and early 40's, poplin jackets and waterproof parkas. During the war years: Eisenhower jackets. Sweaters of all types: cardigans, pullovers, and sleeveless pullovers, however turtleneck sweaters went out of fashion after the 20's.

boys and girls—*overalls and jeans*—Overalls made of blue denim and pants of the same fabric appeared in the boys' section of the *Sears and Roebuck Catalog* of 1923 with this caption "for work or play" and henceforth were a consistent feature of work or play clothes for boys, especially in rural areas. In the 1940's they also appeared as play clothes for girls.

underwear—similar to that for adults. As athletic shorts and sleeveless undershirts became available for men and brief panties for women, they also were made for children.

sleepwear—from the 1920's much sleepwear for young children was in the form of pajamas with feet in them, sometimes called "sleepers." Older boys wore pajamas almost exclusively, whereas girls wore either pajamas or nightgowns.

bathing suits—followed adult styles.

snow suits—little difference between those for boys and girls other than color, pink being reserved for girls. For small children, one-piece snow suits; for older children, two-piece jacket and leggings. In the 1930's water repellent fabrics were used. In the 1940's, hooded jackets were popular.

rain wear—1920's and 30's—rubberized cloth or oiled slicker material. By the late 30's, water repellent fabric replaced oiled slicker fabric. For true water-proofing, rubberized fabrics were required. During the war (in the 40's) when rubber was scarce rain wear was made of synthetic rubber.

the teen-age market—began to grow in the United States in the 1940's as a specialized segment of the fashion industry. Adolescent and college-age girls made skirts and sweaters into veritable uniforms. To the skirt and sweaters they added white ankle socks and either loafers or saddle shoes. The favorite hair style was a long, page-boy cut.

Summary

During the period between the First and Second World Wars, clothing styles for men continued the trends begun before the 1914 War. Clothing for men changed little, and those changes that did take place were relatively minor and gradual. The standardization of wardrobes both for men who were "white collar" office workers and for "blue collar" laborers offered relatively little choice. The former was confined to a suit with vest, white shirt, and necktie for business and the latter to sturdy, washable work clothes. Only in clothing for leisure were men able to exercise a wider degree of selection from a broader range of styles.

Women's clothing in the 1920's incorporated elements that had rarely appeared in earlier historical periods and which provided visible evidence of changes in the roles of women. The radically shorter skirts, cropped hair, acceptibility of cosmetic use, and adoption by women of traditionally masculine garments like trousers showed that women had rejected patterns in feminine dress that had been established for hundreds of years, just as they were rejecting patterns of behavior for women that had confined them to more limited roles in society.

Selected Readings

BOOKS AND OTHER MATERIALS CONTAINING ILLUSTRATIONS OF COSTUME OF THE PERIOD FROM ORIGINAL SOURCES

Fashion Magazines such as *Esquire, Harper's Bazaar, and Vogue.*

General women's magazines such as *Delineator, Ladies Home Journal, McCalls, Women's Home Companion,* etc.

Mail order catalogs.

Pattern catalogs.

Brunhammer, Y. *The Nineteen Twenties Style.* New York: Paul Hamlyn, 1969.

Howell, G. *In Vogue.* New York: Schocken Books, 1976.

Lynam, R. *Couture.* Garden City, N.Y.: Doubleday Company, Inc., 1972.

Robinson, J. *Fashion in the Forties.* New York: St. Martin's Press, 1976.

Robinson, J. *The Golden Age of Style.* New York: Harcourt Brace Jovanovich, 1976.

Schoeffler, O. E. (Ed.) *Esquire's Encyclopedia of 20th Century Men's Fashion.* New York: McGraw-Hill Book Company, 1973.

The 10's, 20's, and 30's. Inventive Clothes 1909–1939. New York: the Metropolitan Museum of Art, N.D.

PERIODICAL ARTICLES

Behling, D. "Fashion Change and Demographics: A Model." *Clothing and Textiles Research Journal.* Vol.4, No.1, Fall 1985, p. 18.

Cohen, R. H. "Tut and the 20's: The 'Egyptian Look'." *Art in America,* Vol. 67 (2), March 1979, p. 97.

"Designer's Delight: The Best of the Great 1920–30 Period." *American Fabrics and Fashions,* Summer 1977, p. 27.

Hall, L. "Fashion and Style in the Twenties: The Change." *Historian,* Vol. 34 (3), May 1972, p. 485.

Kruckeberg, V. L. "Dining in Style: Conservation of a Circa 1920's Velvet Gown." *Dress,* Vol. 9, 1983, p. 21.

Richards, L. "The Rise and Fall of it All: Hemlines and Hiplines of the 1920's." *Clothing and Textiles Research Journal,* Vol. 2 (1), Fall 1983, p. 42.

Simms, J. "Adrian- An American Artist and Designer." *Costume,* No. 8, 1974, p. 13.

"The 1920's." *American Fabrics and Fashions,* No. 106, Winter 1976, p. 20.

Vreeland, D. "Vionnet." *Domus,* No. 534, May 1974, p. 50.

DAILY LIFE

Abels, J. *In the Time of Silent Cal.* New York: G. P. Putnam's Sons, 1969.

Allen, F. L. *Only Yesterday.* New York: Harper and Row, 1931.

Allen, F. L. *Since Yesterday.* New York: Harper and Brothers, 1940.

*Andrist, R. K. (Editor). *The American Heritage History of the 20's and 30's.* New York: American Heritage Publishing Company, 1970.

Boorstin, D. *The American Democratic Experience.* New York: Random House, 1973.

Congdon, D. *The Thirties: A Time to Remember.* New York: Simon and Schuster, 1962.

Graves, R. and A. Hodge. *The Long Weekend: A Social History of Great Britain, 1918–1939.* New York: Norton, 1963.

Jenkins, A. *The Thirties.* New York: Stein and Day, 1976.

Terkel, S. *Hard Times.* New York: Avon Books, 1970.

This Fabulous Century: Volumes 3, 4, and 5. New York: Time-Life Books, 1969.

Wecter, D. *The Age of the Great Depression.* New York: Macmillan Company, 1948.

Werstein, I. *Shattered Decade: 1919–1929.* New York: Charles Scribner's Sons, 1970.

* Also contains illustrations of costumes from contemporary sources.

CHAPTER 18

The New Look, the Fifties, and the Sixties

1947–1970

Historical Background

The first years after the end of World War II were devoted in Europe and Asia to recovery from the devastation of the war, and both in the United States and abroad to the return to a peacetime economy. Soon after the war relations between Russia and the major powers in Western Europe deteriorated to the point where the conflict was spoken of as a "cold war." In China the Communists took power and much of the world seemed to be divided between the ideologies of communism and capitalism. In 1950 an actual conflict broke out in Korea between communist-controlled North Korea and South Korea and the United States became directly involved in the fighting. The Korean War ended in 1953.

Veterans of World War II and the Korean War were entitled to educational subsidies and many of them took advantage of these benefits to return to college. The college students of the immediate post-war period and the generation of college students who followed after the veterans have been described as "studious, earnest, rather humorless, bent on getting an education not for its own sake but because it clearly would, under the emerging national system, lead surely and inevitably to a good

job and the solution to *the* youth problem of not so long before—economic security."[1] These students have since been labeled "the silent generation."

In 1957 the Soviet Union launched the first satellite to orbit the earth and the Space Age began. Americans were shocked at the gap in technology between the U.S. and Russia that this feat represented, and in 1960 President Kennedy vowed that the United States would reach the moon by 1970. The first manned moon landing was made in 1969.

Between 1957 and 1969, the Silent Generation was replaced by young people whose elders frequently wished they would be more silent. The advance guard of the newly-awakened young were the "Beatniks," at first a literary movement. The "Beats" adopted eccentric habits of dress and grooming "—beards, pony tails, dirty sneakers, peasant blouses . . ."[2] They experimented with drugs, turned to Eastern mysticism, especially Zen Buddhism, and rejected the "square" world. The Beatnik phenomenon faded, but as early as 1960 a college student association president was quoted in *The New York Times* as seeing greater concern among

1. J. Brooks. *The Great Leap*. New York: Harper and Row, Publishers, 1966, p. 232.
2. *Ibid.* p. 236.

students with non-college affairs. Some students became involved in the growing civil rights movement which through non-violent resistance and the courts succeeded in ending the most blatant forms of discrimination against black people.

By the mid-60's student unrest on college campuses was drawing more and more media coverage. *The New York Times* spoke of a student "revolt against conformity, boredom, and tediousness of middle-class life" and students began calling for greater voice in college governance.

Another expression of youthful revolt against the values of the adult society, the hippie movement, surfaced in 1966. Young people, most of them from middle class families, responded to the call from Timothy Leary, a proponent of the use of the drug LSD, to "turn on to the scene; tune into what's happening; and drop out—of high school, college, grad school . . ." Beginning in California in the Haight-Ashbury District of San Francisco, the movement, which became a drug-using sub-culture, spread across the country. The hippie philosophy stressed "love" and freedom from the constraints of "straight" society. On Easter Sunday, 1967, in Central Park in New York, 10,000 young people— not all of them hippies—gathered to honor love. In Philadelphia on May 15, of the same year, 2500 hippies held a "Be-in," a gathering honoring the notion that everyone had the right to "be."

Throughout the decade the United States had been becoming more and more enmeshed in war in Vietnam. As increasingly larger numbers of young people were being drafted to serve in Vietnam, student protests against the war began to escalate. The general climate of student unrest and rebellion together with the lessons in non-violent protest and mass rallies that had been learned from the civil rights movement of the 50's and early 60's contributed to a growing activism among college students.

Students were not the only segment of American society to question traditional values. Many women had returned willingly in the post-war period to the home to become wives and mothers, but by the 1960's the number of working women, particularly those who were also married women with children, had begun to increase. Some women began to question some of the assumptions about their traditional roles in the family and the work force. The book *The Feminine Mystique*, a best-seller in the early 60's, seemed to crystalize the dissatisfaction felt by some women, and gradually a Women's Liberation Movement was formed that articulated the point of view that women should have equality

of opportunity in the job market and the right to choose their respective roles in society. This movement gained momentum throughout the latter part of the 60's and was given widespread coverage in the news media.

Some Influences on Fashion

Some of the events outlined above had either direct or indirect effects on fashion, and there were other events or developments over this period that also were reflected in women's, and to a lesser extent men's, clothing styles.

THE MOVE TO THE SUBURBS

The changing patterns of life in Western Europe in general and in the United States in particular were one of the important influences on what people wore. Many women returned to full-time homemaking after working for pay during the war. Families produced a bumper crop of babies. The family orientation of the period was emphasized as women's magazines stressed "togetherness." Many urban families moved to the suburbs. Family travel increased and camping became a popular form of recreation. Domestic help was scarce. The effect of these changes was to create an emphasis on more informal or casual styles. Department stores expanded sportswear departments for men, women, and teens. The proportion of leisure-time clothing in the suburban American's wardrobe increased, a tendency which accelerated as the period progressed.

FASHION INFLUENCES FROM THE YOUNG

Changes in the socio-economic status of adolescents had begun during World War II. Before the war, many young people were wage-earners and members of the work force soon after they entered their teens. But the post-war socio-economic changes kept many young people dependent for a longer period of time—through high school and even beyond—and this accentuated the period of adolescence as a separate stage of development. The teen market in records and clothes grew rapidly and teen-age fashions and fads played an important role in the garment industry.

Not only did adolescents provide a growing market for producers of fashion goods, but they were also responsible for the introduction of new fashions, as well. One notable example was the introduction of longer hair styles for males, a style fostered by the Beatles, a long-haired English singing group, popular with teens of the early 60's.

Other styles adopted by young people before they spread to the older segments of society were the mini skirt, a skirt which ended above the knee, and pants worn in place of skirts for school, work, and social events. In 1968 these garments were causing controversies in schools and offices. Court cases were brought to decide whether banning these garments infringed the rights of students and women workers.

FASHION INFLUENCES FROM PROTEST MOVEMENTS

The young people of the first decade after the war, the so-called Silent Generation, had shown none of the rebellion against the established society that characterized the 60's. The aforementioned Beat poets of Southern California in the late 50's had adopted certain clothing styles: leotards, turtle-necked sweaters, tweed jumpers, and pony tails for girls; blue jeans for boys; and a general emphasis on a scruffy, unkempt appearance, but these styles were popular among a rather limited segment of young people.

In the hippie sub-culture of the latter half of the 60's costume also served to identify members or sympathizers. The press showed photographs of hippies who had bought their clothing in thrift shops or those who had made themselves colorful and imaginative costumes. Men and women grew their hair long—to the shoulders or longer, and men wore beards, head bands, and beads. Women wore long, gipsy-like costumes. Some of the elements of so-called hippie dress were quickly adopted by the fashion industry. The first widespread media coverage of hippies had begun in early 1967 and by 1968 Ken Scott, an American designer, had already designed a collection that included what he called a "hippie gypsy look."

THE IMPACT OF TELEVISION AND THE SPACE AGE

Television became commercially available to the American public around 1948, but in that year only twenty stations were on the air and only 172,000 families had sets. By the census of 1950 five million families had a TV set in the house.[3] Television proba-

bly had an impact on fashion as a medium for the spread of fashion information. Would fashion trends like longer hair, blue jeans, and the hippie look have spread through the population so quickly if news were disseminated only by the written or broadcast media?

The Space Age also influenced fashion. After the spate of manned space flights that began in the early 60's, the French designer André Courrèges designed a line of clothes in 1964 that he called "Space Age." Models came out wearing "space helmets." Plastic was emphasized, and bold, vivid colors stressed.

INTERNATIONAL TRAVEL

The post-war period was also marked by a spirit of internationalism. Air travel made it possible for people to move easily from one place to another and the relatively low cost of this transportation, as compared with ship travel, coupled with an increased affluence for many encouraged more Americans to travel abroad. In 1929, 500,000 Americans visited abroad. In 1958 the number of Americans who went abroad reached 1,398,000 who spent an estimated two billion dollars in their travels.[4] Travelers returned with fashion goods from the countries they visited. They also became more receptive to imported goods sold in the United States.

The quantity of foreign fashion goods being imported into the United States also increased sharply. In 1960 the steady increases in imports were seen by labor and management in the American garment industry as a serious threat. These imports were at first chiefly from Western Europe, but in the 60's the developing countries in Asia and Africa began to export goods that sold for low prices. Retailers liked the imported goods because often they could take a higher mark-up on these items than on domestic goods. Fashion promotions by the sophisticated Western European countries created a demand for fashionable Italian, French, and English goods.

High fashion design took on a more international flavor. The French position as the sole arbiter of fashion for women was challenged not only by American designers who had come of age during the war but also by English, Italian, and even a few Irish and Spanish designers.

The Fabric Revolution—Before World War II clothing was made from a limited number of fibers: the

3. Brooks, *op. cit.*, p. 162.

4. *The New York Times*, Jan. 17, 1960.

natural fibers silk, wool, cotton, and linen, and the man-made fibers rayon and acetate. The successful marketing of nylon, invented before the War but not given wide distribution to the civilian population until after the War, touched off a successful search for other synthetic fibers. Many of these came onto the market in the 50's. The major apparel fibers that appeared at this time included modacrylics (1949), acrylics (1950), polyesters (1953), triacetate (1954), and spandex (1959). Other fibers were also developed, but these either had limited use or were found mostly in household textiles or industrial applications. Many companies that had formerly been chemical companies began to manufacture fibers, since these were chiefly derived from chemical substances.

One of the characteristics of most of the postwar fibers was that they were easy to care for. With the more casual life style that had evolved, and with the virtual disappearance of servants from the middle class household, these fabrics that were easier to maintain rapidly gained consumer acceptance. The expansion of travel helped to promote "drip dry" fabrics. In the late 50's there were "wash and wear" fabrics. In the 60's "wash and wear" was replaced by "permanent press." These were chiefly cotton and cotton blended with polyester. Some wool fabrics were given special treatments to render them more readily washable.

These new fibers may also have contributed to the popularity of some of the silhouettes of the period. The full-skirted styles of the 50's were held out by lightweight, permanently stiffened nylon petticoats. The A-line of the late 50's and 60's and the unfitted shift were, in more expensive garments, backed with supporting fabrics that maintained the shape of the garment.

Some of the new fabrics, like Qiana® nylon introduced in 1968, were promoted by introducing them in a line of high fashion items made by Paris couturiers. In the beginning of the period the couture seemed wary of using synthetic fabrics, but by the end of the 60's they were being widely used in the couture along with more traditional fabrics made from natural fibers.

The Changing Couture—Some individual members of the French couture went on designing in Paris throughout World War II, but most of the couturiers left Paris or closed their ateliers. Mainbocher and Schiaparelli had gone to New York, Balenciaga had gone to neutral Portugal. Chanel gave her last show in 1940. But once the war had ended, the couturiers began to plan for a revival of their businesses. This revival was given an enormous push forward by

the collections of 1947 and the "New Look," the name given by the fashion press to the collection mounted by Christian Dior.

Dior had worked before the war for Piquet and after, briefly, for the house of Lucien Lelong. (Lelong was not a designer but ran an establishment carrying his name.) In 1945 Dior was offered financial backing to open his own establishment and in 1947 the house of Dior made fashion history. The new styles were successful over night, and the house of Dior became one of the most influential of the houses in the haute couture.

Dior remained a major designer until his death in 1957. In the ten years that he ran the house of Dior he helped to develop the establishment into a major business that created and sold perfumes, furs, stockings, gloves, and other accessories under license around the world. After his death Yves St. Laurent, a young protégé of Christian Dior, was named head designer. St. Laurent was drafted soon after showing his first successful collections and in his absence Marc Bohan became head designer. A power struggle developed when St. Laurent sought to return to Dior after his army service. In the end, Bohan stayed with the House of Dior and St. Laurent went off to form his own establishment.

Another major designer of the post war period was Cristobal Balenciaga. Balenciaga was born in Spain and opened his first Paris establishment in 1937. When he returned to Paris after the war he was noticed by Carmel Snow, the editor of *Harper's Bazaar*, and he soon became a favorite of hers. She featured his work often in *Bazaar*. His work showed a mastery of almost sculptural forms and shapes and frequently his styles were well ahead of their time. After being a major force in the *haute couture* for most of the 60's he suddenly and unexpectedly closed his establishment in 1968. Balenciaga died in 1972.

Other important French couturiers of the postwar period included Jacques Fath, Pierre Cardin, and Hubert de Givenchy. Interest in the designs of the couture remained exceptionally high throughout the 50's and early 60's. Department stores in the United States such as Ohrbachs and Alexanders in New York City bought designer original garments and by arrangement with the designer made relatively faithful "line for line" copies which they sold at much lower prices than the originals could command. Around 1954 American stores began a sort of piracy of French designer styles. Low-priced copies were sold as copies of Monsieur X, Monsieur Y, or Monsieur Z. Knowledgeable customers were aware that Monsieur X was Dior, Monsieur Y was Jacques Fath, and Monsieur Z was Givenchy.

In the 1960's a group of young designers who had trained under men like Dior and Balenciaga left these established couture houses and opened their own establishments. The most successful of these young men in addition to Yves St. Laurent were Pierre Cardin, André Courrèges, and Emmanuel Ungaro. In the mid-60's, after being successful in the haute couture, most of these designers expanded in the direction of ready-to-wear (or as the French call it, prêt-à-porter). Both Courrèges and St. Laurent designed lines of ready to wear in the mid-60's. Cardin had opened a men's wear boutique in 1957 and turned his design expertise to a variety of other products as well. In the years since this radical alteration was made in the operation of some of the couture houses, the Paris prêt-à-porter group has become so important that the fashion press goes to Paris not only for the regular shows of the haute couture but also for the opening of the prêt-à-porter collections.

Other Centers of Design for Women's Fashions— In the post war era a number of fashion design centers other than Paris also became important. In the past when travel was by boat or lengthy airplane trips, there was a certain practical aspect to having a single important center for fashion design. In the post war period jet travel made it fast and easy to reach any of the major cities of the world, and the fashion press could cover shows in diverse parts of the globe with ease. In the 50's and 60's Florence and Rome in Italy, and London joined Paris and New York as important centers of fashion design. The showings of styles in each of these cities was covered by the fashion press, and important and influential fashion designers of international reputation worked in each of these places. Nevertheless it was still Paris to which the fashion world looked with greatest interest.

Costume

COSTUME FOR WOMEN

The New Look and the Fifties—Seldom does fashion change almost overnight, but in 1947 an exceptionally rapid shift in styles took place. After the war the Western Nations began to recover from the devastation of the war. The war in Asia had ended in August 1945. After a little more than a year in which there were no major fashion upheavals, the French designer Christian Dior caused a sensation by introducing a line of clothing at his Spring, 1947 show that deviated sharply from the styles of the preceding season and which came to be known as "The New Look." (See Figure 18.1.) It was accepted rapidly and became the basis of style lines for the next ten or more years. In describing the "New Look" Collection, *Vogue* said:

> If there could be a composite, mythical woman dressed by a mystical, composite couturier, she would probably wear her skirt about fourteen inches from the floor; it might have, for its working model, a flower: petals of padding and stiffening sewn beneath the cup of the skirt; or it might be a long, straight tube beneath a belled and padded jacket. Her waist could be as small and nipped-in in cut as tight bodice and padded hips could make it. Her shoulders would be her own (or it would seem so); her arms traced closely in cloth. Her hat engaging but not silly—a gendarme hat; a hat with a broken brim; a mushroom hat which at eye level would have an almost flat surface with crown slipping into brim; or a thicket of straw and flowers. She might wear a high-necked, boned-collar blouse, or she might wear a suit with a low-necked collar; there would probably be a fan of pleating somewhere about her; and she would, without question, wear opera pumps—pointed, high-heeled.[5]

The major style elements of the New Look and the changes that it wrought were these. Skirt lengths dropped sharply. Examination of fashion magazines of the preceding months shows that there was already a tendency toward somewhat longer skirts. Many other designers in the Spring of 1947 also showed longer skirts, but to the woman on the street who had worn her skirts just below a knee for the preceding four or five years, the change was radical. Although there were pockets of resistance to the longer skirts (in the United States groups of women banded together and called themselves the "Little Below the Knee" Clubs and declared that they would not lengthen their skirts) the change seemed irresistible and within a year the longer skirt lengths were widely adopted.

A second major change was in the shoulder line. The square, padded shoulder that had been worn since the late 1930's was replaced by a shoulder line with a round, soft curve also achieved by a shaped shoulder pad. Many designs had enormously full skirts. One of Dior's models had twenty-five yards of fan-pleated silk in the skirt. Other designs had pencil-slim skirts. Whether the skirt was

5. *Vogue,* April, 1947, p. 137.

full or narrow, the waistline was nipped in and small. The rounded curves of the body were emphasized. Many daytime and evening dresses were cut quite low. The curve of the hip was stressed. In jackets which extended below the waist the basque was padded and stiffened into a full, round curve. Once established, the New Look influence permeated women's clothes throughout the greater part of the 50's.

Undergarments—To achieve the fashionable look women returned to more confining corsetry and underclothing than had been seen since before 1920. Fortunately for the comfort of women many of the undergarments required to maintain the soft curves of the New Look were made of newer synthetic fabrics that pulled the body into the requisite shape without the rigid, painful bones and lacing of the early 20th century. The necessary underwear consisted of brassieres that emphasized an "uplift." For wearing under some of the strapless evening gowns, strapless brassieres were available both in short lengths or constructed to extend to the waist. These were boned and although the sections between the bones were generally made of elasticized or synthetic power net fabrics, wearing these confining garments did occasion some degree of discomfort. Many women wore waist cinches of boned or elasticized fabric to narrow the waistline to the desired small size. Corsets or girdles, as they were more likely to be called, generally extended well above the waistline in order to narrow the waist somewhat. These were made of elasticized panels with some stretch combined with panels of firmer, non-stretching fabrics. Some closed with zippers, others had enough stretch to simply pull on over the hips. (See Figure 18.2.)

In order to hold out the skirts of these dresses full petticoats were required. Starched crinoline half slips (at this time crinoline was any open weave, heavily sized fabric) were used, but permanently stiffened nylon plain weave fabrics or nets were generally preferred for these garments because they required less maintenance and were lighter in weight. Beneath the full skirts, slips with full skirts and often a ruffle around the hem were worn while the narrower skirts required a straight slip. Under evening and wedding dresses a hoop petticoat might also be used. (See Figure 18.2.)

Sleepwear also followed the trend toward fuller skirts and figure-hugging bodices, although tailored pajamas were also available. Advertising in fashion magazines and mail order catalogs emphasized nightgowns and a wide variety of sheer and full-skirted models were available. Toward the end of

18.1 Drawing from *Harper's Bazaar*, May, 1947 of a suit from the Dior "New Look" collection of March, 1947. (*Reprinted with the permission of* Harper's Bazaar, *division of the Hearst Corporation.*)

the 50's pastel sleepwear was superceded by more colorful prints in floral and abstract patterns.

1947–1960

Item / Description

daytime dresses—Silhouette often called the period of the "dual silhouette" because both exceptionally full and narrow skirts co-existed. On narrow skirts the length required the bottom of the skirt be slit or have a pleat of some type in order to allow a full stride. Fullness was achieved by goring, pleating, or gathering. (See Figure 18.3.) Some dresses were cut in the princess style.

Small-waists
by JANTZEN

Girdle or panty . . . **10.00**

18.2 (*Above left*) Girdles of the late 40's and the 50's with elasticized extensions above the waist were designed to aid women in achieving the small-waisted silhouette of the period. (*Above right*) Full-skirted, permanently stiffened petticoat was designed to hold out the wide skirts of the same period. (*Courtesy of Stern's Department Store.*)

sleeves—close-fitting. Most often seen were short, cap sleeves just covering the shoulder; short, medium, and longer set-in sleeves that fitted the arm closely; and "shirt sleeves" similar to those on men's shirts but fuller.

necklines—often plain, round or square and ending either close to the neck or lower. Also seen: small and larger collars and Chinese style or "mandarin" standing collars. Some notable *dress styles* included: summer jacket dresses, usually sleeveless and with small straps or halter tops and over this a short jacket or bolero; shirtwaist dresses with full skirts; coat dresses with full skirts, some in the princess style, buttoning down the front. Some dresses of the early 50's had dropped waistlines.

suits—although some full-skirted suits were worn, most tended to be made with narrow skirts. Jackets fitted closely to the waistline, extending below the waist where they either flared out into a stiffened peplum or had a rounded, stiffened, and padded hip section ending several inches below the waist. (See Figure 18.4.) Suit necklines varied in placement, but tended to stand away from the neck somewhat. Collar styles included peter pan, rolled, notched, and shawl types.

separate skirts—either full or narrow.

blouses—Similar in lines to those of dress bodices, i.e. shaped to follow body contours with darts or seams so that they fitted smoothly through the bust and rib cage.

sweaters—worn either tucked into the skirt or out, over the skirt and belted. Fitted closely, many had smooth shoulder lines achieved by knitting sleeve and body in one. Included among the varieties: matching cardigans and pullovers, evening sweaters with beaded and/or sequin decorations, and in the 50's bolero-like cardigans called "shrugs."

evening dresses—usually the same length as daytime dresses. Shorter evening dresses in so-called

18.3 Full-skirted dress of the post-"New Look" period. (*Photograph courtesy of the Smithsonian Institution.*)

18.4 Suits from the 1950's that have narrow skirts, nipped-in waistlines, and rounded, padded extensions of the jacket below the waist. (*Reproduced courtesy of the Butterick Pattern Archives/Library.*)

"ballerina length" predominated, but Paris designers continued to show some long gowns and pattern catalogs included patterns in both lengths. (See Figure 18.5.) Bridal gowns were generally floor length. Wide skirts were preferred for evening but some narrow-skirted styles with elaborate puffs of fabric at the hips or "fish tails" (—i.e., wide areas—at the hem). Strapless ballerina-length gowns with full gored or gathered skirts worn over starched "crinolines" were especially popular among high school and college girls.

outdoor garments—coats either followed the silhouette having fitted bodice areas and full skirts or else were full from the shoulders. Most fitted coats were cut in the princess line and belted;

full coats had a good deal of flare in the skirt. Sleeve styles included kimono and raglan types. Some had turned back cuffs ending well above the wrist and long gloves were worn with these. Fur coats were popular with affluent women. If these followed princess lines they were generally made of less bulky furs. Jackets, ending above the waist, called "shorties," were a convenient way to accommodate wide skirts. Longer jackets, full and flaring from shoulder to hem, were also worn. (See Figure 18.6.)

sportswear—became an increasingly large part of the wardrobe. (See Figure 18.7.)

18.5 Full-skirted evening dress in shorter and longer lengths. This style, often strapless, was characteristic of evening dress in the 1950's. (*Reproduced courtesy of the Butterick Pattern Archives/Library.*)

18.6 A variety of coat styles from 1952. (*Reproduced courtesy of the Butterick Pattern Archives/Library.*)

shorts—in the early part of the period—upper thigh-length and fairly straight. Knee-length *Bermuda shorts* were adopted around 1954 and until the late 50's virtually replaced shorter styles.

pants—narrow, fitting the leg so closely that shoes had to be taken off in order to don the pants. *Lengths:* reaching the ankle; "houseboy" pants ending at the calf; and still shorter pants were given fashion names known as *pedal pushers*. Still other styles had names which changed from season to season, according to the fashion advertising copy writers whim. Loose, printed or knit tops were commonly worn with these pants.

bathing suits—In Europe a scanty, two-piece bathing suit smaller than any that had ever been seen before was introduced.

NOTE: Designer Jacques Heim is credited as the originator of the style, which he called the *atom*. Soon there was a version that was advertised as "smaller than the atom." Eventually the name *atom* was changed to *bikini*. (Bikini was the small coral island in the Pacific where atomic tests were made from 1946 to 1956.) Although it was worn on the beaches of Europe, American women did not adopt the bikini but continued to wear more

covered one-piece suits. Many bathing suits were cut with bottoms like shorts, while others had skirt-like constructions, and a few had full bloomers. Cotton, nylon, and Lastex were the most popular fabrics. (See Figure 18.8.)

golf—played in shorts or trousers or in cotton golfing dresses made with extra pleats of fabric at the shoulders to accommodate the golf swing. Skirts and sweaters were also worn for golf.

18.7 Bermuda shorts (right side) and narrow slacks were important sportswear styles of the early 1950's. (*Courtesy of the Butterick Pattern Archives/Library.*)

18.8 Even the relatively modest bikini's shown on top from the fashion report by Tobé in 1947 were not accepted by American women who, instead, wore bathing suits like those below, which displayed less skin. (*Courtesy of The Tobé Report.*)

skiing—as slacks narrowed, so did ski pants. Stretch yarns, used from about 1956 on, made it possible to make ski pants fit the leg tightly. Closely-woven nylon wind-breakers were worn as jackets, and ski wear was made in bright colors.

(The rapid increase in the numbers of skiing enthusiasts in the United States made for greater variety in ski wear styles.)

hair and head dress—*hair*—short hair had become fashionable with the New Look. In the mid-50's, longer hair regained fashion.

hats—fairly small in scale, but also some large picture hats. In the later 50's hats were consistently small and fitted the head closely, also some turban styles in brightly-colored prints or plain colors.

accessories—gloves in a variety of fabrics and lengths, including some long gloves worn with strapless evening gowns. Handbags, moderate in size and usually with small handles.

jewelry—Necklaces, usually fitting close to the neck, bracelets, and earrings as the predominant forms. Rhinestones, colored stones, and imitation pearls in a variety of colors used for costume jewelry.

cosmetics—Bright red lipstick and face makeup in natural skin tones with mascara on eyelashes and eyebrow pencil. After 1952 eye makeup became more pronounced and some women drew a dark line around the eyes. About 1956 colored eyeshadow began to appear in fashion magazines. Nail polish was available in many shades of pink and red.

18.9 A variety of unfitted "chemise" styles featured in *Women's Wear Daily* in late 1957. (*Courtesy of* Women's Wear Daily, *Fairchild Publications.*)

footwear—Through the 40's and mid-50's, rounded toes and very high heels for dress, with some open-toed, ankle-straps, sling-back or sandal styles. Lower-heeled and flat shoes also available, with more casual styles including moccasins, loafers, ballet slippers, and canvas tennis shoes (sneakers).

Stockings, now inevitably made of nylon, were seamed (more popular) or seamless. Seams were often stitched in dark thread with reinforced heels made in dark yarn and extending several inches up the back of the ankle. About the middle of the decade of the 50's, toes of shoes grew more pointed and heels narrower.

NOTE: High-heeled shoes had "stiletto heels" made with a steel spike up the center of the heel to prevent the narrow heel from breaking. (See Figure 18.18.) Stockings without seams became popular; advances in technology for making nylon stockings made possible the construction of seamless stockings that fit the leg smoothly and without wrinkles.

1960–1970

dresses—The precise dividing line between the end of the styles influenced by the New Look and the unfitted look that became the predominant style of the better part of the 60's is difficult to identify. Balenciaga introduced the unfitted dress style as early as 1954 (his suits were unfitted from 1951 on) and Dior presented the A-line in his collection of 1955. But the unfitted look or chemise styles in dresses as they were called did not catch the public fancy immediately. By 1957 most suits had shorter jackets, loosely fitted and ending shortly below the waist. Some blouson or full-backed styles were being shown and skirts had been growing gradually shorter and narrower. (See Figure 18.9.) Coats were straighter, and hair was longer and showing a tendency to be arranged in styles that were higher and wider around the face.

By 1958 some women had bought unfitted dresses of the chemise-type or the A-line "trapeze," but many others continued to resist the style. (See Figure 18.10.) Throughout the early 60's fashion magazines continued to show both new styles in the unfitted cut together with dresses that followed the narrow waisted full-skirted silhouette. By the mid-60's, however, the unfitted style had supplanted the fitted look of the 50's.

daytime dresses—changed little until the unfitted look became well-established, although skirts gradually shortened. The new styles were either straight and unfitted or princess style with a slight

18.10 A-line dress called "the trapeze" from 1959 was an example of the unfitted styles being introduced at this time. (*Courtesy of the Butterick Pattern Archives/Library.*)

18.11 Mini skirt and matching overblouse, 1969. (*Photograph courtesy of the Smithsonian Institution.*)

A-line in which the waist was loosely defined. The *skimmer*, a sleeveless, princess-line style was a popular example of the latter form.

In the second half of the 60's, dresses with bodices joined to skirts were uncommon. Some dresses fell straight from a yoke at the shoulder; some had empire waistlines; and some were unfitted through the torso and had a flounce joined to the dress all round at the knee.

Gradually shortening skirts were as much as two inches above the knee in the United States in 1966, though more conservative women rarely wore knee-baring styles.

NOTE: The phrase "mini" skirt was coined, and when some women raised hemlines still higher the term "micro-mini" was applied. (See Figure 18.11.)

Short skirts were frequently combined with colored stockings or tights. A commonly worn style among young women was a turtleneck worn with a jumper and tights that matched the jumper.

NOTE: Some designers seemed to derive inspiration from graphic arts: in 1965 St. Laurent showed dresses with geometric blocks of color like those painted by an early modern artist, Mondrian and the boldly-patterned lines of contemporary "optical art" appeared in fabrics for clothing.

pants suits—were introduced in the last two years of the 60's, and unlike earlier pants for women were intended for daytime and business wear. "Double knit" fabrics, especially of polyester were

18.12 Women's pants suit of 1970 from *Butterick Pattern Catalog. (Reproduced courtesy of the Butterick Pattern Archives/Library.)*

18.13 Collarless jacket with braid trim and slightly flared skirt follows the general lines of components of a popular suit style originated by French designer Gabrielle Chanel. (*From* Vogue Pattern Catalog, 1962. *Reproduced courtesy of the Butterick Pattern Archives/Library.*)

often used for inexpensive pants suits. (See Figure 18.12.)

suits—were generally made with loosely fitted jackets. In the early 60's a style originated by Chanel, consisting of a braid-trimmed, collarless, cardigan-style jacket with three-quarter length sleeves, A-line skirt, and blouse with a bow tie at the neck and sleeves extending a little beyond the jacket sleeves was exceptionally popular. (See Figure 18.13.) By the late 60's, pants suits had surpassed skirted suits in popularity.

separate skirts and blouses—of less importance than in earlier decade. Skirts tended to be A-line; many had no waistband, but finished in a facing. Knit tops, especially turtlenecks, were part of a general interest in knitted fabrics.

NOTE: A fashion with a limited following for sheer, see-through blouses and dresses worn without underclothing was reported in the press, but did not spread beyond urban, cosmopolitan areas.

evening dresses—Made in both long and short lengths, but short lengths were preferred. Some of the fashionable styles included: elaborately beaded bodices or overblouses worn with long skirts; straight, short dresses of metallic fabrics, or trimmed with sequins, paillets of plastic, and/or beads. (See Figure 18.14.) In the late 60's, long evening dresses began to supplant shorter ones. Pants suits of decorative fabrics with full-legged trousers were also worn for evening.

18.14 Beaded tulle evening dress, 1966. (*Photograph courtesy of the Wadsworth Atheneum, Hartford.*)

outdoor garments—Overall lines of coats tended to be straight and loose, with an easy fit through the shoulders and a rounded shoulder line. Sleeves were often dropped slightly, or cut in one with the body of the coat; sleeves were wrist length or shorter. Some coats narrowed slightly toward the bottom or, alternately, had a slight A-shape.

High pile coats, some imitating real fur, were made of synthetic fibers. Most were dark or neutral shades, some were made in colors such as red or green.

At the end of the decade, *midi, mini,* and *maxi* lengths were all being shown in coats. (See Figure 18.15.) Long *greatcoats* in double-or single-breasted styles with belted and flared skirts in maxi lengths were inspired by the film *Doctor Zhivago* and its 19th-century Russian styles. Coats in longer lengths were more successful than dresses or skirts although the new length was not immediately established.

Other developments in outerwear included capes, in short lengths in the late sixties, and vinyl-coated fabrics for rainwear.

NOTE: Some manufacturers made coats with horizontal zippers that allowed the wearer to zip off sections at each of the *mini, midi,* or *maxi* lengths.

sportwear—in the early 60's: knitted stretch pants with narrow legs, worn with straight or blouson tops, or knitted tops. Toward the middle of the decade: pant legs grew wide; these styles often had low, hip level belts. Blue jeans became a major fashion item, having first been adopted by counter-culture young people, and then picked up by the fashion industry and heavily promoted. By the end of the 60's persons of all ages, economic, and ethnic backgrounds were wearing blue denim.

NOTE: Blue jeans were adopted by hippies and other young persons who protested against the establishment in general, and the Vietnam war in particular. The choice of these garments was based on the fact that for generations these garments had been associated with farmers and working men. (See Figure 18.16.)

bathing suits—During the early 60's, two-piece bathing suits of relatively conservative cut made a reappearance and, more slowly, but at the same time, the more extreme bikini was becoming acceptable in the United States. Some one-piece bathing suits were blouson, loosely-fitted styles.

ski wear—stretch knits made possible more streamlined ski pants. Synthetic and down fillings quilted into ski jackets and other sportwear provided warmth.

underclothing—made in solid colors and restrained prints in the first part of the decade; in vivid and striking colors and prints in the latter half. Brassieres, underpants, slips, and girdles were the most common items of women's underwear. When skirts grew extremely short, a wide-legged panty was sometimes worn instead of a slip. Sheer, nylon pantyhose as an alternative to nylon stockings held up with a garter belt were first marketed about 1960. (The Sears mail order

18.15 Sketch from *Women's Wear Daily,* September 1971, showing hemline lengths that range from "mini" (far left) to "midi" (center) to "maxi" (far right). (*Drawing by Robert Melendez. Courtesy of* Women's Wear Daily, *Fairchild Publications.*)

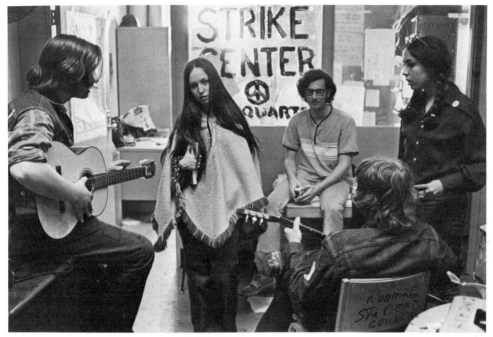

18.16 College students participating in a student strike in May, 1970 have long hair styles characteristic of those worn by young people of that time. (*Courtesy of Queens College office of publications. Eugene Luttenberg, photographer.*)

catalog carried them in 1961.) These garments joined underpants and stocking into one garment and became a virtual necessity as skirts became short.

sleepwear—included both colorful nylon night-gowns ranging in length from the floor to hip-length, "shortie" gowns worn with matching panties, and pajamas. Synthetic pile fabrics and quilted nylon and polyester fabrics were made into warm robes.

hair and head dress—with bouffant hair styles, the fullness achieved by a technique of massing the hair called "backcombing" and/or the addition of artificial hair pieces, more and more women elected to go hatless. (See Figure 18.17.) Those hats that were worn included many with large crowns and small or no brims.

NOTE: Pillbox hats gained notice when they were worn by Jacqueline Kennedy at the time of the 1960 presidential elections and after.

By the mid-60's, girls and young women were allowing their hair to grow straight and long. (See Figure 18.16.) Girls whose hair was not naturally straight pressed the curl out of their hair with clothes irons. Some French fashion designers, particularly Courrèges and Cardin, cut the hair of their models in an almost geometric style for their mid-decade collections. English hair stylist Vidal Sassoon also helped make the geometric cut a popular alternative to long hair.

footwear—changed as skirt lengths changed. Heels lowered, as skirts shortened. By mid-decade, toes were more rounded and less pointed. (See Figure 18.18.) Boots were shown first in the early 60's, and quickly adopted for cold weather. These ranged from ankle-length, short boots worn with stretch pants to calf-high boots. Although the precise form varied from year-to-year, boots remained a basic item of footwear throughout the decade. Colored and textured stockings or panty-hose were worn with short skirts. Knee-length, colored socks were worn by some young girls with mini skirts.

accessories—types and shapes of handbags varied widely, and included small tailored bags, very large bags with round handles and/or shoulder straps. Toward the end of the 60's shoulder bags gained popularity. Materials used included leather and plastic imitations of leather, fabric, and straw.

jewelry—Popular jewelry items included long strings of pearls or other beads similar to those worn in the 20's, earrings either small or long and hanging, necklaces of brightly colored stones, and an enormous variety of costume jewelry at a variety of prices. In the latter part of the 60's large decorative wrist watches were worn and gold-colored jewelry, especially multiple gold chains, seemed to overshadow colored beads.

cosmetics—for those who used cosmetics, bright

THE KENNETH CLUB

Women break diets, they skip exercise classes, think nothing of putting off a visit to the dentist. But cancel an appointment with her hairdresser? . . . no smart woman today would dream of it. In a word: the hairdresser has zoomed into his own. Straightening, stretching, puffing, pulling, changing the line of hair and extending the proportion of a woman's head . . . it's the hairdresser who gives every fashion its ultimate shape. Not since Marie Antoinette took her coiffeur, Léonard, on the flight to Varennes, has the hairdresser been so prized. And possibly not since the Roman Baths has there been anything quite like the hairdresser's salon—a place to meet, to see, to be seen, to unwind, to rewind; a part of everyday life.

No one has had more to do with bringing this about in America than Kenneth Battelle. A serious, unspoiled, hardworking man, with a polite but levelling wit, Kenneth has, at thirty-six, become a kind of hair psychiatrist to dozens of women—changing their looks and, in turn, their lives and careers. While not everyone who "goes to Kenneth" goes in the every-week-without-fail sense, it's probable that almost every famous female head in the world has gone or will go to see what all the talk is about. It's a part of the twentieth-century fashion experience.

For Kenneth's customers there is simply no other haircutter in the world. "The way he puts his fingers through the hair first, before he cuts, weighs it in his hand, touches the scalp," they find unique. To hair that never had body or shape—presto, he gives body and shape. In his hands, hair as wiry and unyielding as a Scotch terrier's coat has been known to swing like velvet. At a fashion-photography sitting Kenneth is adored; he is daring, inventive, sure of the limits. This nice balance of caution and supreme confidence appears to have rubbed off somewhat on the women who come

Mrs Watson K. Blair's pale, strong hair — "best hair in this country" combed straight and round, here, by Kenneth.

DRAWINGS BY HENRY KOEHLER

18.17 Full, bouffant hairstyles like this somewhat extreme example from *Vogue*, July 1963, predominated during the first half of the decade of the 60's. (*Drawing by Henry Koehler. Courtesy of* Vogue. *Copyright © 1963 by the Condé Nast Publications.*)

PARIS OPENINGS

PARIS BUREAU

Paris couturiers have, once again, chosen pumps to be worn by the majority of their mannequins when fall collections open. Both the square toe and the gently rounded toe lend variety to the silhouette. Otherwise, the fashion news lies in the use of materials, colors and details.

1. There is just a seam at back of this black satin pump made by Mario Valentino, Naples, for Michel Goma. Fabric covering shoe and 22/8 heel is in one piece. 2. For Guy Laroche, Charles Jourdan & Fils, Paris, made a pump with flat asymmetric bow cut in one piece with the upper. 3. Serge Matta is fond of bows, self fabric ones on colored satin and black moire pumps, others in satin ribbon which simulates lacing. Heels are 24/8. From Charles Jourdan & Fils.

4. In different shades of brown with gray or red cast, this simple pump is trimmed with self leather and matching color stitchings. For Michel Goma by Mario Valentino. 5. Maggy Rouff also likes soft lines and slim heels in heights varying from 16/8 to 20/8. Quillichini

made pumps with yokes for this couturier. Some in kid are trimmed with stitchings, other models combine leather and grosgrain or satin. Dark gray flannel shade is used for model sketched. Other colors liked are beaver, also yellowish and reddish brown. 6. Pierre Cardin ordered this pump with folds forming an X motif at throat in beet red, olive green, black or brown. From Charles Jourdan & Fils.

7. Mancini's slim squared toes will appear at Balmain for pumps in dressy and casual types. Afternoon model shown here is in black kid with grosgrain trimming in black or beige satin with faille for evening. Heels are 22/8. 8. Toes are softly pointed in slim pumps created for Gres by Massaro. Stripes of black kid simulate lacing along heels and make the two small bows. Heels are 22/8. 9. To accompany Balmain's suits, Mancini combines checked woolen with black kid for this pump trimmed at back with fabric tab passing through leather covered buckle. The 22/8 heel is also covered with black kid. 10. Madeleine de Rauch chose this black patent leather shoe with high straps and grosgrain ribbon bow. Designed by d'Aya.

7/24/59

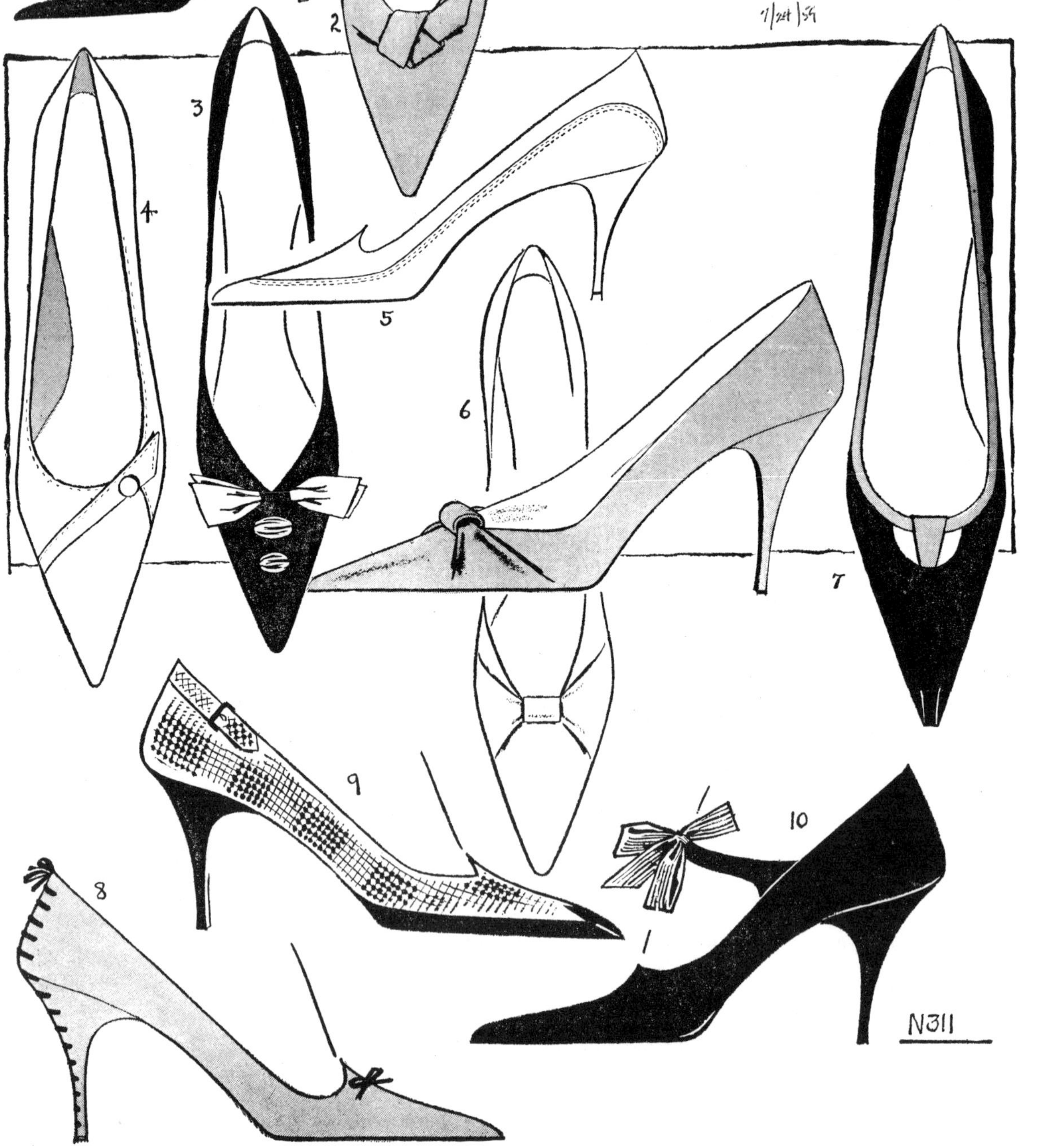

N311

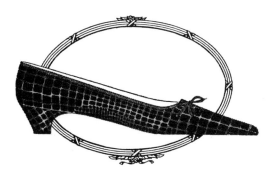

Black or walnut brown
alligator grained calf. $35

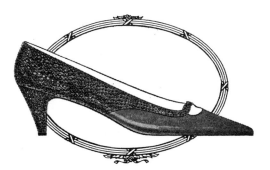

Black, brown, wine, green or gray calf
with matching lizard grained calf. $30

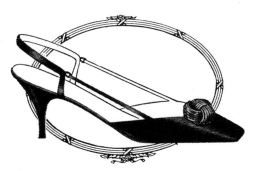

Black satin with a
draped cord trim. $36

18.18 (*Opposite page*) Stilleto heels and pointed toes of shoes shown in *Women's Wear Daily*, 1959, contrasted with lower heels and varied toe shapes (*shown above*) worn with shorter skirts from an ad for Delman Shoes at Bergdorf Goodman that ran in the September 1964 issue of *Bazaar*.

red lipstick was replaced in the 60's by a variety of lighter, paler colors, especially after 1966. Mascara, eye liner, eyeshadow in colors ranging from mauve to lavender, blue, green and even yellow, and false eyelashes were commonly used.

COSTUME FOR MEN—1947–1970

Item / Description

business suits—*Cut:* No post-war change in men's fashions occurred that equaled the radical "New Look" change in women's styles of 1947, although the men's wear industry tried to promote a different look for men. *Esquire*, a men's magazine with a heavy emphasis on fashion, introduced the *Bold Look* for men in October, 1948 (a year after the New Look made its appearance). This was not a radical change in fashion, but rather a continuation of the English drape cut with greater emphasis on a coordination between shirt and accessories and the suit. The coat was broad-shouldered, and the lapel had a long roll, and double-breasted suits predominated. (See Figure 18.19.) Jackets were somewhat longer than during the wartime years. Cuffs returned to most pant legs, and most shirts had wide collars. Shirts were made of nylon as this fiber again became available to the civilian population. Suits moved away from the "English drape" cut in the 50's. Suits had less padding in the shoulders, narrower silhouette. (See Figure 18.20.) Dark gray (called charcoal) was the most popular shade.

NOTE: The 50's are sometimes nicknamed the era of the "gray flannel suit" and fashion promoters called fashionable men's styles the "Ivy League Look."

Shirts worn with the gray flannel suit provided touches of color—sometimes pink or blue, and most often had small collars either buttoned-down style or were fastened together under the tie with tie pins.

Vests—in bright colors also.

In the later 50's, suits altered in cut. Fashion writers called the new suits with shorter jackets, more shaping through the torso, and rounded, cut-away jacket fronts, *continental suits*. (See Figure 18.21.) In the early 60's, continental suits were supplanted by *mod* clothes, English styles with jackets padded slightly at the shoulders, wider lapels, moderate flare to the skirt, and pronounced side or center-back vents. (See Figure 18.22.) Jacket fronts had a moderately cut-away

18.19 Man's double-breasted suit of the immediate post-World War II period. (*Photograph courtesy of the Smithsonian Institution.*)

shape. Suits with body shaping remained fashionable for the rest of the decade.

NOTE: An upsurge of interest in fashion for men was accompanied by heavy press promotion and publicists began to speak of a "revolution in men's wear." Esquire in its *Encyclopedia of 20th Century Men's Fashions* declared, "from grey flannel cocoon stepped a peacock."

18.20 Narrower lapels and single-breasted cut characteristic of the early 1950's. (*Photograph courtesy of Hart, Schaffner, and Marx.*)

The *Nehru jacket* appeared on the scene, based on a traditional Indian jacket that buttoned all the way to the neck and had a small, stand-up collar. The coat was named after the Prime Minister of India, Jawaharlal Nehru who wore the traditional jacket. The style lasted about two years. After Lord Snowdon (then the husband of Princess Margaret of England) wore a formal evening Nehru suit with a white turtleneck, other men combined Nehru jackets with turtlenecks. Turtleneck shirts remained a fashionable item of men's wear even after the Nehru suit disappeared.

NOTE: The Nehru style gained notice when, in 1966 after returning from a trip to India, French designer Pierre Cardin began to wear gray flannel suits made with Indian-style jackets. A spurt in retail sales of men's clothing induced some fa-

18.21 The "continental" cut suit of the later 1950's. (*Photograph courtesy of Hart, Schaffner, and Marx.*)

18.22 1960's suits had slightly padded shoulders, wider lapels, and moderate flare to the skirt. Men wore their hair longer. (*Photograph courtesy of Hart, Schaffner, and Marx.*)

mous designers of women's clothing to enter the men's wear market as well. Cardin was one of the first. (See Figure 18.23.)

casual sportswear—*sports jackets*—reflected the cut of business suits, but used different fabrics. During the grey flannel era, sports jackets of tartan plaids were popular. In the mid-50's, continental-look sports jackets had interesting textures achieved by using raised cord or slub yarns. Leather-buttoned corduroy jackets, checked and plaid and Indian madras plaids were also fashionable. When *mod styles* appeared after 1966, the Norfolk jacket was revived, double-breasted blazers became popular, and bush or safari jackets were worn.

Throughout the 60's, knitted fabrics were also used for sports jackets.

slacks—Casual trousers (slacks) in the 50's were slim and straight. During period of *Ivy League* styles these included chinos (khaki-colored,

twill weave cotton fabric trousers) with a small belt and buckle at the back. These were generally combined with button-down shirts and crew-necked sweaters.

In the late 50's, self-belts and beltless trousers were worn: slacks tapered to the ankles and were cuffless. In the mid-60's: tapered slacks were replaced by those with trouser bottoms that grew wider and included some flared pantlegs and wide, *bell-bottoms.* Blue jeans began to be accepted for fashionable dress in the late 60's.

shorts—About 1954 Bermuda or walking shorts, formerly worn in the 30's, were revived for general sports wear, combined with knee-length stockings. Some attempts were made to incorporate bermuda shorts into *walking suits*, business suits with bermuda shorts instead of trou-

18.23 On the left a patterned sports jacket, characteristic of colorful sportswear adopted by men in the 60's. On the right, a Nehru coat, a style based on the traditional dress of men in India as worn by Prime Minister Jawaharlal Nehru. (*Reprinted from* Sir Magazine, *courtesy of Lopez Publications.*)

sers, but these styles never captured any significant segment of the market.

NOTE: One of the authors remembers seeing a young man appear for a college prom in a tuxedo jacket with matching bermuda shorts instead of long trousers.

sports shirts—in the immediate post war period reflected the wide-collared styling or more formal shirts, made in bright colors; plaids were especially popular. In the 50's, small-patterned fabrics in shirts with buttoned-down collars. In the 60's a great diversity of patterns and textures including Western-style shirts, bright prints, and some shirts cut to fit close to the torso.

Knitted shirts and sweaters of all kinds were worn throughout the period, and included T-shirts, polo shirts, and in the latter part of the 60's, many turtleneck shirts.

clothing for active sports—*swimming*—tailored trunks were preferred in the early 50's, medium length boxer shorts predominating; sometimes sets of matching sport shirts and trunks. By the end of the 50's varieties included those like Bermuda shorts, still-longer *Jamaica shorts* and tailored trunks. In the 60's, the miniscule European knit bikini for men (or, as the European's called it the *slip*) was appearing on American beaches. Synthetic knits were used for bathing suits because they dried quickly and were wrinkle-free.

evening dress—generally consisted of tuxedos or dinner jackets. Tail coats were rare, worn only for very formal occasions. The cut of jackets for evening followed the prevailing cut of jackets for daytime. White dinner jackets were worn in summer. About 1950 a light blue dinner jacket of *French blue* appeared. The trend toward greater color and variety in styling of mens wear had little effect on formal wear until the mid-60's when ruffled shirt fronts and colored evening dress were adopted by less conservative men.

outdoor garments—turned away from the large-scaled, broad-shouldered styles of the late 40's to trimmer, narrower styles. The predominant line of the 50's was a natural shoulder and more slender cut. Some specific styles included tan polo coats; tweed, checked, and small-patterned fabric coats, and raglan-sleeved coats. In the late 50's, the wraparound, belted coat was revived. In the 60's, as in suits, outerwear for business and dress had more definition of waistline and more flared skirts. Coats were made in a variety of lengths, paralleling the mini, midi, and maxi lengths in women's styles. Fur and leather coats, and fur-collared coats appeared in the latter part of the 60's. (See Figure 18.24.)

NOTE: Synthetic fibers were used in pile linings to add warmth. Zip-in linings remained popular, especially for rainwear. Emphases on preservation of endangered fur-bearing animals caused some persons to substitute man-made pile fabric imitations of fur.

Casual coats were made in great variety, re-

18.24 Shorter lengths in women's skirts were paralleled by shorter lengths for men's coats in the mid-60's. (*Photograph courtesy of Hart, Schaffner, and Marx.*)

flecting emphasis on leisure activities. Generally either hip or waist length, made in light or heavy weights, lined or unlined, set-in or raglan sleeves, with buttoned or zippered closings, such coats used a variety of sturdy fabrics. Styles included Western dress influences during the presidency of Texan Lyndon Johnson, *campus* or *stadium coats* that ended below the hip, shorter jackets for bicycling or motorcycling, quilted down or fiber-filled jackets.

underwear—remained much the same—consisting of boxer shorts, jockey-type shorts, athletic shirts, and T-shirts, but the variety of fabrics and colors in which these items were manufactured increased, especially in the 60's.

sleepwear—in the post-war period men seemed to prefer pajamas. The variety of styles increased in the late 50's and 60's with shortlegged pajamas, short nightshirts, and a wide range of colors and fabrics in more traditional styles.

hair and head dress—*hair*—After the war some men continued to wear short "crew cuts" like those given to soldiers. When the hair was cut flat on top, it was called a *flat top*. In the 50's a contrasting style, inspired by singer Elvis Presley, was longer with a curly pompadour in front and hair at the back brushed into a point that resembled a duck's tail. The nickname for this style was "D. A." from "duck's ass."

While crew cuts and D.A.'s were worn by younger men, older men tended to compromise somewhere between the two, with hair long enough to be combed back from the forehead. Radical changes in hair length came in the 60's, and at the beginning were seen as a protest by the young against middle class values. (See Figure 18.16.) Longer-than-shoulder length hair was chiefly limited to high school and college-age youth or older men wishing to dramatize a personal protest against some aspect of contemporary society, but moderately long hair, beards, moustaches, and sideburns had become accepted styles for all segments of society by the close of the 60's. (See Figures 18.22 and 18.24.) The longer hair styles are often said to have been inspired by the singing group, "The Beatles." Fashion-conscious men began to patronize "hair stylists" rather than "barbers."

hats—during the 50's continued to be much the same as in the pre-war period, with the fedora the staple of men's head wear. In 1952 President Dwight Eisenhower helped re-establish the homburg when he wore one to his inauguration rather than the customary top hat. Straw hats for summer followed the lines of the fedora, hat brims decreased in size. Sporty hats for suburban and leisure wear appeared, and these included the Tyrolean hat, a hat with sharply-creased crown, narrow brim turned up in back and down in front, and having a cord band with a feather or bush decoration; flat-crowned caps with visors for sports car drivers; and flat crowned, small brimmed round pork pie hats. For businessmen in winter a narrow, Russian-style hat made of curled astrakan fur or its imitation in synthetic fiber fabrics gained popularity. Some of these were made with ear flaps that tucked inside the hat and folded out for use in especially cold days. When hair styles grew longer, men did not always wear hats.

footwear—continued to stress styles of moccasins, oxfords, and brogues (a type of oxford with perforations at the tip and side seams.) In the 50's lines narrowed. White buckskin shoes were part of the uniform of college students. Imported Italian shoes were fashionable in the mid-50's. In the 60's the classic styles were supplemented by high shoes and boots, seen for the first time since the 30's for street wear, and by the end of the decade most shoes had somewhat squared toes. Hippie influence gave rise to a variety of work shoes and sandals.

Stockings were available in a variety of patterns and styles. Synthetic fibers made possible one-size, stretch stockings. Antistatic finishes were added to stockings to combat the tendency of synthetic fabric trousers to cling to synthetic fiber stockings.

accessories—for men were limited to functional items such as wrist-watches, and jewelry such as rings and identification bracelets, handkerchiefs, tiepins until the latter part of the 60's when new jewelry styles appeared. With turtleneck sweaters and shirts men began wearing necklaces, some bracelets were also seen.

The trend seems to have begun with the hippies who wore beads and other decorative necklaces.

COSTUME FOR CHILDREN

As in all previous periods styles for children displayed many elements of adult styles. The socio-cultural events and technological changes that influence adult clothing are also reflected in developments in children's clothing. For example, the synthetic and synthetic-blend "wash and wear" fabrics of the 1950's and the "permanent press" of the 1960's found a ready market in children's clothing.

In the 1950's plaid vests and miniature gray flannel suits just like those for their fathers were made for boys, while most pattern magazines of the period included several patterns for mother-daughter "look-alike" outfits. One is tempted to see in these styles a reflection of the emphasis on family togetherness that was characteristic of the United States in the 50's.

Yet another instance of the links between adult and children's styles can be noted in the fact that whereas pants were worn for play by girls, they were not generally worn for school until the late 60's, the period during which adult women began to wear pants to their jobs.

infants and pre-school children—Small girls, ages one to about four, were dressed in loose, yoked dresses and boys in romper suits or short pants. Both boys and girls wore long, corduroy pants or overalls.

After the late *1950's*—long pants up to about size three were made with gripper-snap fasteners up the inseam and around the crotch area to facilitate changing of diapers without having to take off the entire garment. For children at the crawling stage, knees were reinforced.

1960's—knit coveralls were made in soft, terry fabrics for infants.

girls—*dresses*—echoed silhouette of adult women's styles. *1940's and 50's*—skirts full, bodices fitted. Princess line styles, full circular skirts, and jumpers all conformed to the predominant shape. (See Figure 18.25.)

1960's—Slightly A-line, princess cut "skimmers" were popular as dresses in summer and jumpers in winter. Skirts shortened, ending well above the knee. (With the short skirts in cool weather, long tights in matching or contrasting colors were worn.)

For the duration of the unfitted line, children's dresses were either straight, unfitted sometimes with a wide ruffle around the hem, or gradually and slightly flared from shoulder to hem.

blouses or tops—tailored shirts, often with rounded "peter pan" collars; knit polos, T-shirts, other knit tops. In the 60's, turtleneck knit shirts. (See Figure 18.26.)

pants—also followed cut of adult styles:
· 1940's and 50's—fuller.
· 1960's—narrower, fitting the leg more closely.
· late 1960's—fuller again.
· Jeans for play and sportswear; stretch pants especially in the '60's.
· For play or active sports, girls wore shorts or pants.
· 1950's—Bermuda or walking shorts, pedal pushers, and other lengths carried the same fashion names as those for women.

hair—until the mid-60's, hair tended to be short. Latter part of the 60's, long hair predominated.

boys—*suits*—like those of adult men.

jackets—younger boys: Eton jackets; all ages: blazers.

shirts—dress shirts with suits and jackets. Most common shirt styles were knit T-shirts that pulled over the head; polos with collars and

18.25 Children's clothing reflected silhouette changes in adult women's clothing. Full-skirted dress of 1962 (*top left*), contrasts with A-line of styles from 1970 (*bottom left*). (*Illustrations courtesy of the Butterick Pattern Archives/ Library.*)

18.26 (*Above*) A "back-to-school" advertisement of clothing for small girls, August, 1961. (*Reproduced courtesy of Saks Fifth Avenue, New York.*)

"Licorice sticks make the best peace pipes"

18.27 Boys' clothing for Fall, 1961. (*Reproduced courtesy of Saks Fifth Avenue, New York.*)

18.28 Children's outerwear, mid-1960's. Girl at left wears a modacrylic pile parka and knitted tights.

buttoned vents at the front; woven sports shirts; and plaid flannel shirts in cold weather. In the late 40's western-style shirts with yoke and cuffs in contrasting colors to the body of the shirt. (See Figure 18.27.)

hair—Until the latter part of the 60's, cropped short or cut in a "crew cut." Toward the end of the 60's, hair was worn longer.

boys and girls—*outdoor garments*—dress coats in miniature versions of classic styles for men and women, and an enormous variety of jackets including: buttoned and zippered jackets with knit waistbands and cuffs made in fabrics ranging from lightweight poplin to leather; hooded parkas; boxy jackets; pea jackets; melton (a dense, wool fabric) toggle coats with wood or plastic "toggle" closings.

1960's—synthetic pile coats and nylon jackets with fiber filling for insulation. (See Figure 18.28.) Hooded sweatshirts.

bathing suits—like those of adults.

teen-age market—Continued to expand. Youthful fads of note were:
- Late 1940's, after the "New Look"—long, full black skirts, worn with leg-of-mutton-sleeved plaid blouses and flat ballet slippers.

- 1950's—fluffy bedroom slippers.
- Early 1960's—white "go-go" boots.
- Late 1960's—blue jeans.

Summary

The adoption of the styles of the New Look in 1947 marked a sharp change in women's fashion and were the beginning of the post-war styles. For another decade the silhouette of women's clothing continued to follow the pattern established by Christian Dior in 1947 of natural curve over the shoulder, a close fit through the bosom, a narrow waistline, and curved hips. Throughout this period the French couture was followed closely by well-to-do women and celebrities who patronized the couturiers and by slightly less affluent women who bought line-for-line copies of Paris designs from American retail stores.

For men, the 50's were the era of "the man in the grey flannel suit." This expression even became the title of a popular novel written in the mid-50's. Clothing for men was conservative in cut and color, with sports clothing the only "bright" spot in most men's wardrobes. In the second half of the decade, men's clothing was influenced by European, especially Italian styles, and the popular suits were labeled "continental" by the fashion press.

The 60's was a period of upheaval in the United States. The civil rights movement, student unrest, women's liberation, and growing dissent over the escalation of the American military committment in Vietnam were accompanied by changes in fashion that contrasted markedly with the styles of the 50's. Skirts for women came to be shorter than at any previous period in the history of Western dress. Trousers for women were accepted for daytime and evening wear in place of skirts. Some young men adopted shoulder-length hair for the first time in almost two hundred years. Men began wearing more colorful and varied clothing for business and leisure than had been seen in all the time since the Industrial Revolution.

And at the time that this period drew to a close, fashion in women's clothing was in a state of confusion. Three skirt lengths: the mini (above the knee), the midi (mid-calf) and the maxi (floor-length) were vying for acceptance as "the" correct length. The controversy had become so intense that the weekly news magazine, *Newsweek*, ran a cover story on the "Midi vs. the Mini" and devoted nine pages of text and pictures to this burning question. The uncertainty of society in general at the end of the 60's might be compared to the uncertainty in fashion.

Selected Readings

BOOKS AND OTHER MATERIALS CONTAINING ILLUSTRATIONS OF COSTUME OF THE PERIOD FROM ORIGINAL SOURCES.

Fashion and general magazines and newspapers of the period.

Pattern catalogs.

Mail order catalogs

Bernard, B. *Fashion in the 60's*. London: Academy Editions, 1978.

Dorner, J. *Fashion in the Forties and Fifties*. New Rochelle, N.Y.: Arlington House Publishers, 1975.

Ewing, E. *History of Twentieth Century Fashion*. London: B. T. Batsford Ltd., 1974.

Lee, S. T. (Ed.) *American Fashion*. New York: Quadrangle/New York Times Book Company.

Schoeffler, O. E. (Ed.) *Esquire's Encyclopedia of 20th Century Men's Fashion*. New York: McGraw-Hill Book Company, 1973.

The World of Balenciaga. New York: The Metropolitan Museum of Art, 1973.

PERIODICAL ARTICLES

Coleman, E. A. "Abstracting the Abstract Gown." *Dress*, Vol. 8, 1982, p. 27.

"Charles James: Architect of Fashion." *American Fabrics and Fashions*. No. 128, 1983, p. 19.

"It was 25 Years Ago: Dior, the New Look." *Harper's Bazaar*, Vol. 105 (3128), July 1972, p. 32.

Martin, R. " 'The New Soft Look': Jackson Pollock, Cecil Beaton, and American Fashion in 1951." *Dress*, Vol. 7, 1981, p. 1.

Ratner, E. "Levi's." *Dress*, Vol. 1, No. 1, 1975, p. 1.

DAILY LIFE

Brooks, J. *The Great Leap*. New York: Harper and Row, 1966.

Crouzet, M. *The European Renaissance Since 1945*. Harcourt Brace Jovanovich, 1970.

Dodds, J. W. *Everyday Life in 20th Century America*. New York: Putnam.

Lefebvre, J. *Everyday Life in the Modern World*. New York: Harper and Row, 1971.

Miller, D. T. and M. Nowak. *The Way We Really Were*. Garden City: Doubleday & Co., 1977.

Obst, L. R. (Editor) *The Sixties*. New York: Random House/Rolling Stone Press Book, 1977.

O'Neill, W. *Coming Apart. An Informal History of America in the 1960's*. New York: Quadrangle, 1971.

This Fabulous Century, Volumes 5, 6, and 7. New York: Time-Life Books, 1969.

* Also contains illustrations of costumes from contemporary sources.

Bibliography

A Selected Bibliography of Books In English That Deal With the Subject of Historic Costume

BIBLIOGRAPHIES, DICTIONARIES, AND ENCYCLOPEDIAS

Anthony, P. and J. Arnold. *Costume: A General Bibliography*. London: Victoria and Albert Museum and the Costume Society. N.D.

Calasibetta, C. *Fairchild's Dictionary of Fashion*. New York: Fairchild Publications, 1988.

Cunnington, C. W., P. Cunnington and C. Beard. *A Dictionary of English Costume, 900–1900*. London: Adam and Charles Black, 1960.

The Costume Society of America Bibliography. New York: Costume Society of America, 1974/1979/1983.

Fairholt, F. W. *A Glossary of Costume in England*. Wakefield, England: E. P. Publishing, 1976 (facsimile of 1885 edition).

Houch, C. *The Fashion Encyclopedia*. New York: St. Martin's Press, 1982.

Kybalová. L., O. Herbenová, and M. Lamarová. *The Pictorial Encyclopedia of Fashion*. London: P. Hamlyn Publishing Group, Ltd., 1968.

Picken, M. B. *A Dictionary of Fashion*. New York: Funk and Wagnalls, 1969.

Planché, J. R. *A Cyclopaedia of Costume or Dictionary of Dress*. London: Chatto and Windus, 1876–1879.

Wilcox, R. T. *The Dictionary of Costume*. New York: Charles Scribner's Sons, 1969.

Yarwood, D. *The Encyclopedia of World Costume*. New York: Charles Scribner's Sons, 1978.

GENERAL REFERENCES AND SURVEYS

Adams, J. D. *Naked We Came: A More or Less Lighthearted Look at The Past, Present and Future of Clothes*. New York: Holt, Rinehart and Winston, 1967.

Arnold, J. *Patterns of Fashion, Vol 1: 1660–1860, Vol 2: 1860–1940*. New York: Drama Book Specialists. 1977.

Baines, V. B. *Fashion Revivals from the Elizabethan Age To the Present Day*. London: B. T. Batsford, 1981.

Batterberry, M. and A. Batterberry. *Mirror, Mirror*. New York: Holt, Rinehart and Winston, 1977.

Bell, Q. *On Human Finery*. Philadelphia: R. West, 1973.

Belkin, K. L. (Ed.) *The Costume Book*. Philadelphia: Heyden and Son., 1981.

Bigelow, M. S. *Fashion In History*. Minneapolis: Burgess Publishing Company, 1979.

Black, J. and M. Garland. *A History of Fashion.* London: Orbis Publications, Ltd., 1975.

Boucher, F. *20,000 Years of Fashion.* New York: Harry N. Abrams, N.D.

Bradfield, N. *Costume in Detail.* London: Harrap Ltd., 1975.

Bradfield, N. *Historical Costumes of England, 1066–1968.* London: Harrap Ltd., 1981.

Bradley, C. G. *Western World Costumes.* New York: Prentice-Hall, 1954.

Braun, L. et al. *Costume Through the Ages.* New York: Rizzoli, 1982.

Braun-Ronsdorf, M. *The Wheel of Fashion.* London: Thames and Hudson, 1964.

Braun and Schneider. *Historic Costume in Pictures.* New York: Dover Publications, Inc., 1975.

Brooke, I. *A History of English Costume.* New York: Theatre Arts, Books, 1973.

Bruhn, W. and M. Tilke. *A Pictorial History of Costume.* New York: Hastings House, 1976.

Callister, H. *Dress from Three Centuries.* Hartford, Conn.: Wordsworth Atheneum, 1976.

Clinch, G. *English Costume from Prehistoric Times to the End of the 18th Century.* London: Rowman and Littlefield, 1975.

Contini, M. *Fashion.* New York: The Odyssey Press. 1965.

Cremers-Van Der Does, E. C. *The Agony of Fashion.* Poole, Dorset, England: Blanford Press, 1980.

Cumming, V. *Exploring Costume History.* London: B. T. Batsford, 1981.

Cunnington, P. *Costume in Pictures.* New York: Herbert Press, 1981.

D'Assailly, G. *Ages of Elegance.* Paris: Librairie Hachette. 1968.

Davenport, M. *The Book of Costume: 2 Volumes.* New York: Crown Publishers, Inc., 1948.

Dorner, J. *Fashion: The Changing Shape of Fashion Through the Years.* New York: Crown Publishers, Inc. 1974.

Evans, M. *Costume Throughout the Ages.* Philadelphia: J. B. Lippencott. 1950.

Fabre, M. *History of Fashion.* London: Leisure Arts, Ltd., 1966.

Fairholt, F. W. *Costume in England: A History of Dress to the End of the 18th Century.* Detroit: Singing Tree Press. 1968.

Fox, L. M. *Costumes and Customs of the British Isles.* Boston: Plays, Inc. 1974.

Garland, M. *The Changing Form of Fashion.* New York: Praeger Publishers. 1970.

Garland, M. *Fashion.* Baltimore: Penquin Books, 1962.

Gorsline, D. *What People Wore.* New York: Bonanza Books, 1952.

Green, R. M. *The Wearing of Costume.* London: Sir Issac Pitman and Sons, Ltd., 1966.

Hansen, H. H. *Costume and Styles.* New York: E. P. Dutton and Company, Inc. 1956.

Harris, C. and M. Johnston. *Figleafing Through History.* New York: Atheneum. 1971.

Hildreth, J. C. *In Pursuit of Elegance: Costume Treasures from American and Canadian Collections.* Phoenix, Arizona: Phoenix Art Museum, 1985.

Hill, M. H. and P. A. Bucknell. *The Evolution of Fashion: Pattern and Cut from 1066 to 1930.* London: B. T. Batsford, 1967.

Kelly, F. M. and R. Schwabe. *Historic Costume: A Chronicle of Fashion in Western Europe 1490–1790.* London: The Art Book Co., 1980. (Reprint of 1929 edition.)

Kelly, F. and R. Schwabe. *A Short History of Costume and Armour, 1066–1800.* New York: Arco Publishing Co., 1973.

Kemper, R. H. *Costume* New York: Newsweek Books, 1977.

Kohler, C. *A History of Costume.* New York: Dover Publications, Inc. 1963.

Laver, J. *Clothes.* New York: Horizon Press, 1953.

Laver, J. *The Concise History of Costume and Fashion.* New York: Harry N. Abrams, N.D.

Laver, J. *Costume.* New York: Hawthorne Books, 1963.

Laver, J. *Costume and Fashion.* London: Thames and Hudson, 1985.

Laver, J. *Costume Through the Ages.* New York: Simon and Schuster. 1967.

Laver, J. *Taste and Fashion.* London: G. C. Harrap Ltd. 1948.

Lester, K. M. and R. Kerr. *Historic Costume.* Peoria, Ill.: Bennett, 1977.

Norris, H. *Costume and Fashion.* 5 volumes. New York: E. P. Dutton, Inc., 1924.

Nunn, J. *Fashion in Costume, 1200 to 1980.* New York: Schocken Books, 1980.

Payne, B. *History of Costume.* New York: Harper and Row, 1965.

Pistolese, R. and R. Horsting. *History of Fashions.* New York: John Wiley and Sons, Inc. 1970.

Rothstein, N. (Ed.) *400 Years of Fashion.* London: Victoria and Albert Museum, 1984.

Russell, D. *Costume History and Style.* Englewood Cliffs, N. J.: Prentice-Hall, 1983.

Selbie, R. *The Anatomy of Costume.* New York: Crescent Books, 1977.

Squire, G. *Dress and Society, 1560–1970.* New York: The Viking Press. 1974.

Squire, G. and P. Baynes. *The Observer's Book on European Costume.* New York: Charles Scribner's and Sons, 1977.

Sronkova, O. *Fashions Through the Centuries.* London: Spring Books, N.D.

Stavridi, M. *The Hugh Evelyn History of Costume.* London: Evelyn, 1966.

Stibbert, F. *Civil and Military Clothing in Europe.* New York: Benjamin Blom, Inc., 1968.

Tilke, M. *Costume Patterns and Designs.* New York: Hastings House, 1974.

Vanity Fair. New York: The Metropolitan Museum of Art, 1977.

Vincent, J. M. *Costume and Conduct in The Laws of Basel, Berne, and Zurich, 1320–1800.* Westport, Conn.: Greenwood Press (reprint of 1935 edition).

Waugh, N. *The Cut of Women's Clothes, 1600–1930.* New York: Theatre Arts Books, 1968.

Wilcox, R. T. *The Mode in Costume.* New York: Charles Scribner's and Sons, 1983.

Yarwood, D. *Costume of the Western World.* New York: St. Martins Press, 1980.

Yarwood, D. *English Costume from the Second Century B.C. to 1972.* London: B. T. Batsford, 1972.

Yarwood, D. *European Costume: 4000 Years of Fashion.* New York: Larousse, 1975.

COSTUME FROM SPECIFIC HISTORIC PERIODS

Antiquity

Abrams, E. and Lady Evans. *Ancient Greek Dress.* Chicago: Argonaut, Inc. Publishers, 1964.

Bonfante, L. *Etruscan Dress.* Baltimore: Johns Hopkins University Press, 1975.

Broholm, H. C. and M. Hald. *Costume of the Bronze Age in Denmark.* Copenhagen: Nyt Nordisk Forlag, 1940.

Brooke, I. *Costume in Greek Classic Drama.* Westport, Conn.: Greenwood Press, Inc., 1973.

Gullberg, E. and P. Astrom. *The Thread of Ariadne.* Sweden: Goteborg. Studies in Mediterranean Archeology, Vol. XXI, 1970.

Hope, T. *Costume of the Greeks and Romans.* New York: Dover Publications, Inc., 1962.

Houston, M. G. *Ancient Egyptian, Mesopotamian, and Persian Costume.* New York: Barnes and Noble, 1964.

Houston, M. G. *Ancient Greek, Roman, and Byzantine Costume and Decorations.* New York: Barnes and Noble, 1977.

Klepper, E. *Costume in Antiquity.* New York: Clarkson Potter, Inc., 1964.

Lutz, H. F. *Costumes and Textiles among the Peoples of the Ancient Near East.* Leipzig: J. C. Hinrichs'sche Buchandlung, 1923.

Sichel, M. *Costume of the Classical World.* North Pomfret, VT: David and Charles, Inc., 1980.

Wilson, L. M. *The Clothing of the Ancient Romans.* Baltimore: Johns Hopkins Press, 1938.

Wilson, L. M. *The Roman Toga.* Baltimore: Johns Hopkins Press, 1924.

Middle Ages

Brooke, I. *English Costume of the Early Middle Ages, 10th-13th Centuries.* London: A. &. C. Black Ltd., 1936.

Brooke, I. *English Costume of the Later Middle Ages, the 14th and 15th Centuries.* London: A. &. C. Black, Ltd., 1935.

Brooke, I. *Medieval Theatre Costume.* New York: Theatre Arts Books, 1976.

Costumes of the Religious Orders of the Middle Ages. West Orange, N. J.: Saifer, 1984.

Cunnington, C. and P. Cunnington. *Handbook of English Medieval Costume.* Northampton: John Dickens and Company, Ltd., 1973.

Cunnington, P. *Medieval and Tudor Costume.* Boston: Plays, Inc., 1968.

De Baille, K. *Medieval Costume.* Raymonds Quiet Press, 1980.

Drobna, Z. *Medieval Costume, Armour and Weapons.* London: Paul Hamlyn, 1962.

Druitt, H. *A Manual of Costume as Illustrated by Monumental Brasses.* London: Alexander Moury, Ltd., 1906.

Evans, J. *Dress in Medieval France.* Oxford: Clarendon Press, 1952.

Goddard, E. R. *Women's Costume in French Texts of the 11th and 12th Centuries.* New York: Johnson Reprints, 1973.

Hartley, D. *Medieval Costume and Life.* London: B. T. Batsford, Ltd., 1931.

Houston, M. *Medieval Costume in England and France, the Thirteenth, Fourteenth, and Fifteenth Centuries.* New York: Barnes and Noble Imports, 1879.

Newton, S. M. *Fashion in the Age of the Black Prince.* Totowa, N. J.: Rowan and Littlefield, 1980.

Piton, C. *The Civil Costumes of France of the 13th and 14th Century.* West Orange, N. J.: Saifer, 1984.

Scott, M. *The History of Dress: Late Gothic Europe, 1400–1500.* New York: Humanities Press, 1980.

Sronkova, O. *Gothic Women's Fashions.* Prague: Artica, 1954.

Renaissance

Arnold, J. (Ed.) *Lost from Her Majesties Back.* Birdle, Bury England: Costume Society, 1980.

Ashelford, J. *The Visual History of Costume: The 16th Century.* New York: Drama Books, 1983.

Birbari, E. *Dress in Italian Paintings, 1460–1500,* London: John Murray, 1975.

Brooke, I. *English Costume in the Age of Elizabeth-16th Century.* London: A. & C. Black, Ltd., 1950.

Cunnington, C. W. *Handbook of English Costume in the Sixteenth Century.*

Cunnington, P. *Medieval and Tudor Costume.* Boston: Plays, Inc. 1968.

Herald, J. *Renaissance Dress in Italy, 1400–1500.* New York: Humanities Press, 1981.

Kelly, F. M. and A. Mansfield. *Shakespearian Costume.* New York: Theatre Arts Books, 1976.

LaMar, V. A. *English Dress in the Age of Shakespeare.* Washington, D.C.: Folger Library, 1958.

Linthicum, M. C. *Costume in the Drama of Shakespeare and his Contemporaries.* Oxford: Clarendon Press. 1936.

Morse, E. *Elizabethan Pageantry.* New York: Benjamin Blom (reprint of 1934 Edition).

Stubbes, P. *Anatomy of Abuses in England in Shakespeare's Youth, A.D., 1583.* New Shakespeare Society, 1877.

Vecellio, C. *Vecellio's Renaissance Costume Book.* New York: Dover Publications, Inc. 1977.

17th and 18th Centuries

Buck, A. *Dress in 18th Century England.* New York: Holmes and Meier, 1979.

Brooke, I. *Dress and Undress* (Restoration and 18th Century). London: Metheuen and Company, Ltd., 1958.

Buck, A. *Dress in 18th Century England.* London: B. T. Batsford, 1979.

Costume of the Western World. New York: Harper and Brothers. 1951.

Cunnington, C. W. and P. Cunnington. *Handbook of English Costume in the Seventeenth Century.* London: Faber and Faber. 1972.

Cumming, V. *A Visual History of Costume: The 17th Century.* New York: Drama Books, 1984.

Cunnington, C. W. and P. Cunnington. *Handbook of English Costume in the Eighteenth century.* London: Faber and Faber, 1957.

Eighteenth-Century French Fashion Plates in Full Color: 64 Engravings from the Galerie des Modes 1778–1787. New York: Dover Publications, Inc., 1982.

Gallery of Fashion, 1790–1822. London: B. T. Batsford, 1949.

Halls, Z. *Women's Costume 1750–1800.* London: Her Majesty's Stationery Office, N.D.

Klinger, R. L. *Distaff Sketch Book: A Collection of Notes on Women's Dress. 1774–1783.* Union City, Tennessee: Pioneer Press, 1974.

Ribeiro, A. *The Dress Worn at Masquerades in England 1730–1790 and its Relation to Fancy Dress in Portraiture.* New York: Garland Publishers, 1985.

Ribeiro, A. *A Visual History of Costume: The Eighteenth Century.* New York: Drama Book Publishers, 1983.

Sichel, M. *Costume Reference, No. 3: Jacobean, Stuart, and Restoration. No. 4. The 18th Century.* London: B. T. Batsford, 1977.

19th Century

American Mail Order Fashions, 1880–1900. Scotia, New York: Americana Review, 1961.

Blum, S. *Fashions and Costumes from Godey's Lady's Book.* New York: Dover Publications, Inc., 1985.

Blum, S. *Victorian Fashions and Costumes from Harper's Bazar. 1867–1898.* New York: Dover Publications, Inc, 1974.

Boehn, M. *Modes and Manners of the 19th Century.* 3 volumes. New York: Benjamin Blom (reprint of 1927 edition).

Buck, A. *Victorian Costume.* Carlton, Bedford, England: Ruth Bean Publishers, 1984.

Caffrey, K. *The 1900's Lady.* New York: Gordon-Cremonesi, 1976.

Coleman, E. A. *Changing Fashions: 1800–1970.* Brooklyn: The Brooklyn Museum, 1972.

Collard, E. *The Cut of Women's 19th Century Dress: The Vertical Epoch. circa 1800–21.* Burlington, Ontario: The Costume Society, 1972.

Collard, E. *Patterns of Fashions of the 1870's.* Burlington, Ontario: The Joseph Brant Museum, 1971.

Cunnington, C. and P. Cunnington. *A Handbook of English Costume in the 19th Century.* London: Faber and Faber, 1970.

Evolution of Fashion: 1835–1895. Kyoto, Japan Kyoto Costume Institute, 1980.

Fashion Plates in the Collection of the Cooper-Hewitt Museum. New York: Cooper Hewitt Museum, 1982.

Foster, V. *A Visual History of Costume: The 19th Century.* New York: Drama Books, 1983.

Gersheim, A. *Fashion and Reality, 1840–1914.* London: Faber and Faber, 1963.

Gibbs-Smith, C. H. *The Fashionable Lady in the 19th Century.* London: Her Majesty's Stationery Office, 1960.

Ginsburg, M. *Victorian Dress in Photographs.* New York: Holmes and Meier Publishers, Inc., 1983.

Hall, C. *From Hoopskirts to Nudity.* (1866–1936) Caldwell, Ohio: The Caxton Printers, Ltd., 1938.

The House of Worth. Brooklyn: The Brooklyn Museum of Art, 1962.

The House of Worth: The Gilded Age in New York. New York: Museum of the City of New York, 1982.

Imperial Styles: Fashions of the Hapsburg Era. New York: Rizzoli, 1980.

Kunciov, R. (Ed) *Mr. Godey's Ladies.* New York: Bonanza Books, 1971.

La Belle Epoque. New York: Metropolitan Museum of Art, 1982.

Lansdell, A. *Fashion A' La Carte: 1860–1900.* Aylesbury, Bucks, England: Shire Publications Ltd., 1985.

Moore, D. L. *The Woman in Fashion.* London: B. T. Batsford, 1949.

Newton, S. M. *Health, Art, and Reason: Dress Reform of the 19th Century.* New York: Schram, 1976.

Sichel, M. *Costume Reference Series: No. 5: The Regency; No. 6: The Victorians.* London: B. T. Batsford, 1977/1978.

Tarrant, N. *The Rise and Fall of the Sleeve, 1825–40.* Edinburgh: Royal Scottish Museum Collections.

Tozier, J. and S. Levitt. *Fabric of Society: A Century of People and their Clothes.* New York: St. Martin's Press, 1984.

Walkley, C. and V. Foster. *Crinolines and Crimping Irons: Victorian Clothes. How They Were Cleaned and Cared For.* London: Peter Owen, Ltd., 1978.

20th Century

American Women of Style. New York: Metropolitan Museum of Art Exhibition Catalog, 1975.

Battersby, B. *Art Deco Fashion. French Designers 1908–1925.* New York: St. Martin's Press, 1974.

Bernard, B. *Fashion in the 60's.* London: Academy Editions, 1978.

Blum, S. *Everyday Fashions of the Twenties as Pictured in In Sears and Other Catalogs.* New York: Dover, 1982.

Bowan, S. *A Fashion for Extravagance: Parisian Fabric and Fashion Designers from the Art Deco Period.* New York: E. P. Dutton and Company, Inc., 1985.

Carter, E. *20th Century Fashion: A Scrapbook.* London: Eyre Metheuen, 1975.

Coleman, E. A. *Changing Fashions: 1800–1970.* Brooklyn: The Brooklyn Museum, 1972.

Collard, E. *The Cut and Construction of Women's Clothing in the 1930's.* Burlington, Ontario: Eileen Collard, N.D.

Collard, E. *Women's Dress in the 1920's: An Outline of Clothing during the "Roaring Twenties."* Burlington, Ontario. Eileen Collard, 1981.

Dorner, J. *Fashion in the Forties and Fifties.* New Rochelle. New York: Arlington House Publishers, 1975.

Dorner, J. *Fashion in the Twenties and Thirties.* London: I. Allen, 1973.

Ewing, E. *History of Twentieth Century Fashion.* London: B. T. Batsford, 1974.

Glynn, P. *In Fashion. Dress in the 20th Century.* New York: Oxford University Press, 1978.

Laver, J. *Women's Dress in the Jazz Age.* London: A Hamish Hamilton Monograph, 1964.

Mansfield, A. and P. Cunnington. *Handbook of English Costume in the Twentieth Costume. 1900–1950.* London: Faber and Faber, Ltd., 1973.

Nuzzi, C. *Parisian Fashion.* New York: Rizzoli, 1979.

O'Donnol, S. M. *American Costume 1915–1970—A Source Book for the Stage.* Bloomington, Ind.: University Press, 1982.

Peacock, J. *Fashion Sketchbook, 1920–1960.* New York: Avon Books, 1977.

Robinson, J. *Fashion in the Forties.* London: Academy Editions, 1976.

Robinson, J. *Fashion in the Thirties.* London: Oresko Books, 1978.

Robinson, J. *The Golden Age of Style, 1909–1929.* New York: Harcourt Brace Jovanovich, 1976.

Schroeder, J. J., Jr. *The Wonderful World of Ladies Fashion.* Illinois: Digest Books, Inc., 1971.

Sichel, M. *Costume Reference Books: The Edwardian's Costume. #7, 1918–1939, #8, and 1939–1950, #9. 1950 to Present, #10.* London: B. T. Batsford, 1979.

Steele, V. *Fashion and Eroticism: Ideals of Feminine Beauty from the Victorian Era to the Jazz Age.* New York: Oxford University Press, 1985.

Stevenson, P. *Edwardian Fashion.* Shepperton, England: Ian Allen, 1980.

Thompson, P. *The Edwardians in Photographs.* London: B. T. Batsford. 1979.

Torrens, D. *A Review of Women's Dress 1920–1950.* New York: Universe Books, N.D.

Vreeland, D. *American Women of Style.* New York: Costume Institute, Metropolitan Museum of Art, 1975.

AMERICAN COSTUME

Brown, M. W. *Dresses of the First Ladies of the White House.* Washington, D.C.: The Smithsonian Institution, 1952.

Earle, A. M. *Costume of Colonial Times.* Detroit: Gale Research Company, 1974.

Earle, A. M. *Two Centuries of Costume in America, 2 volumes.* New York: Dover Publications, Inc., 1970.

Gummere, A. M. *Quaker: A Study in Costume.* New York: Benjamin Blom (reprint of 1901 edition).

Modesty to Mod: Dress and Undress in Canada, 1780–1967. Toronto: Royal Ontario Museum, 1967.

Warwick, E., H. Pitz and A. Wykoff. *Early American Dress.* New York: Bonanza Books, 1965.

Wilcox, R. T. *Five Centuries of American Costume.* New York: Charles Scribner's Sons, 1963.

Worrell, E. A. *Early American Costume.* Harrisburg, Penna.: Stackpole Books, 1975.

CHILDREN'S COSTUME

Cunnington, P. and A. Buck. *Children's Costume in England, 1300–1965.* A. & C. Black, 1965.

Ewing, E. *History of Children's Costume.* London: B. T. Batsford, 1977.

Garland, M. *The Changing Face of Childhood.* London: Hutchinson, 1963.

Guppy, A. *Children's Clothes. 1939–70.* Poole, Dorset, England: Blandford, 1978.

Macquoid, P. *Four Hundred Years of Children's Costume.* London: Medici Society, Ltd., 1925.

Martin, L. *The Way We Wore: Children's Wear, 1870–1970.* New York: Charles Scribner's Sons, 1978.

Moore, D. L. *The Child in Fashion.* London: B. T. Batsford, 1953.

Worrell, E. *Children's Costume in America. 1607–1910.* New York: Charles Scribner's Sons, 1981.

MEN'S COSTUME

Byrde, P. *The Male Image: Men's Fashion in England 1300–1970.* London: B. T. Batsford, 1979.

Coleman, E. A. *Of Men Only.* Brooklyn: The Brooklyn Museum, 1975.

Halls, Z. *Men's Costume. 1580–1750.* London: Her Majesty's Stationery Office, 1970.

Halls, Z. *Men's Costume, 1750–1800.* London: Her Majesty's Stationery Office, 1973.

History of the Men's Wear Industry, 1790–1950. New York: Fairchild Publications, 1950.

Moers, E. *The Dandy.* New York: Viking Press, 1960.

Schoeffler, O. E. (Ed) *Esquire's Encyclopedia of 20th Century Men's Fashion.* McGraw-Hill Book Company, 1973.

Waugh, N. *The Cut of Men's Clothes, 1600–1900.* London: Faber and Faber, Ltd., 1964.

SPECIAL TYPES OF COSTUME.

Accessories

Armstrong, N. J. *A Collector's History of Fans.* New York: Crown Publishers, Inc., 1974.

Armstrong, N. J. *Jewelry: An Historical Survey of British Styles and Jewels.* Guildford, England: Butterworth Press, 1973.

Black, J. A. and M. Garland. *Jewelry Through the Ages.* New York: William Morrow and Company, 1974.

Colle, D. *Collars, Stocks, Cravats.* Emmaus, Penna.: Rodale Press, Inc. 1972.

Corson, R. *Fashion in Eyeglasses.* London: Peter Owen Ltd., 1972.

De Vere Green, B. *A Collector's Guide to Fans over the Ages.* London: F. Muller, 1976.

Ewing, E. *Fur in Dress.* London: B. T. Batsford, 1981.

Flower, M. *Victorian Jewellery.* Cranberry, N. J.: S. Barnes, 1973.

Foster, V. *Bags and Purses.* London: B. T. Batsford, 1982.

Gere, C. *European and American Jewellry.* New York: Crown Publishers, Inc., 1975.

Hinks, P. *Nineteenth Century Jewellry.* London: Faber and Faber, 1975.

Haertig, E. *Antique Combs and Purses.* Carmel-by-the-Sea, CA: Gallery Graphics Press, 1983.

Jewelry Through 7000 Years. London: British Museum, 1976.

Mason, A. F. *Jewellry—An Illustrated Dictionary.* London: Osprey Publishing, 1973.

Newman, H. *An Illustrated Dictionary of Jewelry.* London: Thames and Hudson, 1981.

Von Boehn, M. *Ornaments: Lace, Fans, Gloves, Walking Sticks, Parasols, Jewelry, and Trinkets.* New York: Benjamin Blom, Inc. (reprint of 1929 Edition).

Cosmetics

Angeloglou, M. *A History of Makeup.* London: Macmillan Company, 1970.

Corson, R. *Fashions in Makeup; From Ancient to Modern Times.* London: Peter Owen Ltd., 1981.

Gunn, F. *The Artificial Face: A History of Cosmetics.* New York: Hippocrene Books, 1974.

Footwear

Baynes, K. and K. (Eds) *The Shoe Show: British Shoes Since 1790.* London: The Crafts Council, 1980.

Brooke, I. *Footwear.* New York: Theatre Arts Books, 1976.

Grass, Milton N. *History of Hosiery.* New York: Fairchild Publications, 1955.

Probert, C. *Shoes in Vogue.* London: Thames and Hudson, 1981.

Swann, J. *Shoes.* London: B. T. Batsford, 1982.

Walker, S. A. *Sneakers.* New York: Workman Publishing Company, 1978.

Wilsox, R. T. *The Mode in Footwear.* New York: Charles Scribner's Sons, 1948.

Wilson, E. *The History of Shoe Fashion.* New York: Theatre Arts Books (reprint of 1900 edition).

Hats and Headdress

Amphlett, H. *Hats: A History of Fashion in Headwear.* Chalfont St. Giles: Sadler, 1974.

Asser, J. *Historic Hairdressing*. New York: Hippo-crene Books, 1975.

Charles, A. and R. DeAnfrasio. *The History of Hair: An Illustrated Review of Hair Fashions Throughout the Ages*. New York: Outlet Books, 1977.

Clark, F. *Hats*. London: B. T. Batsford, 1982.

Corson, R. *Fashion in Hair*. London: Peter Owen, Ltd., 1971.

For Heads and Toes: A Selection of Head and Foot Attire. Brooklyn: Brooklyn Museum, 1974.

De Courtais, G. *Women's Headdress and Hairstyles in England: A.D. 600 to the Present*. Totowa, N.J.: Rowan and Littlefield, Inc., 1973.

Prober, C. *Hats in Vogue Since 1910*. London: Thames and Hudson, 1982.

Severn, B. *The Long and Short of It. 5000 Years of Fun and Fury over Hair*. New York: David MaKay Company, Inc., 1971.

The Wigmaker in 18th Century Williamsburg. Williamsburg, VA.: Colonial Williamsburg, 1971.

Wilcox, R. T. *The Mode in Hats and Headdress*. New York: Charles Scribner's Sons, 1959.

Underwear

Crawford, M. D. C. and E. Guernsey. *History of Corsets in Pictures*. New York: Fairchild Publications, 1951.

Crawford, M. C. D. and E. Crawford. *A History of Lingerie in Pictures*. New York: Fairchild Publications, 1952.

Cunnington, C. W. and P. *The History of Underclothes*. London: Michael Joseph, 1951.

Ewing, E. *Dress and Undress: A History of Women's Underwear*. New York: Drama Book Specialists, 1979.

Ewing, E. *Underwear: A History*. New York: Theatre Arts Books, 1976.

Probert, C. *Lingerie in Vogue Since 1910*. New York: Abbeville Press, 1981.

The Undercover Story. New York: Fashion Institute of Technology.

Waugh, N. *Corsets and Crinolines*. New York: Theatre Arts Books, 1954.

Armour

Blair, C. *European Armour*. London: B. T. Batsford Ltd., 1958.

Blair, C. *European and American Arms, 1100–1850*. London, B. T. Batsford, 1962.

Hewitt, J. *Ancient Armour and Weapons in Europe*. North Branford, Conn.: Arma Press, 1975.

Robinson, H. R. *The Armour of Imperial Rome*. New York: Charles Scribner's Sons, 1975.

Wilkinson, F. *Arms and Armour*. New York: Bantam Books, 1973.

CLOTHING FOR SPECIAL OCCASIONS.

Ackerman, E. *Dressed for the Country: 1860–1900*. Los Angeles, CA: Los Angeles County Art Museum, 1984.

Cunnington, P. and C. Lucas, *Charity Costumes*. New York: Barnes and Noble, 1978.

Cunnington, P. and C. Lucas. *Costume for Births, Marriages, and Deaths*. New York: Barnes and Noble Books, 1972.

Cunnington, P. and A. Mansfield. *English Costume for Sports and Outdoor Recreation*. New York: Barnes and Noble, 1969.

Ewing, E. *Women in Uniform Through the Centuries*. London: B. T. Batsford, 1975.

The Gallery of English Costume for Sport. Art Galleries Committee of the Corporation of Manchester, England, 1963.

Kidwell, C. *Women's Bathing and Swimming Costume in the United States*. Washington, D.C.: Smithsonian Institution Press, 1968.

Lansdell, A. *Wedding Fashions: 1860–1980*. Aylesburg, Bucks, England: Shire Publications, 1983.

Mansfield, A. *Ceremonial Costume: Court, Civil, and Civic Costume from 1660 to the Present Day*. New York: Barnes and Noble Imports, 1980.

Probert, C. *Swimwear in Vogue*. London: Thames and Hudson, 1981.

Smith, A. M. et al. *Man and the Horse: An Illustration of Equestrian Apparel*. New York: Metropolitan Museum of Art, 1984.

Stevenson, P. *Bridal Fashions*. Shepperton, England: Ian Allan, 1978.

Stevenson, S. and H. Bennett. *Vandyck in Check Trousers. Fancy Dress in Art and Life, 1700–1900*. Edinburgh: Scottish National Portrait Gallery, 1978.

Taylor, L. *Mourning Dress: A Costume and Social History*. Boston: Allen and Unwin, 1983.

Zimmerman, C. S. *The Bride's Book: A Pictorial History of American Bridal Gowns*. New York: Arbor House Publishing, 1985.

OCCUPATIONAL AND WORKING CLASS DRESS

Barsis, M. *The Common Man Through the Centuries*. New York: Ungar, 1973.

Copeland, P. E. *Working Dress in Colonial and Revolutionary America*. Westport, Conn.: Greenwood Press, 1977.

Cunnington, P. *Costume of Household Servants from the Middle Ages to 1900*. London: Adam and Charles Black, 1974.

Lansdell, A. *Occupational Costume and Working Clothes. 1776–1976.* Aylesbury, Bucks, England: Shire Publications Ltd.

Lister, M. *Costume of Everyday Life.* Boston: Plays, Inc., 1972.

Oakes, A. and M. Hill. *Rural Costume.* New York: Van Nostrand Reinhold Company, 1970.

White, W. J. *Working Class Costume from Sketches of Characters* (c. 1800–1815) London: Victoria and Albert Museum, 1971.

Williams-Mitchell, C. *Dressed for the Job: The Story of Occupational Costume.* England: Blandford Press, 1983.

FASHION MAGAZINES, FASHION DESIGNERS AND THE FASHION INDUSTRY

Blum, S. *Designs by Erte.* New York: Dover Publications, Inc., 1976.

Carter, E. *Magic Names in Fashion.* Englewood Cliffs, N. J.: Prentice-Hall, 1980.

Charles-Roux, E. *Chanel: Her World and the Woman Behind the Legend She Herself Created.* New York: Random House, 1975.

Coleman, E. *The Genius of Charles James.* New York: Holt, Rinehart and Winston, 1982.

De Marly, D. *The History of Haute Couture, 1850–1950.* London: B. T. Batsford, 1980.

De Marly, D. *Worth-Father of the Haute Couture.* London: Elm Tree Books, 1980.

Devlin, P. *Fashion Photography in Vogue.* London: Thames and Hudson, 1978.

Duncan, N. H. *History of Fashion Photography.* New York: Alpine Press, 1979.

Etherington-Smith, M. *Patou.* New York: St. Martin's Press, 1984.

Fashion Illustration. New York: Rizzoli, 1979.

Farber, R. *The Fashion Photographers.* New York: Watson Guptill, 1981.

Holland, V. B. *Hand Coloured Fashion Plates, 1770–1899.* London: B. T. Batsford, 1955.

Howell, G. *In Vogue.* New York: Schocken Books, 1976.

Kidwell, C. *Cutting a Fashionable Fit-Dressmaker's Drafting Systems in the U.S.* Washington, D.C.: Smithsonian Institution Presses, 1979.

Kidwell, C. B. and M. C. Christman. *Suiting Everyone: The Democratization of Clothing in America.* Washington, D.C.: The Smithsonian Institution Press, 1974.

Langley-Moore, D. *Fashion Through Fashion Plates.* New York: Crown Publishers, 1972.

Latour, A. *Kings of Fashion.* London: Weidenfeld and Nicolson, 1956.

Lee, S. T. (Ed.) *American Fashion.* New York: Quadrangle/New York Times Book Company, 1975.

Ley, S. *Fashion for Everyone: The Story of Ready-to-Wear.* New York: Charles Scribner's Sons, 1975.

Lynam, R. (Ed.) *Couture.* Garden City, New York: Doubleday and Company, Inc., 1972.

Osma, G. *Fortuny: His Life and Work.* New York: Rizzoli, 1980.

Thornton, N. *Poiret.* New York: Rizzoli, 1979.

Torrens, D. *Fashion Illustrated.* London: Studio Vista, 1974.

Traphey, J. *Harper's Bazaar: 100 Years of the American Female.* New York: Random House, 1967.

The World in Vogue. New York: Viking Press, 1963.

The World of Balenciaga. New York: The Metropolitan Museum of Art, 1973.

STAGE AND SCREEN COSTUME HISTORY

Bailey, M. J. *Those Glorious, Glamor Years: The Great Hollywood Costume Designs of the Thirties.* Citadel Press, 1982.

De Marly, D. *Costume on the Stage.* New York: Barnes and Noble Imports, 1982.

Leese, E. *Costume Design in the Movies.* Bembridge, England: BCW Publishing, 1976.

La Vine, W. R. *In a Glamorous Fashion: The Fabulous Years of Hollywood Costume Design.* New York: Charles Scribner's Sons, 1982.

McConathy, D with D. Vreeland. *Hollywood Costume.* New York: Abrams, 1976.

Prichard, S. *Film Costume: An Annotated Bibliography.* Scarecrow, 1981.

PERIODICALS

Periodicals Devoted to Historic Costume
Costume
Dress
CIBA Review (no longer published)

FASHION MAGAZINES AND NEWSPAPERS

Ackermann's Repository of the Arts. London: 1890–1829

Almanach des Modes, Paris: 1814–1822

La Belle Assemblee or *Bell's Court and Fashionable Magazine.* London: 1806–18

Cabinet de Modes. Paris: 1785–1789

Delineator. New York: 1873–1937
Demorest's Monthly Magazine. New York: 1865–1899
Elle. Paris: 1945 to present.
Esquire. New York: 1933 to present.
La Galerie des Modes. Paris: 1778–1787
The Gallery of Fashion. London: 1794–1803
Glamour. New York: 1939 to present
Godey's Lady's Book. Philadelphia: 1830–1898
Harper's Bazaar. New York: 1867 to present
Journal des Dames et des Modes. Paris: 1797–1839
Le Journal des Demoiselles. Paris: 1833–1904

Mademoiselle. New York: 1935 to present.
Men's Wear. New York: 1890 to present.
Les Modes Parisiennes. Paris: 1843–1875.
Officiel de la Couture et de la Mode de Paris. Paris: 1921 to present.
Peterson's Magazine. Philadelphia: 1837–1898.
Petit Courrier des Dames. Paris: 1822–1865.
Sir. Amsterdam: 1936 to present.
Vanity Fair. New York: 1913–1936.
Vogue. New York: 1892 to present.
Women's Wear Daily. New York: 1910 to present.

Index